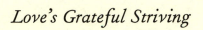

Love's Grateful Striving

love's grateful striving

*A Commentary on
Kierkegaard's*
Works of Love

M. JAMIE FERREIRA

OXFORD
UNIVERSITY PRESS

2001

OXFORD
UNIVERSITY PRESS

Oxford   New York
Athens Auckland Bangkok Bogotá Buenos Aires   Calcutta
Cape Town Chennai Dar es Salaam Delhi Florence Hong Kong   Istanbul
Karachi Kuala Lumpur Madrid Melbourne Mexico City Mumbai Nairobi
Paris São Paulo Shanghai Singapore Taipei Tokyo Toronto Warsaw

and associated companies in
Berlin Ibadan

Copyright © 2001 by M. Jamie Ferreira

Published by Oxford University Press, Inc.
198 Madison Avenue, New York, New York 10016

Oxford is a registered trademark of Oxford University Press.

Library of Congress Cataloging-in-Publication Data
Ferreira, M. Jamie.
Love's grateful striving : a commentary on Kierkegaard's Works of love
/ M. Jamie Ferreira.
    p.   cm.
Includes bibliographical references and index.
ISBN 0-19-513025-1
1. Kierkegaard, Søren, 1813–1855. Kjærlighedens gerninger.
2. Love—Religious aspects—Christianity.   I. Title.
BV4505.K423 F47   2001
241'.4—dc21   00-055734

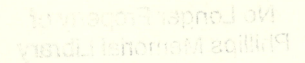

9 8 7 6 5 4 3 2 1

Printed in the United States of America
on acid-free paper

acknowledgments

The Kierkegaard Research Center in Copenhagen has been an invaluable resource for me, and I am deeply grateful to Niels Joergen Cappeloern, the director, for his kind invitation first to be part of a conference where I gave my first paper on *Works of Love,* and then to spend large portions of two summers at the center. He has been a wonderful friend and dialogue-partner; I have learned more from him than he could know. Others at the center have been extremely kind and helpful to me in my work (in particular, Pia, Stacey, Begonya, and Arne). I consider the center a second home, and this book is an expression of my gratitude.

My thanks also go to others here at home (like Walter Jost and Gordon Steffey) who have read and commented on parts of the manuscript, and to those graduate students here at UVA who have shared my excitement about the topic of neighbor-love. Elizabeth McManus helped enormously with her conscientious and patient bibliographical assistance. Blackwell Publishers has kindly granted permission for me to draw on my work originally published in the *Journal of Religious Ethics,* spring 1997 ("Equality, Impartiality, and Moral Blindness in Kierkegaard's *Works of Love*"), and in *Philosophical Investigations,* January 1999 ("Other-Worldliness in Kierkegaard's *Works of Love*"). Mercer University Press kindly granted permission for me to draw on my article, "Mutual Responsiveness in Kierkegaard's *Works of Love,*" in their *International Kierkegaard Commentary* series volume 16. Moreover, both Princeton University Press and Indiana University Press have granted me permission to use their copyrighted material.

George has shown me over the years what love's grateful striving truly means, and I dedicate this book to him.

contents

abbreviations

Works by Søren Kierkegaard

BA   *The Book on Adler. Kierkegaard's Writings* 24. Trans. Howard V. Hong and Edna H. Hong. Princeton, N.J.: Princeton University Press, 1998.

CD   *Christian Discourses/ The Crisis and A Crisis in the Life of an Actress. Kierkegaard's Writings* 17. Trans. Howard V. Hong and Edna H. Hong. Princeton, N.J.: PrincetonUniversity Press, 1997.

CUP 1-2   *Concluding Unscientific Postscript*, 2 vols. *Kierkegaard's Writings* 12. Trans. Howard V. Hong and Edna H. Hong. Princeton, N.J.: Princeton University Press, 1992.

CI   *The Concept of Irony with Continual Reference to Socrates. Kierkegaard's Writings* 2. Trans. Howard V. Hong and Edna H. Hong. Princeton, N.J.: Princeton University Press, 1989.

EO 1-2   *Either/Or*, 2 vols. *Kierkegaard's Writings* 3–4. Trans. Howard V. Hong and Edna H. Hong. Princeton, N.J.: Princeton University Press, 1987.

EUD   *Eighteen Upbuilding Discourses. Kierkegaard's Writings* 5. Trans. Howard V. Hong and Edna H. Hong. Princeton, N.J.: Princeton University Press, 1990.

FSE   *For Self-Examination* and *Judge for Yourself! Kierkegaard's Writings* 2. Trans. Howard V. Hong and Edna H. Hong. Princeton, N.J.: Princeton University Press, 1990.

FT   *Fear and Trembling* and *Repetition. Kierkegaard's Writings* 6. Trans. Howard V. Hong and Edna H. Hong. Princeton, N.J.: Princeton University Press, 1983.

JFY *Judge for Yourself!* See FSE.

JP *Søren Kierkegaard's Journals and Papers.* Ed. and Trans. Howard V. Hong and Edna H. Hong, assisted by Gregor Malantschuk. Bloomington: Indiana University Press, (Vol. 1) 1967, (Vol. 2) 1970, (Vols. 3–4) 1975, (Vols. 5–7) 1978.

MLW *The Moment and Late Writings. Kierkegaard's Writings* 23. Trans. Howard V. Hong and Edna H. Hong. Princeton, N.J.: Princeton University Press, 1998.

PC *Practice in Christianity. Kierkegaard's Writings* 20. Trans. Howard V. Hong and Edna H. Hong. Princeton, N.J.: Princeton University Press, 1991.

PF *Philosophical Fragments* and *Johannes Climacus. Kierkegaard's Writings* 7. Trans. Howard V. Hong and Edna H. Hong. Princeton, N.J.: Princeton University Press, 1985.

"Purity" "Purity of Heart"; see UDVS.

PV *The Point of View. Kierkegaard's Writings* 22, including "On My Work as an Author," "The Point of View for My Work as an Author," and "Armed Neutrality." Trans. Howard V. Hong and Edna H. Hong. Princeton, N.J.: Princeton University Press, 1998.

SUD *The Sickness unto Death. Kierkegaard's Writings* 19. Trans. Howard V. Hong and Edna H. Hong. Princeton, N.J.: Princeton University Press, 1980.

SV *Samlede Vaerker.* Ed. Drachmann, Heiberg, Lange. 14 vols. København: C.A. Reitzels, 1847.

TA *Two Ages: The Age of Revolution and the Present Age. A Literary Review. Kierkegaard's Writings* 14. Trans. Howard V. Hong and Edna H. Hong. Princeton, N.J.: Princeton University Press, 1978.

UDVS *Upbuilding Discourses in Various Spirits. Kierkegaard's Writings* 15. Trans. Howard V. Hong and Edna H. Hong. Princeton, N.J.: Princeton University Press, 1993.

WA *Without Authority. Kierkegaard's Writings* 18, including "The Lily in the Field and the Bird of the Air," "Two Ethical-Religious Essays," "Three Discourses at the Communion on Fridays," "An Upbuilding Discourse," "Two Discourses at the Communion on Fridays." Trans. Howard V. Hong and Edna H. Hong. Princeton, N.J.: Princeton University Press, 1993.

WL *Works of Love. Kierkegaard's Writings* 16. Trans. Howard V. Hong and Edna H. Hong. Princeton, N.J.: Princeton University Press, 1995.

Works by Emmanuel Levinas

BPW *Basic Philosophical Writings.* Eds. and Trans. Adriaan Peperzak, Simon Critchley, and Robert Bernasconi. Bloomington: Indiana University Press, 1996.

EI   *Ethics and Infinity*. Conversations with Philippe Nemo. Trans. Richard A. Cohen. Pittsburgh: Duquesne University Press, [1982] 1985.

EN   *Entre Nous: On Thinking-of-the-Other*. Trans. Michael B. Smith and Barbara Harshav. New York: Columbia University Press, 1998.

FF   *Face to Face with Levinas*. Ed. Richard A. Cohen. Albany: State University of New York Press, 1986.

GCM   *Of God Who Comes to Mind*. Trans. Bettina Bergo. Stanford: Stanford University Press, 1998.

LR   *The Levinas Reader*. Ed. Seán Hand. Oxford: Blackwell, 1989.

NTL   *Nine Talmudic Lectures*. Trans. Annette Aronowicz. Bloomington: Indiana University Press, 1990.

OB   *Otherwise than Being, Or Beyond Essence*. Trans. Alphonso Lingis. Dordrecht: Kluwer, [1974] 1991.

"Paradox"   "The Paradox of Morality: An Interview with Emmanuel Levinas," with Tamra Wright, Peter Hughes, and Alison Ainley, in *The Provocation of Levinas: Rethinking the Other*, pp. 168–80. Eds. Robert Bernasconi and David Wood. London: Routledge, [1986] 1998.

PN   *Proper Names*. Trans. Michael B. Smith. Stanford: Stanford University Press, 1996.

TI   *Totality and Infinity*. Trans. Alphonso Lingis. Pittsburgh: Duquesne University Press, [1961] 1969.

TIME   *Time and the Other*. Trans. Richard A. Cohen. Pittsburgh: Duquesne University Press, [1947] 1987.

"Trace"   "The Trace of the Other." *In Deconstruction in Context: Literature and Philosophy,* pp. 45–59. Ed. Mark C. Taylor; trans. Alphonso Lingis. Chicago: University of Chicago Press, [1963] 1986.

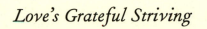

Love's Grateful Striving

introduction

What does the love commandment—'love your neighbor as yourself'—ask us to do? Each of the three elements leaves room for questions: Who is my neighbor? What is love? How should 'as yourself' be interpreted? Dostoyevsky's famous rebel, Ivan Karamazov, confesses to his brother: "I never could understand how one can love one's neighbours. In my view, it is one's neighbours that one can't possibly love, but only perhaps these who live far away. . . . To love a man, it's necessary that he should be hidden, for as soon as he shows his face, love is gone."[1] Ivan assumes the neighbor is the one near to you, and he sees such love as an impossible demand. In *The Idiot*, another of Dostoyevsky's characters locates the domain of the commandment more broadly: for Nastassya Filippovna, the commandment raises the question, "Can one love everyone, all people, all one's neighbors?" She replies: "Of course not, it would even be unnatural. In an abstract love for humanity one almost always loves only oneself."[2] She assumes the neighbor is "all people" and considers the requirement unnatural and evasively abstract. Friedrich Nietzsche admitted to being grateful to Dostoyevsky's psychological insights and seems to echo the conclusions of both these characters— with, of course, his own twist—in Zarathustra's discourse "On Love of the Neighbor."[3] Zarathustra has an idealistic version of Ivan's preference for abstraction: "Do I recommend love of the neighbor to you? Sooner I should even recommend flight from the neighbor and love of the farthest. Higher than love of the neighbor is love of the farthest and the future." He also echoes something of Nastassya's sensitivity to the disguises of self-love when he insists: "Your love of the neighbor is your bad love of yourselves. You flee to your neighbor from yourselves and would like to make a virtue out of that."

So we must ask again—what does the love commandment command us to do? Does it ask us to love everyone at the same time, and with identical expressions? But so many people, so little time! These simple limits should spare us any agony

3

in reading the commandment as one that prescribes a physically impossible task. Is the only alternative an abstract love of humanity? Is this itself, however, an escapist refuge for self-love? Does the commandment apply only to those with whom we come in contact, whose faces we see? But with today's media we see more faces than we can physically attend to. Does it apply only to those in our limited arena of physical contact? Or is this, too, a way in which we escape from more significant or long-range demands on us? Is it the calculated and reasonable reciprocity of the Golden Rule, or is it an *infinite* demand?

Dostoyevsky's questions remain at the heart of an increasing number of contemporary discussions about our responsibility to and for each other. Sometimes these discussions ask the same nineteenth-century question outright: what does the love commandment ask us to do? They contrast *eros* and *agape,* questioning whether agape can do justice to the special relations we have (e.g., to our spouse or child) and whether there are any limits to the sacrifice required. Others use a distinctive idiom to express these concerns—an idiom that speaks about the constitution of selfhood, about respecting the other's otherness (alterity), and about the role of self-esteem. Is love of another possible without seeing the other as *another-me?* On the other hand, if I do see the other as another-me, is love of an *other* possible? Does the alternative of seeing *oneself as another* break through the barriers of sameness or merely reinforce them? If I come to be a self *through* another, a self through a Thou, is self-love still instrumentally using the other? In a world where the atrocities of genocide and 'ethnic cleansing' still haunt us, what does the qualification 'as yourself' amount to? All of them—traditional, modern, and postmodern—ask what is the source of my obligation: does it lie in the other person, in the relation between us, or in an external command?

Søren Kierkegaard's *Works of Love* is a book about relationship that addresses all these questions. Consisting of two series of deliberations on love published under Kierkegaard's own name in 1847, it is about relationship in two distinct senses: it speaks about our relation *to* other persons—in the sense of our responsibility to and for them—and it speaks about our relation *with* another person—in the sense of the qualities that characterize a particular relation with a concrete, distinctive other. Kierkegaard takes to heart the variety of biblical reminders that press the commandment to ever-increasing inclusiveness—from loving those who also love you, to loving those who do not love you, to loving those who persecute you, to loving all people without exception. Moreover, unlike many interpreters of the commandment, he is not afraid to take the 'as yourself' clause seriously. *Works of Love* addresses questions about the character and limits of responsibility to and for others, as well as about the ethical relevance of sameness, commonality, difference, and alterity. It is also a detailed discussion of human interrelation that implies a distinctive understanding of one's relation to oneself, as well as a distinctive understanding of one's relation to the Transcendent or the Source of all selves. Thus, in addition to bringing us into the arena in which contemporary discussions of impartiality, partiality, alterity, and essentialism take place, *Works of Love* engages with contemporary debates about 'gift,' self-sacrifice, and self-esteem, as well as with discussions of ways in which God (or the "trace" of God) figures in human relations for a religious person.

If I am correct in this description of the concerns of *Works of Love*, it should in principle make a significant contribution to these contemporary discussions about what constitutes selfhood and the normative character of the relation between selves. Analytic moral philosophy, existentialism, deconstruction, Marxism, feminism—all of these are seedbeds, which generate different kinds of discussions because of their different vantage points and their different tools and methods of inquiry. Prominent contemporary discussions of selfhood and the relation of one self to another self offer what seem to be quite different (and sometimes incompatible) understandings of the relevance of need, desire, self-esteem, self-sacrifice, violence, mutuality, gift, transcendence, and the extent of responsibility for another. *Works of Love* speaks to all these issues, but it has not often been looked at as a resource for these topics, for two main reasons.

First, there has long been a pervasive sense that Kierkegaard's emphasis, throughout his writings, on both "the individual" and the utter transcendence of God precludes his having anything interesting or important to say about relationships between human beings. Those interested in discovering what Kierkegaard has to say on ethics or relationships between people most often turn to *Either/Or II* and *Fear and Trembling*. But these books are written by pseudonyms, authors created by Kierkegaard, who present partial perspectives on the ethical. Although in the pseudonymous writings one may discern important anticipations of the ethic found in *Works of Love*,[4] I suggest that they can only be appreciated properly when seen in relation to this work. Without moving forward to *Works of Love*, scholarship can only unfairly evaluate Kierkegaard's various contributions to ethics; yet some of the most popular accounts of Kierkegaard's place in the history of ethics have been done solely from the limited perspective of the pseudonymous works.[5]

Many feminist critiques have also suffered from this restricted view of Kierkegaard's accounts of ethics.[6] I cannot do justice to the growing field of feminist ethics in this book, but there is a substantial overlap between feminist critiques of Kierkegaard's ethic and those I examine in detail, especially for questions about sacrifice, mutuality, self-love, and special relations.[7] There is, I recognize, a distinctively feminist concern about the undeniable expressions of misogyny in several of Kierkegaard's writings that can bear on the possibility he allows (or precludes) for a woman to achieve a genuinely ethical self; but since there is no consensus even among feminists on this issue,[8] I will limit my concern to that aspect of feminist critiques that highlights the importance of mutuality, self-esteem, and distinctive and individualized responsiveness to the other. Moreover, I propose that the resources uncovered in *Works of Love* for addressing concreteness and interpersonal relationships should be taken into account by feminist critics as well.

Second, even when *Works of Love* has been recognized as an appropriate resource for exploring Kierkegaard's account of ethical human relationship, it is still not allowed to stand in its own right. Its reputation is presently its greatest liability. Its initial reception in Europe and the United States in the twentieth century was powerfully and negatively affected by some very influential critics—like T. W. Adorno, Karl Barth, and K. E. Løgstrup[9]—to such an extent that many today assume that they know its message and do not actually take the time and trouble to examine it firsthand. They take for granted that what such critics have said—namely, that *Works of Love* presents an ethic that is asocial, otherworldly, nonmutual, and unlivable—obviates the need to bring it into conversation with other ethics, except perhaps as an a priori foil. Its reputation as an example of contempt for the earthly—both socioeconomic conditions and the demands of special relations with family, friends, and the beloved—precedes it and reinforces the general inclination not to look to Kierkegaard for insights into human relationships. This is a particularly pressing issue at the moment since the critique by Løgstrup is presently being given a second life under the auspices of a prestigious American philosopher and ethicist.[10]

Even without this remarketing of Løgstrup's critique, the damage has been done. Too often, when *Works of Love* is included in graduate courses in theological ethics, the selection of the required readings within it often simply perpetuates the way in which the professor first came to know *Works of Love;* thus, certain standard deliberations (the ones that have been most criticized in the past) are chosen for attention, whereas most of the others are ignored. Students end up reading only what will, because it is out of context, apparently reinforce the stereotypes of spiritual dualism and unrealistic demands for impossible perfection.

Although there have been many valuable, recent efforts by fine scholars to undermine interpretations of asociality and acosmism for the rest of Kierkegaard's corpus,[11] less has been done in exploring *Works of Love's* deliberations to assess such challenges.[12] Happily, there has been a quite recent upsurge of attention to *Works of Love*, with impressive and sensitive readings by individual scholars,[13] although there has not been an analysis of all the deliberations in relation to one another. Moreover, the negative picture of *Works of Love* remains the dominant one today for ethicists, and we still find many of the earlier criticisms repeated by contemporary readers. For example, as recently as 1998, in an essay entitled "Something Anti-social about *Works of Love*," Peter George contends that although some of Kierkegaard's later polemical works (like *For Self-Examination* and *Judge for Yourself!*) make a strong case for "social relationships, including an active, open and interactive love-relationship," *Works of Love* does not give evidence of that concern.[14] George is typical of those who argue that Kierkegaard's ethic in *Works of Love* excludes preferential love and reduces all relationships to the God relationship.[15] He concludes that Kierkegaard's commitment to the hiddenness of genuine love results in an ethic "describing the self's relation to itself," a "one-termed relationship," which because it precludes reciprocity, is not a relationship at all.[16] George's evaluation of this ethic is as follows: "Even though love helps, it cannot be a particularly active love if the help remains hidden. Such help is not interactive, for the person who was helped cannot even respond with gratitude. Such a relationship, then, is not two-termed and social, but one-termed and individual."[17]

In the end, according to George, there is something antisocial in *Works of Love* because Kierkegaard is not yet willing to argue "that a social and interactive relationship with other people is necessary if the self is to be authentically spiritual."[18] Sometimes critics have seemed to be attempting to make the case that

Kierkegaard's ethic is not concerned with other people. But this is hard to do once we go beyond the pseudonymous writings. The more interesting debate, as George and others recognize, revolves around whether the concern for others comes only after or independently of the self's project of gaining subjectivity (or being in the right relation to God) or whether concern for others is a necessary and constitutive part of the self's project of becoming a self (before God). In other words, the real question is whether, in Kierkegaard's view, becoming a self only allows concern for others or whether it requires it. It will be the task of this book to provide a reading of *Works of Love* that considers all of its deliberations in detail and in relation to one another for the sake of answering this question.

It is also part of that task to address the perennial criticisms as well—that Kierkegaard's ethic precludes preferential love or puts it in conflict with neighbor love; that it requires a lack of reciprocity; that it is unethically individualistic; and that it is otherworldly, asocial, or acosmic. The fact that these sorts of criticisms of *Works of Love* have had such a long life is significant: it takes two to create such an impression, and there must be something in *Works of Love* that is able to generate or sustain such criticisms. What has long intrigued me is that this extremely negative picture of the ethic in *Works of Love* has come to be the dominant one even though the bulk of textual material found in the fifteen deliberations themselves belies that picture. At the very least there is much to put alongside the few texts that are repeatedly brought forth in criticism. Consider the following excerpts, presented here as a foretaste of the alternative reading I hope to substantiate, a constructive reading that will address in detail the specific, historically important criticisms of *Works of Love*.

Early in the book, Kierkegaard expresses his agreement with the view that "life without loving is not worth living" (WL, p. 38); in the Conclusion, he elaborates: "To love people is the only thing worth living for, and without this love you are not really living . . . to love people is the only true sign that you are a Christian" (p. 375). From beginning to end, Kierkegaard emphasizes how deep and valid is the human need to love and to be loved. When he exclaims: "How impoverished never to have loved" (pp. 63, 101, 175), he is not talking about love for God but is referring to our "innate need for companionship" (p. 154); indeed, "so deeply is this need rooted in human nature, and so *essentially* does it belong to being human that . . . even our Lord Jesus Christ, even he humanly felt this need to love and be loved by an individual human being" (p. 155).

"Kinship" with others is also a constant theme, but a kinship that does not alienate us from other groups. He refers to the "kinship of all human beings," a "kinship secured by each individual's equal kinship with and relation to God in Christ" (WL, p. 69). He speaks of the "inhumanity" and "unchristianness" of "wanting to deny kinship with all people, with unconditionally every person" (pp. 74, 75), and he repeatedly condemns the ways in which people deny "kinship with other human beings" (p. 85).

Moreover, relationships are two-sided—"Without a *you* and an *I* there is no love" (WL, p. 266)—and concrete: "When it is a duty in loving to love the people we see, *then in loving the actual individual person it is important that one does not substitute an imaginary idea of how we think or could wish that this person should be.* The one who does this does not love the person he sees but again something unseen, his own idea or something similar" (p. 164; the emphases here are all Kierkegaard's).

Finally, as if anticipating charges that his ethic polarizes God and human beings or renders the relation to human beings only an indirect one, he insists that "God is changed into an unreal something, a delusion," if a person believes that "the more he rejects those he sees, the more he loves the unseen" (WL, p. 160). Such a view "misrepresents God, as if God were envious of himself and of being loved, instead of the blessed God's being merciful and therefore continually pointing away from himself, so to speak, and saying, 'If you want to love me, then love the people you see; what you do for them, you do for me'" (p. 160).

At the very least, these passages show that the book is not so one-sided as it is reputed to be. Some, however, admitting that *Works of Love* contains these kinds of formulations, have suggested that, as far as it is true, it is evidence of a great contradiction within *Works of Love*. For those who are aware only of the parts of *Works of Love* that are usually targeted for criticism, I want to show in detail some of its richness. For those who see evidence of a contradiction, I want to argue that there is a way to make sense of *Works of Love* as a coherent whole. Moreover, I shall suggest that there are good reasons for *not* dividing the two series into separate and successive concerns with law and then gospel, as has commonly been done.[19]

My examination of these deliberations will highlight four areas of concern, although none of them is absolutely separable from the others. The first area is Kierkegaard's cautions about self-love, which have often been taken to imply a hatred or fear of self, one that precludes self-esteem and caring for the self. I will argue that these cautions are actually in the service of showing how important to him the integrity of the other is, even, or especially, in relationships. That is, his warnings against mistaking relations that are solely preferential for genuine love are ways of safeguarding the genuine otherness of another. *Works of Love* provides overwhelming evidence that Kierkegaard is acutely sensitive to the many and subtle ways in which we turn the other into "another-me," a "second-I," or me with another inflection. Like others before him, he attacks a self-love that can be both devious and ingenious; he uncovers the ways in which relationships based on preference can deepen our restrictive concern with ourself. However, what looks like negativity toward the self can be reconstrued as actually an attempt to safeguard the other's distinctive integrity within relationships—what thinkers today describe as appreciating the other's alterity, or resisting the assimilation of the other into sameness. Kierkegaard's pseudonymous critique of the life lived in purely aesthetic categories imparts the same message indirectly by attacking the aesthete's lack of genuine engagement with another, as well as the manipulative use of the other for one's enjoyment.

Second, for issues of concreteness and abstraction, readings of *Works of Love* have tended to do one of the following: (1) criticize its focus on the abstract category of "human being," ignoring its attention to distinctiveness/difference; (2) defend it from the charge of abstraction by indicating its emphases on distinctiveness and difference, deemphasizing its reliance on assumptions about the "essentially" human; (3) admit emphases on both essence and difference, arguing that they are finally incompatible and irreconcilable; or (4) point to both emphases, assuming that they are compatible without exploring or accounting for the apparent incompatibility. I want not only to argue that *Works of Love* contains resources for an understanding of impartiality that allows moral attention to concrete difference and the distinctive needs of individuals but also to account for the contrasting emphases on abstraction and concreteness, essence and difference.

The third area of concern is the implications of Kierkegaard's ethic for the material, the this-worldly needs of both the other and the self. To cover the various construals of this concern, I examine Kierkegaard's recommendations to ignore "distinctions" and his dismissal of "externals," arguing that when seen in context they do not promote indifference to the material condition of other people or a passive resignation to the status quo. In this respect it is important to appreciate how Kierkegaard's emphasis on reconciliation and forgiveness reveals the value he places on interpersonal relationships. In addition, I address Kierkegaard's understanding of God as "the middle term," arguing that it does not reduce his ethic to one in which we do not *directly* love our neighbor, one in which love for others is so mediated that it results in their being used as stepping-stones in our relationship with God. Finally, I address the question of the role of self-denial, suffering, or persecution in this ethic. In all these ways I will be considering whether this ethic entails an intrinsic opposition for the believer between God and God's creation.

The fourth area of concern is the notion of "infinite debt," found in *Works of Love,* and the question of whether it results in an unlivable ethic. Here the questions are whether the ethic is fulfillable and whether it entails undue sacrifice of self or insufficient self-esteem.

Although *Works of Love* has received increased attention in the past decade, there is still need for a direct grappling with the text in detail, in its entirety, in its own right, and in context. We need to consider anew, as if for the first time, the particular deliberations and comments that have caused the most consternation; we need to set them in the context of the other deliberations, and we need to try to see what is at stake for Kierkegaard and why he is so willing to take the risk of being misunderstood. Like all religious writers, he walks a tightrope, attempting to do justice both to immanence and to transcendence. Texts are responses to particular problems, with particular audiences in mind, and this applies not only to *Works of Love* as a whole but to each of the deliberations as well. Kierkegaard, more than most, is extremely self-conscious of himself as a writer attempting to communicate something that needs to be appropriated. We need to ask of every deliberation what in this text invites criticism, what is its audience, what is at stake, and what are the options for reading it?

Throughout this study I will draw heavily on the text, presenting Kierkegaard's own words at great length. Kierkegaard is an elegant and entertaining and at times mischievous writer, and often there is no sense in trying to paraphrase him since his own words dramatically make his points better than any paraphrase could. My hope is that this generous use of Kierkegaard's own words will tempt readers to begin their own process of engagement with *Works of Love*. I want to provoke a fresh reading, one that challenges the distorting sediment of layers of second-hand criticism passed on uncritically to students and other readers. But I am not concerned only about responding to unfair criticism. This controversial book has had its adoring fans, as well as its harsh and unyielding critics. Despite being grist for the mill of many a critic, *Works of Love* has been seen by many outside the academic community as a rich source of spiritual edification. But uncritical devotion is as bad as unfair criticism. What *Works of Love* has lacked, thus far, has been detailed exegetical attention by sympathetic critics and by open-minded defenders. I hope to facilitate this by providing a sympathetic yet critical reading that proceeds in detail from *Works of Love's* opening prayer through its fifteen separate deliberations and conclusion.

This study will result in a form of detailed commentary on the fifteen deliberations of *Works of Love*, and I will consider them in order, allowing readers to more easily find material relevant to a given deliberation. Because each of my chapters is dedicated to particular themes raised in succeeding deliberations, none of them will give the whole picture on any 'big' question—for example, the status of self-love, the content of our obligation, the question of mutuality, or the implications for the relation to community. Therefore I have provided significant cross references among chapters. Still, because part of the purpose of my study is to show that the separate deliberations need to be read in light of one another, soon after the beginning I call into play material from throughout the entire text. Sometimes deliberations build on one another, one assuming things from an earlier piece or the mention of an issue that will be more fully addressed only later; at other times they mutually illuminate and elaborate one another in other crucial ways. There will, in addition, be a number of different grids involved at the same time: for example, the fifteen explicit topics of the deliberations; the triad of self, other, and God; the contrast (and relation) between inner and outer; and the various dimensions of love, which I term Love's Law, Love's Labor, Love's Gift, Love's Vision, and so on.

Moreover, I plan to take into account the fact that Kierkegaard was working on a variety of other pieces of writing at the same time as he was preparing *Works of Love*, as well as the fact that earlier and later writings address some of the same themes. I will turn to these insofar as they can illuminate what is going on in *Works of Love*. For example, Kierkegaard completed the first series of deliberations in *Works of Love* in April 1847 and the second in August. In March of that same year he published his *Upbuilding Discourses in Various Spirits*, and these three discourses can complement themes in *Works of Love*. Indeed, all of the discourses that he entitles "upbuilding discourses" should be relevant to the deliberation "Love Builds Up." Moreover, in June 1847, he made a sketch of what would become the second part of his *Christian Discourses*, and almost all the chapters of that section (which he completed in November 1847) bear importantly on themes in *Works of Love*. Finally, although some were published much earlier, Kierkegaard wrote a number of other discourses that are relevant to this study; for example, he wrote three separate discourses entitled "Love Hides a Multitude of Sins," which should complement study of the deliberation with that very same title in *Works of Love*.

Looking back on his work, Kierkegaard insisted that there was "a powerful polemic in *Works of Love*."[20] In the chapters that follow I want to explore *Works of Love* precisely as a polemic, illuminating the theological and social context to which Kierkegaard's formulations about the importance of "works" (and the relation between works and love or faith) are a response. I want to explore Kierkegaard's provocative recommendations about "works" of love in the explicit light of what he thought needed to be said about works to his audience, that is, his readers, situated as they were in a religiosity in which, as he says, "the Lutheran emphasis on faith has now simply become a fig leaf for the most unchristian shirking."[21]

To those familiar with the Lutheran tradition, the English translation of the title of this text, *Works of Love*, can be misleading. The Danish word *gerninger*, however, simply means 'deeds' or 'acts,' with no connotations of the question of 'merit' that Luther associated with "works-righteousness."[22] Still, the more general question of Kierkegaard's relation both to Luther's thought and to the Lutheranism of his day is an important one and awaits comprehensive treatment. Throughout this study I hope to show that Kierkegaard was deeply committed to what he saw as the core doctrines defended by Luther—namely, confidence in the God who loved us first, reliance on grace, and the impossibility of merit. Given this fundamental agreement, it seems appropriate to assume that Kierkegaard is not challenging Luther's views unless he makes this explicit. That is, Kierkegaard found in Luther some indispensable shared commitments, which we can expect to be in play throughout the whole of *Works of Love*, even if he does not continue to call them explicitly to our attention. Nevertheless, it is crucial in reading *Works of Love* to appreciate his unmitigated critique of the Lutheranism of his day, as well as the particular nature of his love/hate relationship with Luther's own understanding of Christianity. Without doubt, Kierkegaard sought to redress a Lutheranism that was taking "in vain Luther and the significance of his life,"[23] and the bulk of his journal comments on Luther accuse nineteenth-century Danes of misappropriating Luther; in some comments, however, the blame goes to Luther himself for having been confused or at least for having carelessly occasioned a huge and deadly confusion about faith.[24]

Thus I will be taking Kierkegaard's judgment that Lutheranism (and occasionally Luther himself) made the mistake of taking a "corrective" and turning it into a "norm," and I will be using it as a fundamental hermeneutical principle for reading *Works of Love*. This will lead me to highlight the ways in which certain central assumptions, shared with Luther (within Luther's corrective), inform the entire work, as well as the ways in which Kierkegaard may, in order to provide a corrective, depart from Luther. But just as importantly, it will mean highlighting the ways in which *Works of Love* itself bears the mark of being meant as a corrective with respect to issues of socioeconomic equality and political conformity. Everything he says against 'the world'—the search for worldly equality and the selfishness and irresponsibility of a community of self-lovers—needs to be seen in the light of his fears about the dangers of the particular social and political currents of his age.

Consideration of *Works of Love* in the light of Luther's commitments and

Kierkegaard's response to them is a sine qua non of any full appreciation of *Works of Love,* but I also want to examine Kierkegaard's ethic in relation to the twentieth-century's legacy of inhumanity. For Emmanuel Levinas, the Lithuanian-born Jewish philosopher whose life spanned our century (1906–95), the "essential problem" was whether we could speak "of an absolute commandment after Auschwitz," whether we could "speak of morality after the failure of morality"[25] Levinas's response was an ethic in which we each have *infinite* responsibility for *every other*—every neighbor and every stranger—and it has been criticized for its hyperbolic extremism. Moreover, Levinas, like Kierkegaard, has been criticized for rejecting the notion of "reciprocity" in the ethical relation. These commonalities between Levinas and Kierkegaard suggest that it would be fruitful to consider many aspects of *Works of Love* in the light of Levinas's other-centered ethic.[26] I suggest that Kierkegaard's commitments to notions of commanded love, duty, and infinite debt to the other bring his ethic into productive conversation with those in our day who, like Levinas, argue for the precedence of ethics over ontology.[27]

More radical than Kierkegaard's better-known critiques of speculation and metaphysics, the moral critique in *Works of Love* highlights responsibility for the other as the primary dynamic of human intersubjectivity and focuses on the negative implications of various metaphysical totalizing systems, whose emphasis on being (rather than "becoming") is a way of hierarchizing people. Kierkegaard's critique is in this sense a version of the argument for the precedence of love over being.[28] In my reading, Kierkegaard's emphasis on equality is, at least in part, a polemic against marginalizing those who are at the bottom of the 'ontological ladder'—the poor, the oppressed, the exploited, the 'paltry,' the slave. Although it might take some imagination for those who know only Kierkegaard's other writings to think of him as an advocate of the poor and downtrodden, I encourage readers to be open to the unexpected in *Works of Love.* When Kierkegaard insists that to love the neighbor is "essentially to will to exist equally for unconditionally every human being" (WL, p. 84), he is not mouthing platitudes; he intends the claim for equality to be understood concretely. It is "due to Christianity," he claims, that "the times are past when only the powerful and the prominent were human beings—and the others were bond servants and slaves" (p. 74), and that "the times are past when those called the more lowly had no conception of themselves or only the conception of being slaves, or not merely being lowly human beings but of not being human beings at all" (p. 80). The love commandment is precisely a challenge because many have "inhumanly forgotten" that "whether a person is a man or woman, poorly or richly endowed, master or slave, beggar or plutocrat, the relationships among human beings ought and may never be such that the one worships and the other is the one worshipped" (p. 125).

chapter one

Love's Grateful Striving

Preface, Prayer, "Love's Hidden Life and Its
Recognizability by Its Fruits" (I)

The introduction to *Works of Love* consists of a Preface to the reader, a Prayer, and then an opening deliberation that provides general guidelines, setting the stage for the deliberations proper. I propose to treat these as the introduction to the whole of *Works of Love* for two reasons. When first thinking about this project, Kierkegaard noted his intention to produce a single series of twelve lectures on love (erotic love, friendship, and neighbor love),[1] and although he gave the publisher two series of deliberations, there is no indication that there was any theological or conceptual rationale for the division. Moreover, since there is only one Conclusion to the deliberations, it seems appropriate to treat the whole as a single work.[2]

I. The Preface

The Preface provides guidance for the reader, emphasizing two main points. The first turns on the meaning of the word "deliberations," which is found in the subtitle, describing *Works of Love* as "Some Christian Deliberations in the Form of Discourses." His intended reader is that "single individual" who will first "deliberate" about *whether* to read these deliberations and then "lovingly deliberate" *on* them. In the same year in which he wrote *Works of Love*, Kierkegaard made an explicit contrast in his journals between a "deliberation" (*Overveielse*) and an "upbuilding discourse," which can shed light on his purpose. "A deliberation," he says, "does not presuppose the definitions as given and understood; therefore, it must not so much move, mollify, reassure, persuade, as *awaken* and provoke people and sharpen thought."[3] Whereas an upbuilding discourse about love "presupposes that people know essentially what love is," a deliberation "must first fetch them up out of the cellar" and "turn their comfortable way of thinking topsy-turvy with the dialectic of truth." If we take this seriously we should expect *Works of Love* to provide clarifications of key definitions and concepts necessary to an understanding of the way in which genuine love expresses itself in works; moreover, we should expect it to be provocative and to "awaken" people. We shall see that it fulfills these expectations: it is an unusual combination of thoughtful analyses permeated with the message that "love is a revolution."[4]

How do these deliberations fit into Kierkegaard's authorship as a whole? First, the subtitle and Preface and journal entry contrast deliberations with discourses, so we should note that *Works of Love* is the only book that he entitles "Deliberations," in contrast to a large number of "discourses": *Eighteen Upbuilding Discourses, Three Discourses on Imagined Occasions, Upbuilding Discourses in Various Spirits, Christian Discourses*, and various "Communion" Discourses. All of these, deliberations and discourses alike, are signed "S. Kierkegaard." But most people who have heard of Kierkegaard are probably more familiar with titles like *Fear and Trembling, Either/Or*, and *The Concept of Anxiety*—works that he published under pseudonyms; these are writings authored by a variety of created characters who usually have symbolic names (e.g., Johannes de Silentio, Victor Eremita, and Vigilius Haufniensius). Although these works are now catalogued in libraries and bookstores under "K" for Kierkegaard, it is interesting to note that the original volumes would have been placed in alphabetical order according to the author or editor listed on the book's spine, for example, Victor Eremita. In retrospective accounts of his authorship late in his career, Kierkegaard divided his writings into those signed by him and those put forth under pseudonyms, reminding the reader that both sorts were published in tandem from the beginning to the end of his career.[5] He explains that the pseudonymous writings provide "indirect communication" to an audience of those who are either straightforwardly "aesthetes" or are under the "illusion" that they live in Christian categories when they really live in aesthetic ones; these need to be addressed "indirectly" because one cannot dispel an illusion by a direct frontal attack. The signed writings, by contrast, are said to be religious writings, a form of "direct communication" addressed to those who profess Christianity and know what Christianity is but need to be encouraged or reassured.

The division between signed religious works and pseudonymous aesthetic or ethical works is a time-honored one, but the last decade has seen a variety of attempts to question the status and relevance of the contrast.[6] It is important to note that whether he intended to or not, Kierkegaard himself complicates that simple division in several significant ways. First, although the retrospective account of his authorship, "The Point of View for My Work as an Author," was published under his own name, Kierkegaard dallied with the idea of publishing it under the pseudonym A-O.[7] Moreover, he elsewhere characterized "direct" communication as one that seeks to impart information, and "indirect" communication as one that seeks to communicate a "capability";[8] since it is plausible to assume that all his writings attempt to provoke or facilitate a practical change in the reader's way of living, one could conclude that all his writings are "indirect" in at least that one important sense. Finally, although Kierkegaard himself tells us that we should not attribute any of the words of the pseudonyms to him,[9] he sometimes changes to a pseudonym after he has written the entire book or, alternatively, wishes he had written a pseudonymous work in his own name; occasionally he even seems to have been caught up in the fun of simply experimenting with names.[10] Thus, despite the fact that the pseudonymous authors seem symbolically related to their communications, one cannot simply assume that a given work was prepared from the beginning as the creation of a given pseudonym. That the writings are pseudonymous cannot be ignored, but there is no simple way to positively formulate the relevance of the pseudonyms.

In short, much has been written about the literary status of Kierkegaard's authorship, and there is no consensus about what to make of it. It would be difficult to think of another writer who used such a remarkable variety of literary genres: in addition to discourses and deliberations, there are diaries, novels, aphorisms, reviews, and retrospectives. Or, seen from another angle, the writings range across a dialectical lyric, a venture in experimental psychology, a "mimical monograph," a fragment of philosophy, and a postscript to that fragment that he terms a "mimical-pathetical-dialectical compilation." Moreover, he was unusually self-conscious about questions concerning interpretation of texts and authorial strategies—questions about the autonomy of a text and the authority of an author (or lack of it). All of this makes reading Kierkegaard's works a fascinating (if sometimes dizzying) experience, and the reader who comes to any of his works for the first time needs a little orientation.

For our purposes here, however, we do not need to make any judgment about what the real Kierkegaard believed. The text, *Works of Love,* stands before us as a suggestive proposal that deserves serious consideration by those interested in the commandment to love one's neighbor. It is enough to note that "deliberation" seems to be a middle category, consisting of work signed by him but different from a discourse in its goal. Whereas an upbuilding or Christian discourse presumes an audience that already knows "essentially what love is," and therefore can appropriately "move, mollify [and] persuade," deliberations are intended to awaken people from their comfortable but confused ways of thinking. By presenting *Works of Love* in his own name but as a series of "deliberations" rather than discourses, Kierkegaard supports the inference that we should read the work as an instance of a peculiar category—as addressed to those who live in "inwardness" or "subjectivity" but do not yet know what Christian love 'at work' means. These people need to be awakened, turned topsy-turvy with respect to the limits of preferential loving (erotic love and friendship), but they are already in a position to be directly challenged by the idea of a working Christian love for one's neighbor.

One can also think of the awakening strategy Kierkegaard employs in terms of the Socratic method of maieutics—that of playing midwife, the role not of the one who gives the truth but of the one who facilitates its realization in us, helping the student to draw out what is already there in some form.[11] His method of indirection is a performative strategy in which one facilitates (sometimes through the trauma of paradox) another's self-realization. Kierkegaard's intention to withdraw himself from the reader's focus is apparent in his claim that he is not directly addressing the reader but merely repeating the 'you shall' with which eternity addresses him (WL, p. 90). Behind this strategy is Kierkegaard's assumption that only love can recognize love (p. 16), a strategy that builds up the love it presupposes is already in his readers. That is, *Works of Love* is maieutic in two senses: it employs the loving strategy of maieutics and it helps us to understand how love itself is maieutic.

The maieutic dimension is also seen in his subtitle, which offers the qualification "in the form of discourses." But it is also possible that he keeps these deliberations "in the form of discourses" so that we might remember the kind of advice he gives us elsewhere about the purpose of a discourse and the role of the reader as listener. For example, in the discourse "Purity of Heart," he tells us that to achieve its goal, a discourse must require more of the reader than merely the interpretive activity needed to understand the discourse: it "must *decisively* require something of the listener . . . it must unconditionally require his decisive self-activity, upon which everything depends."[12] First, as we saw, the reader of the Preface to *Works of Love* is addressed as the "single individual"; this category, which is absolutely central to Kierkegaard's thought, highlights both the concrete particularity of the reader and the reader's inalienable responsibility for his or her own judgments and actions.[13] This reader is therefore a listener on whom a practical demand is being placed. Kierkegaard compares the author of the discourse to the concealed prompter one finds in the theater, whispering lines to the actor, adding: "No one is so foolish as to regard the prompter [author of the text] as more important than the actor [the reader-listener]."[14] In other words, the reader is an active listener, not a spectator. The author speaks what the listener should appropriate so that the listener, now speaking in his or her own right, "says it himself to God."[15] The "Purity of Heart" discourse asks you a question, or equivalently "you are asking yourself through the discourse: What kind of life is yours; do you will one thing and what is this one thing?"[16] In other words, a discourse—any discourse—asks you whether a particular question is a genuine question for you; it asks you to put the question to yourself and to be able to answer it, one way or the other. This advice seems appropriate to the question of whether we love our neighbor, and it may account for the "form" that the deliberations on works of love take.

The second point made in this Preface may sound surprising at first. Kierkegaard says: "They are *Christian deliberations,* therefore not about *love* but about *works of love.*" Presumably, it is distinctively Christian to be concerned with love in action, expressed in works; moreover, it is about "works of love" that we need to be challenged. As he notes later in a journal comment, Christ was not concerned with a feeling but rather with action.[17] Kierkegaard admits that these writings cannot do justice either to *all* love's works or to any single one *in depth*—all the more reason for saying that it is not about "love" as such,[18] which would be an even more inexhaustible topic: "Something that in its total richness is *essentially* inexhaustible is also in its smallest work *essentially* indescribable just because essentially it is totally present everywhere and *essentially* cannot be described."

II. The Prayer

Because the introductory prayer is a rich source of insight into the remainder of the work and because it is seldom attended to, it is worth quoting at some length. Kierkegaard opens extravagantly: "How could one speak properly about love if you were forgotten, you God of love, source of all love in heaven and on earth; you who spared nothing but gave everything; you who are love, so that one who loves is what he is only by being in you!" He repeats this refrain, completing his address to the Trinity of Love: "How could one speak properly about love if you were forgotten, you who revealed what love is, you our Savior and Redeemer, who gave yourself in order to save all. How could one speak properly about love if you were forgotten, you Spirit of love, who take nothing of your own but remind us of that love-sacrifice, remind the believer to love as he is loved and his neighbor as himself!"[19] Embedded in this refrain is an implication for the reader: how could one speak properly about these deliberations on love if *this prayer* were forgotten—that is, if one lost sight of the theological commitments embedded in this prayer and assumed throughout the entire work? Kierkegaard continues: "O Eternal Love, you who are everywhere present and never without witness where you are called upon, be not without witness in what will be said here about love or about works of love." And what God is called to witness is that "no work can be pleasing unless it is a work of love: sincere in self-renunciation, a need in love itself, and for that very reason without any claim of meritoriousness!" It is interesting that the prayer is presented only once, at the outset, unlike the guidance for the reader, which is placed before each series. Presumably, readers need to be reminded; God, having heard our prayer once, doesn't. The prayer is important because it embodies crucial assumptions that inform all the analyses and recommendations that constitute *Works of Love;* indeed, it sets in place at the outset the indispensable parameters of Kierkegaard's discussion of love's works.

A. Gift and Striving

Kierkegaard's opening prayer makes it impossible to ignore his wholehearted embrace of the Lutheran principle of the priority of grace, and it is important that this not be forgotten even where it is not explicitly affirmed later on in *Works of Love*. First, in good Augustinian-Lutheran fashion, Kierkegaard assumes that to speak about love or works of love at all, we need to remember THAT GOD LOVED US FIRST. When he says to God in prayer that the "one who loves is what he is only by being in you," he is foreshadowing what will be made far more explicit throughout the deliberations: in the first deliberation we will be told explicitly that God's love is the source, origin, and wellspring of love in us, and in later deliberations we will be reminded again and again that "God loved us first" (WL, p. 336; also pp. 101, 126). It is worth noting that the prayer's appeal to the Trinity reminds us that the love that is God's gift is not only given in creation but also renewed through Christ's death. This dimension of love as GIFT OR GRACE is in place from the outset and is the standard by which we are to interpret any and all references to *our effort*. That is, our effort cannot, as Kierkegaard says, give us any "claim to meritoriousness." We are given love by God (or better, love is the presence of God in us), and we are thereby empowered to love. The theme of gift or grace, enabling and empowering us—which is set forth in the profoundly serious context of a prayer—underlies all the deliberations.

Second, Kierkegaard appeals to the Spirit's reminder that love comes in the form of "love's sacrifice"—in other words, after gift or grace comes works[20]— as well as the reminder that the believer is "to love as he is loved and his neighbor as himself!" The perhaps surprising phrasing—with its "love as he is loved *and* his neighbor as himself," as if there were two separable aspects—recalls the two forms of the neighbor love commandment found in Scripture: "Love one another as I have loved you"[21] and "Love your neighbor as yourself."[22] The double formulation may be intended to remind us that although we are supposed to love our neighbor as God has loved us, there are some things only God can do, and the best we can do is to approach that by loving our neighbor as we love ourselves.

The prayer, with its emphasis on the gift of God's love to us and the commandment to love the neighbor, places the whole set of deliberations within a great parenthesis of GIFT and STRIVING, gifted love and grateful works. In a journal entry from 1847, presumably as he was in the process of preparing for or writing *Works of Love,* Kierkegaard expressed his sense of "the relationship between good works and faith" as follows:

> Good works in the sense of meritoriousness are naturally an abomination to God. Yet good works are required of a human being. But they shall be and yet shall not be; they shall be and yet one ought humbly to be ignorant of their being significant or that they are supposed to be of any significance . . . it is like a child's giving his parents a present, purchased, however, with what the child has received from his parents; all the pretentiousness which otherwise is associated with giving a present disappears when the child received from the parents the gift which he gives to the parents .[23]

In other words, good works are "required," although our ability to do them is itself a gift and does not "merit" grace.

Indeed, in Kierkegaard's journals we find a lovely formulation of this dual commitment: he writes that Christianity is "grace, and then a striving born of gratitude."[24] The implication is that our *effort* is important, although it cannot be meritorious in the sense of entitling us or giving us a right to something from God. Kierkegaard is assuming here the importance of a distinction between what I call *deserving* something from someone in the sense of having a right or entitlement to it and what I call *being gratefully receptive* to it; that is, we may not have deserved or merited some good thing given to us, but we can do something to prepare ourselves for an appropriate reception of the gift, to embrace it gratefully, or to appropriately express our gratitude through the exercise of love. The fundamental presuppositions of both gift and the striving born of gratitude will inform the entire set of fifteen deliberations. Only if we keep these commitments in mind can we go on to explore Kierkegaard's understanding of works of love.

The theology embedded in the prayer raises the question of Kierkegaard's relation to his Lutheran heritage, and at the end of this book I return to that important question. There is, however, one aspect of Kierkegaard's assessment of Luther that will be useful to touch on briefly here, precisely as a way of justifying one of the assumptions behind my reading of *Works of Love*—namely, that we should assume Kierkegaard is in theological agreement with Luther except for those places where he specifically notes otherwise. As early as 1846, Kierkegaard, indicating his familiarity with Luther's theology, described Luther's contribution as follows:

> What Luther says is excellent, the one thing needful and the sole explanation—that this whole doctrine (of the Atonement and in the main all Christianity) must be traced back to the struggle of the anguished conscience. Remove the anguished conscience, and you may as well close the churches and convert them into dance halls. . . . An atonement is necessary only in the understanding of anguished conscience. If a man had the power to live without needing to eat, how could he understand the necessity of eating—something the hungry man easily understands. It is the same in the life of the spirit.[25]

This passage, from the period in which Kierkegaard was beginning to write *Works of Love*, reveals not only a significant appreciation of Luther but also a claim that in the absence of the presupposition that Luther recognized (i.e., the anguished conscience), one can only misunderstand Christianity.

Kierkegaard is both a master psychologist and a master rhetorician—he realizes that some things can be understood only by people who have already had certain kinds of experiences (e.g., an anguished conscience or an experience of the church practice of indulgences as it occurred in Luther's time) and, therefore, one must be sensitive to the audience to which one speaks. Kierkegaard makes a passing reference in *Works of Love* to the experience of an anguished conscience (p. 201), and in the year just before his death he explicitly suggests that since there are no anguished consciences around anymore, the application of Luther's legitimate cure for the anguished conscience now amounts to a simple celebration of secularity. This is at the heart of his late negative judgments about Lutheranism: that "the tragedy about Luther is that a condition in Christendom at a particular time and place is transformed into the normative"; Lutheranism is a "corrective" that is "not qualified to stand alone."[26] But long before Kierkegaard expressed those sentiments he was already deeply troubled by the way in which people failed to appreciate the context in which Luther's protests were

made: "The tragedy of Christendom is clearly that we have removed the dialectical element from Luther's doctrine of faith, so that it has become a cloak for
sheer paganism and epicurianism [because] we completely forget that Luther
urged faith in contrast to a fantastically exaggerated asceticism."[27] As if to account for his own radical strategy, Kierkegaard suggests provocatively that
"Luther's true successor will come to resemble the exact opposite of Luther, because Luther came after the preposterous overstatement of asceticism," whereas
his successor comes "after the horrible fraud to which Luther's view gave
birth."[28]

This general conclusion—that Luther provided a "corrective," which was
taken "in vain" and now needs to be seen and reevaluated in the light of the particular abuses and exaggerations that generated it—is an important Kierkegaardian insight, which I suggest we take to heart in reading *Works of Love*. We need
to read all of Kierkegaard's recommendations in the light of a contrast between a
"corrective" and a "norm." He is himself providing a "corrective," as he sometimes admits, to Luther's corrective, and we should adopt his own awareness of
the ways in which correctives need to be formulated with great care and can, nevertheless, be misleading or misunderstood.[29] Since he is responding to a situation
in which "the Lutheran emphasis on faith has now simply become a fig leaf for
the most unchristian shirking,"[30] his own emphasis on the fruits of love, love in
its "outward direction," and the responsibility of "the individual" are framed
with an eye to the way faith has been taken as an excuse for not striving.

Ironically, however, the irresponsible inwardness that Kierkegaard wants to
correct walks hand in hand with an exaggerated emphasis on "externals" and
"reciprocity." Because in his judgment the appeal to saving grace has been misunderstood so that it amounts to secularity, he must bring in the counterweight of
self-denial. Kierkegaard responds to the particular situation of the audience to
which he speaks—the radicality of *Works of Love* responds to the radicality
of the misappropriation of Luther's thought. The task is a difficult one, namely,
to suggest an understanding of Christian love that embodies a tension between
an outwardness, which appropriately understands the contingency of external
achievements, and an inwardness, which is committed to striving and responsibility to others.

The way to do that is to maintain a dual commitment to striving and gift,
works and grace, law and love. Kierkegaard writes in his journals: "You must go
through this 'You shall'; this is the condition for *unconditional* respect. And behind this 'You shall' lies grace, and there everything smiles, there all is gentleness."[31] This epitomizes the structure of *Works of Love*. The "shall" is not alone:
behind it lies the gracious smile. We shall see that Kierkegaard's "Conclusion"
to *Works of Love* highlights how the love commandment is infinite comfort, as
well as infinite rigorousness, infinite lightness, as well as infinite heaviness. Gerard Manley Hopkins's lovely words, "lightning and love . . . a winter and
warm,"[32] are a precise translation of Kierkegaard's understanding that Christianity is "infinite humiliation and grace." The assumption behind all that Kierkegaard writes is his agreement with Luther about grace. In the end, Kierkegaard
says that he will "stand by the Lutheran principle," which he interprets as re-

minding us: "You are saved by grace; be reassured, you are saved by grace—and then you strive as well as you can."[33] The Kierkegaardian formulation of the Lutheran principle, then, is grace, humiliation, grace, and then a striving born of gratitude.

B. Need

A less obvious theme is introduced in the prayer—the theme of NEED—but its importance will become evident as the deliberations proceed. In fact, one could argue that the theme of need pervades *Works of Love* in various ways. Here Kierkegaard speaks of love's need—"a need in love itself [*en Kjerlighedens Trang*]." It is as yet only implicit, but what this shorthand form means, we shall see later, is that not only are we given love by God, empowered to love, but also there is a need in love *to express itself.* It is interesting to note that the word Kierkegaard uses to speak of this "need" is the strong Danish word *Trang*—a kind of passionate craving, a dynamic impulse coming from within and reaching out. Already we can see hints of what will be clearly stated in the first deliberation; that is, the need to love is generated by positive passion rather than hardship, which can be remedied. In other words, in this sense of the need of love, it is presence, rather than absence, that is the motivation. Moreover, Kierkegaard appears to connect the lack of merit with the need of love to express itself when he writes that a work of love is "for that very reason without any claim to meritoriousness." For both these reasons, the dynamic impulse of need—a theme that is developed in several different ways—will speak importantly to a variety of criticisms of *Works of Love,* including the question of love's motivation and concreteness.

The notion of love's need can be read in two ways—the need of love to express itself and the need for love. The first witnesses to a presence of love that needs to express itself; the second witnesses to an absence that calls out to be satisfied. Kierkegaard will speak of the need of love in both ways throughout *Works of Love.* Keeping these decisive emphases on gift, striving, and need in mind, we turn to the introductory deliberation.

III. "Love's Hidden Life and Its Fruits" (I)

The first deliberation, entitled "Love's Hidden Life and Its Recognizability by Its Fruits," addresses a contrast that underlies all of Kierkegaard's writings—that between inner and outer. In this deliberation, the contrast is presented in visual metaphors: unseen and seen, invisible and visible, hidden and revealed; in later deliberations it will also involve the contrast between blindness and vision. Moreover, in very Lutheran fashion, Kierkegaard presents the contrast as a condition of simultaneity—hidden *yet* revealed—rather than a mutually exclusive either/or. In other words, there is a tension between them, and in this first deliberation Kierkegaard is already indicating the difficulty of expressing the precise relation between the two sides of this tension.

A. Love's Hiddenness

Love, he insists, "dwells in hiding or is hidden in the innermost being" (WL, p. 9): "Just as the quiet lake originates deep down in hidden springs no eye has seen, so also does a person's love originate even more deeply in God's love. If there were no gushing spring at the bottom, if God were not love, then there would be neither the little lake nor a human being's love"—"a human being's love originates mysteriously in God's love" (pp. 9–10). Love's "hiddenness" refers to several things. First, love is hidden because its source is God, who is hidden, who is invisible, a "secret source." Second, love's hiddenness lies in the fact that it is a gift, something, as early mystics used to say, "without a why,"[34] unfathomable in the motivation of the giver. Both of these rationales, which imply the unfathomability of love, were already embedded in the opening prayer. Going beyond these now, Kierkegaard focuses in this deliberation on a third account of hiddenness—the hiddenness that amounts to a lack of certainty about whether love is indeed present (in another or in me), whether it is love that is generating a given attitude or course of action. Love is hidden because there are no guarantees that can infallibly attest to the presence of love—it is "not unconditionally and directly to be known by any particular expression of it" (p. 13). There is, he continues, "no word in human language, not one single one, not the most sacred one, about which we are able to say: If a person uses this word, it is unconditionally demonstrated that there is love in that person." The same is true of works, and "there is no work, not one single one, not even the best, about which we unconditionally dare to say: The one who does this unconditionally demonstrates love by it," for "it depends on *how* the work is done." Thus, two people can use the same word or engage in the same behavior, whereas in one person there is love and in the other there is not; indeed, two people can use opposite words or do opposite deeds and yet each be manifesting love.

Kierkegaard is suggesting that at least in one respect there is a kind of dissociation between inner and outer, and his point is commonsensical. He is reminding us of something we have all experienced—that it is often difficult to tell from observation of externals (the outer) what is really occurring. For example, it is hard to tell just from observing external behavior whether what is being handed to someone is a gift, a bribe, or a payment on a debt. Kierkegaard will bring this problem up explicitly toward the end of *Works of Love*, when he muses on the impossibility of portraying mercifulness: try to paint a woman giving another "the only bread she has," and you will see that although the loaf of bread is visible, the "most important thing," that it is "the only one she has," is not observable from the outside (pp. 324–25). This is an important point to which Kierkegaard returns repeatedly, and it is often the explanation for his emphasis on the irrelevance of externals.

This notion of human love's hiddenness parallels not only the hiddenness of the Godhead but also the hiddenness of the Incarnation of God. The theme of Christ's incognito is treated in the *Philosophical Fragments*, by Johannes Climacus: "Look, there he stands—the god. Where? There. Can you not see him? He is the god, and yet he has no place where he can lay his head."[35] God's love in

Christ wants to reveal itself, yet its revelation is always ambiguous. Just as in works of love, there must be revelation (since God would not have wanted "to walk through the world in such a way that not one single person would come to know it"), yet externals may be misleading.[36]

This opening deliberation thus highlights a common Kierkegaardian theme—the RISK implied by uncertainty. Kierkegaard reminds us about the two sides of risk: that "we can be deceived by believing what is untrue, but we certainly are also deceived by not believing what is true" (WL, p. 5). We risk being deceived in thinking love exists or is present, but we also risk being deceived in thinking it is not. We shall see this theme again explicitly in several deliberations in the second series, particularly the deliberation entitled "Love Believes All Things," in which Kierkegaard anticipates the question of the American pragmatist philosopher William James of whether it is better to be duped by hope or by fear.[37] Kierkegaard asks: "Which deception is the more dangerous?" and thereby reminds us that we can be impoverished by our cautious fear of risking, as well as by our foolhardy daring.

B. Love as Knowable

Despite the inevitable uncertainty that comes from the fact that there is no guarantee, no necessary and sufficient conditions that certify that love is at work, Kierkegaard nonetheless appeals to the scriptural verse that "the tree is TO BE KNOWN by its fruits." Love is indicated, made recognizable by its fruits; if it is able to be known in principle, its fruits must be "recognizable" (WL, p. 11). Kierkegaard sees himself here as in agreement with Luther. In a journal comment from 1849, he indicates his great respect for and forthright approval of Luther's position on to the outward expression of love:

> Here again Luther is completely right. No one can see faith, it is unseen; therefore no one can decide whether or not a man has faith. But faith shall be known by love. Nowadays we have wanted to make love into an unseen something, but against this Luther, together with Scripture, would protest, for love is Christianly the works of love. To say that love is a feeling and the like is really an unchristian conception . . . from a Christian point of view love is the works of love. Christ's love was not intense feeling, a full heart, etc.; it was rather the work of love, which is his life.[38]

Both Luther and Scripture would protest a dualistic spiritualization of love because both understand that love is not "an unseen something." When he calls on Luther (p. 78) explicitly in the chapter in *Works of Love* that he devotes to showing how Christianity is "sheer action," Kierkegaard is telling us not to be misled by the vehemence of Luther's reaction against the "merit" of works into thinking that Luther's alternative is an uncritical rejection of works as such.

Love is, like God, simultaneously hidden and revealed. There are, Kierkegaard insists, two thoughts in one: "When we say that love is known by its fruits, we are also saying that in a certain sense love itself is hidden and therefore is known only by its revealing fruits" (WL, p. 8). Love IS recognizable by its fruits; but this manifest thought contains the hidden one that Love is ONLY recognizable by its fruits. But note that Kierkegaard does not say that love is, or only is, recognized by its fruits; his double thought in fact contains a further hidden thought, which is that Love is only recognizABLE by its fruits, for as he notes later, *"to be able to be known by its fruits is a need in love"* (p. 10; emphasis mine). Fruits are necessary and sufficient conditions of recognizability; the point is to work so that love *"could* be known by its fruits, whether or not these come to be known by others" (p. 14).

Why, then, is there such a strong cautionary warning about our fallibility in recognizing love by its fruits? The answer is, first, because there is no guaranteed expression—no univocal test of either How or What expresses love (WL, p. 13). Second, mistakes are possible in judging, either because one doesn't know what the fruits of love are or because one doesn't judge the situation properly (p. 7). For example, one can fail to understand that callousness or coldness are not fruits of love (p. 7), or one can confuse "fruits" with "words and platitudes" (pp. 11, 12). Thus, the importance of fruits, the requirement of fruits, is not meant to encourage the practice of judging others: so "the sacred words of that text are not said to encourage us to get busy judging one another; they are rather spoken admonishingly to the single individual, to you, my listener, and to me" (p. 14). The importance of fruits is meant to encourage us not to allow complacency with ourselves. Kierkegaard says something similar when, late in life, he writes that "whether I have been treated shabbily by anyone . . . is really not my concern but quite properly is their business."[39] I am not responsible for what the other does, in that sense; it is not my job to judge others but rather to keep myself honest. And with great insight into human nature, he warns us to watch ourselves so that we do not become more concerned that love is known than "that it has fruits and therefore could be known" (p. 14).

What is at stake for Kierkegaard in affirming love's hiddenness? First, he wants to remind us that love is unfathomable (without why) because its origin is God's love. Ultimately, the source or power of the act is hidden (cannot be infallibly known). Second, he wants to ensure that we do not assume that love is equal to its fruits, that it is exhausted by an enumeration of its fruits. But it is important to remember that the emphasis on hiddenness is balanced by an emphasis on knowability. In an important sense the fruits of love cannot be hidden; they must be recognizable, and they must allow grounds for determining, though not infallibly, whether love is our motivation.

C. Fruits versus Consequences

Kierkegaard engages in the double-sided task of emphasizing the importance of fruits of love while at the same time rejecting a consequentialist view of ethics. Love need not in fact be recognized by someone, but it must have fruits that could in principle be recognized. In other words, love must express itself, but it is not invalidated if the love that motivates an attitude or action is not recognized by others as loving or if it is not successful in what it attempts to achieve. "Fruits" must be active and "manifest" (WL, p. 16), as opposed to mere "words and platitudes" (p. 12), yet "fruits" are not necessarily publicly observable external behaviors; it can equally be a work of love to forgive someone a wrong one has done to you as to feed the hungry. Works or fruits of love are not "external"—that is, they will include such acts as "believing all things," "remaining in love's debt," and forgiving another. Lack of love could be shown, as noted earlier, by the coldness or callousness with which a traditionally purported "work of love," like helping the poor, was performed. Kierkegaard later gives a profoundly sensitive example of a 'work of love' that fails to be done with the requisite love: he describes someone who "feeds the poor" but in so doing "sees the poor and the lowly only as the poor and the lowly" (p. 83). His judgment is that such a person has "not yet been victorious over his mind in such a way that he calls this meal a banquet." "The one," he says, "who gives *the banquet* sees the neighbor in the poor and the lowly."

What is at stake in arguing that works of love are neither necessarily external nor able to be judged by observable results or achievements is that so-called works of love can be done unlovingly. What is at stake in the resolute anticonsequentialism that Kierkegaard espouses is that loving works can be thwarted by nature or other people and may not come to observable fruition. I may, for example, bind up the wounds of an injured person and convey him to the hospital for further care, only to find that he later died as a result of an intern's mistake in prescribing medication. However, nothing in this discussion, which emphasizes the limited relevance of consequences or observable results, implies a cavalier attitude toward the concrete needs of other people. In fact, in this deliberation, Kierkegaard anticipates his later comments on love as an outward task when he condemns the thoughtlessness involved in "thinking about [one's] own cares instead of thinking about the cares of the poor, perhaps seeking alleviation by giving to charity instead of wanting to alleviate poverty" (WL, pp. 13–14). This simple distinction between "fruits" and consequences (or achievements) will become important later in clarifying the criticism that in *Works of Love* Kierkegaard devalues this-worldly concrete needs (e.g., when we hear about Christianity's indifference to "externals" or when we come to the much-maligned deliberation in which he contrasts mercy with generosity).

It is worth noting here that in these introductory comments, Kierkegaard contrasts genuine and nongenuine works of love. If this is appreciated early on, it should not produce confusion. Both in the opening prayer and in this deliberation, Kierkegaard distinguishes between what we traditionally term "works of love" (acts of charity like feeding the hungry and clothing the naked) and works actually done in love:

> There are, of course, works that in a particular sense are called works of love [acts of charity, love-works, *Kjerlighedsgjerniger*]. But even giving to charity, visiting the widow, and clothing the naked do not truly demonstrate or make known a person's love, inasmuch as one can do works of love [acts of charity, *Kjerlighedsgjerniger*] in an unloving way, yes, even in a self-loving way, and if this is so the work of love [*Kjerlighedsgjerningen*] is no work of love [*Kjerlighedens Gjerning*] at all. (WL, p. 13)[40]

The physical behavior may be the same, but the "work" is different. Once this contrast is made, Kierkegaard tends to use the words "fruits" and "works" without significant difference in meaning.[41]

To anticipate a little, Kierkegaard's perennial concern with the relation and contrast between inner and outer surrounds the deliberation on the love commandment proper (see WL II, A–C). It comes into play, as we have just seen, in the first deliberation as hidden versus recognizable, and it will be explicitly retrieved and focused on in the two parts of the third deliberation. That is, after examining in detail the love commandment in the three parts of the second deliberation, Kierkegaard uses the two parts of the third deliberation to show once more, in III, A, the importance of *outer action* (as opposed to simple inwardness) and, in III, B, the role of *inner conscience* (as opposed to what is external).

D. Love's Need

This opening deliberation also provides the first discussion of the theme of NEED, which was alluded to in the opening prayer and which will play a crucial role in all the deliberations. Kierkegaard insists that "to be able to be known by its fruits is a need in love," yet this "signifies the greatest riches!" (WL, p. 10). The active force of such a need is illustrated by Kierkegaard's comparison with a plant's need to express its life; to insist on making love unrecognizable is as much against nature "as if the plant, which sensed the exuberant life and blessing within it, did not dare let it become recognizable and were to keep it to itself as if the blessing were a curse, keep it, alas, as a secret in its inexplicable withering!" (p. 11). He compares it to the richness of the poet who has a need to write—"we are saying the utmost when we say of the poet, 'He has a need to write'; of the orator, 'He has a need to speak'; and of the young woman, 'she has a need to love'" (p. 10). In this way it is a "young woman's greatest riches, that she needs [*trænge til*] the beloved," or a devout person's riches that "he needs God" (p. 11). Love's fruits are similarly said to "press forward" (*trænge frem*). The analogy with the plant suggests that in all these cases it is love's presence that presses forward, and this is the same message found in his later claim that "love is a need, the deepest need, *in the person in whom there is love* for the neighbor" (p. 67; emphasis mine). The suggestion that love needs to express itself or it withers and dies binds this use of the verb 'need' to the stronger use found in the prayer—namely, need as craving (*Trang*).

In one of his Christian discourses, Kierkegaard makes an intriguing comment about need that seems to disavow the usual connection between a need and its fulfillment; he writes that "the need brings its nourishment along with it; what is sought is in the seeking that seeks it; faith is in the concern over not having faith; love is in the concern over not loving."[42] In other words, the need in love is a need that is not satisfied in any ordinary way; it does not get filled so that we can stop seeking. The finding is in the never-ending seeking. A contemporary discussion of need and desire can illuminate Kierkegaard's meaning. Emmanuel Levinas, the twentieth-century French thinker who, like Kierkegaard, attacked Hegelian-inspired notions of totalization and systematization, proposed that ethics is more important than ontology; in the process he made an interesting distinction between "need" and "desire" that bears on Kierkegaard's notion of need.[43] According to Levinas, "needs" can be fulfilled, whereas "desire" is a craving for the infinite and, therefore, is insatiable. Thus, for Levinas, what is desired does not fill my desire but "hollows it out, nourishing me as it were with new hungers," with an "insatiable compassion."[44] In other words, as he says elsewhere, "desire in some way nourishes itself on its own hungers and is augmented by its satisfaction."[45] Kierkegaard's idea of the need in love, the craving that nourishes me with new hunger, seems to fit what Levinas means by desire.

A second sense of NEED is found in Kierkegaard's recognition that love generates a CLAIM on us by those we love. In an important but usually unremarked sentence in this opening deliberation, Kierkegaard tells us that we should not "hold back [our] words any more than [we] should hide visible emotion if it is genuine, because this can be the unloving committing of a wrong, just like withholding from someone what you owe him [because] your friend, your beloved, your child, or whoever is an object of your love has a claim upon an expression of it also in words if it actually moves you inwardly"; even more strongly, "the emotion is not in your possession but belongs to the other; the expression is your debt to him." "When the heart is full," he continues, "you should not enviously and superiorly, shortchanging the other, insult him by silently buttoning your lips" (WL, p. 12). That is, others have a right to the expression of our love if we in fact love them. This will have important ramifications when we consider the question of the role of mutuality in Kierkegaard's view of love of one's neighbor.

This understanding of another's need for our response leads into a more prominent and pronounced sense of need to be found in Kierkegaard's claims throughout the deliberations to follow. For example, in later deliberations he will speak of our deep need for "companionship," and he will use Christ's appeal to Peter—"Do you love me *more than* these?"—as the example of how we humans need "to be loved" (WL, p. 154–55). In suggesting that an absence motivates one person toward another, Kierkegaard anticipates Levinas's claim that desire is "desire for the other," for "sociality"; "the ethical relation of love for the other stems from the fact that the self cannot survive by itself alone, cannot find meaning with its own being-in-the-world, within the ontology of sameness."[46] Sometimes both senses of need (love's need to express itself and our need to be loved by companions) are inextricably entwined; the exclamation that "love in a human being is a need, the expression of riches" (p. 67) is made in the context of the discussion of companionship, but it applies as well to love's need to express itself in works. Moreover, in his "Conclusion" to *Works of Love*, Kierkegaard makes an indirect, but nonetheless clear, reference to our need to love and to be loved in relation to the paradox of commanded love—that is, he implies that the real paradoxicality of a commandment to love is found in the fact that "to love people is the only thing worth living for, and without this love you are not really living" (p. 375). It is paradoxical that we should require a commandment at all, given the strength of our need to love and to be loved. From the opening prayer of *Works of Love* to its conclusion, the appreciation of the human need to love and to be loved is front and center in Kierkegaard's mind.

This reference to the paradox of the love commandment—how can love be commanded?—leads us to the tripartite deliberation (WL II, A–C) in which Kierkegaard treats love as command, duty, or law. We will, no doubt, have questions about the source of the love commandment, as well as about the ability to fulfill it; it is important, then, that we keep in mind all the assumptions and clarifications about God's gift of love and about human need to which Kierkegaard has called our attention in the opening prayer and the introductory deliberation.

chapter two

Love's Law—Obligation

"You *Shall* Love" (II, A)

The tension that structured the introductory deliberation, between love's hiddenness and its necessary manifestation in fruits, is one version of the theme of the relation between the unseen and the seen, on which Kierkegaard works a number of variations. In one sense, this theme informs the entirety of *Works of Love*, but it is attended to most explicitly in the next three deliberations, II, III, and IV. The second deliberation consists of three separate discussions, which analyze in detail the love commandment "You shall love the neighbor as yourself." Although one might expect an exploration of the love commandment to be conducted in terms of the biblical image of hearing God's command, Kierkegaard in fact chooses instead to work (mostly)[1] within an idiom of the visual, reflecting on the ways in which human beings themselves embody dimensions of hiddenness and revelation, unseen and seen, invisible and visible. Before considering the ways in which Kierkegaard uses the theme of the seen and unseen to clarify the requirement expressed in the commandment, it is important to consider the form and the status of the second deliberation.

I. The Tripartite Command

The set of three discussions focuses on different elements of the love command, which Kierkegaard chooses to present as follows: (II, A) "You *Shall* love," (II, B)

"You shall love the *Neighbor*," and (II, C) "*You* shall love the Neighbor." Two implications of the form of the presentation are worth noting. First, Kierkegaard does not present the elements in abstraction but highlights them in their place within the command. Kierkegaard was known to be a stickler for typographical details, often giving precise instructions to the printer concerning font sizes, headings, and other ways of indicating relative importance in his publications,[2] so his decision to stress certain elements while keeping them within the unity of the command is important. What is even more important is that the three discussions are presented as parts of a single deliberation. Given the deliberateness of his editorial choices in general, Kierkegaard's decision to have the three parts under the rubric of one deliberation suggests that any judgments we make about anything in any one of them should be made on the basis of the three taken together, qualifying and clarifying one another. The three discussions are remarkably intertwined, so that, for example, important dimensions of the element "neighbor" are found in all three, rather than being restricted to the part that focuses on "neighbor." I propose to highlight and do justice to Kierkegaard's editorial choice by examining the three discussions under the single rubric, "Love's Law," in the following chapters.

What is the status of this second deliberation? It serves the purpose of setting out the indispensable terms for the entire discussion: the nature, object, and subject of obligation. In one sense this might seem to make the second deliberation the heart of *Works of Love*. But this could be misleading about the role these chapters play since, intriguingly, Kierkegaard once considered the option of putting the second deliberation as an appendix to the whole series.[3] That he could conceive of doing this shows that in his view the discussion of the juridical aspects of the commandment is somewhat separable; although he chose in the end not to put it as an appendix, it seems clear that he viewed it as a discrete section intended for conceptual clarification.

My proposal is to read this tripartite deliberation on the love commandment as prefatory to the remaining deliberations, in the sense that it provides a distinctive and separable context for discussion—that is, a context in which the rules are given, the outlines drawn, for the space in which love will later be concretely described. Although I will initially treat each of the three parts separately, I argue that the main purpose of the deliberation as a whole, though not its sole one, is to proclaim the unconditionality and scope of the commandment, the bindingness and extent of the duty, rather than to illustrate love in practice or 'at work.' I suggest that we take as a hermeneutical key Kierkegaard's own proposed distinction between the Law and Love as "sketch" versus fulfilled work (WL, p. 104), a contrast he elaborated on in a concurrent journal comment, saying that "the law is the skeleton, the bony structure, the dehydrated husk. Love is the fullness."[4] Then we can treat *Works of Love* as having two separable contexts of discussion—the context of Law, SHALL, or commandment (the sketch) and the context of fulfillment (the fulfilled work). However, I do not mean to use this contrast as a way of dividing the two series of deliberations. For reasons that will become clearer in chapter 7, I do not agree with those commentators on *Works of Love* who think that the decisive transition point comes between the two series;[5]

rather, I suggest that the transition occurs within the first series itself, with the decisive shift at the fourth deliberation.[6]

A preliminary sketch of what is at stake may be helpful here. Contemporary discussions of ethical relationships tend to focus on the following themes: impartiality and partiality, equality and equity, and commonality and difference. Underlying all these concerns is a fundamental question about abstraction and concreteness in an ethic—how to secure attention to what is distinctive about someone without jeopardizing impartiality; how to combine equality and concrete moral concern; or, in another idiom, how to ensure appreciation of genuine alterity, the radical, nonreducible otherness of the other, without either succumbing to abstraction or losing sight of the relevance of commonality. Our task is to assess how Kierkegaard's understanding of "works of love" fares in this regard, and it has to begin with an assessment of the implications of "commanded love" (WL, p. 19).

II. Self-love and the Samaritan

The title "You *Shall* Love" announces an intention to discuss the duty or obligation to love, the bindingness of the commandment. The scriptural citation that Kierkegaard places directly under the title, referring to the two commandments (to love God and to love your neighbor as yourself), suggests that the emphasis will be on the nature of the love command as an imperative—you ought to love or, even more strongly, you must love. But since we have already noted Kierkegaard's emphasis on love as a gift from God that needs to be expressed, we cannot ignore another potential dimension of the "you shall love"—a dimension that describes both our capacity and our need. This descriptive or declarative dimension of the "shall" (namely, you will be able to) will become relevant as we go on.

Before launching into the discourse proper, Kierkegaard calls the reader's attention to the important strategy of determining what presuppositions might lie behind any discourse. His own "presupposition" is the one embedded in the commandment to love your neighbor as yourself, signaled by the "little phrase, *as yourself*" (WL, p. 17). The presupposition to which he calls attention is found at the end of the formulation of the commandment, but it is, he says, "the starting point" of the deliberation. Highlighting this "little phrase, *as yourself,*" is Kierkegaard's way of broaching the vexing question of the role of self-love in any ethic. Is self-love bad, good, or indifferent? Is self-love as such to be rooted out, or is there a legitimate or appropriate self-love?

Kierkegaard reminds us that love of self is presupposed by Christianity: the phrase "as yourself" unapologetically affirms that "every person loves himself" (WL, p. 17).[7] He tells us straightforwardly that through its emphasis on this phrase, Christianity wants to teach a "proper self-love" (p. 18), and he will later contrast this with "selfish self-love" (p. 151). This should be enough to rebut any charge that Kierkegaard simply condemns self-love as such; but since it is such an important starting point for his ethics and since he continues to be taken as an example of a tradition that urges the rooting out of self-love through an ethic of self-denial, we should look more closely at his description of the commandment's impact on self-love.

The commandment, he says, "wrenches open the lock of self-love" (WL, p. 17), concluding that "when the Law's *as yourself* has wrested from you the self-love that Christianity sadly enough must presuppose to be in every human being, then you have actually learned to love yourself" (pp. 22–23). This is, without doubt, a challenging claim, and it might seem to echo what appears to be Luther's condemnation of self-love. Luther writes that the commandment's "as yourself" shows man "the sinful love with which he does in fact love himself, as if to say: 'You are completely curved in upon yourself . . . a condition from which you will not be delivered unless you altogether cease loving yourself, and forgetting yourself, love your neighbor."[8] But Kierkegaard has no hesitation in affirming the possibility of "proper self-love." Although he is exceedingly sensitive to the dangers of perversions of self-love, he assumes that without proper self-love, one could not properly love anyone else: "[I]f anyone is unwilling to learn from Christianity to love himself *in the right way,* he cannot love the neighbor either" (p. 22; emphasis mine). To "wrest" self-love from you, therefore, does not mean ceasing to love yourself but rather opening the "lock," rendering love inclusive rather than exclusive and competitive. In other words, there is an exercise of self-love that is to be opened up, a "sadly"[9] restricted self-love, yet there is clearly a right way to love oneself. It is crucial in reading *Works of Love* to recognize that Kierkegaard does not come down on the side of those who deny that there is such a thing as proper self-love.[10]

Kierkegaard thus counters Luther's apparently monolithic devaluation of self-love by making a distinction between proper and selfish self-love, but it is important to note that Luther himself had a more nuanced view which supports Kierkegaard's appreciation of proper self-love. In the "Treatise on Good Works," for example, Luther explicitly argues that it is a duty to care for oneself since to fail to take care of oneself is to become a murderer of oneself: anyone whose immoderate sacrifice is ruining his strength "will be regarded as a man who takes no care of himself, and, as far as he is able, he has become his own murderer."[11] Although Luther counsels against being "anxious and greedy," which are signs of a lack of trust in God, he recommends a reasonable care for one's body and mind, a care that would preclude undue sacrifice of self.[12]

By way of prefacing and qualifying the cautionary judgments on "self-love" and the status of "preference," which he will offer in the next chapter, Kierkegaard goes out of his way here, at the outset, not only to admit the legitimacy of self-love but even more to remind us quite poignantly of how sad it is when people do not sufficiently love themselves. He writes that just as often as he feels the need to pull in the reins on one person's selfish self-love, he feels the need to open another person to proper self-love: "Whoever has any knowledge of people will certainly admit that just as he has often wished to be able to move them to relinquish self-love, he has also had to wish that it were possible to teach them to love themselves." The person who "throws himself into the folly of the moment," the person who is suicidally depressed or otherwise self-destructive, and the one who "surrenders to despair" because he has been betrayed—all these are examples of a person who "does not know how to love himself rightly." He concludes: "When someone self-tormentingly thinks to do God a service by torturing himself, what is his sin except not willing to love himself in the right way?" (WL, p. 23). Christianity's doctrine reminds a person to "love his neighbor as himself, that is, as he ought to love himself." Indeed, Kierkegaard even equates them: "To love yourself in the right way and to love the neighbor correspond perfectly to one another; fundamentally they are one and the same thing" (p. 22).[13]

How can self-love be warranted? In principle there are several ways in which a legitimate self-love might be justified. One is formal, a matter of simple consistency—if *no one* is to be excluded from our love, we cannot arbitrarily exclude our own self. Others ways are more substantive. One could argue that it is part of our duty to others that we maintain ourselves, to be able to support others, to have something to give. A variation of this theme is (as Kant suggests) that proper concern for the self prevents the temptation to transgress our duties to others.[14] In a different vein, one could argue that if love's proper object is 'the good' (as Aristotle and Aquinas think), then one must love the good in oneself as much as the good in others.[15] A version of this theme is that if one has reverence for God's creation or God's gifts, one must have reverence for oneself. Any of these rationales could support Kierkegaard's commitment to a proper love of self, and he alludes to most of them, as we shall see later (chapter 8, section VIII) when we consider the question of self-sacrifice.

All such rationales imply that one should love the self, as well as the other. But more is at stake in the commandment's qualification, "as yourself": it requires in addition that we use love of self as an index for our love for another. Proper self-love provides the standard. To one who asks, "How shall I love my neighbor," the commandment "will invariably go on repeating the brief phrase 'as yourself'" (WL, p. 20), and Kierkegaard here reads the phrase as meaning 'as you ought to love yourself' (in other places he will assume the reading 'as you yourself are loved by God'). Kierkegaard follows Luther, who says in the "Lectures on Galatians" that "if you want to know how the neighbor is to be loved and want to have an outstanding pattern of this, consider carefully how you love yourself."[16] What does this pattern involve? Luther's answer is that it requires positive readings of the seven commandments that relate to our treatment of others; that is, it requires that we support, help, increase, protect, and preserve, in addition to abstaining from harm, and we are "commanded to further" the welfare of the other because this is what we would wish for ourselves.[17] His "short conclusion" to the Ten Commandments contains a simple model of how the "as yourself" functions: "[E]verybody seeks love and friendship, gratitude and assistance, truth and loyalty, from his neighbor. And all these are what the Ten Commandments require of us."[18]

One modern discussion of the character of self-love answers the question "How exactly do you love yourself?" with the following description: regardless of fluctuations in feelings, "you naturally love yourself for your own sake. You wish your own good, and you do so even when you have a certain distaste for the kind of person you are. . . . After a failure of some sort . . . you will always lay hold expectantly on *another* possibility of attaining some good for yourself. You love yourself more than you love any good qualities or worth you may possess . . . self-love makes you desire worth for yourself."[19] Another account suggests that "we love ourselves by wanting to be happy, to be fulfilled, to be complete"; that we never abandon that general goal; and that the particular aspects of that general concern include the refusal to abandon it and a willingness to forgive our mistakes as we try to find happiness.[20] The "as yourself" clause provides the following general guidelines:

> It means that one must be willing to support one's neighbor's freedom in seeking fulfillment, but only to the extent that the neighbor's choices are morally permissible. It means that one must be willing to support the neighbor's basic needs, but only to the extent that the neighbor acknowledges these needs. It means that one must be willing to forgive the neighbor, restoring a respectful regard wherever it has been destroyed by wrongs.[21]

Many of the later deliberations in *Works of Love* will explicitly assume a certain model of our love of self; for example, Kierkegaard works with the assumption that we want to be treated with respect, not to be treated condescendingly, and that we forgive ourselves our false starts and weaknesses. All of these provide a pattern or model, so that we are never at a loss about "how" to love the neighbor.

The presupposition of love of self is precisely what, in Kierkegaard's account, should lead us to see our duty to help another in need. He cites the scriptural example of the "merciful Samaritan" as precisely revealing just what it would be to love another "as yourself" (WL, p. 22). Indeed, his reference to the good Samaritan is something that should be emphasized, especially in the face of charges that Kierkegaard's ethic is spiritualized or dualistic. In this example, attending to the person's need means binding his wounds, getting him to a place where he can be cared for, and financially arranging for this care. The merciful Samaritan is not praised for having given spiritual instruction to the wounded man, for reminding him how much he was loved by God, or for providing him with spiritual reading for his stay in the ditch. The Samaritan is praised for having given the man precisely what he needed, which in this case was help for his physical, material, bodily pain and suffering. Kierkegaard may not often give such concrete examples, but the Samaritan is surely an unambiguous illustration of the kind of care for another that he believes is implied by the phrase "as yourself."

These early intimations of the category of neighbor, to be developed further in the second part of this deliberation (II, B), are the context in which Kierkegaard introduces this provocative claim: "As far as thought is concerned, the neighbor does not even need to exist. If someone living on a desert island mentally conformed to this commandment, by renouncing self-love he could be said to love the neighbor" (p. 21). This infamous desert island scenario has been repeatedly targeted for criticism, but it has seldom been considered in context.[22] It is adduced as evidence of both the denigration of self-love and the irrelevance of the actual other in Kierkegaard's ethic, as if it doesn't matter whether there is an actual neighbor or not. But several qualifications need to be noted before this passage can be assessed fairly. First, Kierkegaard begins by restricting the relevance of the claim with the words "as far as thought is concerned"; the context is explicitly limited to a thought experiment: "As far as thought is concerned, the neighbor does not even need to exist," but to love in the actual world (rather than "in thought") the neighbor does need to exist. Or to put it more precisely, whenever there actually is another in the vicinity, one cannot love only "in thought." Second, since this claim is made in the part of the deliberation that focuses on the unconditionality of the command rather than in the part that focuses on the category of neighbor, one could argue that the point is not to speak about the neighbor as such but (given Kierkegaard's acknowledgment of a "proper self-love") to show the importance of renouncing a restrictive self-love. That is, if (counterfactually) there were no other people around us, we could still show our obedient conformity to the commandment by renouncing a restrictive self-love, and we can renounce such self-love in these circumstances by determining ourselves to love, as ourselves, such others as may ever come our way. Thus, this desert island story does not mean to tell us, nor would it allow, that in the presence of another we need only mentally conform to the commandment.

In sum, Kierkegaard distinguishes between two forms of self-love: a "selfish," exclusive love of self, which is at odds with the good of the other, and a "proper," inclusive love of self, which both encompasses the good of the other and is the measure of the good of the other. What makes love of self "proper" as opposed to perverted cannot therefore consist in rejecting, denying, or rooting out love of self. Proper love of self is a safeguard—it must be in place if we are not to love another person *less* than we should (i.e., less than we should love ourselves). The phrase "as yourself" is a reminder that we should love another as we ought to love ourselves, as well as a reminder that we should not love another more than we love ourselves. This suggests that Kierkegaard reads the commandment as requiring equal regard, or parity. Whether or not this turns out to be an adequate characterization, we can conclude that, at the very least, he does not go so far as some thinkers do: he does not think we are commanded either to love ourselves more than others or to love others more than ourselves.

Kierkegaard is aware that many people would take exception to an ethic that requires us to love another person as we ought to love ourselves. Although he does not specifically address it, one can assume that he was familiar with the Thomistic tradition's refusal in Roman Catholicism to read the love commandment as a requirement that we love others as much as we love ourselves. Aquinas defends the conclusion that "a man ought in charity to love himself more than his neighbor."[23] On the other hand, Kierkegaard is also aware that some might object to his ethic for not being austere enough; he explicitly anticipates in this deliberation the objection that some might raise to his conscientious attention to the "as yourself"—namely, "would this really be the highest; would it not be possible to love a person *more than oneself*"? (WL, p. 18). I am going to defer discussion of the challenge posed by an ethic that claims we should love the other more than ourselves; it will more fittingly be considered in my examination of the notion of the "infinitude" of our obligation to the other (chapter 8).

III. The Bindingness and Scope of the Commandment

Kierkegaard turns from his discussion of the "presupposition" of the love commandment to what he terms the chapter's "object of consideration"—the "apparent contradiction" that "to love is a duty" (WL, p. 24). Preference and inclination cannot be commanded; it would indeed be a contradiction if love in that sense were to be commanded.[24] The appearance of contradiction is radically mitigated once we understand that the duty is to love, with an inclusive and enduring love, but it is not an obligation for preferential love.[25] Commanded love may be paradoxical, but not because it obligates us to any kind of preferential response.

There are two important ways in which Kierkegaard presents the "shall" of the command. The first and most obvious way is in terms of its unconditional obligation, and this with respect to both its binding character and its scope. There is no excuse, no respite, no loophole, no exception: the Christian doctrine of the "shall" is "to love the neighbor, to love the whole human race, all people, even the enemy, and not to make exceptions, neither of preference nor of aversion" (WL, p. 19). The *scope* of the commandment is presented in abstract terms: "the neighbor," "the whole human race," and "all people." If this formulation were all we had to go on, there would be reason to wonder whether Kierkegaard's ethic is abstract and unrealistic.[26] But we do have more to go on—the other two parts of the deliberation—and I suggest that II, B, supports a reading of the scope as stressing only that *no one can be excluded*. Until that discussion I propose that we read this reference as a formal reminder that the commandment makes it impossible for you to ever judge that you can rightly exclude anyone who stands before you in need. This is a sufficiently demanding reading of the command to account for Kierkegaard's suggestion that it turns "the natural man's conceptions and ideas upside down" and constitutes a disturbing "offense" (pp. 24–25); the command's strangeness need not be due to its impossible physical demands on us.

Kierkegaard presents the unconditionality of the bindingness of duty as guaranteeing both unchangingness and freedom: *"Only when it is a duty to love, only then is love eternally secured against every change, eternally made free in blessed independence"* (WL, p. 29; emphases Kierkegaard's).[27] As will become clearer in the next two chapters, life presents us with people to love; they are what Kierkegaard calls the objects who are "once given or chosen" (p. 159). Some are "given" to us, and life offers us the opportunity to "choose" others. But once they are given (placed within our moral arena without our choice) or chosen, we are obligated to love them. We haven't yet been told by Kierkegaard what will count as love in any given case, but given his respect for our proper love of self (the commanded "as yourself"), there is no reason to saddle him here with preposterous and untenable claims about unchanging love. For the moment, Kierkegaard's examples should be the guiding principle for determining what duty involves. One example, to which he will later recur, is found in his discussion of two people bound by a chosen commitment, and it is intended to show that genuine love is not simply reactive. Genuine love does not helplessly and automatically go up and down, depending on whether the other loves us (pp. 34, 39). If I have committed myself to someone or if someone is dependent on me, I cannot, in the event that person ceases to love me, exclude the person from the category of "neighbor" to which he or she belongs, whether or not the person loves me. We are responsible for the children we have (given or chosen), bound to love them, bound not to exclude them from our obligation to love, even if or when we dislike them or lose our preferential inclination for them. Kierkegaard ties the concept of unchangeableness to that of independence (pp. 37–39); in other words, I do not have to respond with tit-for-tat ('If you will not love me, then I will hate you'). I am free. I will consider this theme of love's faithful endurance in more detail when it becomes the focus of the later deliberation, "Love Abides" (see chapter 12).

The fact that Kierkegaard emphasizes the "as yourself" of the love commandment is evidence that his ethic is not what Garth Hallett calls one of simple self-denial or even self-forgetfulness.[28] Moreover, Kierkegaard very explicitly makes a contrast between "habit" and the fulfillment of duty (WL, p. 37). Nothing he says here requires that unchangeableness means that a woman should stay in an abusive relationship just because she is married or that a man should make a sacrifice of his life to provide heroin for the addict who is his brother. We need to look carefully at all of *Works of Love* before we can make a judgment about the extent of the sacrifice required in such an ethic, so I will wait until chapter 8 to begin to assess Kierkegaard's resources for putting limits on our sacrifice for others.

What constitutes loving the one who does not love us, loving the stranger, or loving the enemy? Kierkegaard does not announce at the outset whether love is to be understood as disinterested benevolence or as attentive, intimate caring, perhaps because no single description could account for all of the occasions in which we are obliged to love. Some parts of *Works of Love* address the issue of those for whom we have a natural preference, and others address those for whom we have no preference; some parts address our response to those who love us, and others address our response to those who do not love us (or even hate us). In some cases, Kierkegaard's examples tend to be preferential relationships that are elevated or enhanced by eliminating arbitrariness; the enduring aspect of love and the independence of love are qualities that stabilize or enhance inclination. In other discussions he accents the obligation when there is a lack of inclination or a positive disinclination. It is not clear that the same thing will be required in each case. How love is to be expressed in a given case is subject to further determination, and all the remaining deliberations will take part in that task.

In effect, these chapters on the commandment's bindingness and scope tell us *that* we are bound to love without exclusion, but they do not purport to tell us *how* we are to love or what in a given case constitutes a concrete expression of love. I suggest that examples of concrete expressions of love, the "how" and the "what" of love, are first found when Kierkegaard turns in the fourth deliberation to a discussion of "loving the people we see."

IV. The "Shall" of Encouragement

There is a second way (in addition to its unconditionality) in which the commandment to love is treated in this chapter: the "shall" is meant to encourage us and to forbid despair. Kierkegaard makes the point clearly when he says that "when eternity says, 'You shall love,' it is responsible for making sure that this can be done" (WL, p. 41). All of this, he concludes, means that "out of solicitude" for the sorrowing one, eternity commands, "You shall love." Kierkegaard is aware that this notion of command as 'solicitude' is counterintuitive. To say to despairing people that they 'shall' do what they most fear they cannot succeed in doing might seem to be mocking them, but Kierkegaard appeals to our experience of some "dark moment" in which we "learned to love this *shall* that saves from despair," learned that "true upbuilding consists in being spoken to rigorously"(p. 42).[29]

Kierkegaard's claim here has strong echoes of Luther's position, and Luther's formulation may actually make Kierkegaard's message clearer. When in the "Treatise on Good Works" the interlocutor asks: "What if I cannot believe that my prayer is heard and accepted?" Luther's reply is simple: "I reply that faith, prayer, and all other good works are commanded *so that you should know what you can do and what you cannot do.*"[30] I take this to illuminate the value of a commandment to trust, to have confidence, to love—in other words, a commandment, as Luther phrases it, to "receive" from God.[31] The presence of a commandment reminds you that you can trust, that you have the ability to love; the commandment gives you the courage to trust and love. Luther writes that when we are tempted to wonder whether our prayer is acceptable to God, we should "resist the devil and say to him . . . 'I pray and work only because God, of his pure mercy, has promised to hear and be gracious to all unworthy men. God has not only promised it, but most strongly commanded us to pray, trust, and receive on pain of his eternal displeasure and wrath." That is, we must "drive out the devil's suggestion with God's command," the command to "pray, to trust, and to receive from him." When a person doubts—'What if I can't trust, believe, have confidence'—Luther replies: your faith and trust are commanded. 'What if I am not praying rightly?'—your prayer is commanded. In parallel fashion, one could say that in response to the question 'What if I don't think I can love rightly or enough,' Luther would respond: your love is commanded. Kierkegaard echoes this Lutheran confidence; that is, "when eternity says, 'You shall love,' it is responsible for making sure that this can be done." The commandment to love is a reminder that you can, and it gives you courage.

Admittedly, the commandment "constrains" ("Whenever the purely human wants to storm forth"), but more important for Kierkegaard, "wherever the purely human loses courage, the commandment strengthens" (WL, p. 43).[32] If you imagine a situation in which you "sit with someone who deeply mourns," he suggests, you will learn that the response "'You shall sorrow' is both true and beautiful" (p. 43). Note for further reference that Kierkegaard here seems to be assuming the appropriateness of mourning or grieving over a lost love. "So it is with love," he says: "You do not have the right to become insensitive to this feeling [love], because you *shall* love; but neither do you have the right to love despairingly, because you *shall* love; and just as little do you have the right to warp this feeling in you, because you *shall* love."

V. Love's Need Revisited

Thus far in the deliberation we have seen a technical or legislative discussion of the "shall," as well as the claim that the commandment should cause "offense." In the midst of all this, the theme of NEED (*Trang*) appears again. Kierkegaard considers "need" both a blessing and a freedom. He insists that "the expression of the greatest riches is to have a need; therefore, that it is a need in the free person is indeed the true expression of freedom" (WL, p. 38). Such freedom is paradoxical in that "the one in whom love is a need certainly feels free in his love, and the very one who feels totally dependent, so that he would lose everything by losing the beloved, that very one is independent." But the freedom of need depends on a crucial qualification—"yet on one condition, that he does not confuse love with possessing the beloved" since the need to "possess" is precisely a "corruptible," "earthly," and "temporal" dependence (p. 38). Thus, Kierkegaard contrasts the need to love another person with the need to "possess" that person.

Kierkegaard's affirmation of the need to love people might seem to sidestep the issue of a need to be loved. But he affirms that need as well. When he announces there that "a life without loving is not worth living" and claims that "the expression of the greatest riches is to have a need" (WL, p. 38), the need in question is a need *to be loved*. He affirms the need to be loved most clearly when he condemns the kind of "proud independence that thinks it has no need to feel loved": "Sometimes the world praises the proud independence that thinks it has no need to feel loved, even though it also thinks it 'needs other people—not in order to be loved by them but in order to love them, in order to have someone to love'" (p. 39). His judgment is immediate and severe: "How false this independence is! It feels no *need* to be loved and yet *needs* someone to love; therefore it needs another person—in order to gratify its proud self-esteem."[33] When he notes that love can nonetheless "do without it [the love of the other], while it still continues to love" (p. 39), he is not recommending doing without the other's love as the norm but reminding us that what it means to need the other does not preclude a willingness to be hated by the other, should that be the response our love for the other meets.

In the end, the issue of "need" is complicated because Kierkegaard, on the one hand, wants to appreciate the agent's needs, whereas, on the other hand, he wants to avoid approving of the kind of need that renders the other instrumental to the agent's satisfaction. Although it is a complicated issue, Kierkegaard states his position unambiguously in the fourth deliberation, which begins with this beautiful expression: "How *deeply* the need of love is rooted in human nature!" (WL, p. 154). The need to love and be loved is a function of our "innate need for companionship," our "longing for companionship," which even Christ humanly shared since, for example, Christ humanly "felt the need to love and to be loved" by Peter (pp. 154–55).[34]

It seems clear that Kierkegaard does not share Nietzsche's scorn for the need to be loved; he does not consider it "the greatest kind of arrogance."[35] Kierkegaard would agree with a recent account of love that suggests that "one would have to be God in order to be capable of loving without being dependent on being loved in return."[36] That is, Kierkegaard would agree that one ceases to be human when one ceases to need to be loved.

The appearance of the theme of need may seem unexpected within the context of a discussion of duty, but it reinforces the connection Kierkegaard sees between need and command. To understand his sense of the connection, it is necessary to step back a little and consider briefly how Kierkegaard's ethic fits into the framework of contemporary theological ethics. Kierkegaard clearly distances his account from any strictly mutual account—we are not to love others only as they love us (WL, p. 34). Rather, Kierkegaard's ethic is considered to be a classic example of an agapeistic ethic, that is, an ethic that views love in terms of the Greek concept agape (a love that is contrasted with *eros* 'erotic love' and *philia* 'friendship') and considers "'the law of love' as a *practical* doctrine to which Christians are necessarily committed."[37] Agape is commanded love rather than preferential inclination. It looks as if Kierkegaard may be committed to what is called a "divine command ethic"[38] (at least with respect to love) and, if so, to the broader category of a deontological (as opposed to a teleological) ethic. But we should look into this further before drawing any conclusions.

The basic version of a divine command theory claims that ethical rightness and wrongness, ethical duty and ethical prohibition, are constituted by the commands of God.[39] That is, God does not command what is independently right and wrong; God's command makes actions right or wrong. The story of Abraham and Isaac in *Fear and Trembling* seems to portray just such a divine command ethic: what makes it right to sacrifice Isaac is that, and only that, God commands it. But the ethic in *Fear and Trembling,* a pseudonymous account of Christianity by Johannes de Silentio (who admits he cannot make the moves of faith) ought not to be read automatically into *Works of Love*. It remains to be seen whether Kierkegaard maintains a divine command ethic here in this text.

The standard objection to a divine command ethic is that it does not preclude the arbitrary commanding by God of such things as gratuitous cruelty or other acts that conflict with deeply entrenched human intuitions. In the face of such an objection, the account can be modified to include the assumption of a loving God; it can then claim either that ethical wrongness is constituted by the commands of a loving God or that "ethical wrongness *is* (i.e., is identical with) the property of being contrary to the commands of a loving God."[40] Even if this does not beg the question by conceding what is really at stake, such an account can still raise two related objections. The first challenges the loss of human autonomy; such a divine command theory seems to be a purely heteronomous, extrinsic imposition on us, one that encourages servile obedience. The second challenges the motivation for our actions; such a divine command ethic seems to devalue acting charitably out of caring concern for our needy neighbors in favor of acting charitably simply because one has been commanded to do so by God. If it is a divine command ethic, Kierkegaard's ethic is open to such objections.

Kierkegaard's attention to human need, however, seems to indicate an appreciation of the limits of pure command. A command as such cannot create a response of love; it cannot force or enable us to act on our responsibility. That is, a command cannot create the love it demands. The dynamism of need or desire must be assumed prior to the commandment that will guide its expression. Both the actual presence of God's love in us and the fact that this love needs to express itself account for the ability to fulfill the command.[41] In fact, obligation can be understood in terms of the pressing nature of the gift of love's need to express itself: obligation is the description of the need of a gift to express itself or die. In other words, the rightness or wrongness of an act does not, for Kierkegaard, seem to be a simple function of God's *explicit* command.

In creating us, God implanted love in our hearts, and the command presupposes that love. The commandment does not tell us to love; we don't need a commandment for that.[42] Rather, it *guides* 'how' we love (WL, p. 67) and requires us not to restrict it preferentially. God's gift of love was the gift of a need, and the gift is presupposed by the command. The Danish language has the remarkable ability to express this figuratively—the word for task, *Opgave*, includes in it the word for gift, *Gave*. The task that is commanded embodies the gift; we can understand this according to the English expression for assigning a task: 'It is given to you to do X'. It is the point of this deliberation to awaken us to the gift we have been given, the ability we already possess; as Kierkegaard exclaims, "Indeed, what is the highest possession, what is the possession of everything if I never receive the proper impression of my possessing it and of what it is that I possess!" (p. 26). Kierkegaard is once again underscoring the way in which God's gift is the background to God's command, a point that, in one sense, cannot be repeated often enough and, in another sense, is too fundamental to need to be repeated.

Although I have couched my point here in the idiom of "need," it could be made more generally. Arguing that a divine command ethic must be modified to guarantee "the motivational goods of both obedience and autonomy," one author appeals to Paul Tillich's notion of "theonomy."[43] Tillich sees a middle ground between autonomy (man as his own law) and heteronomy (subjection to an external, extrinsic law); that middle ground is "theonomy," which "asserts that the superior law is at the same time, the innermost law of man himself, rooted in the divine ground which is man's own ground."[44] Similarly, and more concretely, the way in which God's gift is the background to the command is important to Kierkegaard's account of the authority of the love commandment insofar as its authority derives from the way in which it reflects the divinely created nature of things. We are created as kin (children of God), so the command to love is not arbitrarily imposed from outside but is grounded in the structure of our humanity. In other words, we can determine the justice of God's authority, and hence the legitimacy of obedience to the command, from the structure of the created world.[45] This seems to echo Kierkegaard's own understanding of the relation between creation and law.[46]

This unexpected and intense focus on the human need to love and to be loved—a need so deep that Kierkegaard calls it a craving—is one of the crucial determinants of Kierkegaard's ethic. It is simply poor scholarship, at the very least, to summarize or assess this ethic (as many do) without taking this Kierkegaardian commitment very seriously. Thus far we do not have reason to consider *Works of Love* as propounding a divine command ethic or a simple ethics of obedience. The remainder of *Works of Love* will contribute to a fuller picture of the status of this ethic, one that allow us to better characterize it in terms of contemporary discussions of egoism/altruism and deontological/teleological ethics.[47] Moreover, Kierkegaard's appreciation of this deep need to love and to be loved is important to the question of mutual responsiveness and reciprocity, so I shall return to it in chapter 15.

This first part of the second deliberation has succeeded in introducing us to both the commandment's indispensable qualification—"as yourself"—and its character as unconditionally binding.[48] The second part of the deliberation will focus more specifically on the concept of "neighbor," but before turning to it, we should note two of the assumptions about "neighbor" that Kierkegaard already reveals in this first part. First, he comments, not surprisingly, on the derivation of the word as follows: *"Who, then, is one's neighbor [Naeste]? The word is obviously derived from 'nearest [Naermeste]';* thus the neighbor is the person who is nearer to you than anyone else, yet not in the sense of preferential love" (WL, p. 21). His second assumption is that the one who is nearer to you than anyone else is at the same time "what thinkers call 'the other'" (p. 21). The following chapter will explore this suggestive tension between nearness and otherness.

chapter three

Love's Law—Equality

"You Shall Love the Neighbor" (II, B)

This chapter begins with the announcement that a new category comes into existence with the commandment—that of neighbor. With deliberate stress, Kierkegaard insists: *"It is in fact Christian love that discovers and knows that the neighbor exists, and what is the same thing, that everyone is the neighbor. If it were not a duty to love, the concept 'neighbor' would not exist either; but only when one loves the neighbor, only then is the selfishness in preferential love rooted out and the equality of the eternal preserved"* (WL, p. 44). In this way he introduces two new themes into the discussion that will illuminate the question of the commandment's scope—*equality* and *preference*. "The neighbor is one who is equal";[1] moreover, love for a genuine other is based in the other's "equality with you before God" (p. 60).[2] Only in "neighbor love," which is "the opposite of preference" (p. 58), can we reach, according to Kierkegaard, "what thinkers call the *'other'*" (p. 21). It is noteworthy that the most crucial division Kierkegaard makes is between nonpreferential love (*Kjerlighed*) and preferential love (*Forkjerlighed*); since the root term is the same, *kjerlighed* or "caring," we can infer that the crucial division is between caring that is not restricted in focus and caring that is restricted.[3] In short, Kierkegaard is here announcing the category of neighbor as one that is intended to safeguard the alterity of the other, to be sure that in love we allow the other to be more than an extension of ourselves. This category is embedded in the commandment, an ingredient in its affirmation of equality. It is a category that coexists with the category of commanded love; without the command, the concept of neighbor does not exist. Of course, suffering people exist whether or not there is a command to love them, but when Kierkegaard says that "no one in paganism loved the neighbor; no one suspected that he existed" (p. 53), he is highlighting the lack of a recognized obligation to care for all without exclusion.

When Kierkegaard says that without the command there would be no category of neighbor, he need not be saying that the divine command is the arbitrary and extrinsic source of the obligation to love others. The category of neighbor, we shall see, is based on the fact of our equality before God, our equality as children of God—our equality as created—and this keeps the commandment from being ungrounded, extrinsically imposed, or arbitrary. The love commandment will assume a kind of grounding in the ontological relation of human creatures to one another as creations of God.

I. Preference or Equality?

Love of neighbor (*Kjerlighed*) is distinguished from preferential love (*Forkjerlighed*) precisely because neighbor is the category of equality before God and preferential love does not do justice to equality. Kierkegaard is unequivocal: "Equality is simply not to make distinctions. . . . Preference, on the other hand, is to make distinctions" (WL, p. 58). In what follows I want to determine precisely what is at stake in the discussion of preference and Kierkegaard's negative evaluation of "distinctions." In particular, I want to suggest that Kierkegaard is offering neither an attack on all self-love nor a denial of the legitimate role of preference and inclination in erotic love and friendship; rather, he wants to preserve the integrity of the other, the genuine 'you.' I shall consider the issue of 'special relations' further in chapter 6, section III.

Kierkegaard's preliminary claim is that love based on inclination or preference is a form of love of self: "[E]rotic love [*Elskov*] and friendship [*Venskab*] are *preferential love,*" and "passionate preference is actually another form of self-love" (WL, pp. 52–53).[4] Preference either expresses or follows inclination. The "beloved is the *other I*"; even in friendship what is loved is "the *other I,* or the first I once again, but more intensely" (p. 57); thus Kierkegaard concludes that "whether we speak of the *first I* or of the *other I,* we do not come a step closer to the neighbor, because the neighbor is the *first you*" (p. 57).

Both here and later, when Kierkegaard says that "erotic love and friendship *as such* are only enhanced and augmented self-love" (WL, p. 267; Kierkegaard's emphasis), he is not saying anything particularly novel. Aristotle's discussion of friendship in the *Nichomachean Ethics* affirms that "friendship is based on self-love."[5] Why?—because a friend is a good for us: "[I]n loving a friend men love what is good for themselves; for the good man in becoming a friend becomes a good to his friend."[6] Aristotle brings out the ambiguity in the phrase "lover of self" and explains the "nature of true self-love": a good man's being is seen by him to be desirable because it is seen by him to be good; therefore "the good man should be a lover of self."[7] Indeed, the model of friendship derives from the characterization of a "good man in relation to himself."[8] It is natural that we should be our own best friend since in our relation to ourselves we can best approach the perfection of mutual good will, mutual aid, mutual delight, and time shared together, which characterize friendship.[9] Aristotle repeats often that "a friend is another self,"[10] and he is unapologetic about the dimension of self-referential preference within friendship, even when it is the friendship of virtue, or friendship directed toward the good (rather than the pleasurable or useful). The love that benefits us because it is directed to the good is genuine and legitimate self-love. Thomas Aquinas, too, concedes the self-interestedness of friendship.[11] Both admit that *as such* they are limited relations—they would agree with Kierkegaard that "erotic love and friendship *as such* are only enhanced and augmented self-love, although erotic love is undeniably life's most beautiful happiness and friendship the greatest temporal good!" (p. 267).

Thus, although Kierkegaard is distinguishing between love based on preference and a kind of nonpreferential love, he is not recommending that relations based on the former should be eliminated or replaced by the latter. Kierkegaard does not deny the beauty, necessity, and "delight" (WL, p. 150) of erotic love and friendship; they are, he says, "life's most beautiful happiness" and "the greatest temporal good" (p. 267). In other words, although he distinguishes the categories of erotic love, friendship, and neighbor love, what is at issue is the contrast between preferential and nonpreferential—not an attack on the erotic aspects of love or the congenialities of friendship. That love of the neighbor and love of the beloved or friend are not mutually exclusive is clear in his later claim in II, C: "Take away the distinction of preferential love so that you can love the neighbor. *But you are not to cease loving the beloved because of this—far from it.* If in order to love your neighbor you would have to begin by giving up loving those for whom you have preference, the word 'neighbor' would be the greatest deception ever contrived" (p. 61; emphasis mine); indeed, he continues, it would be a "contradiction" because it would be preferential (in the other direction) to exclude the beloved.

It is not easy to know how best to describe Kierkegaard's position. In one sense there is a kind of either/or about preference—preferential love can be sharply contrasted *conceptually* with nonpreferential love. Yet he claims that the goal is to preserve love for the neighbor *in* erotic love and friendship—"in erotic love and friendship, preserve love for the neighbor" (WL, p. 62)—and thus they can coincide materially.[12] The elevation or enhancement of erotic love and friendship for one who believes in God, and so sees all as "equal before God," is intended to preclude the arbitrariness and instability of preferential love.[13] One is tempted to say that Kierkegaard wants to ensure that friendship and erotic love are both supplemented by nonpreferential love, but he rejects the language of supplement or addition. He makes this clearer later on when he insists that "there is only one kind of love, the spirit's love" (p. 143). Therefore, neighbor love should "permeate" every expression of love (p. 112); it can and should "lie at the base of and be present in every other expression of love"; "it is in all of them, that is, it can be, but Christian love itself you cannot point to" (p. 146). It is a "misunderstanding" to think that "in Christianity the beloved and the friend are loved faithfully and tenderly in quite a different way than in paganism" (p. 53); neighbor love allows "drives," "inclination," "feelings," "natural relations," and "prescriptive rights . . . to remain in force"; it is not indifferent to "family relations" or "friendship" or "fatherland" (p. 144).

Kierkegaard can agree that friendship—the benevolent, mutual love that results in seeing the other as "another self"—is "the greatest temporal good." His understanding of friendship is no less positive than that of Aristotle and Aquinas, but his aim is to warn against the limitations inherent in relations based on preference. What is at stake for Kierkegaard is not that preferential love should be excluded but that it should not be the determinant of responsibility for the other. The discussion of preference is meant to show that love that is restricted to preference will not apprehend people as equals.

Works of Love has been taken to represent the tradition that reads the love commandment as an instruction to cease entirely loving ourselves, forgetting ourselves for the neighbor.[14] As we saw earlier, Kierkegaard does say that the preferential love should be "taken away," that self-love must be "wrested from us," but his own position does not require us to reject love of self, romantic love, or friendship. What is at stake for him is that self-love must be *unlocked* (WL, p. 17); that is, it must not be restricted to preferential expressions. Here he makes it clear that we must root out "the selfishness in preferential love" (p. 44), not the preferential love itself. We must remove the restrictions of preference when we face someone in need. Erotic love and friendship are not ruled out by Kierkegaard on the grounds that they enhance ourself and are a good for us. The point is that our responsibility is not limited to those we incline to or prefer.

It is important to note that Kierkegaard differs from those who contrast erotic love with other forms of preference, like friendship. By putting both erotic love and friendship in the same category, he avoids the negativity toward sexuality that is found in other accounts. This shows that what he objects to is the preferential aspect, not the sensuality or sexuality associated with erotic love.[15]

When one is in need before me, my response cannot be limited to what I am inclined to do or prefer to do. I must be guided by the other's equality before God, whether or not my inclination goes the same way. Here Kierkegaard is making a version of the Kantian distinction between duty and inclination: a duty has to be fulfilled whether or not we have an inclination or desire to do it; it cannot be fulfilled simply because it is the object of our preference.[16] According to this commandment, I cannot exclude someone simply *because* that person is not an object of preference or inclination. On the other hand, I am commanded to maintain an affirmation of the person as an equal *even if* I am inclined preferentially toward him or her. I must continue to love my spouse both as a spouse and as a neighbor, and my friend both as a friend and as a neighbor—that is, my inclination does not diminish my responsibilities to them as neighbors, equals before God. The point is not to exclude the tenderness and intimacy that are part of erotic love or friendship but to maintain a relation to lover or friend as an equal before God. Kierkegaard's point is clear in the discourse "Purity of Heart Is to Will One Thing," where he notes that "the discourse does not ask you whether you really do love your wife; it hopes so. It does not ask if she really is the delight of your eyes and the desire of your heart; it wishes that for you."[17] Far from recommending that I stop loving my husband with passionate preference, the commandment reminds me that I nevertheless am not allowed to treat him as a sex object or use him solely for my gratification—he is still a neighbor to me.

The discussion of preference thus reveals what I think is the force of the initial formulation of the scope of the commandment found in II, A—"to love the whole human race, all people, even the enemy, and not to make exceptions, neither of preference nor of aversion." The force is that to love "all" people is *to exclude none*. Kierkegaard labors the point that no one can be excluded from having a claim on us simply by virtue of the distinctions that constitute earthly life: "If in connection with Christian love one wants to make an exception of a single person whom one does not wish to love, then such a love is . . . unconditionally not Christian love" (WL, pp. 49–50); "self-denial's boundlessness in giving itself means not to exclude a single one" (p. 52).[18] Preferential love implies making a distinction between what is like us and unlike us, what we like and what we don't like based on similarity and dissimilarity; the other has for us the "distinction" of being tall, gay, blond, bald, black, Catholic, intelligent, or Indonesian. Loving based on preference for these or any other such distinctions excludes those who do not possess them. Preferential love in the form of erotic love and friendship involves a preference for what is like us and an aversion to what is unlike us; in making this kind of distinction, preference denies equality. But every other is my equal before God, and each is the equal of the other before God; and the 'equal before God' just is what we call the neighbor. The wife, the friend, the coworker, the foreigner, the enemy, "the very first person you meet" (p. 51)—anyone who confronts you in need has a claim on your love and is your neighbor.

The radical commitment to human equality at the heart of Kierkegaard's ethic, indeed, of his life, is reaffirmed in one of his later writings. In the Preface (1851) to "Two Discourses at the Communion on Fridays," he asks one indulgence:

> Allow me, however, to express only this, which in a way is my life, the content of my life, its fullness, its bliss, its peace and satisfaction—this, or this view of life, which is the thought of humanity and of human equality; Christianly, every human being (the single individual), unconditionally every human being, once again, unconditionally every human being, is equally close to God—how close and equally close?—is loved by him.[19]

What Kierkegaard means by the "infinite equality between human beings," I shall be arguing throughout, is not a naïve or cavalier dismissal of socioeconomic differences. The ground of this claim lies in the equal closeness of each person to God; the only "difference" is that "one person bears in mind that he is loved . . . [while] another person perhaps does not think about his being loved." Emphasizing THAT each person is loved by God might seem to result in an abstract leveling of human beings. However, THAT each person is loved does not tell us HOW each person is loved, and Kierkegaard will later exult in the way in which God celebrates diversity and loves each of us in our unique distinctiveness (WL, p. 270).[20]

II. Love's Responsibility

Let's return for a moment to Emmanuel Levinas's account of ethical relations because his ambivalence about the word "love" may illuminate something crucial about Kierkegaard's intentions. Levinas's best-known essays are replete with references to the "neighbor,"[21] and at times, especially in his later years, he spoke of "love of the neighbor," which he defined as "love without concupiscence,"[22] "charity," "love in which the ethical aspect dominates the passionate aspect."[23] However, most of the time Levinas preferred a different idiom—that of "responsibility for" the neighbor, rather than that of love. In Levinas's account of ethical relations, responsibility is "the essential, primary and fundamental structure of subjectivity"; "subjectivity is not for itself" but always "initially for another."[24] He learned early on, he says, to "distrust the compromised word 'love,'" choosing instead to speak of "the responsibility for the Other, being-for-the-other."[25] Repeatedly Levinas distances himself from the term "love," which he considers "worn-out and debased," preferring instead "the harsh name for what we call love of one's neighbor," that is, "responsibility for my neighbor."[26] Responsibility is described as a movement: *"Toward another* culminates in a *for another,* a suffering for his suffering."[27] The "substitution for the other," which "lies in the heart of responsibility," is Levinas's name for "Love without Eros."[28]

Like Kierkegaard, Levinas equates the two categories—"the neighbor, the responsibility to the other."[29] In "Ethics as First Philosophy," Levinas details how "the Other becomes my neighbor precisely through the way the face summons me, calls for me, begs for me, and in so doing recalls my responsibility, and calls me into question."[30] Levinas occasionally hesitates about whether the term "neighbor" is the best one to use—sometimes because it seems to obscure the fact of difference[31] and sometimes because it may have lost its legitimate shock value and become taken for granted.[32] Nevertheless, he persists in using it, from his earliest to his latest writings: "It is as a neighbor that a human being is accessible—as a face"; "in this call to responsibility of the ego by the face which summons it, which demands it and claims it, the other (*autrui*) is the neighbor."[33] The term "proximity of the neighbor" means for him "the responsibility of the ego for an other, the impossibility of letting the other alone faced with the mystery of death."[34] Levinas's preference for the term "responsibility," rather than "love" for the neighbor, is understandable. The word "love" can too easily fail to portray what is at stake; it can fail to announce strongly enough that "I am *ordered* toward the face of the other," that my response is his *"right."*[35] In sum, Levinas has what he calls "a grave view of *Agape* in terms of responsibility for the other."[36]

I suggest that reading Kierkegaard's discussion of commanded love in terms of Levinas's discussion of "ordered" responsibility seems to illuminate what is at stake for Kierkegaard. Moreover, it seems to obviate some objections to his account. Love without preference is hard to imagine; on the other hand, the idea of responsibility for the other does not initially raise as many questions as "love" does about the relation between preference and obligation. Obligation and responsibility go together more easily in our minds than obligation and love. We can see this, too, in the case of "care"—it would make more sense to think of commanded care in the sense of caring for someone or taking care of someone rather than caring about someone. If we see the heart of the matter for Kierkegaard as one of responsibility for the other, it does not seem so difficult to understand why we cannot dismiss talk of neighbor love even in the case of a wife or friend; it does not seem so difficult to understand why no one can be excluded, that is, why preference cannot be a criterion for our responsibility.[37] Moreover, Levinas also complements Kierkegaard's account by making clear that in one sense our neighbor, any neighbor, is always in need, in being always vulnerable to death.[38]

Despite Levinas's preference for the "grave" or "harsh" view of love as responsibility for the other, he does fall back time and again to using the word "love": he speaks of love as "peace," love as "the relation with the unique and the other," and "the wisdom of love."[39] Indeed, he says that the "idea of the face is the idea of gratuitous love," and he suggests that faith is "believing that love without reward is valuable"; he goes so far as to say that "that which I call responsibility is a love, because love is the only attitude where there is encounter with the unique."[40] Perhaps this reveals Levinas's sense that there is some value in not simply limiting the language of relations to the language of responsibility. After all, responsibility can be fulfilled grudgingly, hatefully. Perhaps this sad truth accounts for the extremely negative reaction readers often have to Levinas's notion of the self as "hostage" in responsibility;[41] this phrase seems to describe a very unloving situation, putting us at odds with the neighbor—a relation that we would normally condemn. But Levinas makes it clear that "the other is not a being we encounter that menaces us or wants to lay hold of us";[42] Levinas criticizes Jean Paul Sartre's view that the other's gaze is a threat.[43] When Levinas writes, "My ethical relation of love for the other stems from the fact that the self cannot survive by itself alone, cannot find meaning within its own being-in-the-world, within the ontology of sameness," he is revealing a dimension of "need" of the other that makes sense of his own designation of his ethics as "the ethics of the welcome."[44] In fact, Levinas's notion of "hostage" has ties with that of "host"[45] and reminds us not only of the early descriptions he used, in Totality and Infinity, of the self as open in "hospitality" to the other but also of the way he later ties "hospitality" to the extreme sacrifice of "giving to the other the bread from one's mouth."[46] The term "hospitality" reminds us of the graciousness with which responsibility should be fulfilled; it recalls the "gift" of love, which we have been given by God. Levinas explicitly ties responsibility and the gracious gift together when he recognizes that the responsibility of which he speaks "is not a cold juridical requirement"; "it is all the gravity of the love of one's fellowman—of love without concupiscence," and it is accomplished "through all the modalities of giving."[47] The terms "giving" and "gift" call to mind love rather than mere responsibility. Thus, Levinas seems to allow for both dimensions.

Levinas's appreciation that "there is something severe in this love; this love is commanded,"[48] along with the fact that "commandment" has, for Levinas, the very strong connotation of "the right of the human,"[49] allows him to recur at times to the language of love as long as it is commanded. In fact, toward the end of his life, Levinas explicitly comes closer to Kierkegaard in speaking about "the commandment of a gratuitous act" like love; he writes that "commanding love signifies recognizing the value of love in itself" and that "God is a command-ment to love . . . the one who says that one must love the other."[50] We will revisit Levinas's account again when we later consider Kierkegaard's view of love as debt (chapter 8) and as gift (chapter 10). For the moment it is enough to note that although there may be important differences between their ac-counts, Levinas and Kierkegaard both appreciate that the two accents—love and responsibility—need to be part of a full account of the relation to the neighbor. Levinas's preference for the language of "responsibility for the other" clarifies Kierkegaard's understanding of *"commanded* love," and Levinas's appreciation of the strength of "commandment" complements Kierkegaard's understanding of "commanded *love.* "[51]

III. The Blindness of Preference

In his discussion of preferential and nonpreferential love, Kierkegaard uses the image of blindness and "closed eyes." I propose that the metaphors of blindness and vision can be useful tools for exploring his understanding of the ethical rela-tion to the other.

Kierkegaard recognizes a tension between the exclusivity and preference in-volved in erotic love and the responsibility for moral attention to the larger com-munity. He proposes that in erotic love (*Elskov*) one can become "blind from love . . . blind to everything else but this beloved" (WL, p. 68). This is not a contro-versial claim. We have all heard the aphorism that "love is blind," and the nature of that blindness has been the topic of both classic novels and modern self-help books. Martha Nussbaum suggests that Henry James's novels *The Golden Bowl* and *The Ambassadors* address the question of moral blindness (and, indirectly, moral vi-sion) when they highlight a "pervasive tension between love and the ethical, and between the sorts of attention required by each."[52] Love, the novels tell us, con-strains ethical attention in two ways: love asks both that there be "privacy" and "that focus be averted from all else that is outside," and these demands for privacy and exclusivity seem finally incompatible with ethical awareness and responsi-bility.[53] Moral vision is impoverished or distorted because "lovers see, at such times, only one another; and it is not really deep if they *can* carefully see around and about them. That vision excludes general attention and care, at least at that mo-ment."[54] The "exclusivity and intensity of personal love" seem to impede the "just and general responsiveness" that the "gentler feelings" of friendship assist. Nuss-baum concludes that, for James, the different sorts of attention required by the love relation and the general ethical relation allow, at best, only an "unsteady oscillation between blindness and openness, exclusivity and general concern."[55] James re-veals tension, not harmony, in that "so long as our eyes are open, we are wonderful and lovable and finely responsive; but when we immerse ourselves in the most powerful responses, entering silence, closing our eyes, are we then capable at all of asking questions about our friends, of thinking of the good of the community?"[56]

"Closing our eyes" in love is, in James's view, our way of seeing the beloved—or more precisely, seeing only the beloved. Such blindness is the form of devoted attention to the beloved. What is ethically problematical for James is that another kind of blindness—failure to attend to the nonbeloved—follows from seeing only the beloved. That is, for James the preference of friendship is not considered ethically problematical. Moreover, although for James a preference for the beloved is in tension with the more general ethical concern embodied in friendship, he never doubts that such preference is genuine attention to the beloved.

Kierkegaard agrees with James that passionate preference for a beloved can blind us to the needs of our friends. He agrees that "the more securely one I and another I join to become one I, the more this united I selfishly cuts itself off from everyone else" (WL, p. 56). He differs from James, however, in at least two radical ways. Unlike James, Kierkegaard extends that moral threat of the self-absorption of erotic/romantic love to the case of friendship as well.[57] According to Kierkegaard, both erotic love and friendship involve "the *I* intoxicated in the *other I*" (p. 56). More important, Kierkegaard questions whether such preferential exclusivity to the beloved is genuine attention to the 'other' at all. That is, he suggests that such preference expresses self-love because *"erotic love and friendship are preferential love,"* and "passionate preference is actually another form of self-love" (pp. 52–53). The "beloved is the *other I*"; even in friendship what is loved is "the *other I*, or the first I once again, but more intensely" (p. 57); this is true because "[a]t the peak of erotic love and friendship, the two actually do become one self, one I" (p. 56).

Although Kierkegaard's talk of a commandment to love is a world away from the philosopher David Hume's sentiment-based ethic, here he echoes Hume's sensitivity to the fact that even what seems to be sympathetic engagement with another can often be reduced to a modification of self-love precisely because it effects an identity in which genuine otherness is precluded.[58] Hume's attack on the view that ethics is based in self-love in fact reveals the subtle ways in which self-love can be disguised; in the course of that attack it becomes clear that in certain accounts of sympathetic response to others, they are reduced by having to be turned into "another me."[59] Hume indirectly points out the ways in which responses to another can annihilate a relation by eliminating the presence of two separate partners to that relation. Kierkegaard's critique of erotic love and friendship is similarly motivated: as we just saw, his point is to show not only that the "united I" of love and friendship "selfishly cuts itself off from everyone else" but also that "at the peak of erotic love and friendship, the two actually do become one self, one I"; there is no genuine relation because there are not two selves to be in relation (WL, p. 56).[60] As he will later insist: "Without a *you* and an *I* there is no love" (p. 266).

Thus, like James, Kierkegaard speaks of loving attention in terms of blindness to others, but such blindness is found in both erotic love and friendship since they are both expressions of preference or inclination. Moreover, Kierkegaard speaks of the blindness *to* the lover or friend that is a function of the relation between self-love and preference. That is, by suggesting their basis in self-love, Kierkegaard accounts for the way in which erotic love and friendship make one blind *to* the beloved and the friend; preference for Kierkegaard, in contrast to James, is precisely a way of *not* attending to the lover or friend as a genuine other. Kierkegaard complicates James's moral anxiety: there is not only the danger of moral blindness to others when we preferentially love one person to the exclusion of others but also the danger that our preference can so reduce the beloved or friend (to ourselves, to loving what is good for us) that there is no vision—even there— of a genuine other. Kierkegaard concludes that "whether we speak of the *first I* or of the *other I*, we do not come a step closer to the neighbor, because the neighbor is the *first you*" (WL, p. 57).

Kierkegaard is obviously concerned that we reach out to a genuine You and not simply another I; he is concerned, that is, to protect the other's integrity, irreducibility, otherness (or, in the contemporary idiom, the other's alterity). He is concerned that the other does not get submerged or assimilated into the first I. Neighbor love, then, is Kierkegaard's name for that relation to another beyond the self that appreciates the other as a genuine "you"; it is the only genuine alternative to the various ways in which we are tempted to reduce another to "another-I." Kierkegaard claims that preference is self-loving because even if it is not selfish, it remains an expression of "self-willfulness" and "arbitrariness" (WL, pp. 55, 115, 428). For Kierkegaard, passionate preference for the beloved and caring preference for the friend are both rooted in love of self in that they are modes of being 'for myself.' But, as was clear from the ancients on, this is a description of a natural dynamic. Kierkegaard is not rejecting either erotic love or friendship. His intention is to show, with a rhetoric that "awakens" us and turns us "topsy-turvy," that the legacy of sin in us is the temptation to restrict ourselves to preferential love. In this way Kierkegaard condemns one kind of moral blindness: in showing the limits of preference, Kierkegaard is trying to work against blindness to the genuine otherness of the one preferred. But there is still a danger of another kind of blindness in the radical claim he makes in the next chapter—that "one sees the neighbor only with closed eyes" (p. 68). That provocative claim must be explored further.

chapter four

Love's Law—Kinship

"*You* Shall Love the Neighbor" (II, C)

The strident affirmation of equality that informs II, B, is Kierkegaard's version of the general ethical quest for impartiality; it is an attempt to generate a more encompassing perspective and to avoid a reductive self-love ethic. This new chapter, II, C, continues the formal analysis of both the scope and the unconditionality of the commandment. With respect to scope, it continues the analysis of "equality" in terms of the neighbor, the *other*, the object of our obligation. In addition, it introduces a new aspect of unconditionality, from the other direction—that is, the equality of the obligation, with respect to the *agent*, the subject of the "you shall." I shall consider each in turn.

I. The Blindness of Equality

In II, C, the momentum behind Kierkegaard's reminders that preference lies in making distinctions and that equality refuses to make distinctions escalates into the provocative claim that "one sees the neighbor only with closed eyes or by looking *away from* the dissimilarities,"[1] for the neighbor is the human being "taken quite blindly" (WL, p. 68). That is, the concluding claim in II, B, that "equality is simply not to make distinctions" (p. 58) becomes intensified through a striking image of the blindness of equality. Indeed, he proposes that "love for the neighbor makes a person blind in the deepest and noblest and most blessed sense of the word, so that he blindly loves every human being as the lover loves the beloved" (pp. 68–69). Kierkegaard is ruthless in this project, and it is shocking to see what looks like a callous suggestion: if you find it hard to love another, he says, then "shut your eyes"; "when your mind is not confused and distracted by looking at the object of your love and the dissimilarity of the object," you are well "on the way of perfection to loving the neighbor" (p. 68). Such a suggestion should give us pause, especially when it comes in the wake of the claim that "death cannot deprive you of the neighbor" because "if it takes one, life immediately gives you another" (p. 65). We need to ask whether this kind of noble and blessed blindness makes normative an abstract relation to an other whose distinctiveness is irrelevant and who is effectively interchangeable. How much attention to the concrete other is really fostered, or even allowed, in neighbor love by Kierkegaard's suggestion that "in loving a friend you actually hold together with the friend, but in loving the neighbor you hold together with God" (p. 65)?

It is claims like these that have been the occasion for numerous criticisms of Kierkegaard's ethic. From the beginning critics have argued that "Kierkegaard's doctrine of love remains totally abstract" and that, despite "incessant talk" about "that particular individual," the neighbor amounts to nothing more than a general principle of otherness, or the universal human.[2] Does Kierkegaard's emphasis on blindness to distinctions show that such critics are right?

Even readers with only a cursory knowledge of Kierkegaard would probably agree that much of the motivation for his writings lies in an uncompromising rejection of Hegelian abstraction. Moreover, the passionate reminders by the pseudonymous author Johannes Climacus that we have "forgotten what it is to exist" echo Kierkegaard's own journal remarks that deplore his day's lack of spirit or passion;[3] both seem to call us back to subjectivity and concrete particularity. Indeed, Kierkegaard is known for his deliberate cultivation of "the individual."[4] Nevertheless, critics are right to remind us that an emphasis on neighbors as equals or as individuals or as particulars is not sufficient to overcome abstraction; what we need is something to guarantee that these equal individuals or particulars are also recognized in their distinctiveness, that their concrete differences are seen to be morally relevant. In itself the affirmation of individuality and particularity only rejects the "crowd," the "aggregate," the "mass"; it does not guarantee an affirmation of concrete difference.[5] Something more than individuality or particularity needs to be guaranteed.[6] Kierkegaard rejects social abstraction, but the threat of abstract individualism nevertheless looms large. The question is whether the "particular individuals" of whom he speaks are seen as distinctive people embedded in a context of distinctive relations rather than particular *abstract, representative, and interchangeable* individuals. If Kierkegaard's ethic formalizes the relation to the other in a radical blindness to concrete difference or distinctiveness, it will have belied all the verbal assurances he is at pains to offer about his rejection of both self-love and abstraction. The only way in which a genuine appreciation of difference can be incorporated into an account is to provide a way for differences to be *the focus* of loving attention. Later in *Works of Love*, we will find striking affirmations of the importance of vision to interpersonal relationship, and we will need to consider the consistency between these and Kierkegaard's commitment to blindness to all but the essential human being.

It cannot be denied that many of Kierkegaard's claims, when presented in isolation from their context, provide grist for the mill of someone who wants to find fault with this ethic; as a result they should cause at least a prima-facie discomfort and call for interpretation on the part of those who are sympathetic and look to this ethic for insight. An unqualified emphasis on equality can entail a certain kind of moral abstraction that is ultimately as reductive and as destructive as the evil it seeks to avoid. When impartiality is thought to require that all distinguishing characteristics be morally irrelevant, an ethic can achieve universality and neutrality, but only at the cost of being abstract and substitutionist. Whether equality is achieved through submergence or through a distancing and stripping down, the result is the same: with the exclusion of the moral relevance of all distinguishing characteristics, there is nothing to distinguish the purported 'other' from the self, and this unwittingly reduces the other to another self and so reexpresses self-love. Quite simply, an impartiality obsessed with equality and neutrality can fail to appreciate difference. Is concrete attention nothing but moral confusion and distraction? If it is, Kierkegaard's later claim that "the category of neighbor is like the category human being" (WL, p. 141) might be seen simply to transfer the abstractness of the latter to the former. If attention to distinctions and difference is what constitutes immoral partiality, if love looks only at what is essentially the same in us—disembodied, disembedded personhood (created free agency)—how can our moral attention ever be concrete? Kierkegaard is in danger of exchanging the blindness of self-love to the other for an *equally* unloving blindness to the other.

Does Kierkegaard escape this danger? It is important to try to see what is at stake for him in translating the unconditionality of the commandment into an affirmation of equality that requires blindness to the other. What could he possibly mean by saying that we can "see" the neighbor "only with closed eyes"? Can we see anything at all with closed eyes? Could the other be anything to us but an abstraction in such an ethic? Is there no room for loving focus on and attention to morally relevant differences? The question is whether Kierkegaard's affirmation of equality and his recommendation of such blindness preclude or undermine any genuine appreciation of genuine otherness, that is, difference, distinctiveness, and the concrete.

II. Neighbor and Kinship—Blindness toward the Other

The requirement of "blindness" or "closed eyes" can only be properly evaluated if one recognizes that it occurs in a strategic location—in the particular context of formally clarifying the scope and unconditionality of the commandment. In this context of discussion we are urged to close our eyes to dissimilarity and distinction so as not to contract the scope of the commandment; such blindness guarantees that no one can be excluded.

Dissimilarities, distinctions, and differences are, in one sense, neutral; they are necessary if we are even to pick out individuals. Kierkegaard realizes this: "Just as little as the Christian lives or can live without his body, so little can he live without the dissimilarity of earthly life that belongs to every human being in particular by birth, by position, by circumstances, by education, etc.—none of us is pure humanity" (WL, p. 70). Our dissimilarities, according to this passage, constitute the temporal dimension of our existence in that "there is dissimilarity everywhere in temporality—which, after all, is precisely the different, the multifarious" (p. 81). In other words, dissimilarities cannot be denied. What, then, are we supposed to learn from Kierkegaard's recommendations of blindness to dissimilarity and distinction?

In this context of the unconditional scope of the commandment, the distinctions to which we must close our eyes are those that tempt us to disclaim or distance ourselves from one another; "in paganism people are inhumanly separated one from another by the dissimilarities of earthly life" because some ways of construing differences can undermine our sense of "the kinship of all human beings" (WL, p. 69). This is an elaboration of his earlier claim in II, B, that "Christianity's joyful message is contained in the doctrine of humanity's inherent kinship with God" (p. 62). A sense of kinship and solidarity or connectedness is not achieved by imagining an identity that does not actually exist but, rather, by not making those distinctions that alienate one from another.[7] Such distinctions do more than particularize; they particularize in ways that disconnect us. Distinctions that merely particularize can thus be contrasted with distinctions that damage the soul (p. 71), that is, those that "deny kinship" (pp. 74, 85). In one of his early upbuilding discourses, Kierkegaard speaks of "equality's 'divine law to love one's neighbor as oneself' in such a way that no person is so exalted in rank that he is not your neighbor in exactly the same sense as no person is so inferior in rank that he is not your neighbor, and the equality is incontrovertibly demonstrated by your loving him as you love yourself!"[8] Preference for characteristics that are similar to ours, or the kind we value, can lead to exclusion: "If you hold together . . . with some other people of a particular class and with a particular condition in life . . . the things of this world will . . . tempt you comparatively in showing partiality" (p. 78).[9] Differences, in this context, are concrete, and we are to ignore them because they disguise our equality—that is, we are to be blind to them because they blind us to our kinship.

This section, II, C, continues to elaborate the way in which every human being is the neighbor. Kierkegaard is rejecting the partiality associated with kinship in favor of the inclusiveness that kinship promotes. His claim that "the neighbor is the common watermark, you see it only by means of eternity's light when it shines through the dissimilarity" (WL, p. 89)—which has often been taken to be an excessive emphasis on the 'essence' of human nature—looks different when taken in the context of his rejection of what George Eliot calls "love of the clan."[10] It is difficult to imagine an appreciation of community that did not include the acknowledgment that "in being king, beggar, rich man, poor man, male, female, etc., we are not like each other—therein we are indeed different. But in being the neighbor we are all unconditionally like each other" (p. 89).

III. Equality of Obligation—Blindness toward the Agent

The recommendation of "closed eyes" raises the question not only of the abstractness of Kierkegaard's account of the ethical relation to the other but also of whether he devalues earthly or material concerns. In II, C, we find statements of the inevitability of temporal distinctions and Christianity's indifference to the "goal of one temporal condition," which have fueled charges that *Works of Love* dictates a conservative preservation of the status quo and callous indifference to unjust social and economic conditions. On the contrary, I suggest in what follows that the recommendation of indifference to worldly circumstances is an integral part of the strategy for demonstrating the requirement of *equality in the obligation to love;* that it follows directly from it; and that it need not, and is not intended to, support an overall attitude of indifference to physical or worldly needs.

One way to begin this inquiry is to consider for a moment the typographical peculiarity of the title of II, C, "*You* Shall Love the Neighbor," and to ask why there is a third chapter in the deliberation on the love commandment at all. Why isn't the commandment sufficiently clarified once the elements of "shall" and "neighbor" have been clarified? Why is there an additional discussion to highlight the "you"? What is emphasized in the discussion of the "you" that is not emphasized in the discussion of the "neighbor"? If we consider the titles of II, B and C, the most simple and obvious contrast seems to be that B, "You Shall Love the *Neighbor*" focuses on the object of love (the neighbor), whereas C, "*You* Shall Love the Neighbor" seems to focus on the *agent* of the obligation to love. I suggest that the emphasis on "you" provides important guidance in two respects.

First, consider the most explicit clarification of the "you" at the end of this chapter (II, C) in terms of the contrast between "I" and "you." Kierkegaard writes that the "I has no significance unless it becomes the *you* to whom eternity incessantly speaks and says: *You* shall, *you* shall, *you* shall . . . maturity is to understand this *you* personally" (WL, p. 90). Eternity speaks to each of us directly—we are to take the "*you* personally." The point of this admonition is found early on in *Works of Love:* "The divine authority of the Gospel does not speak to one person about another, does not speak to you, my listener, about me, or to me about you—no, when the Gospel speaks, it speaks to the single individual. It does not speak *about* us human beings, you and me, but speaks *to* us human beings, to you and me, and what it speaks about is that love is to be known by its fruits" (p. 14). That is, the commandment does not say, "Everyone shall do X" or "He or she shall do X." It addresses itself to me and tells me what I must do. It does not tell me what others must do; each of us must respond to the "you" that is heard only by a single individual. Kierkegaard will later refer to the way in which Christianity speaks to us individually and tells us things "in confidence" (p. 136).

Kierkegaard goes on to make an intriguing remark: "O my listener, it is not *you* to whom *I* am speaking; it is *I* to whom eternity says: *You* shall" (WL, p. 90). That is, he explicitly attempts to disavow the role of an author who issues directives to the reader. This would be in keeping with his understanding of the need for indirect communication—the impossibility of awakening others directly by issuing an imperative to them. He is, he implies, not issuing an imperative but simply repeating the imperative that is given to him. But it is an interesting question whether he can succeed here; the one who repeats to the reader an imperative issued to himself is still presenting the reader with an imperative. It is not so easy to try to awaken others to the import of a command without instigating a direct confrontation with it. One way to explain why he doesn't seem to see this as a problem is suggested by his discussion earlier in "Purity of Heart," in which he posits the role of the reader as listener and of the author as prompter.[11] Kierkegaard is the prompter who repeats the words of the true Author (God). Presumably Kierkegaard is assuming that when the prompter on the sidelines prompts an actor on the stage, the prompter is mentioning an imperative rather than using one; the prompter is reminding the actor of the Author's words, which the actor is supposed to say. That is, the prompter says the 'You shall,' which repeats the words of the true Author, so that the actor is reminded of the words he is to speak ('You shall'). Just as a prompter is not issuing the directives he reminds the actor to speak, so Kierkegaard is not issuing the directives he reminds the reader of. However, there are times when Kierkegaard seems to be issuing his own 'You shall' to the reader.[12]

In addition to raising this question about the status of the author who is repeating imperatives, the "You" in the title offers even more guidance about Kierkegaard's ethic; it highlights a less obvious but equally important message about the implications of the recommendation of indifference to "temporal" distinctions. The message is about the equality of the *agent's* obligation. In the preceding sections I argued that Kierkegaard's recommendation of "closed eyes" and blindness to "distinction" in II, A and B, does not constitute indifference to the neighbor's particular and concrete distinctiveness. Nothing in such blindness requires us to ignore our neighbor's specific and distinctive needs and desires; it simply requires that we shall not escape from the responsibilities of kinship by focusing on external differences or differences that alienate us from one another. We are told that we cannot make the bargain of simply caring for the people we prefer because they are like us; we can make no exception to who shall be cared for when they are in need. In other words, their condition (in terms of distinctions or dissimilarities) does not affect the unconditionality of our obligation to them. In this chapter, II, C, we are told that there is no exception to the "you" who is obligated; that is, nothing about our condition can affect the unconditionality of our obligation to them. Thus the two chapters are clearly related, but they are related according to the deliberate ambiguity in the term "neighbor"—both the one served and the one who serves could be called neighbor, but in different senses. This is correlated with the difference Kierkegaard himself notes: "The one to whom I have a duty is my neighbor, and when I fulfill my duty I show that I am a neighbor" (WL, p. 22). Insofar as the focus in II, B, is on how one cannot exclude anyone from the category of those who are due our love, and the focus in C is on how one cannot exempt oneself from the command to love, equality in the love commandment has two loci—you and the other. The commandment is to be fulfilled by all equally (without exception) in relation to all equally (without exception).

Christianity, Kierkegaard says in II, C, does not "divisively take sides" on the question of temporal distinctions—"with the calmness of eternity it surveys equably all the dissimilarities of earthly life" (WL, p. 70). He writes in what seems at best a complacent vein that the "dissimilarity of earthly life . . . must continue as long as temporality continues" because it is through overcoming temptations that we become Christian (p. 70). He insists that however "well-intentioned," it is nonetheless "worldliness" to try to achieve "one temporal condition" for all because "worldly similarity . . . is not Christian equality" (pp. 71–72). Christianity "allows all dissimilarities to stand," teaching that "everyone [high and low] is to *lift himself above* earthly dissimilarity" (p. 72). He who loves the neighbor "is at peace by being content with the dissimilarity of earthly life allotted to him, be it that of distinction or lowliness" (p. 84). It is not necessary to "abolish distinctions" precisely because they are mere garments, which if they "hang loosely" enough, allow us to see "that essential other, which is common to all, the eternal resemblance, the likeness" (p. 88).

One way to construe Kierkegaard's resistance to an emphasis on worldly equality (in particular economic equality) is in the light of the standard ethical distinction between equality and equity; that is, he may, like other thinkers view absolute equality as less important than proportionate equity. Similarly, he might have in mind something like the distinction between economic equality and the "doctrine of sufficiency," which requires that every person have enough, assuming that the latter is more important than the absolute equality.[13] But it is likely that the most important explanation of Kierkegaard's attempt to deemphasize socioeconomic equality is found in his perceived need to correct the overemphasis on it found in Europe at precisely the time he was writing *Works of Love*.[14] The point to underscore is that this recommendation of indifference to conditions of rank, birth, and circumstances achieves prominence in the context of the chapter (II, C), where we are led (at least by the title) to expect a focus on the agent. It should not be taken out of that context. I suggest that this focus on the agent points to the equality of our obligation; that is, Kierkegaard's achievement here is to highlight the equality of the demand on us, to insist that we can make no exception to the "you" who is required to act as neighbor to the other.

Moreover, this chapter contains a rationale for the indifference to circumstances that guides and limits how the recommended indifference is to be expressed; we shall find this same rationale in the later deliberation (2:VII) on our duty to be merciful. It is impossible to make an accurate and fair assessment of this ethic without taking special notice of a very unusual feature of *Works of Love*, one that comes to the forefront in II, C's focus on the "you." This unusual feature, which is seldom directly noted, is Kierkegaard's attention to the ways in which the disadvantaged can be unloving. We come face to face with a rather unexpected account of the potential corruptions of the lowly, as well as of the distinguished, because Kierkegaard suggests it would be "cowardly" if he did not "dare to make people aware, the lowly or the distinguished" (p. 85). This account begins with the observation that "one person is haughty and another defiantly envies," but "both ways are in fact rebellion . . . against the essentially Christian" (p. 70); he ends the next deliberation (III, A) with the observation that "a person can inhumanly wish to make himself indispensable by his power, but he can also wish to make himself indispensable by his weakness" (p. 126). In Nietzschean fashion, Kierkegaard reminds us that cowardice, hypocrisy, envy, and "crafty defiance" can all be vices of those who are oppressed or disadvantaged (pp. 70, 74, 80, 84). This results, admittedly, in what may look like advice to the disadvantaged from the advantaged—self-serving advice, at worst, and paternalistic, at best. But I suggest that we take Kierkegaard at his word when he explicitly urges the reader to be as careful in interpreting his distinctions and examples as he was in setting them up (p. 73) and that we reconsider indifference to temporal circumstances in this particular context.

If we do this, we see that Kierkegaard parallels two accounts, both of which begin with a claim that "the times are past" when people can be unsubtle in their failure to love. The first details the ways in which the "powerful and prominent" are tempted to be unloving (WL, p. 74), and the second details the kind of corruption to which the "lowly" are tempted (p. 80). The point is that YOU—high or low—need to be a neighbor to others. YOU, if socially or materially privileged, cannot exempt yourself from loving those less so, as far as you can; but it is also true that YOU, if disadvantaged in these respects, must be able to be a neighbor to others, including those who are socially or materially above you, as far as you can and as far as they need. The former is the obvious reminder to give; the latter is not as obvious but is just as necessary. Kierkegaard's recommendation of indifference covers both reminders.

The implied rationale for the recommended indifference is that insofar as neighbor love is a duty, two things must be guaranteed. First, *ought* implies *can*, so the duty must be *able to be fulfilled* by all, equally. "Eternity," Kierkegaard writes, "assumes that every person can do it and therefore only asks if he did it" (WL, p. 79). This same claim, as we shall see later, is made especially clear in 2:VII, on the duty to be merciful. Second, there must be a distinction between striving and achievement since the consequences of our actions are subject to things outside our control. This is made explicit in this chapter when Kierkegaard reminds us: "What a person will or will not achieve is not within his power" (p. 84). Such a recognition does not, however, preclude responsibility to *strive* to achieve certain ends.[15] I propose that both these factors entail an indifference to social (socioeconomic-political) conditions, but only in very specific senses: (1) indifference to the condition of the one obliged to love and (2) indifference to the condition actually effected by our attempts to fulfill our duty. As for determination of one's obligation to be loving, one's physical circumstances can be ignored; moreover, meritorious fulfillment of duty cannot be conditional on one's particular temporal achievements.

What is at stake is that the duty cannot be biased; there can be no unfair advantages in fulfilling the command. The irrelevance of worldly distinctions is affirmed in the attempt to make clear that the obligation is not conditional on one's particular temporal circumstances. The point is that one's temporal circumstances are irrelevant to one's obligation to love—they can neither make it easier nor harder to fulfill.

But is Kierkegaard being naïve or unrealistic? He is right to point to love's independence from material *determination*, to indicate that given our lack of control over the physical causal nexus, merit attaches to striving rather than to achieving. But is he naïve about what affects striving, about how deeply external conditions can undermine our very energy to continue to strive? It must be admitted that he often exhibits an elitist sense of what constitutes disadvantage, but occasionally he shows a remarkable sensitivity to the power of debilitating or undermining conditions, as when he urges us to imagine "the misery of those who perhaps from childhood or from some time later in life have been so tragically devastated, so badly ravaged, that they are unable to do anything at all, perhaps are even scarcely able to express sympathy in clear words" (WL, p. 325). Whether or not he is correct in his ultimate optimism about our ability to strive even when we are demoralized and our efforts are frustrated, it seems fair to say that he is at least not naïve about the difficulty.[16]

In the context of equality of demand, then, the recommendation of indifference to temporal circumstances serves a purpose that does not entail indifference to worldly concerns or socioeconomic conditions. It is perhaps unexpected to see demands being made on both the "prominent" and the "lowly," but it need not be a proposed justification for indifference to bettering social conditions for those in need. To suggest that the disadvantaged and oppressed must, like the advantaged and oppressors, be warned against being unloving and to suggest that envy is as much to be avoided (is as incompatible with loving) as haughtiness (WL, pp. 70, 80) do not license the inference that one is not obligated to help the needy in the ways one can.[17]

Another factor may be relevant in putting Kierkegaard's conclusions in perspective. One of his assumptions is that the Danes are a "fortunately endowed people."[18] Whether this assumption is elitist, naïve, or realistic, it does help to explain his emphases. I think it is telling that the discussion of indifference to distinction or dissimilarity is explicitly addressed to an audience of those tempted to be haughty or to be envious (WL, pp. 70, 74, 80). His repeated references to "silk and ermine" and "high rank" and "circles" (the distinguished live "in the alliance of their circles" and flee "from one distinguished circle to another"; pp. 74–75) suggest his sense of a society obsessed with prestige and social standing. They suggest an audience, some of whom are tempted to pride themselves on being in the 'right' circles (the country club set, the acknowledged cultural elite), and the rest of whom are tempted to discontent because they want to be in those or other envied circles. Given such an audience, the recommendation of indifference to material distinctions does not warrant the charge of otherworldliness.

Not only is immoral otherworldliness not entailed by the kind of indifference recommended in this chapter of *Works of Love*, but also it does not seem to be Kierkegaard's intention for the book as a whole. Consider his warning in the first deliberation—that acts of charity can be unloving if one is "thinking about his own cares instead of thinking about the cares of the poor, perhaps seeking alleviation by giving to charity instead of wanting to alleviate poverty" (pp. 13–14). This warning is phrased in such a way that the duty of alleviating poverty seems to be assumed. We hear an echo of this when he later warns: "Take care lest being loved is more important to you than that in which you are to love one another" (p. 129). His general commitments to "action" and "actuality" support this demand to "alleviate poverty." His appeal to the example of the Samaritan is fully in line with this emphasis: "Christ does not speak about knowing the neighbor but about becoming a neighbor oneself, about showing oneself to be a neighbor just as the Samaritan showed it by his mercy" (p. 22). Showing oneself to be a neighbor does not involve addressing only 'spiritual' needs; unless one already holds a dualist, spiritualist point of view, one need not see the injunction to serve the neighbor in terms of such dualism.

Kierkegaard's condemnation of the escapism of abstract love is strong and consistently maintained throughout *Works of Love*, and this is in keeping with his view that "actuality" is the source of demand and responsibility. He condemns escapism when he condemns the "worldly way" of closing oneself off from the world, to avoid being contaminated by the rough, the lowly, and the undistinguished (p. 74). If you are not attentive to actual persons and thus fail to respond to the one who walks by you in misery, you have indeed been blind—"but not, alas, in the Christian sense" (p. 75). Kierkegaard criticizes the non-Christian sense of closed eyes precisely because it is that by which one closes oneself off from the world.

These discussions of the three parts of the second deliberation have brought to our attention how Kierkegaard conceptually sets the stage for the remainder of the book. Allow me to review briefly some important dimensions of Kierkegaard's ethic. First, his claim that the preference at the heart of both erotic love and friendship is a form of love of self amounts to the classical admission that a friend (or lover) is "another self." Like Aristotle, Kierkegaard recognizes two kinds of self-love—"proper self-love" and "selfish self-love" (WL, p. 151). Having a friend (or lover) is a proper love of self; loving the friend (or lover) as "another self" is legitimate, an appropriate way of being for oneself; but although it is proper and good, it is still a way of being for oneself and is to be distinguished from neighbor love, which is a way of being for another. He contrasts loving someone as "another self" with loving another "as yourself." Proper love of self is the safeguarding index for love of the other. The love for another "as yourself," which constitutes "redoubling" of the self, preserves the alterity of the other because it has the criterion that one would be willing to give up the other for the sake of the other's good (p. 21), and this is not a criterion of even the highest friendship.[19] Kierkegaard's discussion thus indirectly highlights two contrasting senses of "as yourself": one sense must be in place to ensure that you love the other as much as you should, but the "as yourself" should not assume the form of limiting the relation to that with "another I" (the "as yourself" actually guards the other's alterity).

Second, Kierkegaard's dismissal of the relevance of "distinctions" warns against the limits of preference but does not entail the rejection of preferential relations. The point, as we saw, was to "preserve neighbor-love" in erotic love and friendship. Preference highlights ways in which another is like me or what I like; preference does not do justice to the alterity of the other since it is a way of being for oneself rather than for another. Whereas in II, B, the dissimilarity or distinction we are to look away from is cast in terms of what is like/unlike me in general, relative to self-love's preference, the discussion in C tends to emphasize the dissimilarity or distinction in terms of distinguished/lowly, relative to worldly rank and circumstances. Although the reference of both distinctions may coincide, the sense of each is quite different. It is the former that usually gives rise to the fear that such an ethic does not allow due attention to the distinctive qualities of individuals, and it is the latter that usually gives rise to the suspicion that Kierkegaard is indifferent to the betterment of social or economic conditions.

Third, when the commandment requires that no one be excluded, it does so in two senses: (1) no one can be excluded just because he or she is not naturally the object of my inclination or preference, and (2) no one can be excluded even if he or she is the object of my inclination or preference. In other words, the commandment brings into the circle of my responsibility those who are not the object of my inclination or preference, and it maintains those who are the object of my inclination or preference within the circle of my obligation. The commandment, on the one hand, orders us to love those in need before us even if we are not naturally inclined to love them; on the other hand, where our love is filled with preference, it orders us to be faithful because preference is contingent, changeable, and unstable. In both cases the category of the neighbor is one in which the arbitrariness and the instability of the preferential are eliminated (WL, p. 55); the commandment asks that whether "given" to us or "chosen" by us, a person will never fail to be treated by us with the respect due to an equal before God.

Fourth, Kierkegaard is continually working with a very rich set of contrasts between inward and outward, internal and external. He reminds us of the Samaritan's compassion and the command to "Go and do likewise"—which is clearly different from sitting back and indulging in ineffectual pity (WL, pp. 78–79; also p. 22). In this sense 'hidden' compassion is useless. But the emphasis on action also takes into account the inadequacy of simple outwardness, as is clear from his suggestion that "one who feeds the poor—but still has not yet been victorious over his mind in such a way that he calls this meal a banquet—sees the poor and the lowly only as the poor and the lowly. The one who gives *the banquet* sees the neighbor in the poor and the lowly" (p. 83). What is condemned by implication is a cold, distanced giving. A giving that sees only the poor and unimportant is not a loving giving; it cannot count as a celebration, as a "banquet."

We will need to consider further whether Kierkegaard's commitment to conscientious "inwardness" ultimately supports a charge of acosmic otherworldliness, but at least so far in the deliberations Kierkegaard's evaluation of "distinctions" has not mitigated the obligation of those with privilege to be loving or their responsibility for alleviating the lot of others less fortunate. His recommendation to ignore distinctions does not preclude a basis for programs of socioeconomic change. Moreover, his assumptions about alleviating poverty and being the Samaritan to others could be said to provide the impulse for such programs. Indeed, if he is sensitive enough to condemn the way in which people who are in "alliances of circles" can fail in their duty to love when *they* let "'those people' feel their paltriness" (WL, p. 75), it is difficult to imagine that he could excuse those who fail to provide minimally humane living conditions. Moreover, his description of how the high can incur opposition by loving the low (pp. 74, 85) seems to assume cases in which the high are trying to better conditions for the latter. All of this suggests that we need to read the entire discussion of worldly equality and externals in the light of Kierkegaard's own sense of the need for a "corrective" to a radical overemphasis on them, expressed in the social and political currents of his day. Moreover, Kierkegaard's determination to be even-minded about the obligation to perform works of love means that he cannot allow externals (in this particular sense) to be regarded as important. In any case, these themes of inward/outward, inner/external, are not left behind as Kierkegaard moves on; they remain in an important sense at the heart of the deliberation to which I now turn.

chapter five

Love's Labor—Action

"Love Is the Fulfilling of the Law" (III, A)

One of the most common and persistent criticisms of the accounts of the ethical in Kierkegaard's writings is that they fail to do justice to the value of this-worldly, material concerns. His various accounts of religiousness and the ethical—especially in *Fear and Trembling* (FT) and the *Concluding Unscientific Postscript* (CUP)—with their emphases on inwardness, subjectivity, and the "individual," have seemed to some to be an irresponsible deflection of attention from, and devaluation of, concrete socioeconomic concerns.[1] Whereas the emphasis in *Works of Love* on the neighbor might be thought to be a corrective to such accounts, critics have suggested that it, too, fails to provide for both directness and concreteness in the ethical relationship with others.[2] This third deliberation, coupling the chapters "Love Is the Fulfilling of the Law" (III, A) and "Love Is a Matter of Conscience" (III, B), gives us an opportunity to consider this objection in earnest.

The two parts of the third deliberation illustrate the theme of the first deliberation—the tension between hidden and revealed, inward and outward. Here the outward is represented by the claim that "Christian love is sheer action," and the inward (the hidden) by an appeal to "conscience." Kierkegaard's editorial decision to put the two chapters into a single deliberation is another important strategic move—the two chapters cannot be separated since they provide indispensable counterweights to each other, and for this reason I discuss them together under the single rubric of "Love's Labor" in chapters 5 and 6. One of the main purposes of the third deliberation is to highlight the simultaneity of outwardness and inwardness in works of love: fulfilling the law in action is just as necessary as informing works of love by conscience. Chapter III, A, will tell us that "Christian love is sheer action," and B will tell us that Christianity is not a matter of "externals"; the combination of messages reminds us that the fulfillment of the law in action is not mere outwardness and that the centrality of conscience does not reduce love to mere inwardness. In other words, in this whole deliberation Kierkegaard is walking a fine line—presenting a notion of action that is not simply external, as well as presenting a notion of the role of conscience that is not simply inner.

The charge that religion devalues the concrete socioeconomic concerns of this world is not unique to Kierkegaard's religious ethic; from early on, certain religions have been criticized for promoting an orientation of otherworldliness that implies and supports neglect of (or even contempt for) this-worldly needs. In the case of Christianity, neglect or contempt of this world presumably finds its rationale in the value placed on the world to come, the energy devoted to the heavenly world, where our treasures truly lie (Matthew 6:19–21). Marx voiced the modern criticism of "the other-world": "The struggle against religion is, therefore, indirectly a struggle against *that world* whose spiritual *aroma* is religion."[3] Thirty years later another angry critic of religion, Nietzsche, deplored the "concept of the 'beyond,' the 'true world' invented in order to devaluate the only world there is—in order to retain no goal, no reason, no task for our earthly reality!"[4] He insisted that "if one shifts the centre of gravity of life *out* into the 'Beyond' . . . one has deprived life as such of its centre of gravity."[5] But it is not critics of religion alone who mount tirades against the 'beyond' of another world. Philosophical thinkers like Levinas protest against "seeking the *beyond* as a world behind our world."[6] Religious thinkers, too, reject the metaphysical notion of two spheres. Dietrich Bonhoeffer, for example, argues that "God's beyond is not the beyond of our cognitive faculties," but rather "God is beyond in the midst of our life"; for Bonhoeffer true Christianity affirms that "the beyond is not what is infinitely remote but what is nearest at hand."[7]

Although Kierkegaard does not explicitly espouse any metaphysical thesis about ontological dualism or 'other world,' two early twentieth-century interpretations of his thought focused decisive attention on this kind of criticism and significantly contoured all subsequent reception of his ideas. Martin Buber, the twentieth-century, Jewish, religious thinker, whose master work, *I and Thou,* made existentialist philosophy a household word, offered perhaps the most well-known criticism of Kierkegaard's understanding of the relation to God as "acosmic."[8] In 1936, Buber charged that Kierkegaard's preoccupation with the "individual" or the "single one"[9] pitted God against creation, making it an either/or choice. Kierkegaard did not realize that a God reached by "renunciation of objects" would be an object alongside others: "God," Buber insists, "wants us to come to him by means of the Reginas he has created, and not by renunciation of them."[10] In the end, despite Kierkegaard's splendid preaching about love of the neighbor, he presents a model of "self-relating individuals who look at the world but are in the last instance acosmic, who love men but are in the last instance ananthropic";[11] such a view of the exclusivity of the relation to God (the chosen one) seems to render others (creation) inessential.

Another famous critic, Theodor W. Adorno, one of the leaders of the influential Frankfurt school of philosophy in the first half of this century, brought *Works of Love* to public attention in 1939 precisely as an example of a religious ethic that devalues this world. Adorno's version of the charge is that "Kierkegaard is unaware of the demonic consequence that his insistence on inwardness actually leaves the world to the devil. For what can loving one's neighbor mean, if one can neither help him nor interfere with a setting of the world which makes such help impossible?"[12] Adorno's fear is that the premium Kierkegaard puts on "pure inwardness" can be used to justify indifference to distress, poverty, and oppression. These kinds of criticisms continue to be made, requiring an answer to the charge that he spiritualizes and so devalues God's creation.

Both chapters of this deliberation are crucial background to any consideration of such a charge because they help us assess the relevance of "works" of love by raising the following questions: if Kierkegaard's ethic is anticonsequentialist, how is "action" relevant, and if his ethic is not concerned with "externals," are earthly (socioeconomic) considerations devalued? (We will have occasion to reconsider this question in chapter 13, "Love's Mercifulness," when we examine the deliberation that contrasts mercy with material generosity.) Finally, this third deliberation provides the opportunity for us to consider the much-criticized concept of "the individual" in Kierkegaard's thought to see how it stands with sociality and community.

Stepping back for a moment, we can see that the second deliberation, the explicit formal statement of the commandment, is carefully, perhaps protectively, ensconced between two deliberations (I and III) that explicitly focus on the relation between inner and outer, hidden and revealed. That is, the statement of the commandment is set between two explicit reminders that an ethic of love cannot be one-sided; it can no more be mere inwardness than it can be mere outwardness.

Chapter III, A, addresses the "fulfilling of the law" in a *formal* way—that is, it emphasizes how Christian love takes the form of "sheer action," but it does not yet begin the shift to concreteness, which I will suggest is accomplished when Kierkegaard turns to the fourth deliberation, on "Our Duty to Love the People We See." However, by reflecting in detail on the *forms* that the content of love will take, that is, *action* and *differential expressions of love*, it rounds out the formal statement of the love commandment. These forms point to the way in which love must be both active and sensitive to the distinctive needs of the other and prepare a place for Kierkegaard's later attention to the content of love's labor; they set the stage for Kierkegaard's response to the challenge that, in the words of a contemporary poet, "The world is love's task."[13]

I. Love's (Non-)Promise: Action

Rather surprisingly, Chapter III, A, both begins and ends with a consideration of promises. Kierkegaard first illustrates his view of promise by turning our attention to what he considers to be a neglected biblical story about two brothers. Like a modern-day raconteur, he begins by asking if we have heard the one about the "man who had two sons" (WL, p. 92), and he proceeds to tell the story of someone who did not keep a promise. Kierkegaard focuses, not on the story of the brothers Cain and Abel and not on the story of the prodigal son—who wasted his fortune and came home repentant, to the joy of his father and the dismay of his dutiful brother—but on the story of the two brothers who were asked by their father to work in his vineyard (Matthew 21:28–31). Given his ambivalence toward his own elder brother, Peter Christian, it is perhaps not surprising that Kierkegaard is intrigued by stories about two sons or two brothers. In this particular story, the father asks each of his sons to work for him in his vineyard. The one son (whom Kierkegaard nicknames "the yes-brother") promises, with great solemnity, to do it and then fails to fulfill his promise, whereas the other son initially denies his father's request but then changes his mind and does the work. The point Kierkegaard makes is that promises are not enough; promises do not equal action and as long as one is promising, rather than doing, one is failing to act.

Kierkegaard plays on the various levels of meaning in the notion of a promise. Promises are meant to be kept and are aligned to fidelity in that they seem to secure the thing promised; we shall see that fidelity is a crucial part of love for Kierkegaard. A promise to be faithful to another or to do a good deed—love's promise—seems a good thing. Moreover, the idea of love's promise could refer to the positive potential in love, its potential to grow deeper and more profound. But Kierkegaard brings out another, less positive aspect of promise when he writes that "in a world that deceitfully promises so much, in a generation that is all too inclined to promise and to deceive itself honorably by promising," one must go to the "extreme" of claiming that promises are "far from being honorable" (WL, p. 91). Here is an example of how Kierkegaard's sensitivity to the state of his audience warrants what he admits is an "extreme" claim: when the prevailing state is one in which promises are often escapist maneuvers to avoid action, one must make the "extreme" and provocative claim that "to promise is dishonorable"; under those conditions "true faithfulness is specifically characterized by not making promises; by not flattering oneself by making promises; by not demanding double payment, first for the promise and then for fulfilling the promise."

Since Kierkegaard proposes to clarify what love is by illustrating the case of someone who does not keep a promise, one could say that this is an instance of what he alludes to in this chapter as the Christian method of answering by "swing[ing] away from the direction of the question" to "press the task as close as possible to the questioner, what he has to do" (WL, p. 96). Start with the story of a son who earnestly promises something yet fails to do it—to impress on the reader the contrast between a promise and an action. The "yes-brother," who made a great show of "obedient submission to his father's will," illustrates the seductive danger of promising. Remind the reader that "the one who says yes or promises something very easily deceives himself and easily deceives others also, as if he had already done what he promises, or as if by promising he had at least done some of what he promised to do, or as if the promise itself were something meritorious" (p. 93). The parable wants to point out "the danger of being in too great a hurry to say yes even if it is meant at the moment" (p. 93). Promises give us a false sense of security in our good intention; they can lead to "procrastination and regression" and be a substitute for action (p. 95). Kierkegaard repeats four times the phrase "Christian love is sheer action"; he means that it does not have time for a promise (pp. 98–100).

A more subtle dimension of the story is suggested by Kierkegaard—the way in which the son who says 'no' (because the demand placed on him seems unbearable or otherwise objectionable) understands the demand better than the son who says 'yes' too easily, perhaps with good intentions but without taking full account of what is being asked of him. Kierkegaard writes that "the yes of the promise is sleep-inducing, but the no, spoken and therefore audible to oneself, is awakening, and repentence is usually not far away" (WL, p. 93). The 'yes', the promise, can be escapist or unrealistic, obscuring the distance from redemption, whereas the 'no,' the failure to promise, an act of "actual disobedience," can be more honest and therefore nearer to redemption: "A no does not hide anything, but a yes very easily becomes an illusion, a self-deception." The son who says 'no' reveals that he faces the full impact of what is asked of him, so if he ever does change his mind and fulfill the demand he will truly fulfill it, rather than water it down. Indeed, Kierkegaard says that even if he never does it, he will be the more honest of the two sons and therefore closer to God: "[T]he brother who said no would be closer to doing his father's will insofar as he was closer by being *aware* that he was not doing his father's will" (p. 94).[14] Kierkegaard does not want us to misunderstand, however: "We do not praise the son who said no, but we try to learn from the Gospel how dangerous it is to say, 'I will, sir'" (p. 95).

The second story Kierkegaard uses to show that fulfilling the law is action, rather than the promise of action, is that of the Pharisee who tried to embarrass Jesus and justify himself with the casuistical question "Who is my neighbor?" Kierkegaard suggests that the Pharisee "presumably thought that this might develop into a very protracted inquiry . . . and then perhaps end with the admission that it was impossible to define the concept 'neighbor' with absolute accuracy" (WL, p. 96). In other words, intellectual inquiry into the question "Who is my neighbor," as well as any scholarly attempt to "define the concept 'neighbor' with absolute accuracy" or to criticize a priori an ethic that allows no exclusion, can be an attempt to escape the task of love.

The third example is that of Jesus himself. Jesus Christ is the unique exemplar. The "sheer action" that is Christian love was in Jesus: just as Christ's love was not feeling, but rather the work of love, so, too, Christian love is "not that hidden, private, mysterious feeling behind the lattice of the inexplicable," "not a mood in the pampered soul," and not the "inactivity of a feeling that hunts for words while it lets time slip by, or a mood that is its own gratification" (WL, p. 99).

Possibly thinking of the New Testament story of Christ's chiding of Martha for her busyness (Luke 10:40–42), Kierkegaard adds the important qualification that Christian action is "as far from inaction as it is from busyness"; both extremes need to be corrected. Kierkegaard admits that such love may not exist or may never have existed "in any human being"; he admits that there is "an eternal difference between Christ and every Christian" (since Christ fulfilled the Law in his person), but he adds the consoling, encouraging, and demanding words that "by abiding in love every Christian works so that his love might become like this" (WL, pp. 99, 101).

II. Action and Differential Expressions of Love

The emphasis on "sheer action" in this deliberation is not entirely new. In addition to advancing a formal statement of the bindingness and scope of the love commandment, chapters II, A–C, had already hinted at the form love should take. Perhaps the clearest emblem of love in action is found in Kierkegaard's early reference to the 'merciful Samaritan' in II, A: "Christ does not speak about knowing the neighbor but about becoming a neighbor oneself, about showing oneself to be a neighbor just as the Samaritan showed it by his mercy" (WL, p. 22). This suggests the duty of response directed to the distinctive needs of one who makes a claim on us: the Samaritan provides what this particular stranger needs at this particular moment. In one sense this is perhaps the most concrete moment in the whole of the book, the best example of putting love into practice and acknowledging the importance of a response to a person's distinctive needs, and it should be considered a guiding principle for any interpretation of *Works of Love*. The story of the good Samaritan should continue as a hidden presence as we read, and it should be revisited every time the question of Kierkegaard's ethical abstraction and indifference to worldly concerns is raised. The requirement of action is repeated in II, B, where he charges us to "Go and do likewise" (p. 46), and is formally expanded upon in C, where he insists that "the measure of a person's disposition is this: how far is he from what he understands to what he does, how great is the distance between his understanding and his actions" (p. 78).[15]

All of this formally indicates the requirement of love's practical responsiveness. When Kierkegaard provocatively claims that genuine love is not determined by its object, that its object is "without any of the more precise specifications of dissimilarity," we must read this in light of and must do justice to the claim that follows closely upon it, that "love is not proudly independent of its object" (WL, p. 67). That love of neighbor is determined only by love, not by its object, does not mean that love turns "back into itself through indifference to the object"—no, love turns "outward" (p. 67). The presentation of the commandment through the story of the good Samaritan decisively orients us to the importance of duty in terms of action: action is not mere outwardness but rather practical, engaged, responsiveness. We learned in the first deliberation that there are no abstract expressions of love—no word or act is in itself a word or act of love. The example of the Samaritan highlights the way in which love in action must attend to the distinctiveness of the person to whom we show love; that is, differential expressions of love are required that are sensitive to the needs and condition of the other. The second part of this deliberation, "Love Is a Matter of Conscience" (III, B), will develop this dimension of Kierkegaard's ethic further.

III. God as "Middle Term"

One of the most important themes in *Works of Love* is that God is the "middle term" in our relationships with others: *"Christianity teaches that love is a relationship between: a person—God—a person, that is, that God is the middle term"* (p. 107; emphasis Kierkegaard's). It is also the source of one of the most important criticisms of this ethic, the charge that in Kierkegaard's ethic of love others are not able to be loved *directly, for themselves*. What is at stake for Kierkegaard in this constantly repeated phrase?[16] Does it mean that Ludwig Feuerbach's famous moral challenge to Christianity is correct—that there is a contradiction between love and faith?

> Man is to be loved for man's sake. Man is an object of love because he is an end in himself, because he is a rational and loving being. . . . Love should be immediate, undetermined by anything else than its object—nay, only as such is it love. But if I interpose between my fellowman and myself . . . I disturb the unity by the idea of a third external to us; for in that case my fellowman is an object of love to me only on account of his resemblance or relation to this model, not for his own sake.[17]

In other words, does traditional theology make the other just an occasion for our love of God, a 'stepping-stone' to God? Does this "middle term" mean that Kierkegaard's ethic is premised on an inevitable competition between God and the other for our direct response? One of the passages most often cited as proof of the inhumanness of such a love deserves serious attention. Kierkegaard writes: "As soon as a love-relationship does not lead me to God, and as soon as I in the love-relationship do not lead the other to God, then the love, even if it were the highest bliss and delight of affection, even if were the supreme good of the lover's earthly life, is still not true love." And the reason it fails to be true love is something "the world can never get into its head, *that God in this way not only becomes the third party in every relationship of love, but really becomes the sole object of love, so that it is not the husband who is the wife's beloved, but it is God,* and it is the wife who is helped by the husband to love God, and conversely" (pp. 120–21, emphasis mine). What does it mean for God to be the "sole object of love," so that the wife's beloved is not the husband but God? What does it mean to say, as he does, that Christian love "sacrifices everything to make room for God" (p. 119).

A. Under God's Judgment

The idea of God as the "middle term" must be understood in its context, and I suggest that doing so will divest it of much of what critics find objectionable. For Kierkegaard, what is at stake in this idea is that God should remain the judge of what true love is—for example, that the relationship between husband and wife should remain under God's judgment of what is truly good for each. This means that God's view of what is 'good' is the standard for what we should do for the other or want the other to do for us. The concept of middle term is meant to remind us that "it is not the wife who is to teach the husband how he is to love her, or the husband the wife, or the friend, the friend . . . but it is God who is to teach each individual how he is to love if his love is to stand in the slightest relation to the Law the apostle refers to when he says, 'Love is the fulfilling of the Law'" (WL, p. 113). Kierkegaard describes what he calls the "merely human" view of love, which thinks that true "devotion" consists in the sacrifice of fulfilling the beloved's every wish (p. 107). But this is risky business since it is difficult to determine the other's good in the midst of the tangle of our needs, desires, and wishes. What makes Christian devotedness to the other different is that our determinations of what counts as loving in a given case are stabilized by relating first "to God and God's requirement"; God is the "middle term" in the sense that "as soon as one leaves out the God-relationship, the participants' merely human definition of what they want to understand by loving, what they want to require of each other . . . become the highest judgment" (p. 112). It is in this sense that the "love-relationship requires threeness: the lover, the beloved, the love—but the love is God" (p. 121). God is not the "middle term" by being the direct object of our love in such a way as to marginalize the beloved; God is the "middle term" by being the center of the relationship because "the love is God."[18]

B. Theological Assumptions

Kierkegaard's understanding of God as the "middle term" is encapsulated in this admonition: "Let us give heed to God's explanation" of what love entails (WL, p. 118), because "it is God who has placed love in the human being, and it is God who in every case will determine what is love" (p. 126). In other words, the conclusion that God is the "sole object of love" does not come out of the blue; it comes after some important theological assumptions are described. The first is that God is love and so represents what true love is, and the second is that we all belong to God. I suggest that the view of God as the middle term is the only conclusion that could follow from the theological assumptions Kierkegaard holds. As long as one shares these assumptions about the Creator and creation, one need not read the concept of God as the "middle term" as in any way prejudicial to *genuine and direct* love of neighbor or beloved.

First, God is love. A relationship that is not triadic, that ignores the God relationship and God's judgment of what is love in a given case, ignores the Christian standard of genuine love. The threesome involved is not like a human threesome, where two are vying for another one's attention, nor is it a threesome that uses one as a conduit of our love for the other. If God is held to be Love, then love relationships must be experienced under God's judgment of love.

Second, God as the middle term is the conclusion that follows from our status as creatures of God. Kierkegaard reveals his understanding of how this second theological assumption is tied to the first by connecting God as paradigm of love to God as Creator: "The judgment is this: is it actually love, in the divine sense, to show a devotion such as the object of love demanded? Next, is it love, in the divine sense, on the part of the object of love to demand such devotion? *Every person is God's bond servant; therefore he dare not belong to anyone in love unless in the same love he belongs to God and dare not possess anyone in love unless the other and he himself belong to God in this love* (WL, pp. 107-8, emphasis mine). (It is crucial to note that there is only one love at issue, not competing loves.) Kierkegaard then explains the import of being God's bond servant in terms of how a creature "belongs to God in every thought . . . in every feeling . . . in every movement." He recalls that "the abominable era of bond service is past," but now people want to commit "the abomination of abolishing the person's bond service in relation to God, to whom every human being, not by birth but by creation from nothing, belongs as a bond servant . . . he belongs to God in every thought, the most hidden; in every feeling, the most secret; in every movement, the most inward" (p. 115). This is why "a person dare not belong to another as if that other person were everything to him; a person dare not allow another to belong to him as if he were everything to that other" (p. 108).

This third deliberation, Kierkegaard says, does not seek to judge but rather to "penetrate the illusions" we might have—the illusion that we are self-creations, that we "belong" to ourselves or those to whom we choose to belong (WL, p. 124). To love the other properly is to have no illusion about either the other's status as God's creation or our own status. In virtue of "creation from nothing," each "belongs" to God—so it is a deception if one loves another as if the person 'belonged' to you, rather than to God, or lets oneself be loved as if you 'belong' to the other, rather than to God. It is a deception if you love another as you should love God or allow another to love you in that way. Kierkegaard provokes us: Christianity "wants to make your life difficult." But it is not a manufactured or artificial difficulty; it simply is difficult to live without such illusions.

This same message will be an important part of III, B, where Kierkegaard writes that we are each "bound" to God and that it is insincerity when a person "does not know himself" (WL, p. 151). Genuine love must come out of a "sincere faith": "If two people are to love each other in sincere faith, is it not simply necessary that honesty before God must first be present in each individual? Is it insincerity only when a person consciously deceives others or himself? Is it not also insincerity when a person does not know himself?" (p. 151). What he means is that to know yourself is to know that you are bound to God and that the other is bound to God; therefore, there should be no idiosyncratic determinations of what love consists of; God's judgment should prevail.

The theological assumption that "every person is God's bond servant" does not, for Kierkegaard, mean that we are not acting for the beloved's sake. He explains that Christianity does not simply mean to "collect, as it were, God's outstanding claim (since God, after all, is the bond servant's master and owner) but does it also out of love for the lover, because to love God is to love oneself, to love another person as God is to deceive oneself, and to allow another person to love one as God is to deceive this other person" (WL, p. 108). The point of God as the middle term is movingly summarized by Kierkegaard: "There are people who have inhumanly forgotten that everyone should fortify himself by means of the universal divine likeness of all people"—that is, "whether a person is a man or woman, poorly or richly endowed, master or slave, beggar or plutocrat, the relationships among human beings ought and may never be such that the one worships and the other is the one worshipped" (p. 125). To forget this is to forget that God has "already" installed human beings "in the rights of God" (p. 115). Therefore, Christianity "unalterably and unwaveringly, precisely for the sake of the loved ones," teaches us "to hold fast to the true conception of love" (p. 113).

C. The Implication—That Business about "Hate"

If we recognize that we are under God's judgment of what love is and that we both "belong" to God, there will be times when we simply cannot give what the other asks. It is in this context that Kierkegaard's provocative discussion of "hate" must be understood. And we must consider both the dimension of hating the other and the dimension of being hated by the other.

Kierkegaard reminds us that it is Christianity itself (not he, Søren Kierkegaard) that asks us "out of love and in love to *hate the beloved";* it teaches that the Christian "must, if required, be able to hate father and mother and sister and the beloved" (WL, p. 108). But he immediately qualifies this requirement by asking whether Christianity requires this "in the sense, I wonder, that he should actually hate them? *Oh, far be this abomination from Christianity!"* (p. 108; emphasis mine). As he makes clear a few pages later, we cannot be asked to "refrain from loving them": *"How unreasonable—how then could your love become the fulfilling of the Law"* (p. 129; emphasis mine). Not only can we not be asked by God to actually "hate" father or mother or beloved, but also we cannot even be asked by God to "refrain from loving them"; after all, we are to exclude no one from our love. What then does this "hate" refer to? The preceding discussion of God's judgment of the good and our status as belonging to God gives us a way of appreciating what Kierkegaard means here: insofar as another fails to understand God as the "middle term," that person will see as hate our refusal to always give what he or she asks.

Kierkegaard suggests that "love, faithful and true love, divinely understood, must be regarded by the loved ones . . . as hate, because these refuse to understand what it is to love oneself, that it is to love God, and that to be loved is to be helped by another person to love God, whether or not the actual result is that the loving one submits to being hated" (WL, pp. 108–9). When we cannot fulfill the other's wishes, our love will seem to the other as if it is not love (if one does not see God's judgment as the middle term), and we must be willing to be hated for our love. We must not hate the other, but we must be willing to undergo "the suffering of having to *seem* to hate the beloved" (p. 109; emphasis mine). Christianity "requires only this sacrifice (admittedly the hardest possible in many cases and always very hard): willingly to endure being hated as a reward for one's love" (p. 114). He ends sadly: "I wonder if [in worldly wisdom] you find the suffering of having to *seem* to hate the beloved, of having to have hate as the final and sole expression of one's love, or of having to be hated by the beloved as a reward for one's love because there is the infinite difference of Christian truth between what the one and what the other understand by love?" (p. 109; emphasis mine). He challenges the "earthly alliance in worldliness" (p. 121), which forgets or denies the "universal divine likeness" we share as created by God, and he challenges the blunted sensibility that does not realize that self-love with others is no better than self-love alone (p. 119).

Perhaps Kierkegaard exaggerates what he calls the "collision" between two conceptions of love, "the divine conception and the merely human conception" (WL, p. 109). If, however, the life of Christ is taken as the exemplar of love (p. 110), the unique instance in which love was perfectly practiced, then it seems to be a plausible expectation—Christ, after all, was executed. Moreover, Kierkegaard is following Luther's reminder that Christ told us that we will be hated by all for His Name's sake (Matthew 10:22).[19] Still, most of the time Kierkegaard is only insisting on the requirement of being *willing*, when appropriate, to 'seem' as if to hate the other, or being *willing*, when appropriate, to be hated by the other; he does not claim that it will always be necessary to do so. Although at times he seems to overstate the case, what follows on his own terms is not that opposition is a necessary and/or sufficient condition of genuine love but rather that there is an essential connection between the suffering that follows our attempts to love and the Christian demand on the world; that is, when they do occur together there is a relation that is not accidental, but opposition is not therefore inevitable. He speaks of a "danger," that "even the happiest love between two people still has one danger that . . . the earthly love could become too intense, so that the God-relationship is disturbed, the danger that the God-relationship can require even the happiest love as a sacrifice"(p. 129). He continues: "A consequence of the possibility of this danger is that with concern you must always be on watch . . . although your concern, of course, is not that you might grow weary of your beloved or your beloved of you, but with concern that the two of you might forget God, or the beloved might, or you yourself" (p. 130). There is the "possibility" of a danger, then, but that danger does not by itself require indifference to the other; it is wrong to assume that a "danger" is an inevitability. Remembering God is not necessarily at odds with, or mutually exclusive of, remembering the lover or friend.[20]

We should not end this discussion of the concept of God as the middle term without noting that another way to understand this idea is to see the "middle term" as an intermediary, a means to the goal; in that case we might say that seeing God as the middle term places the neighbor as the direct object of our love, for whom God is a medium. If, however, critics insist on seeing the expression "middle term" as one that marginalizes or diminishes the one who is on the other side of it, we should notice that in at least two instances Kierkegaard refers to the "neighbor" as the "middle term."[21] In the most striking instance, he uses the phrase "middle term" to refer to both God and neighbor as if interchangeably: "Love is qualified as a matter of conscience only when either God or the neighbor is the middle term, that is not in erotic love and friendship as such" (WL, p. 142). If "either God or the neighbor is the middle term," love is a matter of conscience; that Kierkegaard could interchange them in this way suggests that we are not meant to read the idea of the middle term as one that prejudicially divides two people.

IV. The Direction and Content of Love

The view that God is the middle term in our relationships with each other often carries in its train two related objections—that the neighbor is not loved directly, and there is no content to the love for neighbor. A very influential critique of *Works of Love* by Knud Ejler Løgstrup, first published in 1956 in Denmark, makes both objections, concluding that *"Works of Love* is a brilliantly thought out system of safeguards against being forced into a close relationship with other people" and that, for Kierkegaard, "the relationship to God is never purer than in the hate of the loved one."[22] It is worth examining Løgstrup's argument because his conclusion expresses a common concern, and we can learn something from it about how better to address other examples of this critique. Moreover, it is important to examine it because it is currently being re-presented to the English-speaking world under the auspices of the highly respected American philosopher and ethicist Alasdair MacIntyre. With such prestigious sponsorship, it is likely to be considered a standard reference for ethicists interested in learning something about *Works of Love.* Løgstrup's critique, and others like it, have already predetermined for many what they will see when they read *Works of Love;* in other cases, more sadly, they have led people to dismiss *Works of Love* without ever reading it. The criticism that Kierkegaard's understanding of the love command-ment precludes a love of neighbor that is both direct and full of concrete content is serious and deserves to be addressed in depth; I want to consider the warrant used to support such a criticism, and to suggest that it misrepresents Kierke-gaard's position in important ways.

A. An Empty, "Gruesome" Ethic?

Løgstrup charges that Kierkegaard's ethic in *Works of Love* does not allow the human other to be appropriately loved or served because the only content of love for the neighbor is helping the neighbor to love God or, equivalently, because the only content is the negative one of "self-denial." His ultimate starting point is Kierkegaard's striking claim about our duty: *"to help another person to love God is to love another person; to be helped by another person to love God is to be loved"* (p. 107; emphasis Kierkegaard's) or, conversely, that "to love another person is to help that person to love God, and to be loved is to be helped." Kierkegaard re-peats this formulation almost verbatim two more times.[23] Critics like Løgstrup have focused on this kind of formulation of our duty as an example of the indi-rection and emptiness of the love command for Kierkegaard; that is, to love an-other is not to do something directly for the other but only to help the other to love God. Since helping another to love God, for Løgstrup, seems to be different from attending to the other's temporal needs, it looks as if love of neighbor does not entail any genuine content that can concretely benefit the other.[24] If the goal is not to help the other materially, it seems that we are left with self-denial for its own sake. Løgstrup is concerned to reject both the emphasis on self-denial and the private relation to God; and although it is probably true to say that he is argu-ing more against the followers of Kierkegaard than against Kierkegaard himself,[25] he sees places in *Works of Love* that could easily lend support to the views he condemns, and he focuses on those places to the exclusion of everything else. Because, despite his idiosyncratic and admittedly selective use of *Works of Love*, his critique continues to be published and some of the same objections continue to be found in more recent critiques, it is worth considering his argument. In what follows I will address the question of a contentless or spiritualized ethic.[26] Although this is intimately connected with the criticism of Kierkegaard's asceticism and self-denial, I will focus on the latter in more detail in chapter 16, "Love's Transparency," where the question of self-denial comes up more directly for Kierkegaard.

Løgstrup begins with Kierkegaard's view that we know or learn what love is only "in the relationship with God," and from that Løgstrup infers that what we learn is that before God we are "nothing" and are "capable of nothing."[27] Love of God is expressed in self-denial; "it is self-denial that makes up the content of the love of one's neighbor."[28] According to Løgstrup, then, the beginning of Kierkegaard's problem is that he equates love with a self-denial that is directed only to helping the other to love God—that is, a self-denial that has no content that could help our neighbor temporally.[29] As if to compound the error, Kierkegaard makes the mistake of allowing the quality of our self-denial, or our relationship with God, to be determined by the other's response to it;[30] that is, the proof of the genuineness of our self-denial is that our love for the neighbor is met with hatred, opposition, and persecution.[31] This latter idea—that genuine love must be hated—seems to be the heart of what Løgstrup considers the "inner flaw," "the inner contradiction," and even "the obvious absurdity" in Kierkegaard's thinking.[32] Løgstrup takes the view that in Kierkegaard's account, ingratitude and opposition are the "guarantee" of genuine love (as opposed to Kierkegaard's more usual sense that the requirement is not *undergoing* actual hatred but having the *willingness* to be hated[33]). But even if Løgstrup grants this weaker view of the willingness to be hated, he has another concern—that such a criterion means that we can never help others in ways that they might ever recognize or appreciate as helpful.

In Løgstrup's reading, "Kierkegaard ascribes such significance to the difference between the misunderstanding or understanding of others, the difference between their applause and admiration or scorn and contempt, that this difference actually plays a part in deciding which actions constitute love of one's neighbor and which do not. In reality everything depends on being misunderstood and hated."[34] Løgstrup goes on to say that if Kierkegaard were right, "the Christian's task and life would be to bring him or herself into that situation [of being hated]." And it is not only we, according to Løgstrup, who would be damaged by such a policy; the other would suffer as well. The ultimate (and he often says, "gruesome") expression of the problem is that genuine love cannot, in this view, actually ever work for the good of the other in ways the other could ever recognize as good because that would mitigate our sacrifice or self-denial. He suggests that "it is therefore implicit in Kierkegaard's thinking that the worst thing that could happen would be for our neighbor to realize that he or she was the object of love. If our neighbor understood that something was being done for his or her welfare, everything, from a Christian point of view—would be spoiled."[35] To keep our self-denial unlimited we must prevent ourselves from ever fulfilling the other's needs and ever acceding to his wishes, and therefore we end up doing actual injustices to our neighbor.[36] Conversely, our love for another is discredited if it is recognizable and appreciated as love. The two main criticisms, then, are that such a model of love precludes us from helping our neighbor and that it condemns us to total self-denial. In raising these questions about the direction and content of love, Løgstrup's critique also raises questions about the limits of self-sacrifice, as well as about giving and reciprocity, but for the moment I will limit my consideration of his critique to the way it bears on the content of the love command.

B. Resources for Establishing Content

Does Kierkegaard's definition of neighbor love—helping the neighbor to love God—and his corresponding emphasis on "self-denial" result in a purely spiritualized love of neighbor, an atemporal ethic? It is important here to recall the suggestion I made at the outset of this study: we should assume that Kierkegaard is committed to what he takes to be Luther's commitments unless he specifically notes otherwise.

1. God's Love as Model

We have seen that, for Kierkegaard, what it means to love others is a function of their actual condition, as well as our own—that is, our common status as created from nothing, belonging to God. But both Kierkegaard and Luther, as I understand them, would object to Løgstrup's emphasis on our nothingness as the decisive thing we learn in our relationship with God because the most crucial thing for both men is that we learn how God has first loved us.[37] Moreover, in the deliberation "Love Does Not Seek Its Own," Kierkegaard explicitly tells us to imitate God, whose message to us is that we are not "nothing" (WL, p. 272). We learn what love is from seeing how God loves us, not from how we love God. The question, then, is what can we learn from seeing how God loves us? Does what we learn imply that there can be no content directly addressed to the neighbor's needs or that the aim of our love is merely to achieve self-denial? Neither implication follows.

In Kierkegaard's Lutheran terms, God's love for us is an absolute gift: it is not conditional on any response from us; it is given with no claim of a reward. We, too, should strive to love our neighbor in this way. But although God's love for us is unconditional and without limit, surely it could never be seen in terms of self-denial, if self-denial means that God's love should be responded to by hatred. We don't learn from the model of God's love for us that our love for others is genuine only if it is met with hatred or persecution, so God's sacrificial giving is not a model of the goal of self-denial that Løgstrup attributes to Kierkegaard. True, in the relationship with God we are, strictly speaking, capable of nothing; we are, as Kierkegaard is fond of saying, like the child who can give only because it has already been given to.[38] Moreover, we are loved by a God whose love is without the motivation of reward or the fulfillment of conditions. But neither of these characteristics of our relationship with God implies that our model of love should be one in which any positive (appreciative or loving) response by the one loved is ruled out. In our relationship with God, in fact, we ought to recognize His love as the gift it is, and it is appropriate that we respond with love, that is, gratefully use the gift (the resources for love) that we are given by God.[39] Thus the model of God's love for us is not one in which a loving response and gratitude for a gift are ruled out, which Kierkegaard recognizes by speaking of imitation as a "fruit of gratitude."[40] The model of God's love for us does not warrant an understanding of a gift in which its character is lost if the receiver recognizes it as a gift or appreciates it.[41] What we learn from the model of God's love for us, then, is that just as its genuineness does not preclude our loving God, so, too, the genuineness of our love for another does not preclude the other's loving us.

Moreover, the idea that we cannot help others because their appreciation would annul the self-denial of our act confuses two different dimensions of an action—the *end* of an act and the *motive* of an act. Kant is one exponent of such a distinction, and we know that Kierkegaard read Kant and could have had such a distinction in mind. For Kant, every morally relevant act performed by a human being must have an end, or "object," which is constituted by its "material content"; he contrasts this "object" with the determining "ground" of an act.[42] Our actions can have consequences that benefit another, even when our motive is neither the benefit as such nor the requirement of any particular response (but rather our duty). That is, we can be motivated by duty to perform an action that has beneficial consequences. Moreover, this distinction between end and motive makes it possible to understand how we can be benefited by God's love for us without God having the motivation of seeking either reward or an acknowledging response of any kind. So, too, the neighbor can be benefited even if our act is not motivated by the desire for a reward or response. There is a distinction between performing an act of love that is conditional on a positive response by the other and performing an act of love that in fact is responded to with love or to which love is an appropriate response.

Finally, one could say that just as we are empowered to love by being loved by God, so, too, our love of others empowers them to love. Our love is meant to help them to be loving to others, not hateful, and such love is genuine only if it is inclusive (i.e., can include us). Therefore, there is no reason that our love cannot have content that both benefits the neighbor and is recognized as such. Løgstrup is simply wrong to argue that what Kierkegaard learns "in the relationship with God" implies a model of love that precludes our doing good for others that can be recognized by them as good.

2. Scripture

The directness and content of Kierkegaard's ethic is revealed in his appeals to Scripture, the most obvious being the appeal to the good Samaritan.[43] In addition there is a striking rejection (found in the fourth deliberation) of any view in which the directness of our response to our neighbor is undermined. Kierkegaard relies on the biblical message when he issues this reminder: " If someone says of this gift that could help his parents that it is *corban*, that is, intended for God, this is not well-pleasing to God. If you want to show that it is intended for God, then give it away, but with the thought of God. If you want to show that your life is intended to serve God, then let it serve people, yet continually with the thought of God" (WL, pp. 160–61). The explanation is unambiguous: "God does not have a share in existence in such a way that he asks for his share for himself . . . God does not ask for anything for himself, although he asks for everything from you" (p. 161). Kierkegaard condemns the view that "the more he rejects those he sees, the more he loves the unseen, since in that case God is changed into an unreal something, a delusion." To see the idea of God as the "middle term" as precluding direct service to the neighbor "misrepresents God, as if God were envious of himself and of being loved, instead of the blessed God's being merciful and therefore continually pointing away from himself, so to speak, and saying, 'If you want to love me, then love the men you see; what you do for them, you do for me' " (p. 160).

We will also see in the fourth deliberation Kierkegaard's condemnation of the ways in which "high-flying" and "vague" notions of love can be escapist and evasive strategies: "Christian love, on the contrary, comes down from heaven to earth. Thus the direction is the opposite" (WL, p. 173). Rather than visionary talk about soaring up to heaven, we need to be reminded that Christian love "comes down," that "Christianly to descend from heaven is boundlessly to love the person you see just as you see him" (p. 174). Again, Kierkegaard's affirmation of Scripture is evident, as he begins the fourth deliberation with the reference to I John 4:20: How can a man say he loves God whom he does not see, if he does not love his neighbor, whom he sees (p. 155). There is no doubt about the coincidence between love of God and love of neighbor: "'He who sees his brother in need, yet shuts his heart'—yes, at the same time he also shuts out God. Love to God and love to neighbor are like two doors that open simultaneously, so that it is impossible to open one without opening the other, and impossible to shut one without also shutting the other."[44] The point of the story of the final judgment, in which people are told that they fed and clothed God when they fed and clothed "the least" of their neighbors (Matthew 25:34–45), is made explicitly by Kierkegaard, who repeats the words "what you do for them, you do for me" (p. 160).[45]

Kierkegaard's understanding of these texts is informed by the most important of his Lutheran commitments—Luther's insistence that works do not earn "merit." This serves to preclude a problem of competition between God and the neighbor. That is, if works did merit anything from God, we would have a problem of deciding which works were worth more—those directed to God or those to our neighbor. But this difficulty is obviated in an ethic in which no special works obtain God's favor. No work merits God's gracious forgiveness, and all the works of the commandments are equal if done through faith.[46] This ironically provides a freedom that eliminates any temptation to see a choice of doing something for God and doing something for the neighbor. Doing something for God becomes the grateful response of helping those in need.

3. Transitivity

It is interesting that Kierkegaard's appeal to the biblical equation between God and the neighbor ('As long as you did it to one of these, you did it to me') provides another way of finding content in this ethic. We ask this question: What is the content of the task of helping someone to love God? If, as we have just seen, loving God means loving the neighbor, pointing away from God and 'doing for' the neighbor, then by the simple law of transitivity,[47] when we help others to love God we are helping them to help their neighbor; that is, we are pointing them away from God to their neighbor. The world is love's task; the world is not left behind in such an ethic. Kierkegaard says in a later deliberation that "love in all its expressions turns outward toward people, where indeed it has its object and its tasks" (WL, p. 189).

Another version of transitivity appears when we remember that Kierkegaard often prefaces or accompanies his definition of the love commandment with the reminder *"To love God is to love oneself truly"* (WL, p. 107). If to love God is to love oneself truly, to help another to love God is to help another to love himself or herself truly. Kierkegaard gives us some idea of what this might mean: "it is every human being's destiny to become free, independent, oneself" (p. 278), and he reinforces this inference: "The one who loves has understood that it truly is the greatest, the only beneficence one human being can do for another, to help him to stand by himself, to become himself, to become his own master" (pp. 277–78).[48] There is no question of a choice between helping the neighbor to love God and helping the neighbor to love herself or himself truly. Kierkegaard does not, as Løgstrup suggests, make any stark or illegitimate dichotomy between earthly, material help and helping the neighbor to love God; he does not see them as mutually exclusive.[49]

All of the preceding responses suggest why the idea that God is the "middle term" in all relationships does not imply a 'stepping-stone' mentality, an instrumentalizing or marginalization of the other. Outside of *Works of Love* we also find useful formulations of a response to such a criticism. Against the moral critique that God as the "middle term" comes between the other and myself by requiring me to forgo any direct response to the other's needs, in *Either/Or* Judge William likewise insists that God is not so petty or greedy as to demand that we turn away from others in order to turn to God: "It is not in this sense that one is to love God more than father and mother; God is not that selfish. Neither is he a poet who wishes to torment people with the most horrible conflicts, and if there actually were a conflict between love of God and love of human beings, the love of whom he himself has implanted in our hearts, it would be hard to imagine anything more horrible."[50] Even Judge William criticizes the person who "devotes himself one-sidedly to a mystical life" and thus becomes "so alienated from all people that every relationship, even the tenderest and most intimate, becomes a matter of indifference to him."

4. Concrete Imitation of Christ

Finally, another resource for responding to criticism of Kierkegaard's ethic is found in his Lutheran commitment to the "imitation of Christ." Kierkegaard cites with approval Luther's formulation: "Christ is the gift—to which faith corresponds. Then he is the prototype—to which imitation corresponds."[51] "The only kind of adoration God requires is imitation,"[52] and the task is to "put on Christ," to *"re-present"* Christ.[53]

What did Christ do? In what are we to imitate Christ? Is the fulfillment of the law merely Christ's atoning sacrifice? Since we cannot be called to do what Christ did in the sense of imitating his soteriological achievement (we cannot redeem humanity), what we are called on to do is to follow the example he set in his human nature. Kierkegaard sees Christ as the prototype in meeting earthly needs. In an 1849 journal, Kierkegaard chided pastors who spiritualized the example Christ set for us:

> It certainly must never be forgotten that Christ helped also in temporal and earthly needs. It is also possible falsely to make Christ so spiritual that he becomes sheer cruelty. . . . Christ also relieved earthly suffering, healed the sick, the lepers, the deranged; he fed people, changed water into wine, calmed the sea, etc.—but, says the pastor, we dare not expect such assistance nowadays and so it is dropped, and Christ becomes almost more cruel toward us than toward his contemporaries. The answer to this has to be 'No.'[54]

For Kierkegaard, Christ's pattern for us is a down-to-earth one, full of concrete content to be imitated.

"The task," Kierkegaard says, "is not to seek consolation—but to be consolation"; "at the very moment you yourself are suffering most of all, simply think about consoling others, for this is what he [Christ] did" when he sought out the company of "the cripples, the despised, the sinners, and the publicans."[55] Kierkegaard tells us repeatedly that imitation of Christ has more to do with bringing about justice than with subjecting ourselves to self-sacrifice for its own sake. He repeatedly refers to the importance of stressing imitation "in order, if possible, to maintain a little justice in Christendom, and to bring a little meaning if possible into Christianity," to "maintain justice and to set the relationship in order."[56] He Christianizes the Old Testament message of the prophet Micah: imitation of Christ is necessary "to maintain justice ethically."[57] Thus, Kierkegaard does not hold to the stark dichotomy between "helping our neighbor temporally and helping him or her to love God," which Løgstrup attributes to him.[58]

Imitation of Christ is the Christian requirement, but is such imitation possible? Kierkegaard affirms that Christ is "the prototype oriented to the universally human, of which everyone is capable."[59] It is only because Christ "was a human being like everybody else [that] he is truly the prototype"; "he makes the divine commensurable with being a completely ordinary human being," but he also "constitutes the eternal strenuousness in what it means to be a human being."[60] In other words, imitation is strenuous but possible "after grace and by grace."[61]

Thus, consideration of the content of the directive to imitate Christ reveals the concrete content of the commandment to love the neighbor. Coupled with the other resources indicated in this chapter, we can conclude that charges that the love commandment does not have concrete content in Kierkegaard's ethic are not plausible.[62] We could say that Kierkegaard upholds a version of the proverb to which Levinas alludes: "There is a Jewish proverb which says that 'the other's material needs are my spiritual needs'."[63] Moreover, we shall continue to discover resources in the remaining deliberations that will make problematical the recurring charge that this ethic does not do justice to this-worldly responsibility.

chapter six

Love's Labor—Conscience

"Love Is a Matter of Conscience" (III, B)

We saw at the end of the second deliberation that a giving that sees only the poor and unimportant is not a loving giving; it cannot count as a celebration, a "banquet" (WL, p. 83). This illustrates the message of the first deliberation—the giving is not of itself a work of love but must be done in the spirit of love. In addition to seeing this as a contrast between outwardness (action) and inwardness, we can, following Kierkegaard's explicit guidance in this deliberation, see it as a contrast between two kinds of hiddenness: "the inwardness directed outwardly" and "the hidden being of inwardness," which is inwardly directed to the God-relationship (p. 139). The "inwardness directed outwardly" is the concern of III, A, so we turn now to Kierkegaard's discussion in B of "the hidden being of inwardness."

In the previous chapter I attempt to show that Kierkegaard's affirmation of Christianity as "sheer action" concerned with material needs undermines the quietistic implications of his recommendations of indifference to "distinctions" in II, B and C. Indirectly, this responds to a long-standing tradition of criticism of Kierkegaard's thought in general as too focused on inwardness and the individual's relation to God to do justice to concrete, material concerns, a tradition that often takes the emphasis on inwardness found in Kierkegaard's pseudonymous writings, particularly the *Concluding Unscientific Postscript*, and reads it into the ethic in *Works of Love*. In this chapter I want to examine Kierkegaard's disavowal of Christianity's concern with "externals," found in the second part of the third deliberation, to assess its relevance to this traditional criticism. In other words, I see both III, A and B, as providing resources for a response to such criticism—A in terms of "inwardness directed outwardly" and B in terms of "the hidden being of inwardness," which is conscience.

The claims Kierkegaard makes here are bold: "Christianity does not want to make changes in externals . . . it wants only to make infinity's change in the inner being"; it "does not wish to bring about any external change at all in the external sphere" but rather "wants to seize it, purify it, sanctify it, and in this way make everything new while everything is still old" (WL, pp. 139, 145). Appealing to scriptural authority, he affirms that "What Christ said about his kingdom, that it is not of this world, holds true of everything Christian" (p. 138), and the reference to another world is made explicitly: Christianity "wants to be a stranger in life because it belongs to another world, a stranger in the world because it belongs to the inner being." But it is important that we do not identity what Kierkegaard terms "externals" with all outwardness. To say that love is not concerned with changing externals is to say that love is a matter of conscience, and conscience is a category of inwardness. But we have just seen him say in A that Christianity is "sheer action," so we cannot now read its conscientious inwardness as simply negating that.

Some critics have interpreted this refusal to be concerned about externals as emasculating the demand of love and thus fueling the charge of devaluing the world. In particular, such criticism is addressed to two separate issues: the attention to "inner being" leads, first, to indifference to the distinctiveness of the special relations we have (with our child, wife, beloved, or friend), which seem externally conditioned,[1] and second, to indifference to material conditions in this world (conditions of poverty, oppression, or other kinds of suffering). It is important to determine whether Kierkegaard's dismissal of "externals" supports such criticisms because it is obvious that an ethic that undermines either the obligations of special relations or concern for this-worldly welfare cannot be viable. We need to begin with an inquiry into Kierkegaard's understanding of conscience and "hidden inwardness."

I. Conscience as Hidden Inwardness

On the very first page of this chapter, Kierkegaard offers a crucial guide to our interpretation of the text: he says that if one were to "describe in a single sentence" the import of Christianity's commitment to "infinity's change" (as opposed to external change), it would be that Christianity "has made of every human relationship between person and person a relationship of conscience" (WL, p. 135). He adds that "just as the blood pulses in every nerve, so does Christianity want to permeate everything with the relationship of conscience." Such a change "is not in the external, not in the apparent, and yet the change is infinite." What kind of change is radical without being "external" or "apparent"? Moreover, if "love in all its expressions turns outward toward people" (p. 189), what kind of inwardness is supposed to remain hidden? Part of

Kierkegaard's answer to these legitimate questions is found in his discussion of the world's obsession with "visible evidence"; here we can see more easily what is at stake in the emphasis on the inwardness that does not show itself outwardly.

This discussion, which takes place at the middle of the chapter, places directly before us both the situation Kierkegaard finds objectionable and the alternative he proposes. He begins with the claim that there is "something wonderful" about the way Christianity is "so indifferent to acknowledgment in the external world," but he admits that for many it may be "odd" and even "incomprehensible" (WL, p. 144). This probably accounts, he reasons, for the times in history when people have tried to "provide Christianity with a worldly expression in the secular world"—for example, when they "wanted to abolish marriage and indeed lived hidden away in the cloister." Here he obviously echoes Luther's impatience and irritation with what seem to be medieval monasticism's artificial and contradictory attempts to show inwardness. He writes that "compared with true Christian inwardness, the cloister's hiding place in the solitude of the forest or far away on an inaccessible mountaintop and the silent inhabitant's hiding place in the cloister are childishness, just as when a child hides himself—so that someone will come and find him" (p. 144). Ironically, "the cloister's hidden occupant notified the world that he had hidden himself," which for Kierkegaard amounts to not hiding oneself "in earnest," but rather "playing hide-and-seek." It is this kind of outward showing of hiddenness, this hide-and-seek, that Kierkegaard ridicules and opposes when he speaks of the radicalness of change in the internal, inner being and the potential superficiality of change in externals. It is this he is referring to when, in less metaphorical language, he chides the "worldly point of view," which insists on "visible evidence" for everything, this "worldly misunderstanding [which] needs to have it outwardly expressed that love in the Christian sense is the spirit's love"—but this, he insists with barely disguised frustration, "cannot be outwardly expressed, since it is indeed inwardness" (p. 146). Here he echoes the sentiment expressed by Johannes de Silentio in *Fear and Trembling* that the true knight of faith is not conspicuous in the world—he does not stand out because he, like the others, goes for a walk in the woods, and he, like the others, looks forward to a hearty supper. The real difference is not one that should be observable from the outside.[2] The real difference is a matter of the hidden inwardness of conscience.

Another formulation of conscience is found in the Conclusion. There Kierkegaard suggests that "God is the educator" and that our relation to God is "an upbringing"; he refers to "eyes," that "the most competent educator prefers to use his eyes. He takes the individual child's eyes away from him—that is, in everything he makes the child look at him" (WL, p. 377). The way in which a child is taught to look at and look to the adult in charge of his or her upbringing provides the image for the answer to his question "What is conscience?" Conscience is the space in which we look at God, who is looking at us: "In conscience it is God who looks at a person; so now in everything the person must look at him." When we look to God, we come to know with God.[3]

II. Conscience: "The Individual" and Responsibility

The strong emphasis on conscience gives us an opportunity to consider what is probably one of the best-known of Kierkegaard's themes—"the individual" or "the single individual."[4] This theme, often criticized for its implicit inwardness, is found more prominently in Kierkegaard's other writings (and I shall turn to them for further clarification), but it is also found in *Works of Love* and is related here to Kierkegaard's concern with conscience.

The first appearances in *Works of Love* of the phrase "the individual" are in the Preface and in the first deliberation; they are reminders of the active role of the reader as listener, his or her status in relation to the text's message. This use of "the individual" is ultimately related to the question of the accountability of a person for his or her response to the text, but here in the third deliberation there is an even more pronounced emphasis on ethical responsibility in general. Here Kierkegaard makes a direct connection between "the individual" and the more general accountability symbolized by "conscience": *"To question the single individual is the more common expression for the relationship of conscience* (p. 138; emphasis mine). There is no doubt that here the use of the phrase "the single individual" is meant to call to mind—by its association with conscience—issues of responsibility and accountability.[5] The "single individual" is the summoned individual, the one who is responsible—not the 'private' individual. If one had only come across the idea of the "single individual" in the context of this deliberation, it would be a real stretch to turn it (as some do) into a call to asociality or indifference to community. Moreover, the fact that the responsibility is for others becomes accented later in *Works of Love,* as Kierkegaard writes unambiguously that "the single individual is committed in the debt of love to other people" (p. 190). Thus, there is no support here for saddling Kierkegaard's ethic with an interiority that distances people from one another or an interiority that encourages an egocentric concern with one's responsibility to oneself. Instead, there is a positive warrant for understanding our debt of love as a debt "to other people," and the final deliberation of the first series will explore and clarify this debt.

In this deliberation the "single individual" is offered in implied contrast to "the others" (WL, pp. 116, 117). In other writings by Kierkegaard, where there is a connection between "the single individual" and conscience, it is similarly implemented through a negative judgment of "the crowd." Kierkegaard's two notes, collectively entitled "The Single Individual," which were the subject of Martin Buber's influential critique,[6] connect the "crowd" with the majority, the unreflective masses.[7] The "crowd [*Maengde*]" is a quasi-technical term for Kierkegaard. It does not mean other people as such; it means the phenomenon in which one abdicates personal responsibility and listens to the voice of the majority instead of the voice of conscience.[8] In the discourse on "Purity of Heart," the crowd is similarly identified as the locus of "restlessness," "noise," "the crush," and "the jungle of evasions"—the place where one tries to hide oneself from God's voice.[9] Kierkegaard insists that "the voice of conscience must be heard"; "each human being, as a single individual, must account for himself to

God" and therefore resist being dominated by the desire to be in conformity with the popular or majority opinion.

Moreover, "Purity of Heart" gives useful examples of what is at stake for Kierkegaard. When we listen to conscience, we are asking ourselves this question: "Are you now living in such a way that you are aware as a single individual, that in every relationship in which you relate yourself *outwardly* you are aware that you are also relating yourself to yourself as a single individual?" [10] We are called to be "aware" of our "eternal responsibility before God" in a quite practical way; that is, we should ask ourselves if we are "living in such a way that this awareness can acquire the time and stillness and liberty of action to penetrate [our] life relationships." [11] This translates into some very down-to-earth calls to responsibility—for example, "Eternity does not ask whether you brought up your children the way you saw others doing it but asks you as an individual how *you* brought up your children"; [12] in eternity you will not be asked whether you were in agreement with the majority opinion, rather you will be asked "whether you perhaps have corrupted the better part in you" or "whether you perhaps have harmed a good cause because you also judged along with those who did not understand how to judge but who had the crowd's considerable power in a temporal sense." [13] For still another example of how the emphasis on conscience as inwardness is implicitly practical, ask yourself this: *"In the course of your occupation, what is your frame of mind, how do you perform your work?";* "Have you made up your mind about how you want to perform your work, or are you continually of two minds because you want to be in agreement with the crowd [which judges solely by results]?" [14]

"Purity of Heart" assumes that the inwardness that directs itself inwardly does not preclude the inwardness that directs itself outwardly. Kierkegaard asks us to ask ourselves whether "if you live in a heavily populated city and then you turn your attention outward, sympathetically give heed to people and events, do you bear in mind, every time you relate yourself in this way to an outside world, that in this relation you are relating yourself to yourself as a single individual with eternal responsibility? Or do you filter yourself into the crowd, where the one blames the other." [15] Kierkegaard could not be more emphatic about the way in which this inwardness must turn outward: " You are not asked to withdraw from life, from an honorable occupation, from a happy domestic life—on the contrary, that awareness will support and transfigure and illuminate your conduct in the relationships of life. . . . You will find more and more time for your duties and your tasks." [16] "Purity of Heart" is, in the end, a gold mine of resources for clarifying how the phrase "the single individual" is meant to affirm the responsibility of conscience, as well as the fact that the responsibility at issue involves how we treat others.

Like "Purity of Heart," this deliberation thus far tells us two things: first, an appreciation of conscience is an appreciation of "the single individual's" responsibility to others, and second, "the single individual's" responsibility supports worldly tasks and community interrelation rather than undermines them. In other words, everything Kierkegaard says about the importance of action (in III, A) must be carried along as we read his strictures on our responsibility to relate ourselves to ourselves—that is, to conscience—in everything we do.

Kierkegaard's understanding of "the most dreadful responsibility" assigned to each individual[17] anticipates Emmanuel Levinas's understanding of the inalienable responsibility I bear for my neighbor. Levinas describes something parallel to Kierkegaard's notion of the 'single individual': "It is I who support the Other and am responsible for him. . . . My responsibility is untransferable, no one could replace me."[18] Whereas this might sound to some like an arrogant expression of self-centered subjectivity, Levinas is actually trying to put the emphasis on responsibility directly on the agent precisely so that the person in need will be helped. The idea that "no one could replace me" is one way of stressing that I cannot look to others as an excuse for not doing what I should do; I cannot excuse myself by saying that 'that one over there' will help, or 'they' will help. I have to act as if I am the only one who can help because otherwise I may wait irresponsibly for someone else to take care of the person in need. It may well be that neither Kierkegaard nor Levinas adequately appreciates the possibility of social responsibility because they have both lost trust in such a phenomenon, and it may well be that neither of them adequately recognizes that some kinds of human suffering require the concerted effort of public policy change rather than individual response. But it should be clear that both are putting the burden on "the individual" precisely to be sure that we don't succumb to the temptation of looking to others rather than ourselves when suffering needs to be alleviated. In one sense, it puts the spotlight on us. But Levinas specifically intends it to exclude "subjective egotism" and an "egocentric orientation."[19] It is a way of trying to guarantee that whatever happens, the other does not fall between the cracks while each of us looks to someone else to do the job. Thus, Levinas's emphasis on my untransferable, unsubstitutable responsibility for the other reinforces the suggestions Kierkegaard makes about the inalienable responsibility of "the single individual," the responsibility that cannot be abdicated.

When Kierkegaard ties the category of "the single individual" to the category of "conscience," he reveals a crucial way in which the former phrase has social implications. In chapter 7 we will see another important use of this category in terms of the concreteness and distinctiveness of the individual.

III. Hidden Inwardness and Special Relations

One of the most persistent criticisms of the ethic in *Works of Love* concerns special relations (spouse, child, and family).[20] The questions that are asked repeatedly about the status of preferential love obviously hold most strongly in the case of special relations: Does this ethic exclude preferential loves?[21] Does it forbid a discriminate response to special traits and actions?[22] Is it possible or desirable to love without making distinctions?[23] Don't I have special obligations to my family that override any obligation to others? Isn't it better to love my child because he is my child than because I have a duty to love him? Chapter 3 has already provided part of Kierkegaard's response to such questions, with the claim that neighbor love is to be preserved in erotic love and friendship; a number of later deliberations will answer these questions more directly, either by telling us that we are bound to love the people we see—precisely as they are—or by providing concrete illustrations of sensitive responses to the distinctive needs of others. This deliberation addresses the question of special relations in a somewhat indirect way, which it is, nevertheless, important to explore.

Kierkegaard explicitly connects the childish misunderstanding of Christian inwardness and outwardness (the game of hide-and-seek he made fun of earlier) with the way in which some people assume that Christianity is out to change externals in human relationships. He states that "through a similar piece of childishness, people thought it was Christian to . . . express in a worldly way Christianity's indifference to friendship, to the family relationships, to love of the fatherland" (WL, p. 144). But this, he says vehemently, is "indeed false, because Christianity is not indifferent in a worldly way to anything." As in the earlier example of hide-and-seek, "to express one's indifference in such a way that one is eager for the relevant persons to find out about it is certainly not being indifferent" (p. 145).[24] That is, Christianity does not want to be distinguished by bringing about "external change in the external sphere," and this holds true of personal relationships as well. He states time and again that "Christianity has not come into the world to teach this or that change in how you are to love your wife and your friend *in particular*, but to teach how you are to love all human beings *universally-humanly*. It is in turn this change that Christianly changes erotic love and friendship" (142-43). He explicitly reminds us that "Christianity has not changed anything in what people have previously learned about loving the beloved, the friend, etc., has not added a little or subtracted something, but it has changed everything, has changed love as a whole. Only insofar as a change of inwardness in erotic love and friendship results from this fundamental change, only to that extent has it changed these" (p. 147). This is why he said earlier that we must preserve neighbor love (*Kjerlighed*) in erotic love and friendship (p. 62), and this is why the only radical change involved is the change of making love, even when it includes erotic love and friendship, a "matter of conscience." As I noted earlier, "Purity of Heart" brings home the same message: "The discourse does not ask you whether you really do love your wife; it hopes so. It does not ask if she really is the delight of your eyes and the desire of your heart; it wishes that for you."[25]

The temptation to ask for "visible evidence" (WL, p. 145) leads us to expect to see outward expressions that would distinguish Christian love from erotic love and friendship—that is, peculiar behavior that makes the relation of erotic love or friendship stand out because it differs from the ordinary tenor of such relationships. This peculiarity could then be attributable only to Christian love. But Kierkegaard says we cannot *see* Christian love as such; it is like the notion of "humanity," which we cannot see as such even though it is the essential determinant of each human being we do see (p. 147). On the contrary, such peculiar distinguishing features would amount to a denial of the inwardness. To show the distinctiveness of Christian love by requiring of erotic love or friendship marks that are at odds with them would be comparable to the ways in which, he says, those going into the medieval cloisters announced that they were "hidden" (pp. 144, 146). Christian love of one's wife does not require one to forgo natural drives and inclinations[26] or to hold back the tender expressions of intimacy that are appropriate to lovers. Nor does it require one to treat a friend in ways at odds with friendship to ensure that such friendship entails Christian love as well; friendship implies the desire to spend time together, enjoying common interests, and to withhold or exclude such mutual enjoyment would be attempts to mark outwardly the special inwardness that would in fact deny the inwardness.

What, then, should we make of the admittedly "strange, chilling inversion" by which "in loving the beloved we are first to love the neighbor" (WL, p. 141)?[27] Kierkegaard does indeed take us aback at least momentarily when he declaims: "Your wife must first and foremost be to you the neighbor" and "the man who does not see to it that his wife is to him the neighbor, and only then his wife, never comes to love the neighbor, no matter how many people he loves—that is, he has made his wife an exception" (p. 141). Does this empty out all distinctive responses from our varied relationships? On the contrary, for Kierkegaard, what it means to say that someone is "first and foremost the neighbor" is that with respect to each person we must consult with our conscience (p. 140). Because every person "belongs first and foremost to God before he belongs to any relationship," every person, regardless of the particularities of the relationship, must "consult with God"; this consultation is a consultation with conscience since "to relate to God is precisely to have conscience" (p. 143). Kierkegaard makes no bones about the reason for this: "The reason for its being a question of conscience is that a human being in his erotic love belongs first and foremost to God" (p. 143). This elaborates his discussion (see chapter 5, section III) of how we "belong" to God. Here he phrases it in the idiom of being "bound" to God; because we are "infinitely bound" to God, "if a pure heart is to be given away in erotic love the first consideration must be for your soul as well as for your beloved's! This consideration is the first and the last" (p. 149). The "eternal love-history" to which erotic love and friendship contribute, is the history of an "infinitely bound heart"—a heart that has a "prior history" precisely because it was called "into existence out of nothing" (p. 150).[28]

This shared equality before God (each created out of nothing or, alternatively, out of God's love) does not need to change any of the external expressions of the love in the sense that it denies intimacy to the lovers or friends. Kierkegaard says, first your wife is your neighbor, and then she is your wife, but as husband and wife you inhabit a particular kind of relationship—"that she is your wife is then a more precise specification of your particular relationship to each other" (WL, p. 141). This more "precise specification" will make a difference—"the wife and friend are not loved in the same way, nor the friend and the neighbor." That is, the relationship will be carried out in ways that differ from another specific relationship to someone to whom one does not have particular conjugal or familial ties. The distinctive external expressions of your love are not to be excluded: "Christianity has nothing against the husband's loving his wife in particular, but he must never love her in particular *in such a way that she is an exception to being the neighbor that every human being is*" (pp. 141-42; emphasis mine). I take this to be Kierkegaard's way of reminding us that a man can no more take advantage of his wife, because she is his wife, than of another neighbor. We cannot make a sex object out of our wife or husband; we cannot emotionally or physically abuse our spouse because, however intimate and specific the relationship is, each remains a neighbor, an equal before God. The apparent abstractness of the claim "Each one of us is a human being and then in turn the distinctive individual that he is in particular, but to be a human being is the fundamental category" (p. 141) is meant to guarantee the fundamental respect appropriate to our equality before God. The 'first, then' language is not meant to be taken as a temporal qualifier. There is no instant at which we are only the abstract determinant 'human being'; we are always in some kind of special relation, even if it is only the relation of being someone's child.

Erotic love and friendship are not excluded from the Christian change in all love—to make love a matter of conscience. The standard of conscience is the standard of reference to the judgment of the God who created us "out of nothing," and the "glad message" of love's "delight" (since "erotic love and earthly love are the joy of life") must always be held in tension with the rigorous message of love's conscientiousness. This ethic, as a Christian ethic, is not meant to change external expressions of our love—"a wife has her most intimate relationship, humanly speaking, with her husband"—and this ethic is not meant to challenge that intimacy (WL, pp. 151–52). Christianity makes a change *in* erotic love and friendship, but not by preventing them from being erotic love and friendship. Christianity sanctifies marriage, but not by requiring the couple to behave as if they were not married. For Kierkegaard, Christian love is the "foundation" of every particular love (p. 141); it does not ask for the sacrifice of all particular loves.

The character of Christianity's lack of concern for "externals" is clear from Kierkegaard's discussions. When he writes that the "merely human point of view conceives of love *either* solely in terms of immediacy, as drives and inclination (erotic love), as inclination (friendship), as feeling and inclination, with one or another differentiating alloy of duty, natural relations, prescriptive rights, etc., *or* as something to be aspired to and attained because the understanding perceives that to be loved and favored, just like having persons one loves and favors, is an earthly good," he concludes that "Christianity is not really concerned with all this" (WL, p. 144). But he immediately explains in the next sentence that this means that "Christianity allows *all this to remain in force* and have its significance externally, but at the same time . . . it wants to have infinity's change take place internally" (emphasis mine). Indeed, there is no question that "the Christian may very well marry, may very well love his wife, especially in the way he ought to love her, may very well have a friend and love his native land"—"but yet in all this there must be a basic understanding between himself and God in the essentially Christian" (p. 145). Kierkegaard recognizes, however, the "earthly good" of being loved and favored, as well as of having people to love and favor, and all of this is just what one would expect given his early appreciation of how one's response is *claimed* by another: "[Y]our friend, your beloved, your child, or whoever is an object of your love has a claim upon an expression of [your love]," and not to express it would be "withholding from someone what you owe him" (p. 12). In this way, Kierkegaard hints at the importance of differences that he thinks should not be ignored; in doing so, he allows room for, although he does not yet elaborate on, the concreteness of loving attention.

Kierkegaard is objecting to the relationship that does not have conscience at its heart. When Christianity teaches us to love every human being "conscientiously," including our wife and friend, it is trying to correct our purely human view of what is owed to beloved and friend. Identifying with the weakness of human lovers, Kierkegaard writes that "when we speak about conscientiously loving wife and friend, we usually mean loving in a divisive way or, what amounts to the same thing, loving them so preferentially in the sense of an alliance that one has nothing at all to do with other human beings" (WL, p. 142). But this is "simply a lack of conscientiousness." To know yourself, as a sincere love requires (p. 151), is to know that you are bound to God and that the other is bound to God; therefore, there can be no idiosyncratic determinations of what love consists in. God's judgment of how to love another conscientiously should prevail.

In the end, then, one implication of Christianity's indifference to "externals" is that it is not meant to distinguish itself in a worldly way by challenging the natural expressions of erotic love and friendship, drives and inclinations; Christianity is not out to make "outward" changes in the expressions of our loves. Thus, the discussion of "externals" and "hidden inwardness" has implications for the way in which this ethic sustains the concrete intimacy of love relationships and, therefore, for the way in which "special relations" are not excluded. The sanctification it seeks is to "make everything new while everything is still old" (WL, p. 145). The result is that Christianity "has not changed anything" in the content of love and friendship, whereas it "has changed everything, has changed love as a whole" (p. 147). I take these affirmations of unchanged content (i.e., "everything is still old") to suggest that the appropriate understanding of neighbor love does not rule out attention to concrete differences; the concreteness of such attention is appropriate to the different people we love.

IV. Only One Kind of Love

It might be thought that Kierkegaard simply describes the differential expressions of love that obtain in the world but that in his own terms are not legitimate. To better appreciate how family ties or role responsibilities could rightly make a difference in the response we are supposed to make to others in need, we should focus for a moment on one of Kierkegaard's crucial principles (which he puts before us twice)—that there is "only one kind of love" (WL, pp. 143, 146).

Kierkegaard was at pains throughout the second deliberation (A–C) to remedy a variety of "misunderstandings" of the status of genuine love and thereby reinforce the hint implied in the example of the good Samaritan that a loving response is distinctively responsive to particular needs. He does this by formally (grammatically) locating the concept of love and then by indicating that it maintains a concrete engagement. He insists that it is a "misunderstanding" to think that "in Christianity the beloved and the friend are loved faithfully and tenderly in quite a different way than in paganism" (WL, p. 53)[29]—which suggests that normal preferential relations of attachment persist. It allows for special relations to make a difference. Neighbor love, *Kjerlighed,* is not a "higher" love that should replace or be added to erotic love and friendship (pp. 45, 58). Kierkegaard says quite straightforwardly that the goal is to preserve love for the neighbor in erotic love and friendship (p. 62). Nonpreferential love is to "permeate" all expressions of love—to transform them—yet not in the sense of adding something to them, as if you could love the beloved or friend adequately by yourself (p. 112).

Love for the neighbor is not a different "type" or "kind" of love (WL, p. 66) because, as the second part of the third deliberation makes clear, there is "only one kind of love, the spirit's love" (pp. 143, 146).[30] Neighbor love can and should "lie at the base of and be present in every other expression of love . . . it is in all of them—that is, it can be, but Christian love itself you cannot point to" (p. 146). "Infinity" makes its change in erotic love (*Elskov*); Christianity makes *Elskov* transcend its limits, without depriving it of its special distinctiveness. We have one and the same love, not competing loves: "Every person is God's bond servant; therefore he dare not belong to anyone in love unless *in the same love* he belongs to God and dare not possess anyone in love unless the other and he himself belong to God *in this love*" (108; emphasis mine).

V. "Externals" and Socioeconomic Change

The claim that lies at the heart of III, B, that Christianity is not out to change externals, has often been taken to mean that Christianity or Christian love conservatively affirms the political, social, and economic status quo and that it is unconcerned with external circumstances regardless of how much oppression, exploitation, or other suffering is involved. Perhaps this is due to a statement early in the chapter of Christianity's advice to the "poor charwoman who earns her living by menial work" (WL, p. 136). Kierkegaard tells the charwoman that Christianity says: "Do not busy yourself with changing the shape of the world or your situation, as if you . . . instead of being a poor charwoman, perhaps could manage to be called 'Madame'." Does this advice require us to read Kierkegaard's notion of inwardness as a recommendation that we should refrain from attempting to change either our condition or that of others? Such an "inwardness"—"Indeed, what else is Christianity but inwardness!" (p. 137)—seems to make normative a passive affirmation of the status quo, urging that we (and others) rise above the temporal conditions we (and others) face rather than challenge them. (This recalls his earlier emphasis on blindness to distinctions of rank and status.) Do such remarks support the criticism that *Works of Love* embodies an ethic in which the inwardness of love amounts to an indifference to external circumstances, which can be used to justify an indifference to physical distress, poverty, and oppression? Do they entail a passive acceptance of the socioeconomic status quo? Do they rule out or undermine any struggle to remedy inequity and injustice and oppression?

Such a conclusion would, of course, be peculiarly at odds with Kierkegaard's recommendation of the action of the good Samaritan, which clearly does tell us to care about and improve the circumstances of those who have been hurt by the greed of others. I suggest that if we attend carefully to the context of the story of the charwoman, it need not have the horrendous consequences for Kierkegaard's ethic that some have suggested. In fact, the whole of III, B, tells us a much more nuanced story about Kierkegaard's view of inwardness and externals.

At the very least, Kierkegaard tells us that Christianity's indifference to externals means that it is not out to "topple governments" and so install itself in the leadership position (WL, p. 135); neither a church state nor a state church is a goal of Christianity. But setting aside such imperialistic political designs, there is still a question about socioeconomic improvement, whether through change in public policies and institutions that deal with public welfare or through individual efforts to improve the socioeconomic situation for oneself or others.

First, we should pay attention to the very specific context in which Kierkegaard offers advice to the charwoman. After announcing the difference between inner change and external change, he introduces her as follows (I cite this at some length because it is so often misrepresented):

> Take the most lowly, the most disregarded servant, take what we call a rather simple, indigent, poor charwoman who earns her living by the most menial work—from the Christian point of view, she has the right, indeed, we most urgently beseech her in the name of Christianity to do it—she has the right to say, as she is doing her work and talking to herself and to God, something that it no way slows up the work, "I am doing this work for wages, but that I do it as carefully as I am doing it, I do—for the sake of conscience." (WL, p. 136)

His point is that such a woman is the equal of a king in this respect—she, too, can say what the king can say: "I am doing it for the sake of conscience." The language Kierkegaard uses in this instance—"that lowly woman has the right" to say this—recalls his earlier discussion (in II, C) of how the lowly and the elite both have the same obligations, how they are equally bound to the commandment. Lowliness does not excuse one from the commandment any more than privilege does. If 'ought implies can,' then another way of saying this is to say that the lowly have the same right and relevant ability as their superiors. Indeed, this is exactly the way in which Kierkegaard will proceed in the second series, as he considers the duty of both the high and low to be merciful. His concern there is that the lowly should not be deprived of thinking that they have the ability to fulfill the command to be merciful just because they have little to give. Indeed, as we shall see later, you can hear him saying in both cases: "That lowly woman has the right to. . . ." He seems to be doing the same thing when he says here: "To obey—for the sake of conscience—must be granted to everybody" (p. 137).

Perhaps that doesn't seem a good enough reason to advise the charwoman not to busy herself with changing the world or her "situation." But in the same paragraph in which this advice is given, Kierkegaard is also making a point about how "secrets of inwardness" lose something by being made public. Presumably, Kierkegaard is here making a parallel case to that of the monk whom he chastised earlier for losing the secret of inwardness by publicly lodging himself in the 'hidden' cloister. In this context of an emphasis on hidden inwardness, what does it mean to tell the charwoman not to busy herself about changing her situation? Kierkegaard's precise words are these: "Christianity's divine meaning is to say in confidence to every human being: 'Do not busy yourself with changing the shape of the world or your situation, as if you (to stay with the example) instead of being a poor charwoman, perhaps could manage to be called 'Madame'." Having seen Kierkegaard's earlier concern with the way in which distinctions can obscure or undermine our kinship with one another as equals under God, we can assume that this remains his concern. Thus, he is saying, do not think that changing such external distinctions can make it easier for you to fulfill your obligations of love. Do not be envious of the "Madame" as if it would be easier to be a better Christian if one were also a "Madame." Do not busy yourself about changing these external distinctions as if you need to be located higher in the circles of those with mink and ermine to be able to say, with truth and pride, "I am doing this work for the sake of conscience."

Admittedly, Kierkegaard walks a fine line here. What is true may nonetheless be inappropriately said in certain circumstances; some things can be understood only by those prepared by experience to hear them, and some reminders should be voiced only by those who have reached a certain point in their own ethical development. There is always the danger that one may take what is offered as a reminder to someone else as an excuse for oneself; reminders of the potential vices of the disadvantaged should be offered very cautiously, if at all, when the audience also includes better-off people who could use those reminders in a self-serving way against the disadvantaged. But Kierkegaard is himself fully aware, and reminds the reader, that the same expression can mean something different depending on who says it. At a simple level, an expression like "the multiplicity of creation," for example, "means something very different, depending on who the speaker is" (WL, p. 282). More to the point, words that seem to mitigate the rigorousness of the command to love can be misunderstood. We need to attend to the experience of the speaker, to whether the words "are the beginning of the discourse about love" or its "completion" because "that which is truth on the lips of the veteran and perfected apostle could in the mouth of a beginner very easily be a philandering by which he would leave the school of the commandment much too soon and escape the 'school-yoke'" (p. 376).

It is against this background of Kierkegaard's rhetorical sensitivity to his audience that advice to the "lowly," "disregarded servant," the "indigent, poor charwoman who earns her living by menial work," should be understood (WL, p. 136). He reminds her that Christianity says: "Do not busy yourself with changing the shape of the world or your situation, as if you . . . instead of being a poor charwoman, perhaps could manage to be called 'Madame'," but he also notes that it speaks "in confidence to every human being." This recommendation of indifference is addressed to her in her particular circumstances, and thus it is a warning against the envious thought that an advance in social standing will help her to be more loving—as if the two were necessarily connected. It is offered "in confidence" to her; it is not a reminder offered to her stingy employer (to mitigate his responsibility), nor is it advice her stingy employer can appropriately offer to her. The recommendation of indifference to temporal circumstances is not appropriately offered by the slum landlord to his tenants; indeed, the inappropriateness of a given recommendation of indifference is revealed by "the bitterness of the mockery, by the aridity of the sensibleness, by the poisonous spirit of distrust, [or] by the biting cold of callousness" (p. 7) that motivates it. So, too, the recommendation of indifference is not meant to be taken by the slum landlord as an excuse for allowing substandard housing conditions.

Not only is immoral otherworldliness not entailed by the kind of indifference recommended in this chapter, but also it does not seem to be Kierkegaard's intention for the book as a whole. Consider his warning in the first deliberation—that acts of charity can be unloving if one is "thinking about his own cares instead of thinking about the cares of the poor, perhaps seeking alleviation by giving to charity instead of wanting to alleviate poverty" (WL, p. 13–14). This warning is phrased in such a way that the duty of alleviating poverty seems to be assumed.

His example of the Samaritan is fully in line with this emphasis: "Christ does not speak about knowing the neighbor but about becoming a neighbor oneself, about showing oneself to be a neighbor just as the Samaritan showed it by his mercy" (WL, p. 22). Showing oneself to be a neighbor does not involve addressing only 'spiritual' needs; unless one already holds a dualist, spiritualist point of view, one need not see the injunction to serve the neighbor in terms of such dualism. If Kierkegaard were saying that we should each be so satisfied with our lot in life that we never try to improve it or help others improve their own lot, he could not in conscience recommend the example of the good Samaritan. In that case the good Samaritan would have been a busybody who should have said to the man in the ditch: "Don't busy yourself about getting out or getting healed or otherwise changing your situation." What is at stake here for Kierkegaard is obviously something other than that kind of message.

Kierkegaard's condemnation of the escapism of abstract love is strong and consistently maintained throughout *Works of Love*, and this is in keeping with his view that "actuality" is the source of demand and responsibility. He condemns escapism when he condemns the "worldly way" of closing oneself off from the world, to avoid being contaminated by the rough, the lowly, and the undistinguished (p. 74). If you are not attentive to actual persons and thus fail to respond to the one who walks by you in misery, you have indeed been blind—"but not, alas, in the Christian sense" (p. 75). The non-Christian sense of closed eyes is criticized because it is that by which one closes oneself off from the world. Kierkegaard chastises the Pharisee's intellectualizing about who his neighbor is, suggesting that the Pharisee asked the question "in order to find an escape" from the task it might reveal (p. 96). Kierkegaard warns that "the most dangerous of all escapes as far as love is concerned is wanting to love only the unseen or that which one has not seen" (p. 161); this escapism is tempting because it is "intoxicating," but *Works of Love* will warn us that such loving "flies over actuality completely" (p. 161). Thus, Kierkegaard's dismissals of the relevance of temporal distinctions in II, B and C, and of "externals" in III, B, do not support a charge of acosmic otherworldliness because they do not in themselves mitigate the obligation of those of privilege to be loving or to alleviate the lot of others less fortunate.

In sum, the second deliberation formally specifies the scope and bindingness of the commandment and introduces the forms that the content of love will take, and the third deliberation reinforces those forms. Both deliberations, therefore, make room for, and even seem to call for, an appreciation of the concrete to complement the abstract formality of the rule. This complementary appreciation of concrete particularity is developed in the subsequent deliberations of the first series, beginning with the fourth, which reorients the discussion toward the concreteness of "actuality" and what is "seen." This shift (which, to repeat, occurs in the first series) introduces a changed context in which a clarity of vision is appropriate—a context that supports the claim that love appreciates, even cherishes, the concrete differences. Since this fourth deliberation often goes unremarked in discussions of *Works of Love*, I want to stress its importance as strongly as possible. To do so, I place Kierkegaard's explicit turn to moral concreteness and vision in relation to his abstract formulation of the commandment.

chapter seven

Love's Vision

"Our Duty to Love the People We See" (IV)

Despite intimations of the concrete content of the love command in the second and third deliberations, it is true that in an important sense these deliberations are abstract, the abstractness of a formal clarification of the law. The "closed eyes," which are required in the context of commandment, are closed to all preferential or temporal distinctions that could be used as an argument for making an exception; they are closed to what would alienate or repudiate kinship. In such a context, the neighbor is *potentially* every person; therefore, love ignores concrete differences that could be the basis for excluding anyone. This is the context for the claim that every individual "is something particular, represents something particular, but essentially he is something else [which] we do not get to see here in life" (WL, p. 86). Thus the moral focus is on what is common to all persons—essential humanness, which we do not see. What is not visible is "seen" only if we close our eyes to the (visible) appearances that can divide us. But suddenly we come face to face with a magnificent sight—a deliberation on "Our Duty to Love the People We See." Moreover, it opens with pages of impassioned expressions of the depth of our "craving" for companionship, our longing to be with one another—in sum, a deep, desiring need "to love and be loved." This looks like a place where attention to concreteness should be found, if there is any. It looks like a new beginning.[1]

In other words, although the preceding deliberations have not totally lacked references to and examples of the concrete (we found the Samaritan, and his presence is crucial), the dominant theme of the second and third deliberations is the *form* of relation between people. Kierkegaard describes the relation that obtains formally between us 'as equals before God,' but he does not explore the relation as it is actually played out between two concrete people. If ever Kierkegaard is going to consider the warmth, the caring, the tenderness, and the intimacy that we associate with love, it should be in this deliberation, whose first words are "How *deeply* the need of love is rooted in human nature!"

If *Works of Love* proposed only that equality is "simply not to make distinctions" and that we need to "look away" from dissimilarities to love as we ought, Kierkegaard would be rightly criticized for advocating a form of moral regard that is so interiorized and so essentialized that it denies the moral relevance of differences. Such an ethic would be indefensibly abstract. But Kierkegaard's position is undeniably more complex because if we have to love those "we see," we must, presumably, have to *see* those we love. In other words, loving must involve a kind of *seeing*.[2] We could, of course, claim that blindness to what obscures the equality of kinship amounts to a seeing, that is, seeing the other as kin. But Kierkegaard's emphasis in the earlier deliberations is on closing our eyes to the concrete differences among us, which are visible here in this life in order to be able to see the common humanity that is invisible in this life. I suggest that attention to ethical concreteness begins in earnest precisely in this fourth deliberation because here, as we shall soon see, we are urged to "love precisely the person one sees," to attend to people "as they are." Before I explore this recommendation, however, I will indicate why Kierkegaard would have separated the different emphases—that is, why it is not surprising that we should have to look outside the statement of the commandment to find his explicit attention to concreteness.

I. The Skeleton of Law and the Fullness of Love

After the statement of the love commandment and its tripartite analysis in the second deliberation, the third deliberation introduces a distinction between law and love (WL, p. 104). I have waited until this chapter to examine that distinction because it helps explain why Kierkegaard would have adopted the strategy of separating the discussion of formal abstraction from that of specific concreteness. He describes the distinction between "the Law" and "love" as a contrast between a "sketch" and its fulfillment in the "work," suggesting that the sketch remains "indefinite" until the work is finished, when we can we say that "there is not the slightest indefiniteness, not of a single line nor of a single point" (p. 104). He concludes that "the Law defines and defines but never arrives at the sum, which is love" (p. 105). This same kind of contrast is formulated strikingly in his journal characterization: "[T]he law is the skeleton, the bony structure, the dehydrated husk. Love is the fullness."[3] We are meant to think of a sketch as a skeletal structure of lines, outlines, and contours; the contrast would be the fulfillment in the form of a concretely fleshed-out, filled-in painting, with color, texture, or depth. Thus Kierkegaard would probably believe that the work of clarification had to be achieved by *both* a *formal* analysis (a formal statement of the law) and a *material* analysis (a description of concrete love, a fulfilled duty).

Kierkegaard's understanding of the relation between the law and love has two important dimensions. First, he rehearses a litany of ways in which they contrast with each other; for example, the law is death and love is life, the law is hunger and love is satisfaction, the law requires and love gives, and the law is rigorous and love is gentle. There is a clear contrast to be drawn when the law is presented as a requirement by itself. Yet, like the artist's sketch and its fulfillment, "there is no conflict" because they both come from the same source (WL, p. 105). That is, there is no conflict "in love" because the law is taken up into love (p. 106); from the perspective of the fulfilled law, the fulfillment "is one and the same" with the requirement. For Kierkegaard, the statement of the law already implies grace (p. 106), but it is nevertheless important to distinguish the hunger from the satisfaction. The importance of maintaining a conceptual contrast between law and love is supported by draft comments in which Kierkegaard contrasts talking about love as "duty" to talking "about love to the neighbor."[4] The model of the law and love in terms of sketch and fulfillment, skeleton and fullness, prepares us to expect two different rhetorical contexts, or contexts of discussion. Using (what we shall see are) Kierkegaard's own words, we can describe these formal and material contexts as *commandment* and *"fulfillment"* or, alternatively, a context that focuses on (formal) *unconditionality* and one that focuses on (material) *"actuality."*

Other scholars have divided up *Works of Love* in ways that might at first sound similar to this (e.g., into a series on "Law" and a series on "Gospel," or a series on "Law" and a series on "Love"), but my proposal differs markedly from previous ones since it is central to my reading that the difference in rhetorical contexts does *not* coincide with the difference between the two series of deliberations. One of the early descriptions of *Works of Love* divided the two series as follows:

> Part I chiefly concerns itself with that person who, by having dealings with the love command, discovers the position he must be placed in to fulfill that command and sees his only possibility for doing so in the prayer that God will grant him the reality of love. Part II has as its essential theme "the lover," who sees the purpose of his existence as fulfilled by living in grace, and who therefore constantly takes his stand on God's love as his only possibility for loving unconditionally. Only in virtue of being "the lover" can he practice "works of love" at all, just as only the good tree, without being commanded to, bears good fruit. In contrast to Part I in Part II the imperative tense is almost never used.[5]

A variation is that the two series are divided into a concern with law as "theory" and a concern with the Gospel as the "practice" enabled by grace[6] or, similarly, that the first series represents a statement of the law and the second, a description of love.[7] It has also been suggested that the first series is about the *"duty* to love," emphasizing self-renunciation, whereas the second "is edifying or constructive," emphasizing "the return to the world"; the relation between the two is seen as paralleling the double movement of faith described in *Fear and Trembling*.[8] Finally, it has been argued that the first series is guided by the grammar of "Shall," whereas the second is guided by the grammar of "Can."[9] A glance at the lists of chapter titles in the first and second series might seem to support such proposals since most of the titles of the first series focus on duty, law, conscience, and imperatives; none of the titles in the second series includes such categories but seem, on the contrary, to be descriptions of features of love. I argue against such proposals, however, for a variety of reasons.

First, the language of "duty" is found in the text of the chapters in the second series, and a Kantian anticonsequentialism is maintained there as well. Second, it is precisely Christian love that is addressed in the first series: the "royal Law [is] the love commandment" (61), requiring love of one's enemy. Third, the description of love begins even in the first series. Finally, Kierkegaard first described his intention to do a single series of lectures on works of love,[10] and there is no evidence that the decision to publish two series was guided by any theological or conceptual rationale. Thus, although I fully agree that there is a progression from concern with the law as "the skeleton" to love as the "fullness," from a statement of the law to a description of love, I argue that the division of rhetorical contexts occurs in the first series (through the shift signaled in the fourth deliberation of this series) rather than between the first and second series of deliberations.

Because the fourth deliberation is so seldom appreciated in context, I will juxtapose it explicitly with the second deliberation. Using Kierkegaard's contrast between law and love, we see that chapters II, A–C, can constitute the description of a *rule* for determining the category "neighbor"—"all" has the force of "no exceptions." The purpose of these chapters is not to delineate the character of a substantive response to the other but to delimit a category by stipulating that no one can be excluded from this category on the basis of difference or dissimilarity (or included in it simply on the basis of similarity). According to Kierkegaard, the commandment contains "provisions"; however, despite the fact that it "defines and defines," it remains "indefinite"—it "cannot say everything" (WL, pp. 104–5). The analysis of the rule (the sketch or the skeleton) is not meant to give us a complete picture of his view of love. The specification of the rule is rhetorically and categorically different from the description of its fulfillment. The context of discussion in which fulfillment is described is appropriately found after the analysis of the rule as such, beginning explicitly in the fourth deliberation.

II. Love's Vision—The Duty to Love the People We "See"

Kierkegaard's early promissory note—that when one "goes with God," one is "compelled to see and to see in a unique way" (WL, p. 77)—is redeemed in this fourth deliberation, which elaborates "Our Duty to Love the People We See." This deliberation opens with a biblical reference to the contrast between the "unseen" God and the "seen" neighbor. Kierkegaard quotes the first letter of John:

"If anyone says, 'I love God,' and hates his brother, he is a liar; for how can he who does not love his brother, whom he has seen, love God, whom he has not seen" (I John 4:20). A person, Kierkegaard says later, should begin by loving the unseen God, presumably because it is from God that we learn what it is to love, "but that he actually loves the unseen will be known by his loving the brother he sees" (p. 160). Here we are to learn what it means to love the brother one sees; in particular, this deliberation is intended to clarify what it means to have a "duty" to "love precisely the person one sees" and "to love him just as you see him" (pp. 173, 174).[11] I suggest that Kierkegaard's account of the ethical relation to the other in terms of *seeing* the other is richly suggestive and worth exploring in its own right. But what makes it particularly relevant to contemporary reconsideration of ethical abstractness and concreteness (impartiality and partiality, sameness and difference) is that Kierkegaard couples (even equates) our duty to "love precisely the person one sees" with the duty "to find actuality with closed eyes" (p. 163). Discovering how these two aspects of our duty fit together is not only a crucial part of assessing *Works of Love* but also can contribute to contemporary discussions of ethical relationship. Before addressing this further, however, it is worth commenting on the theme of need, which opens the deliberation.

A. Need and Duty

It is striking that Kierkegaard begins this deliberation on our *duty* to love those we see, with repeated references to the human *need* he had introduced in the prayer and the first deliberation—the strong need that amounts to craving (*Trang*). Here, love's need to express itself becomes love's need for love. He alludes to "the first remark . . . made about humanity"—God's judgment that "it is not good for the man to be alone" (WL, p. 154). Even when we are tired of "the busy, teeming crowd," the crush of society on us, the solution is not to separate ourselves from others in unloving isolation but rather to withdraw enough to be able to appreciate again our "longing for companionship [*Selskab*]." Every word Kierkegaard ever spoke against "the crowd" and every criticism ever raised against him for encouraging asociality need to be reassessed in the light of this unqualified affirmation of our need for companionship.

And it is not just the need of physical presence around us, of casual concern, that he is referring to. He is quite clearly talking about the craving "to love and be loved." This need is so deeply rooted in human nature, he says, that even Christ, because he was "an actual human being," "even he humanly felt this need to love and be loved by an individual human being" (WL, p. 155). In one of the most touching moments in *Works of Love*, Kierkegaard recalls the poignant exchange between Christ and Peter, in which Christ asks Peter: "Simon, son of John, do you love me more than these?" Kierkegaard comments: "How moving that is! Christ says: Do you love me *more than these*? Indeed, it is like an appeal for love; this is the way of speaking that characterizes one for whom it is of great importance to be the most loved" (p. 155). Speaking as if from experience, he notes that "even though a person otherwise knows that he is loved because he has heard the yes before, he is very eager to hear it and therefore wants to hear it again . . .

[indeed, is] craving to hear it" (p. 155). And remember, Kierkegaard had early in the first deliberation reminded us that we should not hold back genuine words of love or genuine emotion "because this can be the unloving committing of a wrong, just like withholding from someone what you owe him" (p. 12).

Surprising as it may be to those who have heard only the passages quoted by critics of his ethic, Kierkegaard is using the example of Christ (who is the proto-type to be imitated) to make the points that (1) it is ineradicably human to crave to "love and be loved," and (2) "to love humanly is to love an individual human being and to wish to be that individual human being's most beloved" (WL, p. 156). His ethic simply cannot be assessed properly if these commitments are not given the importance they deserve.

Moreover, something about this need or craving is related to the fulfillment of the love command. Love as such is not commanded; it can only be commanded to direct itself unselfishly. Love has a need to express itself. It shocks Kierkegaard how many people contrive to deprive themselves of the blessing of loving and being loved (WL, p. 157), how many are willing to waste God's gift, the "incom-parable" gift of love "which he implanted in the human heart" (p. 163). He is sadly bemused by the thought of people who apparently "want to be exempt from loving"—"as if it were a compulsory matter," a "burden," to keep loving (p. 172). He is implying that we do not need a law to keep loving because to keep loving is in one sense the most natural thing—it is love's need to keep loving. Without the dynamism of this need or desire in us, it is difficult to see how a command as such could motivate us.

It is worth noting here that Kierkegaard's references to Peter as the "indi-vidual human being" show another side of the category of "the individual." Here Kierkegaard is using it to highlight love's appreciation of the concreteness, particularity, and distinctiveness of a person.[12] That is, not only does the cate-gory of "the individual" reinforce the notion of our responsibility for others, even when the majority opinion goes against us (which we saw in chapter 5), but it also reinforces the concrete way in which a person is unique in the eyes of an-other. Both dimensions of "the individual" are necessary if we are to have genuine community, so ironically the stress on "the individual" is an indirect way of affirming a loving community. In neither case does the category of the indi-vidual support criticisms of individualism and asociality.

B. The Strategic Shift to Vision

This deliberation is the site of an important shift in focus, which Kierkegaard sig-nals by explicitly suggesting that this deliberation is a *different* discussion from those that precede it; that is, he says that this duty is not to be construed "as if the discourse were about loving all the people we see, since that is *love for the neigh-bor, which was discussed earlier*" (emphasis mine); rather, "the discourse is about the duty to find in the world of actuality the people we can love in particular and in loving them to love the people we see" (WL, p. 159). The injunction to love all people (even to love "all the people we see") states the rule that prevents us from excluding anyone. But "all" can only be abstract and potential. This new injunction—to "love precisely the person one sees" (p. 173)—obtains its force in a different way. Coming after earlier clarifications of the unconditionality of the commandment and its formal requirement of expressing love in action, this fourth deliberation focuses on the character of those expressions of love. It begins to make concrete the earlier warning that "at a distance all recognize the neighbor. . . . But at a distance the neighbor is a figment of the imagination" (p. 79). In other words, whereas it is easy to affirm duty in the abstract, duty can only be fulfilled in the actual relation to concrete humans, and Kierkegaard correlates "actuality" with what is "seen."

On the basis of this deliberation, it is plausible to argue that Kierkegaard's Christian ethic is one of *vision*. It is true that the centrality of the commandment implies a kind of aural metaphor—hearing the command or being deaf to the command—but from the very first page of *Works of Love* Kierkegaard shows that he is struck with the notion of vision, of ethics in terms of the seen and unseen.[13] In an 1843 discourse entitled "Love Will Hide a Multitude of Sins," Kierkegaard remarks that "it does not depend, then, merely upon what one sees, but what one sees depends upon how one sees; all observation is not just a receiving, a discovering, but also a bringing forth, and insofar as it is that, how the observer himself is constituted is indeed decisive."[14] Reminding us that to the pure all things are pure, he notes that "an evil eye discovers much that love does not see," and he defines stinginess in terms of vision: "[S]tinginess lives in the heart, when one gives with one eye and looks with seven to see what one obtains in return."[15]

Later on we will see that Kierkegaard considers love in terms of hiding sins and suggests that loving forgiveness is a way of making something seen into something unseen: in forgiveness "what is seen is nevertheless not seen" (WL, p. 295). Moreover, in both this early discourse on hiding sins and in the deliberation in *Works of Love* entitled "Love Hides a Multitude of Sins" (2:V), he suggests that the term "multitude" is important because it is an example of a determination that depends on the condition of the observer. The same expression means something very different, depending on who is determining the multitude; the isolated, uninformed hermit or the well-traveled, scientific researcher will mean different things when each speaks of the "multiplicity of creation" (pp. 283, 294). In other words, Kierkegaard is alluding to the indisputable fact that observation is 'theory-laden'—what we bring to a situation will influence what we see there. What we see when we come lovingly, generously, will differ from what we see when we come deliberately looking for something to find fault with, gossip about, or condemn.

Many of Kierkegaard's writings before *Works of Love*, as I have discussed elsewhere,[16] treat the ethical as a way of life to which vision is crucial—whether in terms of the concept of "transparency," for example, or the way in which qualitative transformations of our manner of seeing things are modes of self-development. In addition, Kierkegaard's reliance on the theme of vision is indirectly revealed in his frequent references to the notion of "illusion" to be dispelled; both elsewhere and in *Works of Love*, the theme of vision is implied in the theme of obscured vision or illusion.[17] It has also been argued that the normative or ethical significance of vision in *Works of Love* is found particularly in the way in which Kierkegaard often treats unloving actions in terms of seeing wrongly.[18] For example, in the third chapter of the second deliberation (1:II, C) , Kierkegaard discusses the negative attitudes of arrogance and envy, which can be interpreted as ways of seeing another in relation to oneself. The nuanced way in which Kierkegaard treats our vision of others as a concern with *the way we see others seeing us* has been termed a "dialectic of recognition"; arrogance, for example, is an attitude that tries to "tell other people how they should see themselves in seeing oneself, to *make* them see oneself as superior."[19] But even if we ignore the technical dialectic, we can say that for Kierkegaard the problem of affirming another is a problem about ways of seeing; that is, we can see others in ways that demean them or affirm them. And this probably accounts for his repeated negative assessments of "comparison" throughout *Works of Love:* comparison is a way of seeing others in relation to ourself or seeing how others stack up against one another in terms of our preferences.[20]

Kierkegaard seems to have a fondness for explicating love's positive attitudes (hope, trust, and mercy) indirectly by reference to negative ones (envy, mistrust, and arrogance), and we shall see this strategy at work in the second series of deliberations. But he does not limit himself to examples of seeing wrongly to make his point; we shall see positive examples in the second series, as well as negative ones. In any case, probably the most decisive positive discussion of ethics as a kind of seeing is found in this fourth deliberation, where to be ethical is to see the other just as he or she is, in all his or her distinctive concreteness.

I consider this deliberation a decisive turning point in *Works of Love* because the shift in context coincides with a shift to a different view of the moral relevance of concrete differences; the descriptions of the fulfillment of love that begin here support the idea of an impartiality (or equal regard) that includes loving the differences (even while it excludes preference).[21] Kierkegaard insists that our duty is not to set about looking for some lovable persons to love; rather, "the task is to find the once given or chosen object—lovable" (p. 159). Precisely the way in which Kierkegaard formulates the duty as finding "in the world of actuality the people we can love in particular and in loving them to love the people we see" reveals how in this deliberation his concern is with our response to those who constitute our arena for moral action, those who constitute "actuality" *for us.*

Limiting the moral arena in this way mitigates the abstraction of the commandment's scope, but does it contradict Kierkegaard's emphasis on nonpreferential love? Is this implied "proximity criterion" at odds with non-preferential love?[22] Does Kierkegaard's acknowledgment of the fact that we are situated in a particular historical and spatial context amount to a disguised expression of preference that is inconsistent with equality? There are two ways to address such an objection. First, it is important to note that *Works of Love* does not argue that simple proximity—without need—would generate a demand on us.[23] That is, proximity in itself without need would not take precedence over a relatively more distant person in need.[24] Second, we must reconsider what is at stake in the notion of preference. In the second deliberation, as we saw, Kierkegaard claims that preference is self-loving because even if it is not selfish, it remains an expression of "self-willfulness" and "arbitrariness" (pp. 55, 115); in other words, such preference excludes impartiality by definition. In the fourth deliberation, on the contrary, the phrase "those once given or chosen," which he repeats (pp. 159, 166), explicitly excludes the dimensions of willfulness or arbitrariness that constitute the preference to be avoided. The stranger who falls ill at our feet on our way to work is "given" to us. Moreover, once "chosen," our wife or friend becomes a "given" for us as well—one who places a demand on us regardless of our convenience. Even if the call on us by all is equal in principle, our duty is to respond to need as manifested in our "actuality," and Kierkegaard most often contrasts "actuality" with the idealized situation (pp. 77–78). Our responsibility is to serve without willful or arbitrary preference, to avoid preferring someone "in contrast to all others" (p. 19); this is not inconsistent with the tragic fact that, because of the limitations of our finitude, some persons will de facto be served at the expense of others.

III. The Tragedy of Responsibility

Kierkegaard does not develop his sense of this tragedy, but recently Jacques Derrida has provided an account of this other (tragic) side of our responsibility that can complement and illuminate Kierkegaard's claim. In an article entitled "Whom to Give to (Knowing Not to Know),"[25] Derrida comments sympathetically on the discussion (in Kierkegaard's *Fear and Trembling*) of the Old Testament story of Abraham and Isaac.[26] He suggests, rather provocatively, that the scenario in which Abraham is asked by God to sacrifice his son Isaac illustrates "the most common and everyday experience of responsibility"—the "sacrifice of love to love."[27]

Derrida suggests that when I fulfill one duty, "I am sacrificing and betraying at every moment all my other obligations: my obligations to the other others whom I know or don't know . . . each of whom is the only son I sacrifice to the other, every one being sacrificed to every one else."[28] The place of God is taken by the particular proximate other who calls on us; the place of Isaac is taken by the other others. Derrida illuminates the nature of the tragedy that exists because we are finite—that to sacrifice ourselves for one of the others, we have to sacrifice all of the other others: "I can respond only to the one (or to the One), that is, to the other, by sacrificing that one to the other. I am responsible to any one (that is to say to any other) only by failing in my responsibility to all the others, to the ethical or political generality." This will be the case even if we manage to help many people; all the rest will have to wait. And what Kierkegaard shows so well in Johannes de Silentio's account is why Abraham can neither explain nor seek comfort in the understanding of others. Derrida recognizes sadly that "I can never justify this sacrifice . . . I can never justify the fact that I prefer or sacrifice any one (any other) to the other."[29]

Derrida suggests that the truth in the Abraham story is that "I cannot respond to the call, the request, the obligation, or even the love of another without sacrifice of the other other, the other others."[30] This just marks the tragedy of finitude, and "as a result, the concepts of responsibility, of decision, or of duty, are condemned a priori to paradox, scandal, and aporia." Derrida says what Kierkegaard implicitly has to acknowledge: "As soon as I enter into relation with the other . . . I know that I can respond only by sacrificing ethics, that is, by sacrificing whatever obliges me to also respond, in the same way, in the same instant, to all the others. I offer a gift of death, I betray." The language Derrida uses is hyperbolic, but no more so than Kierkegaard's understanding of paradox and offense. Derrida concludes: "What can be said about Abraham's relation to God can be said about my relation without relation to every other one as every bit other, in particular my relation to my neighbor or my loved ones who are as inaccessible to me, as secret and transcendent as Jahweh. . . . From this point of view what *Fear and Trembling* says about the sacrifice of Isaac is the truth."[31] There are sympathy and respect in Derrida's account of this dilemma, enacted daily, yet nonetheless profoundly tragic.

Kierkegaard, and presumably Derrida, know that this "irresponsibility" that inheres in "responsibility" can be used as an escapist rationale, much like the escapist strategy of the Pharisees, who wanted to be objectively certain which of the many was their neighbor—a theoretical determination that can eternally postpone service to anyone. But that not everyone can be helped should not be allowed to excuse us from doing what we can for the ones for whom we can do something. Perhaps Kierkegaard's fear that we are all too ready to make such an excuse explains why he does not advert to the tragedy or exhibit the same sadness Derrida does. That he does not, however, need not mean that he cavalierly dismisses those who are not helped at any given time. But there is something to be said for Derrida's honesty—it seems right that we should not ignore the sad truth. We should, at least periodically, acknowledge—with the pain of the sympathy that attends the acknowledgment—that what we do for one is inevitably at the cost of what we could do for another.

IV. The Concrete Other

We still need to ask, though, how concrete, in Kierkegaard's account, is the response to those who call on us if our duty is "to find actuality with closed eyes" (WL, p. 163). I suggest that the "closed eyes" he is urging in this context is importantly different from that developed in his earlier recommendation that our eyes be closed to distinctions of status and advantage. In this context, he recommends the "closed eye of forbearance and leniency that does not see defects and imperfections" (p. 162); he suggests that "in love you do indeed close [your eyes] to weakness and frailty and imperfection" (p. 163).[32] It is quite natural to wonder, on hearing these comments, whether Kierkegaard's ethic allows us to really see the actual other person. It is also natural to wonder whether this ethic recommends a morally culpable blindness, whether it proposes that we ignore moral failings in the other person. We can consider these in turn.

A. Love's Acceptance of the Actual Other

To assess what is at stake for Kierkegaard in the requirement of blindness to "defects and imperfections," we need to understand precisely what attitude he has in mind as the alternative to such blindness. Kierkegaard's commitment to concrete acceptance of the actual other is in evidence every time he refers to our duty to love people "as they are" (WL, p. 166), "to love precisely the person one sees" (p. 173), or "to love the person you see just as you see him" (p. 174). What is at stake for him is made clear in his striking and repeated contrast between loving someone "just as you see him" and seeing him as you want him to be, which is a way of *not* seeing *him,* for "does it not amount to the same thing—*to see a mirage*—and: *not to see?*" (pp. 162, 164). He notes, with what I think is remarkable psychological insight, that we are prone to love the self-generated image of the other person, but, he insists, this is not loving the actual other person at all. On the contrary (and the emphasis is Kierkegaard's), *"in loving the actual individual person it is important that one does not substitute an imaginary idea of how we think or could wish that this person should be.* The one who does this does not love the person he sees but again something unseen, his own idea or something similar" (p. 164). This just repeats what he had put in italics earlier: we must *"first and foremost give up all imaginary and exaggerated ideas about a dreamworld where the object of love should be sought and found—that is, one must become sober, gain actuality and truth by finding and remaining in the world of actuality as the task assigned to one"* (p. 161).

The new formulation of "closed eyes" in this deliberation addresses something other than the blindness to distinction recommended in the second deliberation (1:II, B and C) because the moral focus here is not on loving what we cannot see but on loving what we can see. Since the model is one of loving "precisely the person one sees," what we must see is actuality, and to do that we must be blind to "imaginary and exaggerated ideas" of what the other is or should be. Kierkegaard stresses repeatedly that loving must be a kind of accurate, honest seeing.

Yet Kierkegaard jars us slightly when he suggests that one can only see someone just as he or she is precisely by closing our eyes to weakness, frailty, defects, and imperfections. One way to make sense of the goal of finding actuality with our eyes closed to imperfection is to consider that to see imperfection is not exactly like seeing blue eyes or blonde hair; in an important sense, imperfection is seen as such only by reference to another image that serves as a standard of perfection. We are urged to be blind to imperfections only in the sense of being resistant to their pressure to distance and repel us, a pressure that is generated by the actuality's contrast with the standard of perfection we think we deserve to have embodied in the one whom we will love.

There are different ways of not truly seeing another person. Sometimes, our refusal to accept that someone is not simply a concatenation of "lovable perfections" (WL, p. 164) leads us to separate ourselves from the person. But other times, more sadly, our refusal to accept this leads us to torment the other in various, often subtle ways; our unwillingness to accept the fact that we are not somehow entitled to the perfect mate causes us to be so offended at the other who does not live up to our expectations that we "cunningly demand to see something else" (p. 164). We can "volatilize," he says, the actual other by making his or her form "vacillating or unreal" because we cannot make up our mind just exactly what we want: such an attitude "cannot really make up its mind but at one time wants to have a defect removed from the object and at another wants a perfection added— as if the bargain, if I may put it that way, were not as yet concluded." The implied, contrasting view of genuine love's affirmation of the other could be summarized in the poetic fragment by e e cummings: "As yes is to if, love is to yes."[33]

The person who can't make up his mind "does not love the one he sees and easily makes his love as loathsome to himself as he makes it difficult for the beloved" (WL, p. 165). This is a theme close to Kierkegaard's heart; we will see that he later provides graphic pictures of the domineering tyrant who "wants everyone to be transformed in his image, to be trimmed according to his pattern for human beings," that is, demands that others fulfill his or her ideas of them (p. 270). A loving person, on the contrary, is flexible and has a liberating awareness of others—in other words, sees and appreciates them as they are.

Eyes closed to defects are eyes closed to an imagined or wished-for perfection. In this sense, being blind to defects is not being blind to what is actual, as it was in the earlier context of discussion, but rather to fantasy and abstraction. In the context in which love in "actuality" is described, our eyes are closed to what is not actual in order to see things just as they are, to focus lovingly on what may be different from our dreams. The closed eye of forbearance means that love is an honest, inclusive seeing, which is a concrete seeing. In other words, in the context of the rule, *blindness to distinction* provides a space for concrete seeing, although it does not actually foster it; when we are blind to all except what people have in common, what we can see is too abstract to be responded to. In the context of actuality, on the contrary, *blindness to imperfection* is meant to be a way of fostering concrete seeing. Just as Kierkegaard can speak of love as being blind to imperfections and weaknesses, he can also call it loving the person "just as you see him, *with* all his imperfections and weaknesses."[34] In the end, this same kind of affirmation is central to his discussion, in the opening deliberations of the second series, of how we build up others by our love.[35]

B. Love's Challenge to the Other

We might still be wondering whether this ethic asks us to deny the reality of the defect or imperfection. Is it recommending a kind of dishonesty or, at best, a naïve ignorance? We will see that Kierkegaard addresses such questions more directly in an upcoming deliberation, by considering love in the light of the "love of truth"; in examining that deliberation, I will consider his denial that he recommends intellectual dishonesty and his suggestion that we must sometimes deal "mercy's blow" to others by reminding them that what they are doing is not good.[36] Still, it is possible to get a significant sense of his position simply on the basis of what he says here.

What we learn here is that love is not only accepting but also *challenging*.

Kierkegaard admits that sometimes our sense of someone's imperfection is not the result of our "fastidiousness" or our narcissistic and unrealistic expectations (WL, pp. 158, 166). Sometimes it is precisely because we have found "the firm footing of actuality" (p. 163) that we do "see the defect" (p. 167). Although not all judgments of inadequacy need to be the fantastic result of self-love, which ones are self-serving and which are not has to be determined conscientiously in each case.

A striking formulation of the role of challenge in love's acceptance is found in the following passage:

> [T]he relationship itself will with integrated power *fight against the imper-fection, overcome the defect* . . . the two are to hold together all the more firmly and inwardly in order to remove the weakness. As soon as the rela-tionship is made equivocal, you do not love the person you see; then it is in-deed as if you demanded something else in order to be able to love. On the other hand, when the defect or the weakness makes the relationship more inward, not as if the defect should now become entrenched but in order to conquer it, then you love the person you see. (WL, pp. 166–67; emphasis mine)

This reinforces my earlier suggestion that we are not urged to be blind to the fact that those we see have habits that ought to be changed; being urged to love others "as they are" (p. 166) does not entail a passive approval of or even resignation to whatever they do or are. On the contrary, we are encouraged to "fight against the imperfection." In these cases love is challenging *because* it sees; it can only chal-lenge what it sees. To be precise, love is challenging even (and only) while it loves the person it sees, as the example of Christ's love for Peter effectively shows. Kierkegaard reminds us that Christ "did not say, 'Peter must first change and become another person before I can love him again'"; rather, "he said ex-actly the opposite, 'Peter is Peter, and I love him. My love, if anything, will help him to become another person.' . . . He preserved the friendship unchanged and in that way helped Peter to become another person" (p. 172).[37]

Ironically, in his own anti-Kierkegaardian account of interpersonal relations, Martin Buber puts forth what is simply a version of Kierkegaard's position in *Works of Love*. He speaks of "goals even deeper than acceptance":

> I not only accept the other as he is, but I confirm him, in myself, and then in him, in relation to the potentiality that is meant by him and it can now be developed, it can evolve, it can answer to the reality of life. . . . Let's take, for example, man and a woman, man and wife. He says, not expressly, but just by his whole relation to her, "I accept you as you are." But this does *not* mean "I don't want you to change." Rather it says, "Just by my ac-cepting love, I discover in you what you are meant to become."[38]

It is difficult to see how Buber differs from Kierkegaard in this respect, and it is unfortunate that Buber's concentration on an extremely limited number of Kierkegaard's texts blinded him to this congeniality. In any case, it seems clear that for Kierkegaard inclusive acceptance and challenge are both expressions of seeing the concrete: one is to love a person "just as you see him, with all his imperfections and weaknesses" (p. 174) at the same time as one is encouraged to "fight the imperfection" (p. 166). In the context of fulfillment of the command, therefore, "closed eyes" are eyes that are closed to what is not actual—closed either to what appear to be defects only in relation to an imagined perfection or to what appear to be incorrigible defects (since this, too, is an imaginative projection). But our eyes are to be open—wideopen—to the other in the service of a realistic apprehension of the truth. The particular kind of blindness Kierkegaard proposes is intended to facilitate concrete vision and distinctive response—a vision of and response to others "just as they are."

C. Love's Celebration of the Concrete

We can assume that seeing a person as she is, if she is our daughter or wife, will mean seeing her as our daughter or wife. The particularities of the relation must make some difference in the character of our response, both in terms of what is seen to be needed by those to whom we stand in special relations and what I can more easily do for them because of proximity or greater knowledge of their situation. The discussion of special relations in chapter 6, sect. III, is relevant here. Moreover, the sense that Kierkegaard intends love's acceptance to be *detailed* and *specific* is validated if we look ahead for a moment to the fourth deliberation in the second series, "Love Does Not Seek Its Own." Here Kierkegaard makes especially clear love's appreciation of distinctive detail: we are to love *"every human being according to his distinctiveness; but 'his distinctiveness' is what for him is his own; that is, the loving one does not seek his own; quite the opposite, he loves what is the other's own"* (WL, p. 269; emphasis Kierkegaard's). He illuminates the character of true human love as one that focuses on concrete differences when he describes God's generous love, which is to be our model:

> There is no difference in the love, no, none—yet what a difference in the flowers! Even the least, the most insignificant, the most unimpressive . . . it is as if this, too, had said to love: Let me become something in myself, something distinctive. And then love has helped it to become its own distinctiveness, but far more beautiful than the little flower had ever dared to hope for. What love! First, it makes no distinction, none at all; next, which is just like the first, it infinitely distinguishes itself in loving the diverse. (p. 270)

Although "before God there is no preference" (p. 63), there is an appreciation (even celebration) of differences. Kierkegaard unapologetically affirms differentially expressed love, distinctive in its response, saying that love aids in the process in which one becomes "something distinctive." Divine love "makes no distinction" yet it builds up differentially, responding to need. Thus, genuine human love, emulating divine love, should love the differences and build up differentially, responding to different needs. Kierkegaard affirms our commonsense connection between concreteness and difference. Moreover, when he uses the example of God's love for us to show that not all "distinctive" response is preferential, he is making a crucial distinction between impartiality and disinterestedness, and it is just this sort of distinction that critics are often asking for.[39] Whatever distinctions are ingredients in differential expressions of love, suited to each recipient, are differences allowed to be morally relevant?[40]

V. Love's Reconciliation of Concreteness and Abstraction

Readings of *Works of Love* have tended to do one of the following: (1) criticize its focus on the abstract category of "human being," ignoring its attention to distinctiveness/difference;[41] (2) defend it from the charge of abstraction by indicating its emphases on distinctiveness and difference, deemphasizing its reliance on assumptions about the "essentially" human;[42] (3) admit emphases on both essence and difference, arguing that they are finally incompatible and irreconcilable; or (4) point to both emphases, assuming that they are compatible without exploring or accounting for the apparent incompatibility.

Since it is difficult to deny that both emphases can be found, the compelling question is whether these emphases on the concrete and the abstract, on difference and essence, are fully compatible, and if so, how. Some commentators have argued that they are not compatible. Adorno began the charge of contradiction, suggesting that Kierkegaard's "unyielding abstractness" undermines his insistence on "the 'practice of real life'"; a more recent charge is that where Kierkegaard's affirmation of concreteness is found, it "contradicts his basic emphases," yet "he [Kierkegaard] fails to perceive the incompatibility between the two approaches."[43]

Other scholars have rightly asserted their compatibility but without providing a satisfying explanation of how the two can, in fact, be held together in such a way that neither undermines the other. For example, it has been suggested that *Works of Love's* ethic corrects postmodern, neofeminist radicalizations of difference by incorporating a significant appreciation of both difference and essential humanness.[44] But when such an account concludes that "while we certainly love people in our special relations differently from the way we love others, this difference is not essential,"[45] we have cause to wonder whether Kierkegaard's account of essential human nature can leave room for more than lip service to the importance of difference. We do find in *Works of Love* both kinds of claim: (1) differences should "hang loosely" so that we can perceive "in every individual that essential other person, that which is common to all men"; (2) Christianity "makes infinite distinctions in loving the differences." Moreover, Kierkegaard's claim—"Because of his dissimilarity, every single one of these innumerable individuals is something particular, represents something particular, but essentially he is something else. Yet this you do not get to see here in life" (p. 86)—appears to combine both appreciations. However, if one takes seriously the phrase "essentially he is something else," which "you do not get to see in this life," it sounds disturbingly like the view that differences are "a disguise," that they mask the morally relevant self. Such a view would undermine the verbal assurances Kierkegaard gives about appreciating differences; he would be acknowledging differences but would not be allowing a positive appreciation of them in this life. The result is that only essence would remain morally relevant.

In an effort to supplement and refine those correct readings of *Works of Love*, which see both affirmations of concreteness and abstraction, I am trying to account for these contrasting emphases on difference and commonality by highlighting the strategic importance of the precise location of claims in the text. I have suggested that a focus on the metaphors of blindness and vision (closed eyes and seeing) that are used throughout *Works of Love* alerts us to separate textual centers of attention to ethical abstraction and ethical concreteness. The key to resolving the apparent contradiction lies in drawing a careful distinction between two rhetorical contexts—one, the context in which the unconditionality and scope of the commandment are legislatively analyzed, and the other, the context in which the manner of the command's fulfillment is described as outward, particular, concrete, and distinctive. The two contexts of discussion are in effect a context that emphasizes abstract obligation and one that emphasizes concrete, distinctive response. For example, Kierkegaard's emphasis on the essential human nature, which we do not see in this life, is in the context of describing the unconditional scope of the commandment, whereas the reference to loving the differences comes in the context of fulfillment. Even for the word "essentially" we can find different uses in different contexts: essential human sameness is highlighted in the context of the description of the commandment as rule, whereas in the context of fulfillment, beginning in 1:IV, Kierkegaard complicates the notion of what is essential when he notes that "the beloved, the friend, is of course a human being also in the more ordinary sense and exists as such for the rest of us, but *for you he should exist essentially only as the beloved*, if you are to fulfill the duty of loving the person you see" (p. 165; emphasis mine).

A further layer of complexity is revealed if we go on to align the abstract context with the discussion of blindness (to distinction) and the concrete context with the demand of vision (of the other as he or she is). In the context of the *unconditional statement of the law*, the recommended blindness is blindness to concrete distinctions that obscure the vision of an admittedly abstract commonality. In the abstraction of unconditional obligation, differences only deceive; in this context, the metaphor for the morally relevant object is the "common watermark" (WL, p. 89) on the sheets of paper.[46] By looking closely at the situations that form the contrast to the blindness that Kierkegaard recommends, I have shown that blindness to distinctions is not inconsistent with the "partiality" of a concrete and distinctive loving response. What is at issue in the context of the statement of the law is blindness to what would prompt exclusion, and this does not entail blindness to concrete needs. In the context of *fulfilling the commandment of love in actuality*, concrete differences are not to be ignored; we are not to look behind or beneath them; we do not need to discard a façade to see clearly. In this context the metaphor for the morally relevant object is the distinctive message on a sheet of paper, which, rather than the watermark, indicates what particular response is appropriate. In this context of "actuality" (description of loving response), we find both celebration of distinctiveness and commitment to challenge; hence, we find an emphasis on vision of concrete needs. The blindness recommended here is called blindness to defect, but it is explained as blindness to fantasy and abstraction. It should be clear that any talk of a love that is challenging means (1) that we are not blind to moral defect and (2) that people "as they are" does not refer to the abstraction of personhood. In sum, one context of discussion focuses on the commandment's scope and unconditionality as a way of precluding that anyone can be excluded from being the object of obligation or the subject of obligation; in that context Kierkegaard emphasizes blindness to distinctions. The other context of discussion focuses on the substantive response of fulfillment of the love command; in that context, Kierkegaard requires a clear, honest, inclusive vision of the person just as he or she is.

Finally, one more variation is possible in which we recognize that both contexts actually imply moral vision, that is, the converse of blindness to distinction is concrete vision of kinship, and the converse of what Kierkegaard calls blindness to imperfection is concrete vision of the other just as he or she is. These contexts of discussion could also be considered as two different levels of discussion—a meta-level discussion of a rule and a first-order level of discussion that exemplifies applications.

It should be noted that the two rhetorical contexts I have proposed are not the same as the contexts of universality and particularity since the concept of particularity does not necessarily capture the dimension of concreteness, which is important; as we saw earlier, particulars can be treated abstractly, as loci of rationality or free agency. In addition, this distinction between a context of discussion that precludes exclusion and a context of substantive response does more to explain how affirmations of essentiality and affirmations of concreteness could be consistently incorporated within one account than does an appeal to 'the way the universal is expressed in the particular'; such an appeal has little explanatory value (it is, after all, paradoxical). Moreover, what need to be reconciled are commitments concerning universality (sameness) and concreteness (distinctiveness) made within the first series itself, not only different commitments in each series, so I have located the shift in contexts within the first series.

This detailed attention to the fourth deliberation has revealed the appreciation of concreteness in Kierkegaard's account of the Christian ethic of love. Moreover, my reconstruction of a contrast between the rhetorical contexts of the abstract unconditionality of the commandment and its concrete fulfillment provides a way in which these two emphases can be consistently joined. Thus far, I have argued that *Works of Love* contains resources for an understanding of impartiality that allows moral attention to concrete difference (and hence an interested impartiality), and I have also accounted for the contrasting emphases on commonality and difference in terms of their strategic location. I have also suggested that the image of "closed eyes" or "blindness," which is used in contrasting ways in the two contexts of discussion, provides a fruitful point of departure for exploring the relevance of concrete difference (dissimilarity, and distinction).

Genuine love, in this account, amounts to an honest, nonselective vision of concrete individuals, focusing on them "as they are" rather than trimmed to our measure or imagined according to our wishes. The recognition of the two rhetorical contexts for discussion of moral blindness that I have identified does not obviate the difficulty of fulfilling the commandment, but it may dissolve a perceived inconsistency in the love ethic itself. The love ethic remains an "offense" because it "wrenches open the lock of self-love," not because it exhibits a contradiction. Moreover, in the end, it seems that Kierkegaard sees vision as primary in the Christian ethic commanded by God: "If you want to love me, then love the people you see; what you do for them, you do for me" (WL, p. 160).[47]

chapter eight

Love's Debt

"Our Duty to Remain in Love's Debt to One Another" (V)

As the preceding chapters have shown, Kierkegaard maintains a forthright commitment to seeing God's love for us as an absolute, radically pure 'gift.' God's love for us, of which creation is the first example, is not something that we could ever earn or merit, nor is it something to which we could ever be entitled. As absolutely originary, preceded by nothing that implies indebtedness, God's gift of love is able to be contrasted, unproblematically, with the fulfillment of a debt. In the realm of love between human beings, however, the notion of gift assumes a problematical dimension when we recognize that any gift we give to another is only possible because we have already been gifted; we are always already embedded and implicated in a network of both physical and spiritual indebtedness. Rodolphe Gasché points out, "the donor is always already a *donnée*,"[1] and this is true whether or not we subscribe to a theistic worldview since, at the very least, we are indebted to our parents and to our society. For this reason, it is not so easy in speaking of our love for others to see gift and debt as mutually exclusive. The commonsense contrast between "gift" and "debt" that is suggested in the opening paragraph of Ralph Waldo Emerson's essay on "Gifts"—that "it is always so pleasant to be generous, though very vexatious to pay debts"[2]—may be psychologically accurate, but the line between the two is not always a clear one.

This recognition informs Kierkegaard's strategy in the deliberations: although he will go on in *Works of Love* to discuss our love explicitly in terms of giving to another, calling attention to various ways in which gifts can be given and received and raising questions about the kind of relation that obtains between giver and receiver (questions about mutuality, reciprocity, symmetry, and gratitude, for example), he restricts the focus in this deliberation (1:V) to the way in which love for another needs first to be acknowledged as a "debt," indeed an "infinite debt." In the process of exploring this provocative proposal, I will continue to refer to Emmanuel Levinas, who similarly appeals to the notion of "infinite" debt to the other (the stranger, the poor, and the neighbor) and who insightfully appreciates the relation between debt and gift: "I did not know myself so rich, but I no longer have the right to keep anything."[3] My hope is that their accounts may, in their distinctiveness, mutually illuminate each other on the notion of "infinite" obligation to the neighbor.

I. Our Debt to the Other

One of Kierkegaard's first allusions to the notion of a debt comes early in *Works of Love*, when he suggests that "your friend, your beloved, your child, or whoever is an object of your love has a claim upon an expression of it also in words if it actually moves you inwardly" (p. 12). Although we do not like to speak about debt with respect to those we love, he suggests that we do owe those we love an outward expression of our love. But what about a debt to those we do not love— do we owe everyone love? In the fourth deliberation Kierkegaard spoke of our duty to love those we see as "an outstanding debt to which God obligates you" (p. 163). Since he heads this fifth deliberation with the Pauline text "Owe no one anything, except to love one another" (Romans 13:8), he sees the notion of love as a debt to everyone as part of the scriptural message.

At this point we might ask why we *owe* another human being anything at all. Clearly, Kierkegaard believes that God commands us to give to the other, but God's command does not in itself create a situation of indebtedness to the other (although it might suggest that we owe God something). Kierkegaard also believes that we have been given everything we have by God, but being given a gift from God does not in itself create a debt to others. Although it is good to pass on gifts, it would be hard to say that we owe others the gifts that we have been given. Kierkegaard's only attempt to explain why he finds the scriptural and Lutheran notion of owing a debt to others an apt expression is found just before his reference in the fourth deliberation to the "outstanding debt" to others to which God obligates us: "Usually people piously warn against wasting God's gifts, but what gift of God is comparable to love, which he implanted in the human heart—alas, and then to see it wasted in this way!" (WL, p. 163). One does not, as some people believe, waste love by loving those who are imperfect or weak; such love, Kierkegaard says, is "applying one's love, making use of it." The tragedy comes about when we fail to love those we see; that, he insists, is "truly to waste it." We have an obligation not to waste God's gifts, the highest of which is the love implanted in us, so we have an obligation to exercise this love. Although we are obliged not to waste the God-given gift of material prosperity (i.e., we are obliged to use it), the gift in itself does not create a debt to share it with others. The God-given gift of love, on the contrary, is wasted if we do not exercise it in relation to others.

Another rationale for the notion of debt comes directly from Kierkegaard's Lutheran inheritance. In Luther's reading of the seventh commandment, 'Thou shalt not steal,' we are commanded to have "a willingness to help and serve all men with one's own means," even our "enemies and opponents."[4] Luther cites St. Ambrose: "Feed the hungry: if you do not feed him, then as far as you are concerned, you have killed him," and he concludes: "If your enemy needs you and you do not help him when you can it is the same as if you had stolen what belonged to him, for *you owe him your help.*"[5] The assumption that Luther found in Ambrose, that not giving to others is equivalent to stealing from them, means that since we owe it to them not to steal from them, we can be said, equivalently, to owe it to them to give to them. Although Kierkegaard does not go so far as to say that not giving to others is equivalent to stealing from them, one could argue that this Lutheran legacy explains the ease with which Kierkegaard employs the notion of debt.

II. Our Infinite Debt to the Other

Kierkegaard, however, goes beyond saying that we have a debt to others. He highlights our duty to remain *always* in the debt of love to others, and thus he introduces the theme of a never-ending duty to remain in debt, or an "infinite debt." He puts before us the challenging notion of love as an infinite debt with decisive typographical emphasis, stating that *"the one who loves by giving, infinitely, runs into infinite debt"* (WL, p. 177). Explicitly acknowledging that it might strike us as counterintuitive to hear love described as "an infinite debt" that is generated in the lover, he reminds us of the phenomenological truth that we may well have experienced, the admittedly "amazing" truth that "when a person is gripped by love, he feels that this is like being in an infinite debt." He admits that "ordinarily we say that a person who is loved runs into debt by being loved," and he concedes that although "this is indeed true," still "such talk is all too reminiscent of an actual bookkeeping arrangement: a debt is incurred and it must be paid off in installments." What is shocking is that he is not "speaking about that, about *running into debt by receiving"; "no,"* he insists, "the one who loves runs into debt." He proceeds to formulate his claim with great care: "To give a person one's love is, as has been said, the highest a person can give—and yet by giving it he runs into an infinite debt. Therefore we can say that *this is the distinctive characteristic of love: that the one who loves by giving, infinitely, runs into infinite debt.*"[6]

Kierkegaard denies that he is doing anything more than simply explicating the traditional Christian commandment's affirmation of the nature of genuine human love: Christianity, he claims, "says exactly the same thing about remaining in debt as a noble human love says ardently, but it says it in a totally different way. Christianity does not make a big fuss about it at all. . . . It says it is a duty and thereby removes from love everything that is inflamed, everything that is momentary, everything that is giddy" (WL, p. 188). Kierkegaard is here referring once again to one of the functions of the commandment noted earlier: "If the love in us human beings is not so perfect that this wish [to remain in love's debt] is our wish, then the duty will help us to remain in debt" (p. 179). This "shall" reinforces our efforts and encourages us.

One important feature of this deliberation is that Kierkegaard is locating our infinite debt, or the infinite requirement of love, in relation to the human other rather than to God. Earlier in *Works of Love* he had spoken of our infinite debt to God (pp. 102–3, 132), and his journal comments are ambiguous as to whether he is referring to our love for God or our love for the neighbor. But in this deliberation there is no doubt about the reference—it is the neighbor to whom I owe an infinite debt of love.

III. Without Repayment, Bookkeeping, or Calculation

What is at stake in this radical notion of "infinite" debt is that we remain *always* in debt, and always in an *unlessening* debt; the one who loves can never say 'enough.' This rules out certain ways of loving, and Kierkegaard's examples usefully clarify the irrelevance of certain responses in relation to an "infinite" debt. He asks what we would think of someone who, after that person had done something that "was humanly speaking, so magnanimous, so self-sacrificing" that we stood in awe, "added, 'See, now I have paid my debt'" (WL, p. 178). "Would this not be," he asks, "speaking unlovingly, coldly, and harshly?" But the refusal to admit that our debt is infinite is just another form of this unloving attitude. Resistance to the idea that our debt to another is infinite implies that we want to give with this unspoken addition: "See, now I have paid my debt" or at least made an "installment payment" on it (p. 182).

Just as "an actual bookkeeping arrangement is inconceivable, is the greatest abomination to love," so too is the idea of "calculation"; such categories are incommensurable with the category of infinity. Indeed, Kierkegaard thinks it is clear that "to calculate with an infinite quantity is impossible, because to calculate is to make finite"; thus the one who loves "does not waste a moment calculating" (WL, p. 181).[7] When Kierkegaard rejects the notion of calculation, he also rejects the notion of "comparison" (p. 182). If I appeal to "comparison" to see how much I am loving or how much another is loving, then love is "dwelling on itself"; he compares such self-absorbing analysis to the attempt of an arrow in flight to reflect on its motion (p. 182). One gets a more graphic sense of how deadly such an attempt is if we extend his analogy to a bird in flight: in the attempt to assess precisely where it is and how it is doing 'by comparison' at that particular instant, the forward thrust, the momentum, will cease; and the bird, like the arrow, will simply fall to the earth. When we try to compare our love with the love others have or with deeds of love we have previously done, we fall—out of love; in Kierkegaard's words, when one is "counting and weighing, he is starting to get out of the debt, or in immense self-satisfaction perhaps is al-

ready more than out of the debt—that is, more than out of love" (p. 183).[8] He
concludes that "in comparison, everything is lost, love is made finite, the debt is
made something to repay—exactly like any other debt" (p. 183); hence, "for his
own sake the lover wishes to remain in debt; he does not wish exemption from
any sacrifice, far from it" (p. 178).

Clearly, Kierkegaard is rejecting an economic model in which our love is seen
as repayment on a debt, an "installment payment" that lessens the debt. When we
consider later deliberations, we will see that he goes even further, suggesting that
genuine love of another cannot *demand* any *repayment* by or from the other, even
the repayment of the other's love. His polemic against repayment is two-
pronged: he rejects the idea of love understood as repayment on a debt to another, as well as the idea of love as motivated by the thought of repayment
from the other. The latter issue will require us to consider in detail whether even
gratitude and mutual love are ruled out by such a stark notion of love; indeed, it
will eventually raise the question of whether a work of love is necessarily validated either by a lack of gratitude or by the positive presence of opposition or
persecution—or more provocatively put, whether love is invalidated by a grateful or loving response. We will begin to consider such questions when we arrive
at Kierkegaard's examination of the relevance of the response of the loved one
(which he first alludes to in the second deliberation in the second series), but for
the moment we will remain with the challenge inherent in the notion of an "infinite debt" to the other.

IV. An Infinite and Fulfillable Requirement

Kierkegaard is aware of the human temptation to think that the "infinite" requirement is meant to be motivating precisely by being falsely exaggerated, deceiving us about its expectations. "After all," he notes, "many people think that
the Christian message (i.e., to love one's neighbor as oneself) is purposely a little
too rigorous—something like the household alarm clock which runs a half-hour
fast so one does not get up too late in the morning."[9] Such people think the demand is inflated in order to be a pedagogical device, unfulfillable but usefully motivating. Others, like Sigmund Freud, will later agree that the demand of the love
commandment is inflated, but they will not find it a useful motivational tool;
rather they will point to the excessiveness of the demand as cruel and dysfunc-
tionally guilt producing.[10]

To speak of "infinite" demand is not, for Kierkegaard, an instance of rhetorical hyperbole that can motivate us despite its unfulfillability. The demand, he insists, remains both *infinite* and *fulfillable:* "To pare down the requirement in order
to be able to fulfill it better (as if this were earnestness . . .)—to this Christianity in its deepest essence is opposed."[11] In an 1850 assessment of his authorship, Kierkegaard remarks: "It certainly is no exaggeration for infinity's requirement, the *infinite* requirement, to be presented—*infinitely*"; indeed, only when
it is "heard and affirmed in all its infinitude" does grace offer itself.[12] "Christianity," he asserts, "is gospel——but, but, nevertheless Christ declares that he

has not come to abolish the law but to fulfill it, make the law more rigorous, as in the Sermon on the Mount."[13] Here Christ's fulfilling of the law is precisely what makes it more rigorous. For example, as we will see later,[14] part of this rigorousness involves the Christian "like-for-like," according to which God measures out to us the same as we measure out to others; it involves the "heightened inequality" that magnifies our faults when we find fault with our neighbor. The demand is, nevertheless, *fulfillable, but only because it has been fulfilled:* "Christ's own life as the prototype was the very fulfilling of the law."[15] Here Christ's fulfilling of the law is precisely what allows us to fulfill it. Following in Luther's footsteps, Kierkegaard reminds us that we are like the child who can give his parents a gift, but only because they have already given him an allowance.[16]

The idea that the requirement is infinite is found in Kierkegaard's journals as well, where the judgment that "the requirement is and remains the same, unaltered, perhaps even sharpened under grace" is followed by the conclusion that even with grace there is "not the slightest abatement of the law's demand."[17] The discussion that intervenes might seem to imply that with the advent of grace it is no longer a matter of "fulfilling the requirement of the law," but Kierkegaard's point is not that we are no longer obligated to strive to fulfill the law; the point is that grace frees us from an unendurable anxiety in which our "salvation is linked to the condition of the fulfilling the requirement of the law," which so undermines us that we become "utterly incapable of fulfilling even the least of the law's requirements."[18]

As if in anticipation of the one-sided and cruel misreading of the demand's infinitude, which follows if we take it out of the context of grace, Kierkegaard stresses the gentleness of the law: "God is no cruel creditor and mortgage holder, nor should a human being presume to want to be more than a human being."[19] The poignancy of this recognition is obvious in his warning against exaggerating the religious demand, making it "too rigorous and too morose."[20]

Earlier I stated that for Kierkegaard the demand is infinite yet fulfillable, but only because it has been fulfilled. Christ's fulfilling of the law is precisely what allows us to fulfill it. However, we still need to ask: how do *we* fulfill it?

V. Fulfillment as Imitation

At one level, fulfillment of the command is made possible by Christ's fulfilling of the law. At another level, however, we need to make sense of how we relate to Christ's fulfillment, how Christ's fulfillment can be our fulfillment. The possibility of fulfilling the command is implied in the Christian directive to *imitate* Christ. In considering the way in which Kierkegaard's commitment to the imitation of Christ bears on the content of the command to love the neighbor (in chapter 5, section IV, B, 4), I noted that Kierkegaard's goal was "to apply the Christian requirement, imitation, in all its infinitude, in order to place the emphasis in the direction of grace." That discussion is useful background to this examination of *fulfillment* through imitation.

Since Christ is "the prototype oriented to the universally human, of which everyone is capable," fulfillment of the Christian requirement is imitation "of which everyone is capable" because of grace.[21] When Kierkegaard writes that "as the prototype Christ gives absolute expression to that which naturally no human being achieves: absolutely holding to God in all things,"[22] it is not clear whether we should focus mainly on the term "naturally"—and thus read the claim as allowing that supernaturally, *with grace*, we can imitate Christ's perfect "holding to God in all things"—or whether Kierkegaard means that we can never (even with grace) succeed in being as perfect as was Christ in his human nature's holding onto God. In either case, whether or not Kierkegaard thinks we can succeed in being as perfect as was Christ in his human nature,[23] if the commandment requires an imitation "of which everyone is capable" we can infer that the only imitation of Christ that is required of us is possible for us as grace-filled humans.

We are obligated to imitate Christ, but what did Christ do? We saw in the earlier discussion of imitation that we imitate Christ when we follow his example of compassionate response to those in need. Kierkegaard reminds us of that here: "When it is a duty to remain in the debt of love to one another, *then to remain in debt is not a fanatical expression, is not an idea about love, but is action*" (WL, p. 187).[24] Remaining in the debt of love is not only not "fanatical" but also not theoretical: the debt is fulfilled in "action." At issue is "an *action* and not an expression about, not a reflective view of, love"; it is "a new task."[25] We must "occupy love incessantly in action" (p. 188). Early on Kierkegaard shared Nietzsche's fear that Christianity as it is practiced debilitates its adherents: "When I look at a goodly number of particular instances of the Christian life, it seems to me that Christianity, instead of pouring out strength upon them—yes, in fact, in contrast to paganism—such individuals are robbed of their manhood by Christianity and are now like the gelding compared to the stallion."[26] Kierkegaard now insists, however, that like a skilled rider true Christianity "does not take the fieriness away from the horse, but by controlling the fieriness only refines it"; thus, "Christianity knows how to control love and to teach it that there is a task at every moment" (p. 189). Echoing the message of IIIA, he writes that "love in all its expressions turns outward towards people, where indeed it has its object and its tasks" (p. 189).

Sometimes Kierkegaard seems to make a Kantian move by suggesting that God can take our striving for the required perfection; he tells us that *"Christianly* the emphasis does not fall so much upon to what extent or how far a person succeeds in meeting or fulfilling the requirement, if he actually is striving, as it is upon his getting an impression of the requirement in all its infinitude so that he rightly learns to be humbled and to rely upon grace."[27] But Kierkegaard is not, like Kant, making a point about our temporal succession and God's atemporal glance.[28] Kierkegaard's point is that the striving must be both "actual" and unending—we can never stop or say we have done enough—and only this kind of striving amounts to "getting an impression of the requirement in all its infinitude" and being appropriately "humbled" to know our total reliance on grace.

Kierkegaard certainly shares some of Luther's sensitivity to our anxiety in the face of the law: The leniency or gospel in the law consists in the fact that

Christianity thinks somewhat along these lines: It is anxiety which makes him unable to do it; it is anxiety which makes him totally incapable of doing it—take the anxiety away, and then you will see that he can do it all right . . . at least a good share of it. It is the same with Christianity and grace. Take away this anxiety for the salvation of his soul—this is what makes him incapable. This is removed by grace—you are saved by grace, by grace through faith. Take this anxiety away, and you will see that he can do it, all right.[29]

That is, we can strive when we are not despairing. Kierkegaard tells us that "Christianity's idea is that precisely [the idea of grace] should give a man the courage and the desire to exert himself [so that he] can then venture all the more intrepidly."[30] But he goes on to lament how instead of "'grace' as the basis of courage," "we have used 'grace' to prevent acting."

The point, then, is the attenuation of anxiety rather than mitigation of the law; we do not have to want to be more than a human being to fulfill the Christian requirement. This means that the command is fulfillable, but only if it is seen in its entirety, that is, in the context of grace; outside that context it makes no sense to say that we can fulfill the requirement.

VI. Infinite Responsibility for the Other—A Livable Ethic?

The combination of the claim that our duty to love is infinite and the claim that such love is to be expressed in action amounts to the view that the love commandment requires infinite practical responsibility for the other. The claim that the practical responsibility is infinite may sound extreme: can one live such an ethic? Can one ever fulfill an infinite debt or an infinite demand to love, in a practical way, the neighbor?

As we saw in chapter 3, Emmanuel Levinas has proposed an ethic that sounds similar to Kierkegaard's with respect to our responsibility for others independent of preference; it also sounds similar with respect to the infinitude of the obligation. Once again, I suggest that it is useful to compare their commitments in tandem. Throughout his writings, Levinas argues that we are infinitely obligated to the other, that we are called, without our choosing, to a life of responsibility and responsiveness to an infinite demand. He writes repeatedly that "the *I* before the Other is infinitely responsible" and that "the proximity of a neighbor is my responsibility for him."[31] He describes responsibility for the other as a "passion,"[32] indeed as the "infinite passion of responsibility,"[33] and he sees responsibility as totally inclusive—"for my neighbor, for the other man, for the stranger or sojourner."[34]

Levinas's second major work, *Otherwise than Being or Beyond Essence*, encompassing his seminal essay "Substitution," provides the most fruitful counterpart to Kierkegaard with respect to the infinitude of the obligation. There Levinas, like Kierkegaard, explicitly uses the metaphor of 'bookkeeping': he condemns "strict book-keeping" in relation to others, as well as the "balance of accounts in an order where responsibilities correspond exactly to liberties taken, where they compensate for them," and he argues that "freedom in the genuine sense can be only a contestation of this book-keeping by a gratuity."[35] In responding to the demand placed on us by the other, we "open an unlimited 'deficit,' in which the self spends itself without counting, freely"; our "responsibility for another [is] an unlimited responsibility which the strict book-keeping of the free and non-free does not measure."[36] Similarly, the essay "God and Philosophy" highlights how we are always "already in debt," how everything in us is "debt and donation."[37]

What is at stake for both Kierkegaard and Levinas in rejecting calculation and bookkeeping is guaranteeing that the notion of infinite debt to the other is not diluted or mitigated. Levinas's account of the practical living out of an infinite demand can shed some light on Kierkegaard's understanding of infinite responsibility. Levinas echoes the implications of Kierkegaard's notion of an "infinite debt" of love to the other: "There is an incessant solicitude for solicitude . . . [that is] as responsible, I am never finished with emptying myself of myself. There is infinite increase in this exhausting of oneself."[38] In fact, he insists, "the more I am just the more I am responsible; one is never quits with regard to the Other."[39] When asked if there is "an infinity in the ethical exigency in that it is insatiable?" Levinas responds forthrightly: "Yes. It is the exigency of holiness. At no time can one say: I have done all my duty."[40]

Levinas highlights the rigor of the demand—it is insatiable, inexhaustible—at the same time as he claims that it is in fact able to be fulfilled. When he was challenged with the question "Is it really possible to fulfill such a radical demand?" his answer was yes, "I do think that the *unlimited* responsibility for another . . . could have a translation into history's concreteness," or it took this form: You are fulfilling it now, or you do fulfill it in the simplest acts of kindness to the other.[41]

Levinas's formulations suggest a way to reconcile the tension between the fulfillment and the infinitude of a demand, and this can be clarified by the ambiguity in the notion of "fulfillment," which I think parallels the ambiguity that Kant called to our attention in the notion of the "highest." In his *Critique of Practical Reason,* Kant focuses on the concept of the "highest good" (*Summum Bonum*) and notes that "the concept of the 'highest' contains an ambiguity which, if not attended to, can occasion unnecessary disputes"—that is, "the 'highest' can mean the 'supreme' (*supremum*) or the 'perfect' (*consummatum*)."[42] In other words, one can, roughly speaking, distinguish between a good that achieves its qualitative standard and a good that is completed. Virtue is not the "entire" good for a human being, Kant insists; the entire, consummated good requires happiness as well. Obviously, Kant is talking about a completion in terms of the presence of both elements of the highest good, but we can transpose his distinction between the supreme and the perfect to the case of fulfilling a duty. One could say that, for Kant, the perfection of a moral act is achieved when one acts with the incentive of duty as the determining motivation—I can fulfill the law perfectly at this moment if and only if I perform the act in this way. The act is perfectly moral if performed rightly; there are no degrees of morality in this respect. The completion of my duty, however, is a separate question; there is always, as long as I live, more to do, another work to be performed lovingly. In Levinas's words, it is an infinite commandment ("I am never finished," I am "never quits," and at "no time can one say I have done all my duty"), yet it can be fulfilled.

This distinction shows how the duty can be absolutely radical yet fulfillable: although it is an inexhaustible duty (and so cannot be fulfilled in the sense of completed), one can at a given moment perform a perfect act of love (and so fulfill it in the sense of meeting its demand perfectly at a given time). Levinas clearly thinks the command is fulfillable in the latter sense. Such a distinction, as employed by Levinas, seems effectively to obviate the criticism that such an ethic is unlivable. Whereas we might wonder at first whether Kierkegaard's Lutheran commitments would allow him to believe that an act of love could ever be perfect, it seems appropriate to extrapolate a positive reply from his claim that the Christian demand is fulfillable—with grace (although unfulfillable without grace). Moreover, Kierkegaard does indicate something rather similar to Levinas's answer: "In everything done for you by the one who loves, in the least little triviality as well as in the greatest sacrifice, there is always love along with it" (WL, p. 181). Again, he notes that "the least little expression of love is infinitely greater than all sacrifices, and all sacrifices are infinitely less than the least little bit in part-payment on the debt!" (p. 182). In the light of Levinas and Kant we can reconstruct and clarify a Kierkegaardian answer to the objection that his ethic is unlivable.[43]

We can also find reason outside of *Works of Love* to think that Kierkegaard assumes this distinction between perfect and complete fulfillment of the commandment. For example, Johannes Climacus suggests that Christianity requires "infinite passion" or "infinite subjectivity,"[44] and contemporary commentators charge the impossibility of such a rigorousness requirement. Robert M. Adams, for example, argues that Kierkegaard's Climacan proposal of a life lived with "infinite passion," which he construes as a "striving . . . in which, with the greatest possible intensity of feeling, one continually makes the greatest possible sacrifices on the smallest possible chance of success," is "an impossible ideal."[45] He writes: "Certainly much religious thought and feeling places a very high value on sacrifice and on passionate intensity. But the doctrine that it is desirable to increase without limit, or to the highest possible degree (if there is one) the cost and risk of a religious life is less plausible (to say the least) than the view that *some* degree of cost and risk may add to the value of a religious life. The former doctrine would set the religious interest at enmity with all other interests, or at least with the best of them."[46]

The charge that Climacus's "all or nothing view" about passion and sacrifice is an impossible and undesirable ideal is a version of the charge that the "infinite" requirement of Christianity is an impossible and undesirable ideal. To be fair to Kierkegaard in this regard, we should note that Anti-Climacus, the most idealized Christian in Kierkegaard's corpus, offers a description that suggests that Kierkegaard managed to capture the dialectical nature of the "infinite requirement." Anti-Climacus writes that "what it means in the strictest sense to be a Christian, is to confess honestly before God where he is so that he might still worthily accept the grace that is offered to every imperfect person—that is, to everyone. And then, nothing further—then, as for the rest, let him do his work and rejoice in it, love his wife and rejoice in her, joyfully bring up his children, love his fellow beings, rejoice in life."[47] What is normatively urged is not a matter of extreme psychological engagement to the exclusion of other concerns: "The requirements of ideality," which "should be heard, be heard again and again in their entire infinitude," can be "required of everyone" precisely because they command a deepening of our joy in life, rather than a compartmentalization or alternation of moments of intense subjectivity with moments of ordinary daily life. To repeat, it looks as if Kierkegaard feels at home with the distinction between perfect fulfillment and complete fulfillment.

VII. Infinitude, Alterity, and Offense

When we look at Kierkegaard's account in the light of Levinas's, it becomes clear that both of them are acutely sensitive to the ways in which even those who see relation as essential to subjectivity can interpret the claim that 'one becomes a self through an other' so that, their protestations notwithstanding, it amounts to a self-serving, instrumental use of the other to enhance ourselves. Both men have at the center of their projects a condemnation of arbitrary, selective love—as well as a condemnation of a self-serving appropriation of difference—and everything in their accounts of relationship is at the service of this attack on selfish self-love.[48] It is clear that for Levinas, the attack on self-love is his way of emphasizing the alterity of the other, of precluding a reduction of the other to oneself or an assimilation of the other to the same. Though we might not initially think of Kierkegaard as a champion of the alterity of the other, such a reading of his attack on self-love becomes plausible when we consider in tandem Kierkegaard's and Levinas's shared vehement attack on the variety of ways in which we disguise self-love, on the subtle ways in which we attempt to reduce the other to the self (the same). Similarly, Levinas's emphasis on the "height" of the other and the inability to claim reciprocity are presented as a way of protecting the alterity of the other—the infinitude of the other, the transcendence of the other. Thus, the rationale of Levinas's account alerts us to some deeper commitments that Kierkegaard may share with him; it suggests that it might be possible to read Kierkegaard's emphasis on the infinite debt as similarly in the service of safeguarding the alterity, the irreducibility, of the other.

My presentation thus far of Levinas's commonality with Kierkegaard on issues of fulfillment of infinite demand and the radical alterity of the other is in tension with most of Levinas's explicit evaluations of Kierkegaard's thought, and this needs to be explained. Admittedly, Levinas acknowledged finding an ally in Kierkegaard for a host of beliefs.[49] Nevertheless, Levinas was extremely critical of what he saw as a subordination of the ethical in Kierkegaard's writings, such as that implied in the category of a "teleological suspension of the ethical" in *Fear and Trembling*.[50] This is not the place to decide whether Levinas's commitment to the "trace of God" similarly qualifies the absolute priority of the ethic he espouses and reduces the divergence between him and Kierkegaard;[51] what we can say for sure is that Levinas's concentration on the account of the ethical found in Kierkegaard's pseudonymous writings (*Fear and Trembling* and *Either/Or*) obscures the commonality between them on the character of ethical relation to the other, which appears as soon as we turn to *Works of Love*. Here we find an understanding of ethics and the love relation that seems much closer in important ways to Levinas's own proposal. One can plausibly argue that the notion of the absolute and unconditional duty to love all without exception, dominating self-love's selfish preferential love (which we find in Kierkegaard), is parallel to the notion of absolute and unconditional and infinite demand placed on us by the very existence of the other (which we find in Levinas).[52]

In the end, the only alternative to not wanting to remain in debt is wanting love to be limited in its demands. But limited love is, for Kierkegaard, an oxymoron. Love lives in infinitude: "Love's element is infinitude, inexhaustibility, immeasurability" (WL, p. 180), and when it is treated as finite, it withers and dies, like a fish out of water. His conclusion is that "to be and to remain in an infinite debt is an expression of the infinitude of love; thus by remaining in debt it remains in its element" (p. 181). It sounds as if Kierkegaard is saying that the debt is infinite because love as such is infinite, but he goes on to suggest that the two infinitudes are separable and compound each other: when something "intrinsically infinite" (like love) also has "an infinite debt behind it," it is made infinite a second time—"the debt is the propelling force a second time" (p. 187). Although Kierkegaard denies that such a doubled infinitude is either "fanatical" or unduly "extreme," he does admit that it is radical—so radical that "we almost prefer to warn," he says, rather than to "entice anyone" (p. 197).

In other words, Christianity properly understood is something to be warned against because it is coextensive with "offense" (WL, p. 198).[53] Kierkegaard claims that the Gospel message must always be accompanied by the announcement of the "final danger"—namely, the "double danger" (pp. 192, 194, 204) that if we love, we will "fare badly in the world," that "good is rewarded with hate, contempt, persecution" as well as with "ingratitude, opposition, and derision" (pp. 191, 192, 194). When he says that "self-denial that finds support in the world is not Christian self-denial" (p. 196), he is making the strong statement that the world's "opposition" is not contingently related to Christianity; but as we saw earlier, more often than not, he intends the only necessary condition to be that we are willing to suffer opposition (and this fits with his claim that it is a "danger").[54]

The "earnest conception" of Christianity's demand on us is in many ways terrifying, and so it should be—the Christian requirement should not be able to be accepted as a matter of course by those who are not willing to follow in the footsteps of Christ. Kierkegaard likens Christianity to "a very sharply honed two-edged instrument"—it is "in the human sense, an extremely dangerous good"—which we would not hand over to others without warning them of its potential danger (p. 198). Indeed, he can imagine that under certain conditions "the highest responsibility" might require him even to "preach *against* Christianity . . . in *Christian* sermons." The presentation of Christianity is a unique kind of recommendation; it cannot be directly recommended because "it does not recommend itself directly but first startles people—just as Christ recommended himself to the apostles by predicting in advance that for his sake they would be hated" (p. 199). The "opposition" and "persecution" of the world to which Kierkegaard often refers are not the goal of Christianity, but they are the consequence of following in Christ's footsteps. Such "opposition," however, is not the only reason we find it hard to want to remain in love's debt to the other. When we instinctively flinch in horror at the notion of an "infinite" debt to the other, when we desperately try to convince ourselves and others that it is only rational that there should be restrictions on love's scope or length or depth, we are reacting to our vision of the worst-case scenario—we fear that a commandment of love in terms of infinite debt effectively renders us subject to self-sacrifice without end or total self-annihilation. And Kierkegaard's ethic, like any ethic, needs to deal with this understandable terror.

VIII. The Limits of Love's Sacrifice

The "anxiety" that Kierkegaard refers to about fulfilling the law can be seen not only as anxiety about whether we CAN do all we think we should but also anxiety about the implications of what happens IF we strive that much—namely, the possibility that we may need to sacrifice ourselves utterly for the other, that there will be no place at which we can stop, no standard we can use to discriminate between demands of the other for which we ought to sacrifice ourselves and demands that should not require sacrifice. Are there no limits on the sacrifice of self that genuine love must endure? In what sense is my obligation to love unconditional, or as readers of Levinas often poignantly ask: "But if one fears for the Other and not for oneself, can one even live?" or 'Do I ever have a place in the sun?'[55] This is a version of what Gene Outka calls the "blank check objection," the charge that an ethic of love allows no limits to "self-exploitation"; the question at issue is whether "agape as equal regard in itself allow[s] for any way to differentiate between attention to another's needs and submission to his exploitation, and any warrant for resisting the latter?"[56] More broadly put, the objection is that whether or not another is actually trying to exploit us, there seems to be no way to put a limit on the self-sacrifice that attention to the other's needs might entail.

Addressing this question—of the character of the sacrifice love must make for the other and the possibility of limits on that sacrifice—is an indispensable part of evaluating Kierkegaard's ethic in *Works of Love*. The good news is that the challenge is not peculiar to Kierkegaard's ethic. It is a challenge to any ethic that bases love on the model of God's love for us; it asks whether the model of such a love without limit and without restriction can inform a livable ethic.[57] Although Kierkegaard's commitment to such a model is not new, his account provocatively presses us further than many others do because of its explicitness: how can the notion of any limits at all on self-sacrifice even come up if the debt to the neighbor is admittedly "infinite"? We shall see that Kierkegaard's response reveals important dimensions of the addition "as yourself" and invokes a strong contrast between love and justice.

A. The Limits Implied in the 'As Yourself'

1. Not More than Yourself

One part of Kierkegaard's resources for justifying some restrictions on self-sacrifice becomes apparent when he objects early in *Works of Love* to a hypothetical account of the love commandment that may well call up our deepest fears—an account that claims that our unconditional responsibility is to love the other *more than ourselves*. This raises the question of symmetry and asymmetry in the ethical relation, which I deal with in greater detail in chapter 15. For the moment I am concerned only with Kierkegaard's rejection of such asymmetry as it bears on the limits on self-sacrifice. Although Kierkegaard was not in a position to know of Levinas's twentieth-century elaboration of such an account, he nevertheless anticipated it in his discussion (in the second deliberation) of the love of neighbor 'as oneself.' When he asks: "Would this [love of neighbor as oneself] really be the highest; would it not be possible to love a person *more than oneself?*" (p. 18), he is in effect engaging Levinas's challenge.

At its heart Levinas's ethic elaborates a responsibility to the other in which "I am not his equal, I am forevermore subject to him": "I must always demand more of myself than of the other"; "the Other is higher than I am"; "I owe him everything."[58] He never abandons his early claim that "goodness consists in taking up a position in being such that the Other counts more than myself."[59] This list clearly catalogues a radical forgetfulness of self, one that Levinas himself calls a "miracle"—"the miracle of the ego (*moi*) which has got rid of the self (*soi*) and instead fears for the Other."[60] Our responsibility is to sacrifice for the other, to the point of "substituting" ourselves for the other,[61] if we can thereby help her or him. The question this raises is whether Christianity's "as yourself" shackles its love commandment, clips its wings, so to speak, so that love for another cannot soar to its possible heights.

Kierkegaard, himself often the target of charges of extremism and excessiveness, refuses to read the infinitude of the love commandment as requiring us to love another more than ourselves. Why? His explanation for this qualification is as follows: "There is only one whom a person can with the truth of eternity love more than himself—that is God. . . . A person should love God unconditionally *in obedience* and love him *in adoration*. It is ungodliness if any human being dares to love himself in this way, or dares to love another person in this way, or dares to allow another person to love him in this way" (WL, p. 19).

To appreciate what is at stake for him in condemning such "ungodliness," we should pay close attention to the examples he uses. To love others more than yourself would mean that you would be unwilling to refuse them anything they asked, even if you think it is harmful. To love others more than yourself is to fail to have an appropriate or due respect for them as equals and to have an uncritical concern for them—indeed, it is "adoration." What is being excluded here by Kierkegaard is very specific: "If you can perceive what is best for him better than he can, you will not be excused because the harmful thing was his own desire, was what he himself asked for. If this were not the case, it would be quite proper to speak of loving another person more than oneself, because this would mean, despite one's insight that this would be harmful to him, doing it *in obedience* because he demanded it, or *in adoration* because he desired it" (WL, p. 20).[62]

Kierkegaard makes clear that "it is by no means love to indulge human weakness."[63] Although he is making this point in the context of a reminder that we should not let others idolize us (by exempting us from our duties to them), it is plausible to think that the sacrifice we are obliged to make for others is also limited by this recognition. We are never allowed to obey another human unconditionally: if someone asks of you something that you, "precisely because you honestly loved, had in concern considered would be harmful to him, then you must bear a responsibility if you love by obeying instead of loving by refusing a fulfillment of the desire" (WL, p. 20). Such a relation to others, trying to love them more than yourself, is effectively not loving them at all; in this way, the "intoxicated expression—to love another person more than oneself "—which is the love celebrated by poets, is "secretly self-love" (p. 19).

Thus, in denying that we ought to love another more than ourselves, Kierkegaard is denying a particular kind of willingness to do or give whatever the other asks for when it is a "harmful thing," when our best judgment is that "this would be harmful to him" because we ought not to do that to ourselves. The "as yourself" here serves as an index to our love for the other. To love someone more than yourself would mean to accede to his or her wishes in adoring obedience, but Kierkegaard says that "you expressly have no right to do this" (WL, p. 20).

Consider the test case in which we are faced with a demand from another that as far as we can conscientiously judge is contrary to the person's best interest—for example, an addict's pressing demands for more heroin. Does unconditional love for others mean fulfilling all their desires or needs? Kierkegaard has no trouble in his ethic in concluding that he should not fulfill the addict's demand.[64] The explicitly theological warrant is that fulfilling the demand despite our best judgment that it would be harmful to the other would be equivalent to an obedience or adoration that is due only to God. But more important for our purposes here, the rejection of the "more than yourself" amounts to recommending that the crucial criterion is the determination of harm to the other.

It is worth considering at this point whether Levinas's position would require something more radical than Kierkegaard's—that is, whether when Levinas claims that one must love the neighbor more than the self, that the neighbor's needs always take precedence over yours and can even demand that you sacrifice yourself, he is advocating a higher standard of love than Kierkegaard is or perhaps recommending what Kierkegaard calls unloving "adoration" of the other? The only way to decide is to ask what Levinas would on his own terms actually recommend that we do in the heroin addict case. Like Kierkegaard, a Levinasian can plausibly argue that putting the other's needs first and above our own does not preclude, and certainly should involve, doing what we can to wean someone from self-destructive habits. And the rationale for that in Levinas's case is implicit in the way he reads the love commandment as the commandment not to kill, that is, not to contribute to harming the other. Although Kierkegaard may not thematize this rationale as graphically as Levinas does (for the prohibition on murder), he assumes this same justification for limits on self-exploitation.

Thus, for Kierkegaard, the "as yourself" generates at least one limit on what the other can require of us—a limit determined by reference to what would harm her or him, a limit whose index is the proper love of self. As such, our responsibility for the other is measured by appropriate care of self. This addresses one dimension of the "blank check" objection—the fear that there are absolutely *no* grounds for discriminating among demands placed on us by the other, and hence absolutely *no* way to limit one's sacrifice of self. There is at least one way. What if, however, the other's demand does not harm him or her but entails great sacrifice on our part? Is there ever a way in such a case—legitimately and lovingly—to put a limit on the sacrifice of self? Kierkegaard's response to this question highlights his commitments to equality and the love of self, and both of these have implications for the troubling remainder of the 'blank check' objection.

2. The Limits Implied by Equality

Kierkegaard's emphasis on the "as yourself" highlights the equality of the self and the other as children of God. By itself the commandment to love the other, without the addition of the "as yourself," reveals to me (if I judge it to be authoritative) that I am subject to God's commands; that is, I belong to God. It tells me that I am commanded, and therefore affirms my status as a creature, someone's creation. When the "as yourself" is added to the command to love the other, it reminds me that there is a "we" and we are both under the rubric of God's creation—we are equals before God. This emphasis on equality guarantees that we cannot exclude anyone from the scope of those we are unconditionally obliged to love. One implication of this for Kierkegaard is that the exclusion of no one means that *I too* am not excluded. Our equality precludes any prejudicing of myself in this relation. Kierkegaard often appeals to the standard of consistency, and in this case the upshot of applying the standard consistently is that I must love myself. That he explicitly thinks of consistency as an argument is clear when he claims that it would be a "contradiction" to exclude the beloved from the love command "since inasmuch as the neighbor is all people surely no one can be excluded" (WL, p. 61).[65] Thus, some restrictions on self-sacrifice will be generated when I apply this criterion to a situation.

B. The Limits Implied by the Value of the Gift of Createdness

Another way of applying the consistency criterion involves Kierkegaard's theological view of created-ness, or creation as God's gift—a gift to be valued, appreciated, and protected. He inherits a strong Lutheran appreciation of the gift of creation and the gratitude appropriate to it, noting that "'thanksgiving' is essentially the God-pleasing 'sacrifice'."[66] Modern accounts of the ethical concur in this rationale for valuing the self. Although he does not always seem to draw its implication, Levinas, too, is committed to the value of the gift of creation: "The marvel of creation does not only consist in being a creation *ex nihilo*, but in that it results in a being capable of receiving a revelation, learning that it is created, and putting itself in question. The miracle of creation lies in creating a moral being."[67] The miracle of creation is the I with the potential to become a self. We are guardians of potential selves, and our own createdness is the one with which we are most intimate and knowledgeable (most near and most neighbor). Although Kierkegaard does not use the language of "duties to the self" or "self-esteem," as other thinkers do, there is a sense in which cherishing the gift of creation in all its manifestations seems to include much of what is at stake in their idea of "self-respect" or "self-esteem." For example, Paul Ricoeur's ethic of reciprocity depends strongly on the notion of "self-esteem," which for him is the self's interpretation of itself, esteeming its "capacities" (rather than its achievements).[68] One could argue that Kierkegaard, too, sees the self's interpretation of itself as created as the source of self-esteem; although Ricoeur's Kantian-inspired model may well differ in significant ways from Kierkegaard's understanding of the self's capacities, it is like Kierkegaard's in allowing that the primacy of the other does not entail self-hatred.[69]

C. The Derived Limit on Self-Sacrifice—Providing for the Other

Still another way in which the notion of consistency can generate a restriction on the sacrifice of myself is to see it as deriving concern for the self from the need to be able to continue to give to the other—that is, a duty to maintain the self in order to have something to give to the other, to be responsible for the other. A responsibility to help others (e.g., to help them stand by themselves) requires that we do not allow ourselves to be so undermined that we cannot help others or accurately see them in their need. Paul Ricoeur makes the first point when he asks pointedly: "Must one not, in order to make oneself open, available, belong to oneself in a certain sense"; he highlights the second by suggesting that "resources of *goodness*" are freed in us by the other's initiative, and that someone who detests himself could not even hear "the injunction coming from the other."[70] Though it is often not apparent, Levinas has a similar commitment in that "my responsibility for all can and has to manifest itself also in limiting itself. The ego can, in the name of this unlimited responsibility, be called upon to concern itself also with itself."[71] He is implying that we must maintain ourselves in order to support the other; the I can only support the other if it has something to give.[72] Levinas makes this more concrete, reminding us that "love means, before all else, the welcoming of the other as *thou*"; he asks: "Can that welcome be carried out empty-handed?"[73] The theme of "incarnation" is crucial to Levinas's thought because it is "the body which makes giving possible," and for Levinas our neighbor's first needs are often as mundane as food and drink.[74]

D. Levinas and Kierkegaard—
Different Attitudes to Love of Self

Kierkegaard's interpretation of the love commandment, requiring that we love the neighbor 'as ourself,' sounds rather mild when we put it next to Levinas's claim that we should love the other more than ourselves. Is Kierkegaard's interpretation even compatible with an ethic of infinite duty to the other? Clearly Levinas would never have spoken as Kierkegaard did about love of self; instead, he described our activity in being responsible to the other in terms of "the self emptying itself of itself," highlighting how "the self is absolved of itself," "forgetful of itself," and "divesting itself, emptying itself of its own being."[75] Kierkegaard, in contrast, emphasizes that the little phrase "as yourself" implies that the commandment to love another assumes and requires genuine love of self, and he confirms this need by claiming that an independent whole self is a necessary condition of love because "without a *you* and an *I*, there is no love" (WL, p. 266). The limits on self-sacrifice or exploitation implied in the "as yourself" are the same limits implied in the need for a You and an I in the love relationship. Although Levinas refuses to affirm the love of self, he does assume that the I must maintain its integrity in a relation so that "the fullness of power in which the *sovereignty of the I maintains itself* extends to the Other, not in order to conquer it, but to support it"; moreover, the self is not destroyed by being put in question by the other but is rather engaged in a certain "tension."[76] Ultimately, one gains one's life by losing it: "In substitution my being that belongs to me and not to another is undone, and it is through this substitution that I am not 'another,' but me."[77] Nevertheless, for Levinas, the necessary attack on selfish self-love leaves no room for any salutary reminders about the need to love oneself properly. And he is no doubt right that it is dangerous to remind people who are inclined to be self-centered anyway that they must not forget to love themselves.

Why, then, despite Kierkegaard's equally uncompromising denunciation of selfish love (the subtle ways in which we reduce the other to the needs of the self), does he openly place himself in the potentially dangerous position of recommending the love of self? It is one thing to say in passing, being careful not to dwell on it, that the commandment says: 'You shall love your neighbor as yourself.' Why does Kierkegaard go further, reminding us in no uncertain terms that "if the commandment is properly understood it also says the opposite: *You shall love yourself in the right way.* Therefore, if anyone is unwilling to learn from Christianity to love himself in the right way, he cannot love the neighbor either" (WL, p. 22). Why does he say, with sadness: "Whoever has any knowledge of people will certainly admit that just as he has often wished to be able to move them to relinquish self-love, he has also had to wish that it were possible to teach them to love themselves" (p. 23). Whatever the reason, his conclusion is that we need to be reminded to let ourselves love ourselves because "the most dangerous traitor of all is the one every person has within himself," and there is as much "treachery" in "selfishly not willing to love oneself in the right way" as in "selfishly loving oneself" (p. 23).[78]

Perhaps what is at stake for Kierkegaard, what makes it worth insisting on this potentially dangerous addition to the commandment, is that the "as yourself" not only puts me and the other 'under God,' reminds me that there are two of us of equal status under God (as I suggested earlier), but also reminds me that I have been loved and therefore am able to love; that is, *the Author of my being is also the Source of love in me*. Kierkegaard's Lutheranism allows him to take seriously two variants of the commandment's "as yourself": (1) as you (ought to) love yourself and (2) as you yourself (have been loved). Not only does it remind us of the equality of the other, and so provide the standard for love of the neighbor (neither more nor less than proper self-love), but also the second variant reminds us of the essential Lutheran commitment—God has loved you first; God is the origin and source of the love in you which God commands you not to limit preferentially. I can only love because I am loved; I cannot love of my own resources, on my own initiative, so to speak. When the commandment exists without the reminder that we are loved and so are able to love, it could suggest that the individual is left to his own resources.[79] The "as yourself" reminds me both of my creation and of the gift of love to me, and so takes me out of myself, exteriorizes and desubjectifies my response to the other. It reminds me that God is the enabling source of love in me and so serves as well to de-center the self.

E. The Role of Justice

A third justification for the restriction on the sacrifice of self is the legitimacy or necessity of resisting exploitation for the sake of those others affected by the actions of the particular other with whom I am engaged.[80] This leads us to consider the concept of justice and Kierkegaard's view of the relation between love and justice.

The deliberation in the second series, "Love Does Not Seek Its Own" (2:IV), marks the first time that Kierkegaard calls attention to the realm of justice. He does it by contrasting justice sharply with love: "Justice is identified by giving each his due, just as it also in turn claims its own"; that is, "justice pleads the cause of its own, divides and assigns, determines what each can lawfully call his own, judges and punishes if anyone refuses to make any distinction between *mine* and *yours*" (WL, p. 265). He continues: "As soon as someone is defrauded of his own, or as soon as someone defrauds another of his own, justice intervenes, because it safeguards the common security in which everyone has his own, what he rightfully has." Although he does not say a lot about justice, since this is, after all, not a book about justice but about works of love, Kierkegaard does acknowledge the importance of its demands.[81] On the other hand, Kierkegaard sees love as a relationship in which "mine" and "yours" do not apply: keeping "the work of sacrificially giving of oneself in mind," he insists that *"there are no* mine *and* yours *in love"* since *"'mine' and 'yours' are only relational specifications of 'one's own'"* (p. 265). He adds later that "the one who truly loves . . . knows nothing about the claims of strict law or of justice, not even the claims of equity" (p. 269).

This absolute dichotomy between love and justice is, however, necessarily mitigated. As Levinas noted, qualifying his own dichotomy between love and justice, in practice there is never not a third; that is, "in the relationship with another I am always in relation with the third party," who "is also my neighbor."[82] Thus, although the conceptual contrast between love and justice remains a stark one, it becomes clear that in daily life the situations in which justice is relevant are by far the norm.[83]

We have now seen several reasons invoked by Kierkegaard to support the possibility of restrictions on the sacrifice required of us even as we attempt to fulfill an "infinite" demand. The primary one seems to be an immediate recognition of the value of the gift of creation, which we find in ourselves. Moreover, when equality is seen as a feature of creation, we can then derive our responsibility to ourselves from the responsibility to the other, who needs our support. That is, the implied equality can be extrapolated to include those cases in which we must take care of ourselves, refusing certain kinds of exploitation, precisely in order to be responsible for the other, to have something to give to those in need. In all these ways, Kierkegaard is asserting that a necessary dimension of personal relationship is lost if we forget the self or forget to love the self appropriately. In sum, whereas Kierkegaard does refer to and acknowledge how the demands of justice put limits on what we are obligated to do for another, one point of *Works of Love* is to emphasize that even before we approach the realm of justice, there are limits to what we can be expected to do when we love another as we ought to love ourselves.

chapter nine

Love's Venture

"Love Builds Up"; "Love Believes All Things—
and Yet Is Never Deceived"; "Love Hopes All
Things—and Yet Is Never Put to Shame"
(2:I, II, III)

The second series of deliberations, which Kierkegaard gave to the printer four months after the first series, begins with his guiding hint that we shall be continuing a game he played in childhood, "the game of Stranger" in which one "play[s] Stranger with the old and familiar" (WL, p. 210). The "old and familiar," which he will try to make strange or new to us, refers in general to the metaphors of Scripture whose "quiet, whispering secret" needs to be heard, metaphorical words that are not "brand new words but are the already given words" (p. 209).[1] In particular, the "old and familiar" refers to the famous description of love in the thirteenth chapter of St. Paul's first letter to the Corinthians. I am putting the first three deliberations of this series under the single rubric of "Love's Venture" because they share strategies for exploring and clarifying how love is a venture, a risk we take. They could, however, as will become clear, equally well have been put under the rubric "Love's Upbuilding."

I. "Love Builds Up" (2:I)

Kierkegaard begins the series with a deliberation that focuses on the claim earlier in Paul's letter (1 Corinthians, 8)—that "Love Builds Up"—and the deliberations that follow this one will explore what Paul means when he says that "love believes all things"(II), "love hopes all things" (III), "love does not seek its own" (IV), and "love abides" (or "endures") (VI). Although in the fifth deliberation Kierkegaard uses the formulation found in the first letter of Peter, the message— that "love hides a multitude of sins"—is also Pauline. In short, Kierkegaard expressly says that Paul's description in I Corinthians 13 gives us "simply more precise specifications of how love acts in building up" (WL, p. 219).

A. Hiddenness and Recognizability

Note that "works" of love are here illustrated by tasks that do not necessarily involve publicly observable behaviors. Just as it can be a work of love to give food to the hungry, it can equally be a work of love to "presuppose love in another," to "believe" or trust in another, or to "hope for another." It might look as if the latter kind of "work" cannot be done unlovingly, but Kierkegaard maintains his earlier insistence that we cannot tell from the outside what is done lovingly and what unlovingly. There is a striking echo of the first deliberation in Kierkegaard's reminder that "there is no word in the language that in itself is upbuilding, and there is no word in the language that cannot be said in an upbuilding way and become upbuilding if love is present" (WL, p. 213).[2] He explains that "there is nothing, nothing at all, that cannot be done or said in such a way that it becomes upbuilding" (p. 212); "everything that any human being undertakes, anything that any human being says, can be upbuilding" (p. 215). Just as even loving an enemy can be done unlovingly (e.g., if it is done condescendingly),[3] so, too, even praising or commending oneself can be done "for upbuilding" (p. 215). He imagines a "baby sleeping on its mother's breast" and claims that in itself, this is just a "friendly, benevolent, soothing sight"; it becomes "upbuilding" only if "you see love present" (p. 214). In effect, the mother's love is both hidden and recognizable. Kierkegaard compares love to the forces of nature, which work unnoticed as they bring about "the beauty of the meadow and the fruitfulness of the field": "Love acts in the same way; it presupposes that love is present, like the germ in the grain of wheat, and if it succeeds in bringing it to fruition, love conceals itself just as it was concealed while it worked early and late" (p. 218). In the light, then, of this sensitivity to the hiddenness of love's activity, we begin to learn what Kierkegaard sees as the work of love which consists of "building up" another person.

B. A "Being-for-the Other quality"

Kierkegaard suggests that when we apply attributes to someone and say that she or he is wise or loving, we do not sufficiently appreciate a crucial difference between these kinds of qualities. Wisdom is an example of a "being-for-itself quality" (WL, p. 223)—a quality a person has for oneself, even if he or she also uses it for others. What distinguishes a "being-for-itself quality" is that possession of it can be attributed to you independently of whether you attribute it to others; as Kierkegaard explains: "To be wise does not mean to presuppose that others are wise." However, there is at least one attribute that you cannot be said to possess unless you presuppose that others possess it too—"to be loving is to presuppose love in others." Kierkegaard concludes: "Love is not a being-for-it-self quality but a quality by which or in which you are for others" (p. 223).

The language of love as being *"for others"* is quite striking, and Kierkegaard will go on to repeat it (WL, pp. 248, 255, 281) and to flesh out what it means to be "for others" in succeeding deliberations. Here he is content to say that "building up is love's most characteristic specification" (p. 216), so love, in its capacity to build up, is most characteristically "for others." How does love build up others? His answer is that love "builds up love"; "to build up is to build up love" (p. 215). More specifically, to build up love is to "to presuppose love" in another, to "love forth love" (*opelske*) in another (p. 223).[4] Another way of answering the question 'what does love build up and how?' is suggested if we look ahead to the fourth deliberation, "Love Does Not Seek Its Own" (2:IV); there Kierkegaard examines the most important work one person can do for another—to help another be independent, "to help another stand alone" (pp. 277–78).[5] This is another example of how it is useful to read deliberations in tandem, to treat them as complementary discussions.

C. God the Source of Love

The first qualification Kierkegaard makes about the task of upbuilding others is that one human being cannot "implant love in another being's heart"; "it is God, the Creator, who must implant love in each human being, he who himself is Love" (WL, p. 216). Our task is to cultivate the love that is already present because, although we have been gifted, love is "never completely present in any human being" (p. 218). Our task is "to find in all things the love that is presupposed in the ground" (p. 220). Kierkegaard writes in his journals that "in relation to upbuilding, the task is exactly to *develop* the desire or the need [*Trangen*] which everyone should have, and more and more deeply."[6] The potential to be fully present needs to be actualized by being "loved forth" by us, which implies that we first acknowledge the ground of love in others. The importance of this is evident in Kierkegaard's summary: "No human being can place the ground of love in another person's heart; yet love is the ground, and we can build up only from the ground up; therefore we can build up only presupposing love. Take love away—then there is no one who builds up and no one who is built up" (p. 224).

D. Responsiveness and Mutuality

To presuppose love in others is to affirm them as creations of a loving God; it is to affirm in them the actuality of love and the potential to love more fully even if appearances suggest otherwise. It is to trust them, to have more confidence in them than they have in themselves. To "love forth love" is to "draw out the good" (WL, p. 217), to call forth the best in them; to love forth love is to remind them of their status and potential and to encourage them to actualize it. Educators have long known what Kierkegaard finds especially true in the case of love—that negative expectations kill striving, cause despair, and are self-fulfilling prophecies. In Kierkegaard's view, our positive expectations of others mirror God's encouraging "shall."

One could construe upbuilding as a repetition of the divine creative act, which affirmed creation as 'very good.' A modern author Josef Pieper, develops this idea as follows: "All human love is an echo of the divine, creative, prime affirmation by virtue of which everything that is—including therefore what we *in concreto* love—has at once received existence and goodness."[7] Pieper adds a qualification that might well be said to inform Kierkegaard's own emphasis on upbuilding: "[If] all goes happily as it should, then in human love something *more* takes place than mere echo, mere repetition and imitation. What takes place is a continuation and in a certain sense even a perfecting of what was begun in the course of creation." He goes on to explain that what matters to us more than mere existence is the "explicit confirmation: It is *good* that you exist; how wonderful that you are. In other words, what we need over and above sheer existence is: to be loved by another person . . . the fact of creation needs continuation and perfection by the creative power of human love."[8] Another author, describing the mutuality of ethical relationship as a "dialectic of giving and receiving," suggests that "a capacity for giving in return [is] freed by the other's very initiative."[9] Kierkegaard's notion of nurturing the capacity of another person to love by presupposing love in that person seems quite close to this idea of freeing the capacity for giving in return (although, of course, Kierkegaard would strongly qualify what "in return" means).

The hint of mutuality that this implies is actually developed elsewhere. Although in this deliberation Kierkegaard addresses what it is to build someone else up, many of what he calls his "upbuilding" discourses, particularly his *Christian Discourses,* address a related theme—what it is to *let oneself be built up.* The two themes are intertwined, however, because when we presuppose love in another person, as the foundation that can be developed, we are affirming that same foundation in ourselves. Kierkegaard is suggesting that we ourselves are built up when we build up another person. The practice of upbuilding both identifies and reinforces an equality between us: when we presuppose love in another person, we presuppose it in ourselves. Moreover, upbuilding turns out to be an implicitly mutual relationship between two people because when we build up others we are allowing them to be able to build up others, including us, as well.[10]

E. Like for Like

In the earlier chapter on "Love's Debt," we saw Kierkegaard's reference to a "marvelous like for like" (WL, p. 181), in which there is infinite concern from both sides of the relation[11]—a kind of symmetry compatible with the notion of "infinite debt." The theme of 'like for like' turns out to be a very important one in *Works of Love,* and we have just seen it in the claim that when you presuppose love in another person, you presuppose it in yourself. But there is another version that Kierkegaard brings to the fore even more explicitly here: this "like for like" expresses a direct connection between what one presupposes in the other and what arises in the other—that is, "the more perfect the loving one presupposes the love to be, the more perfect a love he loves forth" (p. 219). In other words, there is a tight correlation, so that the result "accurately corresponds to what was presupposed." This is a connection between one's generous positive expectation of the other's capacity and the magnitude of the gift one thereby gives the other (by loving forth love). We will see further variations on the theme of the 'like for like' in succeeding deliberations, including those on believing all things and hoping all things.

F. Building-up as Self-denial

Nietzsche wrote that to build a temple we have to destroy a temple.[12] Kierkegaard says that the context of love is the only one in which this relation does not hold—the only time that building up does not involve a correlative tearing down (WL, p. 219). Building up does not first involve finding fault or weakness; it is not a case of pulling out the splinter first (pp. 218–19). But Kierkegaard not only contrasts building up with its opposite, tearing down, he goes on to contrast two ways of building up—to build up by "doing something to the other person" and "to build up by conquering oneself" (p. 219). The first is an attempt to control the other; the second is a way of "controlling oneself" (p. 217). Such self-control is self-denial.

"Presupposition first and last is self-denial" precisely because we are continually tempted to think that we can create love in another: "[It] is specifically unloving and not at all upbuilding if someone arrogantly deludes himself into believing that he wants and is able to create love in another person" (WL, p. 216). We are to build up the other, but not by "doing something to the other." Our task is to "draw out the good." Upbuilding is not about an egotistical transformation of the other or an exercise of power in which we produce love in another. We need to be sure that we are not deluding ourselves into thinking that we actually have control, and that takes great self-control (p. 217). We must encourage others, affirm others, and support others, without controlling them, in the ways brought out in "Our Duty to Love the People We see" (1:IV); building up love in others means not trimming them to our measure, not trying to turn them into what we would like them to be.

Presupposing love in another means not taking credit for the upbuilding because one cannot take credit while one says: 'I presupposed it all the time'; therefore, "the one who loves has no merit at all" (WL, p. 217). The work of presupposing love in another does not provide any source for self-congratulation; we cannot point to the built-up other and say he or she is our product. The other is not like "a monument to the builder's craft" (p. 217). Here we find anticipations of Kierkegaard's later account of the controlling character of the domineering tyrant (pp. 277–78). Moreover, one way to avoid a controlling kind of building up is to recognize the equality that is implied in the presupposition of love in another person and to appreciate the way in which the one being built up is precisely being enabled to build up others (including oneself).

Not only does Kierkegaard affirm the inwardly turned self-denial of giving up control, but also he affirms the outwardly turned self-denial of bearing another's burden. To presuppose love in another is self-denial because it is to "bear another person's burdens" (WL, p. 220). True love must be patient and not stipulate a deadline for the result (p. 219). It "bears the other person's misunderstanding, his ingratitude, his anger," as well as his failures, his false starts, and his naïveté. It is ultimately to forgive the other as we forgive ourselves. Here Kierkegaard anticipates self-denial as forgiveness in "Love Hides a Multitude of Sins" (2:V).

Kierkegaard makes clear in his *Christian Discourses* that it is "terrifying" to let oneself be built up because it requires one to recognize one's own sinfulness.[13] Now we can begin to see something of the response to upbuilding that might occur—the response of offense. Letting oneself be built up, having love presupposed in one, is letting oneself be placed under a stringent demand; early in *Works of Love* Kierkegaard notes that "the true upbuilding consists in being spoken to rigorously" (p. 42). When one tries to build up another, the other can respond to this as a threat and take offense; thus, the result of our attempts to build up others may be opposition or persecution. Conversely, when we build up others we nurture their capacity to build us up, thereby putting us under a similarly stringent demand.

II. "Love Believes All Things— and Yet Is Never Deceived" (2:II)

In his well-known essay "The Will to Believe," William James posed a provocative dilemma: since we can always be wrong, he asks, is it better to be duped by hope or by fear? James writes: "Scepticism is not avoidance of option; it is option of a certain particular kind of risk. *Better risk loss of truth than chance of error.*" But, James continues: "Dupery for dupery, what proof is there that dupery through hope is so much worse than dupery through fear?"[14] In this he echoes Nietzsche's own challenge—isn't it better to perish through passion than through weakness?[15] Kierkegaard here proposes a variation on these themes: "We human beings have a natural fear of making a mistake—by thinking too well of another person. On the other hand, the error of thinking too ill of another person is perhaps not feared, or at least not in proportion to the first. But then we do not fear most to be in error, then we are still in error by having a onesided fear of a certain kind of error" (WL, p. 232). Like James, Kierkegaard reminds us that there is a possibility of deception either way. In this deliberation the continuing question of the relation between hidden and manifest, inner and outer, invisible and visible, receives an epistemological twist—it becomes the question of knowledge, belief, and deception. Trust and mistrust become the linchpins of the discussion; trust and mistrust are attitudes we have to the "enigmatic world of the hidden" (p. 229), and our trust and mistrust disclose or manifest ourself.

There are two separable discussions going on in this deliberation. In the first Kierkegaard highlights the apparently inevitable risk of deception, and in the second he examines the possibility of avoiding it.

A. Risk of Deception

Kierkegaard enlists the skeptic's aid: we are fallible, and the outer does not necessarily reveal the inner; our purported "knowledge" remains indeterminate. Hence, we can always be deceived. However, he explicitly narrows the arena in which this skepticism should be considered operative: what is at stake for him is that it is difficult to judge another's intention or motives. Our efforts to understand what others feel or think are limited: "How much that is hidden may still reside in a person . . . how inventive is hidden inwardness in hiding itself and in deceiving or evading others" (WL, p. 229). Experience shows us time and again that we never completely understand another person because "it is always possible that the most indisputable thing could still have a completely different explanation, since an assumption can indeed explain a great number of instances" (p. 229). That is, several hypotheses may account for what appears; our ability to rule out those that do not succeed in being explanatory may well come late in a given case, or never. Thus, Kierkegaard draws the provocative conclusion:

> If, then, someone can demonstrate on the basis of the possibility of deception that one should not believe anything at all, I can demonstrate that one should believe everything—on the basis of the possibility of deception. If someone thinks that one should not believe even the best of persons, because it is still possible that he is a deceiver, then the reverse also holds true, that you can credit even the worst person with the good, because it is still possible that his badness is an appearance. (p. 228)

Intriguingly, Kierkegaard is, on this matter, siding with as unlikely an ally as Thomas Aquinas. In his *Summa Theologiae*, Aquinas raises this question: "Whether Doubts Should Be Interpreted for the Best?"[16] The objection he considers is a commonsensical one: "It would seem that doubts should not be interpreted for the best. Because we should judge from what happens for the most part. But it happens for the most part that evil is done. . . . Therefore doubts should be interpreted for the worst rather than for the best." Another objection that he considers draws (ironically) on the commandment to love one's neighbor "as oneself," suggesting that with regard to ourselves we should not give ourselves the benefit of the doubt, and so this should be extrapolated to apply to the neighbor. But Aquinas resists both these objections and concludes: "Doubts should be interpreted in the best sense." His rationale is that when "a man thinks ill of another without sufficient cause, he injures and despises him. Now no man ought to despise or in any way injure another man without urgent cause: and consequently unless we have evident indications of a person's wickedness, we ought to deem him good, by interpreting for the best whatever is doubtful about him." Aquinas realistically admits that by using this policy we will be deceived "more often than not," but he insists that "it is better to err frequently through thinking well of a wicked man, than to err less frequently through having an evil opinion of a good man, *because in the latter case an injury is inflicted*, but not in the former" (emphasis mine).[17] For Aquinas, there is an important difference between judging things and judging people. In addition, there is a crucial asymmetry in the consequences of our being wrong about people; that is, although Aquinas doesn't use the terms 'justice' and 'injustice,' it does seem that his case rests on the assumption that injustice is a greater evil than intellectual error.

Even though Kierkegaard seems to play the game on the skeptic's epistemological board, we must remember that he is talking about cases of judging people's motives and intentions—the board is a moral one. He could avail himself of Aquinas's rationale to support his claim that "the loving person truly fears being in error; therefore he believes all things" (WL, p. 232). "Knowledge" in such cases, for Kierkegaard, can at best be indeterminate. The best "knowledge" we can obtain is simply an "equilibrium of opposite possibilities (pp. 227–28) or "opposite possibilities in equilibrium" (p. 231). Belief, on the other hand, or what we conclude on the basis of the information we share, is a *choice*: "Mistrustingly to believe nothing at all . . . and lovingly to believe all things are not a cognition, nor a cognitive conclusion, but a choice that occurs when knowledge has placed the opposite possibilities in equilibrium" (p. 234).

Whereas someone like William James would argue that it is not our fear of error but our love of truth that should lead us to be generous in our believings,[18] Kierkegaard's view is that the fear of misjudging someone, of attributing fault where it is not justified, should lead us to be generous in our believings. And Aquinas makes more specific what the fear of misjudging someone could mean—our fear of being unjust to another should incline us to be generous in our judgments.

B. Security against Deception

Kierkegaard's first discussion has reminded us that there is a possibility that we can be deceived either way—either by trust or by mistrust, by hope or by fear. The second discussion makes a different point: it suggests that under certain conditions there is no possibility of being deceived.[19] He says that it is in a certain sense true that we are deceived and in a certain sense not true (WL, p. 235). One option for believing prevents deception from occurring, that is, we cannot be deceived while we continue to love. This theme that we are secure in certain circumstances is a continuing one; what makes this formulation of it distinctive is that here Kierkegaard suggests that the possibility of deception is tied to the demand for reciprocity. That is, Kierkegaard is suggesting that deception is not possible if we see our loving the other as a gift (p. 242), as something that is not intended to secure a particular repayment.

An important strategy for making his point is found in Kierkegaard's frequent analogies with "money matters." His example in this chapter assumes that love is like money. He compares being deceived by loving one who does not love you to being given money by the thief: "[I]f it were possible to deceive someone in money matters in such a way that the so-called deceived one kept his money, would he then be deceived?" (WL, p.239) He adds that: "to deceive in this way—is it not like sticking money in a person's pocket and calling it stealing!" (p. 241). Another version of this comparison with money is the following: "In money matters, for example, someone who in order to obtain money for himself applies to a man on whom he had depended and who he believed had money is duped if the man is then insolvent and has no money. But some one who wants to *give* his money away and does not in the slightest way wish or demand to get it back is certainly not duped—because the recipient has no money" (pp. 241–42; emphasis mine). In other words, only if one is out to get something for oneself can one be deprived of it. The only way we could be deceived is if we were tricked out of loving: "Even though one is not deceived by others, is one not deceived, most terribly deceived, by oneself, to be sure, through believing nothing at all, deceived out of the highest, out of the blessedness of giving of oneself, the blessedness of love!"(p. 235).[20] He thus repeats his early claim that only we can deceive ourselves (p. 6).

In sum, this section of the deliberation emphasizes the themes of risk and venture.[21] Anti-Climacus's sentiment, expressed in *Sickness unto Death*, helps make Kierkegaard's point about the risk of being duped by hope or fear—"by not venturing, it is so dreadfully easy to lose that which it would be difficult to lose in even the most venturesome venture, and in any case never so easily, so completely as if it were nothing . . . one's self. For if I have ventured amiss—very well, then life helps me by its punishment. But if I have not ventured at all—who then helps me?"[22] But the theme of risk is in tension with the theme of "security" against deception, and this threatens Kierkegaard's position in two ways. First, it seems to simply undermine the concept of risk conceptually. Second, the unilateralism it seems to imply can easily assume either arrogant or Stoic overtones.[23] Several elements however, mitigate these dangers. Kierkegaard says late in *Works of Love* that the "security" we gain is the security involved in the promise 'be it done to you as you believe or do' (p. 379). This kind of guarantee is a peculiar one: it bears its own hiddenness, and the kind of certainty we gain is found only in continual "struggle" (p. 380). Moreover, Kierkegaard's acknowledgment of the grief and sorrow we "ought" to feel when our love is rejected or our lover lost (pp. 42–43) seems to belie the unilateralness of the relation.[24]

C. Another Like for Like

Kierkegaard introduces still another variation on the theme of the 'like for like' when he tells us that our judgments of belief in the face of risk reveal us for what we are: "In the very same minute when you judge another person or criticize another person, you judge yourself, because when all is said and done, to judge someone else is to judge yourself or to be disclosed yourself" (WL, p. 233). Since neither the response of trust nor that of mistrust is entailed by the "knowledge" we gain, the inner becomes the outer—that is, "to live is to judge oneself" (p. 228). The claim that as we judge, as we respond in either trust or mistrust, we are judged, is a negative formulation of the injunction to love another 'as yourself.' The Conclusion to *Works of Love* repeats this same version of the 'like for like' more explicitly; that is *"to accuse another person before God is to accuse oneself, like for like"* (p. 381).

Kierkegaard has mentioned a variety of themes that will come up again in the next deliberation. One is that our venture is a "choice"(WL, p. 234), another that it takes "courage" (p. 244). In addition he repeatedly qualifies the claim he is making about trusting others—he wants it be perfectly clear that he is not urging blindness to what others do or fail to do (pp. 225, 228, 239).

III. "Love Hopes All Things— and Yet Is Never Put to Shame" (2:III)

In line with the earlier suggestion that we need to make the familiar become strange or new to us, Kierkegaard suggests that periodically we need a breath of "fresh air," which can range from "a refreshing, enlivening breeze" to "a mighty gale." We need "the enlivening prospect of a great expectancy" if we are not to "suffocate" in the stagnant, "poisonous" air of worldly "complacency" (WL, p. 246). That is, we need HOPE, and the hope we need is a hope for others—"love, which is greater than faith and hope, also takes upon itself the work of hope, or takes upon itself hope, hoping *for others*, as a work" (p. 248, emphasis mine); if one is loving, "he also hopes *for others*" (p. 255; emphasis mine), whereas "despair hopes nothing at all for others" (p. 254). Since a "deliberation" is the proper literary vehicle for provoking and awakening us, for turning us "topsy-turvy," we are invited to a deliberation that should cause us to rethink our notions of "possibility" and "imagination."

This deliberation has obvious parallels with the preceding one. Kierkegaard repeats the same qualification he made earlier about the one who believes all things: "[N]ot everyone who hopes all things" does so as a fruit or work of love (WL, p. 248). Some instances of hoping can be unloving. Neither indiscriminate believing nor indiscriminate hoping is being recommended. Moreover, he repeats the themes of choice and courage and elaborates the themes of risk and security. Finally, his claim that even if we have nothing else to give to the other, hoping for the other is "the best gift" (p. 258) anticipates the idea that love can be merciful despite an inability to be generous.[25]

A. Love's Choice

As with believing all things, so too hoping all things is a "choice" (WL, 249–50), and for precisely the same reason: just as we are faced with the "equilibrium of opposite possibilities," which require us to choose either trust or mistrust, so we are faced with the "duality" of possibility, for "the possible as such is always a duality"(p. 249). In "mere possibility," the "possibilities of the good and of the evil [are] equal," and "choice" is the "differentiating" option to expect one or the other (p. 250). Just as when faced with the same information and the same recognition of the possibility of deception we can make a choice to trust another rather than to mistrust, so when we are faced with a possibility that could be either good or evil we can make a choice to hope rather than to fear.

B. Love's Imagination

Hope and fear in this deliberation parallel the attitudes of trust and mistrust in the preceding one; here it is made clear that the choice to believe and to hope requires *imagination* because it goes beyond what is seen. Although Kierkegaard does not use the term "imagination" often in these deliberations, it is implied in his repeated insistence on "possibility." Imagination is crucial to love's work in hoping precisely because imagination is necessary for appreciating the possibility in its duality, going beyond what is actually seen: "[I]f there is less love in him, there is also . . . less of a sense of possibility" (WL, p. 258), hence less hope, because hope is affirming "the possibility of good" (p. 259).

This deliberation, which constitutes an accolade and analysis of hope, opens with a bold announcement: "Christianity's hope is eternity" (WL, p. 248). It then works its way back to this conclusion, first with an ode to possibility: "Possibility, this marvelous thing that is so infinitely fragile . . . so infinitely frail . . . and yet, brought into being and shaped with the help of the eternal, stronger than anything else, if it is the possibility of the good!" (p. 251). Then he makes this more specific: "To relate oneself expectantly to the possibility of the good is to hope" (p. 249); conversely, "anyone who lives without possibility is in despair" (p. 252). Indeed, Kierkegaard makes the perceptive comment that people can unfortunately "misuse the powers of the imagination" to limit imagination (p. 254); this is one version of the "wanton misuse" of imagination's powers, which he refers to later when he speaks negatively of imagination. That is, like the skeptic we can use our imagination to become obsessed with all the scenarios in which we could be wrong, and thus limit our "sense of possibility" (p. 258).

Throughout his writings, both pseudonymous and signed, Kierkegaard alerts us to the negative connotations of aesthetic possibility, with its danger of dissipation and loss of self, but he nevertheless carves a significant place for a positive concept of possibility in both ethical and religious development.[26] One rich locus for this positive concept is *The Sickness unto Death* by Anti-Climacus (admittedly a pseudonym, but an unusual one[27]): "What is decisive is that with God everything is possible. . . . This is the battle of *faith*, battling, madly, if you will, for possibility, because possibility is the only salvation."[28] In ways reminiscent of Kant's formulation of the dilemma posed by radical evil—that we cannot understand how we can do our duty, but we must nevertheless affirm that it is not impossible[29]—he continues that "the *believer* sees and understands his downfall, human speaking . . . but he believes. . . . He leaves it entirely to God how he is to be helped, but he believes that for God everything is possible. To *believe* his downfall is impossible. To understand that humanly it is his downfall and nevertheless to believe in possibility is to believe."[30] In the end, to believe is to believe in possibility.[31]

As we saw, "to relate oneself expectantly to the possibility of the good is to *hope*." An imaginative appropriation of possibility is equally crucial to love's work in presupposing love in the other and in believing good rather than evil of the other. In short, these are all cases of positive expectations: presupposing love, believing good of the other, hoping for the good of the other—all build up by loving forth love.

C. Love's Courage

Although Kierkegaard does not explicitly link courage with hope here, as he had done earlier with belief, the connection is implied. Hoping for another is the activity of giving the other hope, and it is a work of love that requires courage; hoping is not simply "wishing, craving, expecting."[32] Just as it takes imagination to see either good or evil beyond "the seen," it takes courage to choose to respond to the dual possibility by affirming the possibility of the good.[33] Kierkegaard explores briefly what makes it difficult for us to hope for others, to give them hope by presupposing the love in them: "There is a *worldly, conceited mentality* that would die of disgrace and shame if it were to experience making a mistake, being fooled, becoming ludicrous (the most terrible of all horrors!) by having hoped something for another person that did not come about" (WL, p. 257). He condemns the self-protectiveness that amounts to "simply stealing one's existence from God" (p. 261).

Although Kierkegaard emphasizes the duality of possibility, he intriguingly suggests that "the possibility of the good is more than possibility, because when someone is so bold as to *assume* the impossibility of the good, possibility dies for him altogether" (WL, pp. 253–54). When one deliberately takes hope away from someone, by assuming the impossibility of the good, one annihilates the possibility. "There is," he notes, "an anger and a bitterness that, even if it does not get a murder on its conscience, hopelessly gives up on the detested person, that is, it takes possibility away from him. But is this not murdering him spiritually, hurling him spiritually into the abyss" (p. 257). Taking possibility or hope away from someone is an act of spiritual murder. The radicalness of calling this murder is something he inherited from Luther, who similarly condemned our ill will toward others.[34]

D. Love's Security

As with believing and not being able to be deceived if we keep loving, it is the case that our hoping can never bring us shame if what we hope for is not worthy of shame (WL, pp. 261, 263). The example of the 'prodigal' son's father is used both here (p. 263) and in the preceding deliberation (p. 221)—to hope is to presuppose love, to trust. Kierkegaard's earlier claim was that we can only be deceived if reciprocal love is our demand, and although genuine love takes joy in being loved, it does not demand love.[35] Here, we can only be shamed if our goal is to gain our own advantage in the first place (p. 258).

In this chapter Kierkegaard makes his point with another contrast between love and "money matters." He points out the illusion of assuming that we are in control of our love the way we are in control of our money: "Ordinarily we speak . . . in a domineering and unloving way about our relation to the love within us, as if we ourselves were the masters and autocrats over our love in the same sense as we are over our money" (WL, p. 255). Just as we can stop giving money to one person and keep it for ourselves or others, we assume that if we stop loving another person, we still remain loving (just not to that other person) (p. 255). Kierkegaard suggests that if you think that the other is the loser (rather than you) when you stop loving him, you are like "the speaker [who] is of the opinion that he himself retains his love in the same sense as someone who has assisted another person with money and says, 'I have stopped giving this assistance to him;—so now the giver keeps the money himself that the other received previously"; in such a case "the giver is of course far from losing by this financial shift" (pp. 255–56). But, Kierkegaard insists, "it is not this way with love" (p. 256). Love is not something we get to keep for ourselves by withholding it from another. If we cease to love one person, we do not remain loving because we have made our love arbitrarily preferential. If we despair of any single person we are in despair because we have closed the door to the possibility of the good, and it cannot simply be shut for one person without excluding all the others.

E. A New Like for Like

The work of hoping is to hope "all things," "always," "for others" (WL, p. 248). But the "as yourself" of the love commandment comes into play—in the work of hoping the lover hopes "for himself" as well (p. 259). Kierkegaard explains that to hope all things for oneself and to lovingly hope all things for others are "indeed one and the same"; it "follows . . . from what love is" that they are "altogether one and the same" (p. 259). In fact, there is an important kind of 'like for like' here. The earlier admonition, that when you judge others you are yourself judged, becomes here a positive reminder—that "in the same degree to which he hopes for others, he hopes for himself" (p. 255) and, vice versa, "to the same degree one hopes for oneself, to the same degree one hopes for others" (p. 260). As he says earlier, "No one can hope unless he is also loving; he cannot *hope for himself* without also being loving, because the good has an infinite connectedness" (p. 255). His explanation, it should be noted, is that the good has "an infinite connectedness"—that is, if we love the good as such, we will love the good in ourselves, as well as in the other; we will hope for the good for ourselves, as well as for the other.

That we live "for others" (WL, p. 248, 259) is part of what love means, but if we don't know what it is to hope for ourselves, if we cannot hold open the possibility of the good for ourselves, we cannot hope for another. Anticipating his example in the fourth deliberation, Kierkegaard puts down the *"cowardly, timorous, small-mindedness* that has not had the courage to hope for anything for itself" and wonders "how could it hope for the possibility of the good for others" (p. 257). Holding open the possibility of the good is like opening a door through which we can both walk; unless I know what it is to hold it open, I cannot hold it open for you. If I hold it open for you, if I choose to hope, even despite appearances, in the possibility of good for you, I am affirming the possibility of the good, and I am necessarily embraced in this affirmation. That is, if I can hold it open for you, I, too, can walk through it. The combination of claims that our hope for ourselves implies our hope for the other, and our hope for the other implies our hope for ourselves, is one way in which the notion of "like for like" is used by Kierkegaard. It is not a case of tit-for-tat between two people; it is rather the "like for like" that is revealed in the commandment's phrase "as yourself."

The category of the "like for like" has thus far in *Works of Love* assumed two main forms—when you judge, you are judged, and when you hope for another, you hope for yourself. Both examples involve simultaneity and equality. On the one hand, they could be described in contrasting ways: in the first case, one could say that what one does to another, God does to you; in the second case, one could say that the very same loving hope has two different objects. On the other hand, one could argue that they are both examples of how love does unto you just as you do unto others. Such a "like for like" has a kind of shock value even here, but the importance of this theme does not become fully apparent until Kierkegaard reaches his Conclusion, where he gives what is perhaps his fullest treatment of the "like for like" and his considered judgment of its value. We will see that he introduces it as it if is an afterthought: "Just one more thing, remember the *Christian like for like, eternity's like for like*" (WL, p. 376), but it is not an afterthought at all. Instead, it is "such an important and decisive Christian specification" that he would like to use it to end "if not every book in which I develop the essentially Christian, then at least one book"—presumably this book. The theme of the "like for like" will come up again in succeeding deliberations, and I consider it in detail in chapter 17.

Kierkegaard noted in the deliberation on upbuilding that a discourse about "what can be upbuilding" would be an "interminable" one, "inasmuch as everything can be that" (WL, p. 215). This suggests that neither the analysis of how love builds up by presupposing love in others nor the analyses about presupposing love in others when we believe and hope for them can really end. All the deliberations are instances of Kierkegaard's own concern to upbuild his readers, and most of them are implicitly discussions of what it is to build up another. *Works of Love* is, in effect, a set of deliberations that presupposes love in us and repeats the message that love presupposes love in others.[36]

chapter ten

Love's Gift

"Love Does Not Seek Its Own" (2:IV)

"Love is a revolution," proclaims Kierkegaard, a revolution that causes confusion and upheaval in the ordered world of 'mine' and 'yours,' the world in which one's "own" is the center of attention.[1] Despite the negative phrasing of its title, this deliberation turns to the positive notion of love as *giving* in a way that affirms not one's "own" but the other's "own." At the outset of this study, in analyzing the opening prayer, I suggested that the notion of "gift" would be in play from then on, as one of the crucial parameters of all the deliberations. The idea that God's gift of Godself to us is love and that this gift at the same time enables us to love others has, indeed, always been in the background. But here, in this deliberation, Kierkegaard begins to elaborate this idea by explicitly setting out two dimensions of giving. The first—"Love does not seek its own"—uses "own" as shorthand for all the things I want to think of as 'mine,' as contrasted with 'yours': The second—"Love loves what is the other's own"—uses "own" to refer to what is distinctive about the other. Together they tell us both that love is giving and that our giving is directed to the welfare of the other.

Lying at the heart of this deliberation are Kierkegaard's proposals that love is "sacrificially giving of oneself" and that love *gives in such a way that the gift [Gave] looks as if it were the recipient's property*" (WL, p. 274). That is, love gives, and it gives in such a way that the gift does not look as if it is a gift at all. This claim, which he makes repeatedly, puts Kierkegaard right in the middle of a contemporary discussion about what constitutes a "gift," how it fits within an economy of "exchange," and indeed whether a "gift" as such is even possible; I will refer to this debate toward the end of this chapter. At a minimum, Kierkegaard has already made the notion of love as a gift of ourselves problematical by the way in which he has insisted, at the end of the first series, on our "infinite debt" to the other. We normally do not term what we owe to another person a "gift." Yet Kierkegaard affirms the obligation to give to others, and he has said that we remain in the debt of love by giving—so our giving must be compatible with our infinite debt. Love cannot help but appear to be different against the background of an "infinite debt," and this deliberation's foremost objective is to get us to ask ourselves if we really know what a 'gift' is and 'how' to give to another.

This deliberation should not be isolated from those preceding or following it because they, too, bear on its central concern, either by raising the question of whether love's genuineness depends on the response of the other (particularly, the negative response of hatred, ingratitude, or persecution) or by indicating more clearly why giving requires a sensitive concern for the other's self-respect.[2] Thus, the question of gift is one that runs deep in *Works of Love*, and this deliberation is particularly significant for the way it causes us to question the relation between gift and debt. In sum, the emphasis on gift in this deliberation allows Kierkegaard to develop further what he meant by his earlier rejection of "repayment," as well as to explore in some detail the relation between gift and debt, which begins the process (to be completed in later deliberations) of bringing us face to face with perennial questions about mutuality and symmetry in ethical relationships.

I. The Sacrifice of Giving

The claim that love "does not seek its own" is a very Lutheran way (following St. Paul) of affirming love's unselfishness. But Kierkegaard imagines the reader asking, doesn't God who is Love seek to be loved? True, God seeks our love, and Kierkegaard has already admitted that Christ sought the love of Peter (WL, pp. 155–56), so he takes this opportunity to qualify the way in which God, and God in Christ, are models for us. The feat of seeking love while not seeking one's own is possible only to a being who *is* love. Since none of us *are* love, Kierkegaard says, we can't directly seek love without seeking our own. The weight of sin's influence on the world drags us down so that we tend, he implies, to treat love as an "object" that we can seek and possess (p. 265). We must, therefore, reorient ourselves and appreciate that love is not an object that we can seek like other objects. Like happiness, it cannot be found directly. For us, love must involve the abandonment of a search for love; it must be a "sacrificial giving of oneself" (pp. 265, 268).

But at the same time as he says this, Kierkegaard reminds us that our sacrifice does not mean that we lose all possibility of being loved by others.[3] After all, he has repeatedly affirmed our need to be loved, and he expects that we will find joy in being loved by others.[4] He makes it clear that "in the eyes of the world," we will look like the "unconditionally injured," the ones made fools of, tricked, and deceived. But although it does involve a reordering of values in relation to the love of others, sacrificial giving does not constitute annihilation of earthly life because the strong leitmotiv of the "like for like" weaves its way in and out of the deliberations; that is, as we shall see more clearly in chapter 11, section II, one receives what one gives.[5] This important version of a "like for like," which we have seen many times, is expressed in Kierkegaard's confidence that the one "who loses his soul will gain it" (WL, p. 268).[6] Courage to seek nothing at all for oneself is buoyed by the knowledge that "everything becomes the true lover's" (p. 268). In any case, Kierkegaard's rhetoric about sacrificial giving should not obscure the fact that he has already laid great stress on proper love of oneself, our need to be loved, and our equality with others before God.[7] Presumably, he thinks he does not need to remind us of these things again; these deliberations are written as a series and we should remember what has been accomplished in the earlier ones.

But there is something more that Kierkegaard does need to tell us. We cannot understand what sacrifice of self and what self-denial mean without learning more about why they are to be brought about, that is, to what end. Sacrifice and self-denial are ways in which our life is, as Kierkegaard hyperbolically says, "completely squandered on existence, on the existence of others" (WL, p. 279). Such squandering refers not to waste but to the generous abandon with which we live for others, not counting or calculating what we give. Sacrifice and self-denial are not a goal in themselves but the substance of forgetting one's own in loving the other.[8]

II. The Content of Giving

The sacrifice and self-denial we experience are the other side of giving to the other. What do we give? Kierkegaard calls it loving "the other's own": *"Love does not seek its own. The truly loving one does not love his own distinctiveness but, in contrast, loves every human being according to his distinctiveness; but "his distinctiveness" is what for him is* HIS OWN; *that is, the loving one does not seek his own; quite the opposite, he loves what is the other's own"* (WL, p. 269). In the contemporary idiom, we might well call this appreciation and cultivation of others' "own"-ness, an appreciation and cultivation of their alterity, their otherness. Kierkegaard's assumption is that "it is every human being's destiny to become free, independent, oneself" (p. 278). Loving the other's own amounts to loving the other's distinctiveness, which Kierkegaard first emphasized in the deliberation "Our Duty to Love the People We See" (1:IV), and loving the other's distinctiveness will entail the sacrifice and self-denial of not seeking one's own.

Kierkegaard's first illustration of seeking one's own in contrast to loving the other's own is that of "the rigid, the domineering person." It is worth citing at length since, first, it shows something of what is at stake for Kierkegaard when he condemns seeking one's own as unloving, and it indicates the kind of sacrifice involved in giving up such a self-centered existence; and second, there seems no paraphrase that could do it justice or make it clearer:

> *The rigid, the domineering person* lacks flexibility, lacks the pliability to comprehend others; he demands his own from everyone, wants everyone to be transformed in his image, to be trimmed according to his pattern for human beings . . . he thinks of something definite about this person and then insists that the other shall fulfill this idea. Whether this is the other person's distinctiveness or not makes no difference, because this is what the domineering person has supposed about him. If the rigid and domineering person cannot ever create, he wants at least to transform—that is, he seeks his own so that wherever he points he can say: See, it is my image, it is my idea, it is my will. (WL, p. 270)

Kierkegaard's example is not at all farfetched; it should hit close enough to home to give each of us pause. This "tyrant" tries to reduce the other's own to his own, tries to reduce the different to the same, "domineeringly refusing to go out of oneself, domineeringly wanting to crush the other person's distinctiveness or torment it to death" (p. 271). Even when he or she does not go to the extremes of tormenting the other or does it in more subtle ways, which have become socially acceptable, such a person needs to be reminded of the other's distinctiveness, of what is the other's own. To cease seeking one's own in this way will amount to self-denial, that is, a denial of self-seeking.

Another way in which we seek our own by trying to trim people to our measure, to turn them into what we want them to be, is what Kierkegaard calls "smallmindedness." The "enviously imperious, cowardly timorous" person cannot believe in his own distinctiveness, so he "cannot believe in anybody else's either" (WL, pp. 271–72). Such a person clings "to a very specific shape and form that he calls his own; he seeks only that, can love only that." Whether one is a domineering tyrant or a small-minded tyrant, it will be a costly sacrifice to give up one's restrictive, reductive attitude to others. This is how self-denial comes into play; it is not a game in which one denies oneself for the sake of denying oneself. The daily effort to appreciate and cultivate the distinctiveness of the other entails sufficient sacrifice; we do not need to go around looking for special ways to sacrifice or deny ourselves. Here Kierkegaard is echoing Luther.[9]

In a passage that is so striking that I cannot omit any of the details, Kierkegaard suggests that appreciation of the distinctiveness of others imitates God's gift:

> With what infinite love nature or God in nature encompasses all the diverse things that have life and existence! Just recollect what you yourself have so often delighted in looking at, recollect the beauty of the meadows! There is no difference in the love, no, none—yet what a difference in the flowers! Even the least, the most insignificant, the most unimpressive, the poor little flower disregarded by even its immediate surroundings, the flower you can hardly find without looking carefully—it is as if this, too, had said to love: *Let me become something in myself, something distinctive. And then love has*

helped it to become its own distinctiveness, but far more beautiful than the poor little flower had ever dared to hope for. What love! First, it makes no distinction, none at all; next, which is just like the first, it infinitely distinguishes itself in loving the diverse. Wondrous love! (WL, p. 269–70, emphasis mine)

Moreover, the God who created "out of nothing" affirms the creature's distinctiveness, "so that the creature in relation to God *does not become nothing . . .* but becomes a distinctive individuality" (pp. 271–72, emphasis mine). But the "small-minded" person tries to excuse his own fear of difference, his own resistance to otherness, by trimming even God to his own measure; his understanding of Christian love "distorts God, as if he were also small-minded, as if he could not bear distinctiveness—he who so lovingly gives all things and yet gives all things distinctiveness" (p. 271). Our gift to others, then, is to help each "to become its own distinctiveness," so that no one thinks he or she is "nothing." This is what the unselfishness and self-denial of love amounts to; this is what constitutes squandering our life on the "existence of others" (p. 279).

Although his scenarios of self-denial never quite match the style and wit of his accounts of the domineering and the pathetic tyrants, Kierkegaard does give a positive example of what is involved in loving another, and it is a striking example of paradox. Moreover, it is just the same sort of paradox found in the idea that we should love another in such a way that "it looks as if the gift were the recipient's own property." So it is worth considering just how these two things relate. As in the temporal realm, so, too, in the world of spiritual things, Kierkegaard says, "to become one's own master is the highest—and in love to help someone toward that, to become himself, free, independent, his own master, to help him stand alone—that is the greatest beneficence" (WL, p. 274). This is another variation on the theme that love "builds up," which we considered in chapter 9, and these two deliberations are mutually illuminating in this respect. He repeats: "The one who loves has understood that it truly is the greatest, the only beneficence one human being can do for another, to help him to stand by himself, to become himself, to become his own master" (pp. 277–78). In other words, the greatest love we can show to another is to help the other stand alone. But the paradox in this effort is clear: to help another stand alone is to *help* another to be *independent.* Kierkegaard is not unaware of the peculiarity of giving such a gift to another; he calls it "the greatest contradiction" (p. 275).

This paradox recalls Kierkegaard's journal comments on the relation between power and dependence. He writes, anticipating the phrasing in *Works of Love:*

The greatest good, after all, which can be done for a being, greater than anything else that one can do for it, is to make it free. In order to do just that, omnipotence is required. This seems strange . . . but if one will reflect on omnipotence, he will see that it also must contain the unique qualification of being able to withdraw itself again in a manifestation of omnipotence in such a way that precisely for this reason that which has been originated through omnipotence can be independent.[10]

This "withdrawal" is crucial in allowing independence, and Kierkegaard concedes that its perfection is not possible to finite being. Finite power is informed by finite self-love because "only omnipotence can withdraw itself at the same time it gives itself away, and this relationship is the very independence of the receiver."[11] And then appears the crucial phrase echoed in *Works of Love:* "For goodness is to give away completely, but in such a way that by omnipotently taking oneself back one makes the recipient independent." Finite power cannot make someone free, for "only omnipotence can make [a being] independent, can form from nothing something that has its continuity in itself through the continuous withdrawing of omnipotence." Although we cannot do it perfectly, it is nonetheless the goal for which we should strive—the goal of being able to withdraw ourselves in such a way that the gift seems to the recipient to be his or her own.

III. The 'How' of Love's Giving

What we are trying to do is to help the other to be independent in such a way that our helping does not make that person dependent. What we give to the other, therefore, is closely tied to *how* we give to the other—"to help the other to stand alone, cannot be done directly" (WL, p. 274). Kierkegaard invokes a host of terms to indicate this indirection: he talks about hiding our help, being shoved aside, and being unnoticed or invisible (pp. 274, 275, 278). Kierkegaard connects the "how" and the "what" as follows: the "highest that one human being can do for another" is to make him "free, independent, himself, his own master, and *just by hiding his help* [one] *has helped him to stand by himself*" (p. 275; emphasis mine). Giving the gift implies hiding the help. Therefore, he continues, in the phrase "to stand by oneself—through another's help!"(p. 275), the dash represents a qualitative break; it signals the hiddenness of the help. By means of the dash, he says,

> the greatest contradiction is surmounted. He is standing by himself—that is the highest; he is standing by himself—more you do not see. *You see no help or support*, no awkward bungler's hand holding on to him, any more than it occurs to the person himself that someone has helped him. No, he is standing by himself—through another's help. But *this other person's help is hidden from him*—the one who was helped? No, from the eyes of the independent one (for if he knows that he has been helped, then in the deepest sense he of course is not the independent one who helps and has helped himself); it is hidden behind the dash. (p. 275, emphasis mine)

He continues: "So it is with all the work of the one who loves. Truly, *he does not seek his own, because he gives in precisely such a way that it looks as if the gift were the recipient's property*. Insofar as the loving one is able, he seeks to encourage a person to become himself, to become his own master" (p. 278; emphasis mine).

In this way "the loving one, the hidden benefactor, is shoved aside, since it is every human being's destiny to become free, independent, oneself."

So far this seems commonsensical enough: true love gives without making itself the center of attention, and Kierkegaard recognizes that even in sacrifice we can call attention to ourselves. But then he adds: "If it is noticed that the one who loves has helped, then the relationship is disturbed, or else the helper has not lovingly helped, the one who loves has not helped properly" (WL, p. 279). This last remark makes us acutely aware of the peculiarity he has been insisting on—the hiddenness of the gift. It forces us to ask why it must be hidden. In the process of addressing this question, we will find two distinctive dimensions of Kierkegaard's understanding of "gift" coming to the forefront, both rooted in his theological commitments: first, the importance of simple human compassion for another when one is giving a "gift" and, second, a sense in which only God can give a "gift."

Before exploring Kierkegaard's rationale for the hiddenness, we need to ask a 'so what' question. What is at stake in this discussion of gift? One consequence is that we could place Kierkegaard in relation to the twentieth-century discussion in which gift is contrasted with "economic exchange" in such a way that the concept of gift is seen as unintelligible, self-canceling, or 'the impossible.' Does Kierkegaard's idiom of 'hiddenness' amount to a theoretical or conceptual dilemma: if a gift must be hidden, then when it is received as a gift it ceases to be a gift?

A more practical consequence is that it helps to assess the criticism that Kierkegaard's insistence on the invisibility of the help (otherwise "the relation is disturbed") precludes one from giving any benefit that the other "notices" or can recognize as such. Does the emphasis on hiddenness mean that gratitude or appreciation or grateful use of what one gives invalidates it? We saw earlier (chapter 5) that a similar question has been raised by critics like Løgstrup. Løgstrup argued that in Kierkegaard's ethic the genuineness of love is determined by the response of the other and that the ethic implies the morally unacceptable consequence that hatred and misunderstanding were the "guarantee" of genuine love. This implies that we are precluded from helping others in ordinary, temporal ways because such benefits would be recognized as helpful, and therefore we should strive to create situations in which others hate and misunderstand us, rather than situations in they can be more loving. In other words, he is in effect charging that Kierkegaard makes the other's indifference, ingratitude, or hatred the necessary condition of our giving lovingly, so we are precluded from giving the good things that we are Christianly supposed to give to others (because they would recognize them as good and so not respond with indifference or ingratitude or hatred). This would mean that the other's appreciation would invalidate the putative gift by depriving it of its necessary condition. In this context, it would mean that we cannot genuinely give to another. Given the ethical relevance of the answers to both versions of the question, it is a pressing task to assess whether Kierkegaard's claim here, that we ought to give to others "in such a way that it looks as if the gift were the recipient's property," entails such consequences.

IV. Two Dimensions of Gift

It is crucial to look closely at what is at stake for Kierkegaard in his insistence on the hiddenness of the giver and/or the gift. He is once again remarkably graphic in describing what we shouldn't do or be. He begins by describing a "clammy, uncomfortable anxiety" in the face of "strange distinctiveness" (WL, p. 272) and an "asthmatic tightness which gasps for relief" (p. 273)—such attitudes, which express fear of the other's distinctiveness and a desperate holding on to what is ours, are incompatible with a loving giving. The alternative is found in openness, gracious generosity or welcoming embrace.[12]

But there is something far more decisive in Kierkegaard's model than these psychological criteria. Probably the most important dimension of giving, if we judge by its emphasis and repetition, is the proposal that love *"gives in such a way that the gift looks as if it were the recipient's property"* (WL, p. 274).[13] Kierkegaard writes: "The greatest benefaction, therefore, cannot be done in such a way that the recipient comes to know that it is to me that he owes it, because if he comes to know that, then it simply is not the greatest beneficence" (p. 275). Why not?

A. Compassionate Giving

The first reason for insisting on hiddenness involves the hiddenness of the giver and focuses on our concern for the other's self-respect. Kierkegaard's insistence that the other should not know he or she has been helped is based on the need for compassion for the other person, concern either for what will happen to the other as a result or for how the other views himself or herself.[14] The general message is to give to another in such a way that the other is not made to feel the gift as a burden, in terms of debt, dependence, or obligation. Given the number of times Kierkegaard accents it, the avoidance of making someone feel dependent seems very important: "[T]he one who loves also knows how to make himself unnoticed so that the person helped does not become dependent upon him" (WL, p. 274); "the true way makes itself invisible and thus . . . in this way exempts from all dependence the world as well as the persons involved" (pp. 274–5).[15]

There are, however, other ways in which we can make a gift to another a burden, and Kierkegaard shows that he is sensitive to these as well. We just saw his remarkable description of how God's love for creatures builds them up, affirms their distinctiveness, so that even the most insignificant can say to themselves: I am "something in myself, something distinctive"; that is, God reminds them that they are "something," not "nothing."[16] By alluding to the sensitive way in which God's creative love builds up (while withholding God's omnipotence), Kierkegaard indirectly foreshadows something he will make far more explicit in the eighth deliberation, "The Victory of the Conciliatory Spirit in Love"—that we can give to another in unloving ways, in humiliating and condescending ways. This eighth deliberation, which I shall consider at length later (chapter 14), illuminates the present deliberation by showing us another way in which "the one who loves hides himself" (WL, p. 340). It tells us that love or forgiveness—by implication, everything we give to the other—must be given in ways that "prevent humiliation" (p. 342). The eighth deliberation repeatedly emphasizes how we should avoid humiliating other persons when we overcome the evil they have done and try to bring them to love the good, or when we reconcile ourselves to them in forgiveness (pp. 338, 339, 342). Kierkegaard reminds us how unloving it is to savor a victory in a condescending way, how unloving to use the power of forgiveness "to master another person" (p. 339). He urges us to be "dexterous" in the ways in which we give to another (p. 340), ingenious in the ways in which we can avoid appearing superior—that is, ingenious in the ways in which we can hide ourselves in our giving, even to the extent of trying to free someone from thinking with sadness of the forgiveness he or she needs. The eighth deliberation as a whole is a testament to the importance of giving in such a way that it does not seem to the other to be a "gift," and it nicely complements the discussion here of what it is to love the other's own, to appreciate and respect his or her distinctiveness.[17]

Thus the first dimension of 'gift' implies that in addition to the minimum condition of being a benefit, a gift requires only that it be given in a particularly loving way. Hence we can give gifts. This is in keeping with the way in which Kierkegaard contrasted a gift with "exchange" in "Love Believes all Things" (2:II). He had alluded to the gift of love when he argued that the one who gives a gift can never be deceived or exploited because such a person is not "demanding reciprocal love," not "requiring reciprocal love," not giving *so that* he or she will receive in return (WL, pp. 237, 242). He concluded that a loving person "can no more be deceived out of his love than a man can be tricked out of the money he tenders as a gift and gives to someone" (p. 242). But in addition to this possibility that we can give gifts if only we do it in the right way, Kierkegaard also seems to rely on a notion of gift that would deny that we can give gifts.

B. Gift as Gratuity

The second reason for insisting on hiddenness involves the way in which what is given is hidden *as gift*. Kierkegaard's claim is clearly that what we lovingly give should not be given in such a way that it is seen as a gift; rather the one to whom it is given should see it as his or her own.[18] But in the light of Kierkegaard's deep commitment to the loving "gift" of Godself by God, it is difficult not to see a gift as a good thing. And if it is a good thing, there is no reason why it should not 'look' as if it were. In truth, a gift should look like a gift. Given the "love of truth" of which he so often speaks, there must be something else going on here. I suggest that what is at stake for Kierkegaard here is the realization that in his theological framework, only God can give what is strictly speaking a "gift." Kierkegaard is not recommending that we give a "gift" that should not seem like a gift. Rather, this deliberation elaborates another dimension of the notion of our "infinite debt" to the other—that everything we have is given, so what we give is already a gift, and what we give is what we owe the other. In other words, what we give is not, strictly speaking, a "gift" to the other, which is why it should not look like one. Let me explain further.

We can infer that for Kierkegaard we learn what a gift is from considering

God's gift to us, which is the paradigmatic exemplification of a gift. What we learn is that a gift, as such, is a gratuity; something that, when done, is freely done because it is not owed. God's love for us is an absolute gratuity, for which it is perfectly appropriate for us to feel grateful and indebted. The appropriateness of such a response is due precisely to the absolutely gratuitous character of the act. If we think of the term "gift" as a formal designation for a *gratuitous* act that benefits the receiver, it becomes clear that not every benefit is a "gift." At least the two conditions of gratuity and benefit must be met.

In other words, the second dimension of Kierkegaard's understanding of gift implies that the notion of 'gratuity' is essential to a "gift" and thus theologically restricts the appropriateness of the term "gift"; it is not appropriate for the case in which we 'give' what we have already been given. In this view, someone may give another a good thing, a benefit, that is not a "gift" (and so should not be seen as one). When would it be a bad thing for something (X) to look like a "gift"? Presumably when, although it benefits the receiver, it is not a gratuitous act. That is, if X is owed to you, then when I give it to you, I should do it in such a way that it does not appear to be a "gift"—a gratuity for which the appropriate response is indebtedness. Why is it good to be reminded that it is not technically a "gift"? Because that reminder serves as a reminder at the same time of my infinite debt to you.

Consider the following remark by Kierkegaard once more. He writes that "the greatest benefaction, therefore, cannot be done in such a way that the recipient comes to know that it is to me that he owes it, because if he comes to know that, then it simply is not the greatest beneficence." When we ask why this is so, we can see that one answer is that what the recipient should come to know is that ultimately God is the giver; Kierkegaard says that "every human being stands by himself—through God's help" (WL, p. 278). Unless I give to another in such a way that the other sees that what I have given has been a gift from God to me, a gift enabling me to give to another, and that it is ultimately to God that the recipient should feel indebted, then I have misled the recipient—and that is a form of harm.[19] Later in the eighth deliberation of this series Kierkegaard will make clear that loving persons do not attribute to themselves the good they do but rather refer to the "third" (goodness or God) (p. 339).[20] If I do not give credit to God I am trying to take credit for giving what another gave to me;[21] Kierkegaard assumes he can count on the outrage you would feel at the dishonesty of a person who has received a great gift from you and who then proceeds to give it to another and to take full credit for it.

Consider a mundane example. Imagine that a person comes to share with me an apartment that has been generously given for my temporary use (set up with soap and toothpaste). She has forgotten to bring toothpaste and obviously feels in need of it. What are the various ways in which I could benefit her by providing some toothpaste? I could, of course, give her the tube that had been left for me, while putting myself at the center of attention as the "generous" one and making her feel stupid for not remembering something as indispensable as toothpaste, or even cheap, implying that I think she simply hoped someone else would provide it. I can be so condescending that she would perhaps rather go without than take the toothpaste from me. If she did take it, she would have received a good thing, but she would have seen it as something for which she was supposed to feel indebted and grateful (i.e., as a "gift" that put her in my debt). I could make it seem even more like a gift in this sense if I were to make it very clear that I was grudgingly sharing the last ounce of toothpaste I had or that I was in fact resentfully going to have to go without when I gave it to her. That would make it seem like a gift in the negative sense in which Kierkegaard is using it here.

More important, I don't need to give the toothpaste grudgingly for it to seem to her like a negative gift. I could give her the toothpaste with great kindness but still make it seem like a gift by making sure she understands clearly how difficult it will be for me to get some more for myself; I could give it willingly, even happily, but still make her feel that she is somehow depriving me of something and thus owes me something. We all know far too many ways in which we can give a good thing to another in a way that manages to burden that person.

I could, of course, prevent anything from being seen as a gift, just by not giving anything. But this is not what Kierkegaard is recommending—he wants us to give without making it seem like a gift. How can I do that? I can give it to her kindly and not take the credit for it, so to speak. I could say that an extra tube had been placed in the bathroom by whoever prepared the apartment for me to take over (and in fact the apartment lease itself was a gift, so the toothpaste is not part of any payment I have made for the apartment). If I give it to her while making clear that it was a gift to me, she need not feel indebted or humiliated. Another thing I could do is give it to her with the clear message that it is an extra tube I carry along for emergencies such as this, and I would be just as happy not to have to carry it home with me again when I leave. Once again, she could benefit from the thing I gave her but she needn't think of it as a gift (she could even think she was doing me a favor). I have given in such a way that I have freed her from the need to think of it as a gift. Ideally, if I saw her need I should give it to her before she had to feel uncomfortable by asking for it. Kierkegaard is recommending that I make it clear, with any good thing I give to another, that this was indeed a gift to me, meant to be handed on and so not a deprivation or loss to me. My obligation can be understood as the pressure, inherent in the gift we have been given, to express itself, to pass itself on, to be shared.

All of this sounds like caring, practical advice on how to give gifts, like love and forgiveness. And it sounds as if it would serve equally well as caring advice about how to give food to the hungry and shelter to the homeless. It sounds like a challenge to how we give, alerting us to the ways in which we can put people subtly in our power by making them dependent or humiliated. In other words, it seems quite a stretch to turn such passages as we find in Kierkegaard into an ethical thesis whose implication is that we are not allowed to benefit others. The answer to such a criticism is that we can give good things to others even if they are not technically a gift because we can give a good thing in a way that focuses on the other and takes us as much as possible out of the center of attention. Gratitude and appreciative use of the good thing will not invalidate it as a work of love. Kierkegaard is making a very practical point: we are all gifted by God, and to dare to give anything to another condescendingly or begrudgingly is to deny our own indebtedness to God. That is, we need to remember that we owe the other more than we could ever give (chapter 8). In this matter of giving to the other, we must avoid being "noble rogues" whose payment is the self-satisfied smile that puts the focus on us rather than on the other.[22]

It also seems, it should be said, quite a stretch to turn Kierkegaard's point into a philosophical puzzle whose implication is that there cannot, for humans, be a genuine gift. The paradoxical aspects of gift giving to which he calls our attention are not for him part of an intellectual conundrum or a philosophical thesis but a way to highlight our infinite debt; the problem is simply the practical one of making ourselves as hidden as possible.

V. The Gift and Love of Truth

Whether something should 'look like a gift' is not about external appearances but rather about the giver's theological convictions about the gift, the recipient, and the Ultimate Giver. It is, in the end, a question of truth. When God confers a benefit on me, it is a gratuity for which I should feel indebted and grateful. When I confer a benefit on you, however, the good thing I do for you is not a gratuity but something owed to you. This, I think, is the intuition behind Luther's suggestion that if I do not give you what I can, I am actually stealing from you.[23] The question at issue, then, is not the ambiguous one, whether I can give a gift that doesn't seem like a gift, but rather the clearer one—how can I give something good to someone in such a way that it doesn't seem to that person that I have thereby put him in debt or made her dependent on me?[24] How can I do something that helps you without turning it into a burden for you? Or alternatively, how can I give you something that you are owed so that it will be clear to you that it is rightfully yours. In other words, Kierkegaard's concern about how to give you something good "in precisely such a way that it looks as if the gift were [your] property" is a concern about affirming the truth.

Moreover, the question of truth comes into play in another sense as well. To help the other to be his own master means to help the other to have the courage to be himself "before God" rather than to try to "create himself" (WL, p. 271).[25] This can involve depriving others of their "fatuities" (p. 277); that is, helping others to be themselves includes depriving them of illusions, of inaccurate pictures of themselves. An appreciation of this intellectual honesty is indicated in the fourth deliberation in the first series, for part of "Our Duty to Love the People We See" is to challenge them while accepting them as they are.[26] Moreover, Kierkegaard will say in the tenth deliberation, on praising love, that self-denial is itself a form of "the love of truth."[27]

There is, of course, a potential danger in being reminded that everything we have has been given to us and that everything we give is therefore owed to the other rather than being a "gift," and it is a danger for both the giver and the receiver. The danger is that something of the joy of giving a gift and the joy of receiving one, the joy of generosity and the joy of gratitude, could be lost. There is technically no generosity and therefore technically no place for gratitude. It could be a grim picture. But Kierkegaard's emphasis on our concern for how the other feels should be reassuring in this respect. The bond between two people is not changed 'externally' by Christianity, he says, and this means that there is no change in the situation of gift giving in an external sense. My theological commitment is not a psychological phenomenon that interferes with the pleasure I have in either giving or receiving. Moreover, Kierkegaard is much more concerned about the times when it is not pleasurable to give because I don't want to give to the other. Here the reminder that we are gifted by God and that our gift is meant to be exercised, passed on, or shared is a vital motivating factor.

VI. The Work without Return and the Impossible Gift

A remarkable attention to the category of "gift" has emerged in the last few decades; prompted by earlier anthropological analyses of gift giving and commodity exchange, a variety of disciplines has taken an interest in the conditions of giving and receiving.[28] Current literature on intersubjectivity, as well as philosophical ethics, is very much interested in the notion of the 'interestedness' of gift giving, and it may well illuminate *Works of Love* to consider how Kierkegaard's position relates to this current intellectual landscape.[29]

In his 1963 article, "The Trace of the Other," Levinas introduces the notion of a work "without return,"[30] an idea that can be helpful in appreciating Kierkegaard's view of love as a gift that must not be seen as a gift. Like Kierkegaard, Levinas was from the beginning committed to the idea of a "gift of self": "To recognize the Other is to give"; being "for another" is the "giving" in which "a subject becomes a heart, a sensibility, and hands which give."[31] Echoing Kierkegaard's claim that love must be recognizable in its fruits, Levinas notes that without "works," "goodness is but a dream without transcendence, a pure wish."[32] He characterizes a "work" as follows: "[A] work conceived in its ultimate nature requires a radical generosity of the same who in the work goes unto the other"; again, *"a work conceived radically is a movement of the same unto the other which never returns to the same."*[33] A work that does not return to us, a work "without return," is a "one way movement" rather than "a reciprocity." Indeed, in words that could have come from Kierkegaard's mouth, Levinas insists that a work of love is not a work that "chases after merit" or "recompense"; it is not "absorbed again in calculations of deficits and compensations, in accountable operations."[34] Such a work, or loving response, must go on without being able to see "the triumph of its cause"; indeed, it must be content to "renounce being the contemporary of its outcome, to act without entering the promised land." Nevertheless, Levinas claims that a work is "not realized in pure loss"; he explains that "a work is neither a pure acquiring of merits nor a pure nihilism" since in both cases people take themselves to be "the goal" of their action.[35]

Levinas's article also raises the question of the relevance of the other's response. He suggests provocatively that the "radical generosity" of a work actually "requires an *ingratitude* of the other" because "gratitude would in fact be the *return* of the movement to its origin."[36] The work would lose its "absolute goodness" or its "radical generosity" if there were any kind of reciprocity, even the reciprocity of gratitude. This implies that a work of love is validated by such ingratitude, that such ingratitude is a necessary condition of a genuine work of love—which calls to mind the criticism we saw Løgstrup level against Kierkegaard's ethic. And it is true that Kierkegaard often speaks as if ingratitude is the only response a work of love will receive; he often phrases it in the idiom of "persecution" or "opposition" (WL, p. 193, 196). However, I suggest in chapter 5 that Kierkegaard is not committed to seeing hatred and opposition as either a necessary or a sufficient condition of love; more important to him is the requirement that we be *willing* to be hated or persecuted. Moreover, there is reason to think that Kierkegaard is himself aware of the fallacy in the reasoning that makes the genuineness of an act conditional on the kind of response that follows. As I noted earlier, his Lutheran background should have made him aware that such a necessary connection between love and ingratitude or opposition does not follow in an ethic premised on the model of God's love for us; God's love for us does not require ingratitude as a validation for its genuineness. In fact, Kierkegaard appeals to Luther's reference to Psalm 50, concluding that "'thanksgiving' is essentially the God-pleasing 'sacrifice'."[37]

Moreover, in a journal comment in 1851, Kierkegaard reveals the error in making ingratitude a mark of a work without return. Commenting on Savanarola's remark that "a great benevolence can be repaid only by great ingratitude," Kierkegaard re-presents Savanarola's position: "Excellent! For a benevolence which obtains for me another kind of benevolence, a direct payment, is certainly *eo ipso* not such a great benevolence. Suppose it to be a great benevolence—but it is rewarded with much gratitude—it becomes somewhat less. No, when it is rewarded with ingratitude, then only is it altogether a benevolence; if it is rewarded with much ingratitude, then it is quite truly a great benevolence."[38] But he continues, sarcastically: "Payment I have, then, at any rate. For from the recipient's great ingratitude I have the payment that my great benevolence becomes in truth a great benevolence." In other words, Kierkegaard realized that ingratitude can serve as a kind of repayment; ironically, ingratitude can perform the function of returning us to ourselves by guaranteeing our work (without return). In this respect, Kierkegaard seems to end up differing from Levinas on the issue of ingratitude.

Jacques Derrida is a current thinker whose conclusions about "the gift" have been provocative, to say the least. It has been suggested that his discussion of the gift is "perhaps Derrida's most Kierkegaardian gesture" and that "traces of Kierkegaard could be located on nearly every page" of the two texts that focus on gift.[39] Derrida concludes that "the gift is the impossible." He is careful not to say that a gift is impossible; what he says is that "the gift is the impossible," "the very figure of the impossible."[40] So Derrida is not out to deny the obvious—that there is a use of the term "gift" that refers to an economic notion tied to exchange or reciprocity, a cultural phenomenon in which a giver gives to another and the other recognizes it as a gift, generating a kind of obligation to repay in some form. We do give presents (*cadeaux*) to each other according to the customs of our respective societies; still, for Derrida "the gift" (*le don*) is the symbol for something that goes beyond that, for the kind of giving that is not caught up in an economy of exchange. What Derrida is pointing to is a notion that is by definition both economic and yet qualitatively other than economic—a gift that is not a gift: the impossible. Where does Derrida get such an idea? He certainly does not get it from observing practices of gift giving; he can't derive the qualitatively different notion of pure gift/nongift by quantitatively extrapolating from actual samples. He can't derive the noneconomic from the economic; he can't derive "the impossible" from the actual. So how could he come to conclude that "the gift is the impossible"? Why does he long for something that transcends the economic gift, and why does he try to formulate this conceptual problem with the notion of gift (i.e., that "the simple identification of the gift seems to destroy it"[41])? Is it anything other than arbitrary stipulation that affirms that there should be some noneconomic example of what is paradigmatically an economic concept?

As I read him, Derrida is not primarily concerned to stipulate some idiosyncratic notion of gift. Nor do I see him seeking a bizarre intellectual thrill from playing word games about gift and reciprocity that give counterintuitive results. He may be, of course, but he doesn't have to be. One way to make sense of his conclusion is to suppose that, like Kierkegaard, he is sensitive to the spectrum of ways in which things that are objectively benefits to the other are given. Like Kierkegaard, he is sensitive to the nonloving ways in which we manipulate, humiliate, or undermine the one to whom the thing that looks like a gift is given; and like Kierkegaard, he is aware of the compassionate ways in which we can try to hide ourselves in our giving. If we imagine to ourselves a picture of what the worst case of putative gift giving would be like and then abstract progressively from that picture all of the things that make it bad, we could in principle or theoretically extrapolate to a case in which absolutely nothing is allowed to influence the giver and nothing is given by the other in response—not appreciation, gratitude, or even acknowledgment of the gift. Presumably such abstraction is one way in which one can derive the conclusion that a gift can be given only if it is not seen as a gift; therefore, a gift as such is "the impossible." If we abstract and purify cases of bad gift giving and so arrive at a theoretically pure case, we end up concluding that to intentionally give a gift conceptually implies the correlative acknowledgment of it as a gift—and so disallows it as a gift. In this kind of extreme extrapolation, then, one could conclude that giving is so conceptually tied to a kind of reciprocity (at least the reciprocity of the acknowledgment of the gift) that it undermines its own possibility.

But why try to formulate this logical conundrum? What is the source of Derrida's impulse? It is easy enough to see that in Kierkegaard's case the paradox of the gift is tied to the notion of an "infinite debt." This may perhaps suggest one motivation of Derrida's commitment to the gift as "the impossible," one that he shares with Kierkegaard (and Levinas)—the sense that the idea of "gift" is problematical if in fact we are in a situation of infinite debt to one another. I think the danger sensed by each is that if the notion of gift is not understood to be excluding any and all reciprocation, we will forget the debt we owe to the other. Or at least we will forget that it is an infinite debt, and we will, whether we intend to or not, begin focusing on the response to the gift, counting and calculating and making excuses for ourselves.[42] This might justify Derrida's effort to show that the gift is "the impossible" on conceptual or theoretical grounds. But although Kierkegaard is as concerned as Derrida is about maintaining the integrity of the infinite debt, he nevertheless does not undertake the task of showing conceptual impossibilities in the concept of gift.

Of course, if we take the notion of infinite debt seriously, there can be no intelligible talk of gratuity, excess, generosity, extravagance, or squandering. Everything is already owed. Kierkegaard says, as we saw, that we must give, but we must give in a particular way—not in a way that means we cannot give, but rather in a way that puts every gift *sub specie aeterni:* under the particular light of a unique (divine) giving that can, so to speak, absorb the risk and safeguard the giving. That is, Kierkegaard's theological commitments to an infinitely giving God, and the need in love to express itself on pain of withering and dying, support (and even require) his affirmation of the possibility of love as giving. These commitments—the gift and the gift's need to give itself—preclude his denying the possibility of genuine giving.[43] And we have seen that the way in which he does this is by taking the giver out of the center of attention. The program is as follows: remove, as far as possible, concern for the giver and the giving so that we are not asking questions about them. Focus on the other's need. Let go of the idea of "return" in such a way that we don't keep asking if we have let go of it. The answer to the theoretical conundrum is simply to cut the knot that keeps us bound to evaluating the motivation of the giver—because that effort to make sure the gift is 'pure', to make sure that the receiver gets a 'pure' gift, still manages to keep the attention on us, the giver.

We are obliged, therefore, to give while hiding ourselves. That it is difficult to hide ourselves does not let us off the hook of the obligation to give. A completely unmotivated giving is a contradiction in terms—it could not be an action. The point is to guide the motivation—not that there is no giver, and not that there is no giving, but rather the concern is with the other, not to let the other feel indebted, dependent, humiliated, "nothing." The intellectual conundrum in which something is both motivated and nonmotivated, economic and noneconomic, plays the role that the question of the Pharisees played—it postpones the giving.

In sum, Kierkegaard insists that love is a matter of giving to the other, and the content of that giving is not spiritualized but concerned with the person's well-being in various senses (e.g., one cannot be free, independent, or oneself if one is oppressed by certain material conditions). Although in one sense the word "gift" is technically inappropriate for what we give to others (because it is what they are owed), once the focus shifts to compassionate concern for their feelings, it begins to seem natural to call love or forgiveness or material help a gift on condition that it is a benefit that is lovingly given. In that case whether something is a genuine gift would depend on how the benefit was given or done. Kierkegaard's example of the child who gives his parents a "gift" from the allowance they have already given him shows both sides of the pictures—both why we might want to continue to call it a gift and why we could understand someone who insisted it wasn't a gift.[44] In either case, the command to give to the other remains unconditional.

There are two main positions on the gift. (1) The gift is impossible because a genuine gift must be without return of acknowledgment or appreciation, so any response on the part of the other invalidates it. It is invalidated if there is any return. (2) The gift is possible, but it is only a gift if it is without the return of making us feel superior or giving us the credit due to God. To give a gift is to give without making it conditional on a return, however subtly one may conceive it. In this view a gift is not invalidated by the return of appreciation or gratitude or use; it is invalidated only if a return is claimed or demanded. This view, Kierkegaard's view, distinguishes between the result or natural outcome of our giving and the requirement or demand for such a result or outcome.

Kierkegaard's claim that love is a giving of oneself and his advice on how to give have implications for the question of mutuality in a relation. In the end, then, the question about whether acknowledgment or appreciation invalidates a gift becomes the question of whether Kierkegaard's account of love for the other can do justice to the mutuality that we feel in our heart of hearts is part of a genuine relation. But we leave that discussion for a later time (chapter 15). Right now we have to deal with the fact that attention to the other's distinctiveness has been emphasized so strongly in this deliberation that Kierkegaard feels the need to assure us that there is still a significant contrast between nonpreferential love and preferential love.

VII. Love's Appreciation of Distinctiveness

A. The Contrast with Preference—Sacrifice Again

Erotic love and friendship are examples of preferences for certain kinds of distinctiveness in the other. The discussion of the gift we give to the other in terms of appreciating the other's distinctiveness raises the question of whether neighbor love has then collapsed into preferential love. Is it distinguishable from erotic love and friendship? We have already seen that one way of distinguishing the attentiveness of neighbor love from the attentiveness of erotic love or friendship appeals to the arbitrariness of the latter. Here Kierkegaard suggests another way of distinguishing them: in contrast to neighbor love, "erotic love and friendship have limits" (WL, p. 273). They love the other's distinctiveness, but they will not give up the love or friendship even if "the other's distinctiveness requires this very sacrifice." In this way the deliberation returns again to its opening—true love does not seek its own; true love sacrifices itself for the sake of the other. But does that mean that we are not to love our own distinctiveness?

B. Loving Our Own Distinctiveness—"As Yourself" Again

Kierkegaard does in fact say that we are to love the other's distinctiveness rather than our own (WL, p. 269). Such a claim seems to challenge what we have concluded about his affirmation of "proper self-love." But if we take his discussion in its entirety, we can see that it actually supports the idea of proper self-love. In his own terms, we must love our own distinctiveness because it is what comes from God's hand, because "distinctiveness . . . is God's gift by which he gives being to me, and he indeed gives to all" (p. 271). One's goal is "before God to be oneself." To love one's own distinctiveness is "to know what God has given him" (p. 271). All of this retrieves the theme of the "as yourself" again—it would indeed be inconsistent to be obliged to love the other's distinctiveness, as what is God-given, but to reject the idea of one's own creation as the gift of our distinctiveness.

The content of our love, our gift, is being "for others," which finds expression in all the ways in which we can help others to be themselves. Suffering is usually the concomitant of such efforts to help others. Kierkegaard will elaborate this in the following deliberation, when he explains how the one who loves "forgets himself" in order to think of someone else's misery or suffering or loss (WL, p. 281).

chapter eleven

Love's Forgiveness

"Love Hides a Multitude of Sins" (2:V)

It could easily be argued that the themes of forgiveness and reconciliation are at the heart of the deliberations in the second series. Not only do the next two deliberations, "Love Hides a Multitude of Sins" (2:V) and "Love Abides" (2:VI), offer a variety of perspectives on love's forgiving relation to others, but also the deliberation entitled "The Victory of the Conciliatory Spirit in Love, Which Wins the One Overcome" (2:VIII) is an explicit treatment of forgiving reconciliation. All three deliberations offer recommendations, both directly and indirectly, for cultivating loving relationships—ways that minimize divisiveness and maximize reconciliation. In other words, all three deliberations, like the earlier deliberations on presupposing love, believing the other, and hoping for the other, give indisputable evidence of Kierkegaard's concern with interpersonal relationships.

In this chapter and the following I will examine two deliberations that focus on forgiveness in two particular forms: love's covering up or forgetting the sins or weakness of another and love's openness to reconciliation. (The eighth deliberation, which I will consider in chapter 14, describes not only openness to reconciliation but also a positive effort to bring it about.) Put negatively, these two deliberations—"Love Hides a Multitude of Sins" and "Love Abides"—focus on the refusal to look for or to highlight sin or weakness and the refusal to withdraw from love in the face of another's rejection. These are paradigmatic examples of what Kierkegaard calls "love in its outward direction," that is, "works of love"

(WL, p. 282). Moreover, both deliberations raise a question we need to address: the question of whether Kierkegaard's ethic advocates works of love that involve an unhealthy kind of blindness or wishful thinking or an intellectual dishonesty at odds with Kierkegaard's express commitment to seeing people just as they are.

I. Inner and Outer—"Redoubling"

Kierkegaard opens this deliberation (V) in a provocative way: "[W]hat love does, that it is; what it is, that it does—at one and the same moment" (WL, p. 280). This is a way of challenging us to rethink the relation between inner and outer. He explains that what love does in an "outward direction" effects a "redoubling" in "an inward direction back into itself" and suggests that these two movements are "simultaneously one and the same." This is provocative because it gives us a different perspective on the relation between inner and outer than we have seen thus far in these deliberations. In fact, it sounds a little like the claim that Kierkegaard, in various pseudonymous works, attributes to Hegel and then rejects— that 'the inner is the outer and the outer is the inner.'[1] In Hegel's thought, presumably the claim meant that the end result is only an unfolding revelation of what was already there in the beginning: Spirit actualizes itself by manifesting itself and returning to itself.[2] Kierkegaard and some of his pseudonyms saw this as a mistaken identification (or the making commensurate) of the inner with the outer, a conflation of the two that ignored the ways in which the outer could be at odds with the inner (as when monastic behavior belies its inner ideal) or the ways in which there could be a qualitative break in which an outer (revelation) goes beyond what can be discovered by turning inside.[3] In any case, Kierkegaard began *Works of Love* by complicating his own rejection of Hegel's view of the identity between inner and outer: he insisted in the first deliberation that love must bear fruits, must be recognizable in its fruits, even though there is not a single word or deed that necessarily guarantees whether love is present. In other words, he admitted that there is some kind of relation between inner and outer in which the inner must (necessarily) be manifested, but he warned against certain kinds of attempts to determine the relation. Most of the deliberations that followed the first one can be understood as performing some variation on this theme (hidden/manifest, inward/outward, unseen/seen, or invisible/visible). This deliberation continues that task (especially in relation to the themes of the "like for like" and the "as yourself"), but it does so by initially proposing a simultaneity between inner and outer.

II. "Redoubling"—Like for Like

The concept of "redoubling"[4] has already been mentioned in the first deliberation, where Kierkegaard notes both that the concept "neighbor" is a redoubling of oneself and that the love commandment's "as yourself" is a redoubling (WL, p. 21).[5] It is also scattered throughout Kierkegaard's entire authorship.[6] In this deliberation he initially gives three examples of "redoubling" or the "double mode" of inward/outward: (1) the one who gives bold confidence to others experiences bold confidence for herself or himself; (2) the one who saves another from death, saves herself or himself from death; (3) the one who remembers others is remembered by God. These are meant to illustrate the abstract formula that "love is always redoubled in itself" (p. 282) or, more concretely, the principle that "the one who loves receives what he gives" (p. 281). This provides us with the generalized formulation of the "like for like," which we considered earlier in its negative form (pp. 233, 256). It is strange, Kierkegaard admits, but in the case of love, one "acquires" or "retains" what one gives. In the case of love, "this giving and this receiving are one and the same"—"I myself receive what I give to another" (p. 282). These repeated claims are important, not least because they bear on the question of self-sacrifice and love of self; they suggest that in the case of my love for another there is no zero-sum game. I do not make a sacrifice without being benefited in some way. This is yet another way in which Kierkegaard's account maintains its emphasis on the "as yourself" part of the love commandment. It is, in some sense, an important affirmation of symmetry in relation (a topic to be considered more fully in chapter 15, "Love's Asymmetry").

This particular formulation of the "like for like," which runs through all the deliberations, raises the specter of "exchange," which Kierkegaard has already declared to be at odds with genuine love. Does confidence in the "like for like"— one gets what one gives—turn neighbor love into a kind of "profit" transaction"?[7] The only way to avoid concluding that it does is to focus on the nature of what one 'gets.' The benefit received is one that is not extrinsic to what one gives; in other words, I will be benefited, but the value of that benefit will, of course, depend on my already having a certain hierarchy of values. The benefit of forgiving is being forgiven by God, but this will only seem a benefit if my values are religiously ordered. That is, when Kierkegaard says that we get what we give, he is highlighting the other side of the scriptural promise that he noted earlier—we save our life (only) if we lose it.[8] We may have confidence that we will get what we give, but it is not a case of calculated exchange precisely because what we get is not extrinsic to our giving. Moreover, it takes courage to have this confidence; this is precisely the "struggle of faith" (WL, p. 380). Where what one gets is conditioned on having certain values, and where risk is involved there is no simple exchange.

Consider in detail what we learn from one of Kierkegaard's examples of love's redoubling—that "the one who loves, who forgets himself, is recollected by love" (WL, p. 281). Kierkegaard claims that the one who loves "forgets his suffering, in order to think of someone else's, forgets all his misery in order to think of someone else's, forgets what he himself loses in order lovingly to bear in mind someone else's loss, forgets his advantage in order lovingly to think of someone else's—truly such a person is not forgotten. There is one who is thinking about him: God in heaven, or love is thinking about him" (p. 281). In other words, while the one who loves forgets himself or herself in order to think of the other person, God is thinking of the one who loves (p. 281).[9] The theme of what it is to live "for others"—a theme that has been especially prominent in the last few deliberations[10]—finds remarkable expression here. And the social implication (i.e., the purpose of forgetting oneself is to be able to remember others) is reinforced by Kierkegaard's reminder of the content of imitation of Christ: "[A]t the very moment you yourself are suffering most of all, simply think about consoling others, for this is what he did. The task is not to seek consolation—but to be consolation."[11] In addition to illustrating the "like for like" principle, this example also has implications for the social and material caretaking implied in this ethic.

The presupposition of the believer's freedom to forget self and think about the suffering of others is that I do not need to obsess about myself; I do not need to be anxious about making sure I have enough for me because God doesn't forget me. I can afford to be generous since in an important sense I do not need to provide for myself. If we are busy remembering ourselves, we are striving for self-sufficiency; there is no need for God to remember us. As Kierkegaard colorfully puts it: "The self-lover is busy; he shouts and makes a big noise and stands on his rights in order to make sure he is not forgotten—and yet he is forgotten" (WL, p. 281). If we are busy grasping and hoarding for ourselves, not only is there no need for God to fill our hands with what we need but also he cannot do so; only when our hands are empty can they be filled again. The believer's forgetfulness of self does not amount to the threatening sacrifice it would otherwise be because we are already and always provided for. It has been argued that this generous (ungreedy or ungrasping) attitude to the "struggle for life" and the "pursuit" of happiness is the mark of a distinctively Christian ethic.[12] At the very least it is a hallmark of Luther's own emphasis on our confidence in God.[13]

Kierkegaard began this deliberation with the announcement of the redoubling "like for like," and he concludes the introductory part with the suggestion that the way in which "love is always redoubled in itself" also holds true "when it is said that love hides a multitude of sins" (WL, p. 282). In other words, the fourth example of redoubling, which he will now attend to in detail, is the following "like for like"—the one who hides a multitude of sins finds that his or her sins are also hidden.

III. Love Hides Sins

Kierkegaard's suggestion that love "hides" sin is actually only his endorsement of the scriptural message in the epistles of Peter and Paul, repeated by Luther.[14] But since it has been criticized as a recommendation of dishonesty or self-deception, unfair both to ourselves and to others who are affected by the one whose sins we hide, it is crucial to see what is actually at stake for Kierkegaard in this traditional recommendation to hide sins. It should be noted that this theme was not a new one for Kierkegaard: in 1843 he produced two discourses, both entitled "Love Will Hide a Multitude of Sins."[15] In addition, four years after *Works of Love* was published, he published a third discourse entitled "Love Will Hide a Multitude of Sins."[16] I will consider those treatments of the theme insofar as they illuminate this deliberation.

Kierkegaard himself provides an interpretive tool for examining the ways in which love hides sins when he takes up the visual metaphor implied in the categories of the unseen and the seen. Some ways of hiding sin concern sin that is not seen and some concern sin that is seen. The first way of "hiding" sins might be called the way of *nondiscovery*. Kierkegaard takes "discovery" to be an active verb, implying a "conscious and deliberate effort to find" something (WL, p. 285). Although technically it makes no sense to say that we can hide what we don't actually see, Kierkegaard's point is the more general one—love hides sin when we lovingly refuse to go looking for it. It is, in effect, hidden from us when we fail to see it, so we contribute to hiding sin when we refuse to either look for or highlight people's weaknesses, faults, and sins. In one of the 1843 discourses, Kierkegaard makes our active role in seeing sin even clearer: "It does not depend, then, merely upon what one sees, but what one sees depends upon how one sees; all observation is not just a receiving, a discovering, but also a bringing forth, and insofar as it is that, how the observer himself is constituted is indeed decisive."[17] Thus, in *Works of Love* Kierkegaard is condemning the tendency we have to take pleasure in learning about the dark or seamy underside of people's lives—their sins and their weaknesses. It is the tendency to think that it is sophisticated to discover weakness and sin, whereas it is gullible and "shallow to believe in the good" (p. 284). Kierkegaard here effectively repeats Luther's interpretation of the fifth and eighth commandments: it is wrong to "censure one's neighbour's sins or transgressions, and not to overlook or minimize them"; it is wrong to "explain away and lampoon the goodly life, words or works of one's neighbour," and to "speak of any evil."[18] In short, Kierkegaard concludes that to look for the worst (the shabby or the petty) in others to look good by comparison is "a bad way to become better" (p. 286).

Kierkegaard makes quite clear that when he is condemning this response to the neighbor's faults and weaknesses, he is ranting against the vanity or self-indulgence that motivates a calculated effort to "discover" sin in others. This exploring tendency we have, whether born of idle curiosity or deliberate malice, finds its extreme expression in "slander, defamation, and lies" (WL, p. 287); when it wants to discover evil badly enough, it will embellish what it finds or sometimes simply make it up, believing what it wants to believe. Kierkegaard's condemnations of this unloving exercise are unusually strong: "discovery" of sin is something we do "craftily, mistrustingly" (p. 283); it is "shrewd, sly, foxy" and tends to "corrupt" (p. 283); it is a "malignant curiosity about evil" or "cunning's reconnoitering for an excuse for one's own faults" (p. 286). In other words, he is not talking here about the sin we come across by accident. He is exposing a deliberate activity that is clearly antithetical to the goal of cultivating interpersonal relationships or community.

To repeat, strictly speaking, one cannot "hide" what one does not see, but Kierkegaard's point is that sin is hidden (unseen) by love. It is hidden by love's refusal to set out on a sordid voyage of discovery; since love does not go looking for sin, it does not see the sin it would have seen had it persisted in its unloving detective work. In this sense sin remains unseen because it is hidden by the failure to discover it.

A second way in which sin is hidden by love involves the prevention of sin. Kierkegaard says that hiding sin is achieved by preventing the sin from coming into existence, by being careful not to provide "occasions" for sin (WL, pp. 297, 299).[19] In one of the 1843 discourses on hiding sin, Kierkegaard similarly suggests that one hides sin by reducing sin ("refrain from disputes and you will reduce sins") and by turning a sinner "from the error of his ways."[20] In these cases we could say that sin remains unseen because it is hidden by the attempt to prevent it.

These ways of hiding sin, or rendering it unseen, by lack of discovery or by prevention refer to the sin we do not actually see; therefore, they do not offer any evidence for the charge of willful blindness or intellectual dishonesty.[21] However, some ways of hiding sin presuppose that the sin is clearly seen. Kierkegaard suggests that what love "cannot avoid seeing or hearing, it hides," and it does so in three ways: (1) by silence, (2) by mitigating explanation, or (3) by forgiveness. In all these cases we clearly see the sin; thus, only in such cases is the charge of intellectual dishonesty even relevant. We need to determine whether Kierkegaard renders plausible these recommendations for hiding sins we see.

First, love hides sin by being silent—that is, by not spreading the news of the neighbor's faults, not repeating gossip or spreading rumors about faults and weaknesses, whether or not they are true (WL, pp. 289–90). The refusal to be silent in this respect, whether careless or malicious, tends to "corrupt people" and certainly provides occasions for more sins. Kierkegaard condemns the casual way in which people ruin other people's lives by careless gossip, and he vehemently expresses his contempt for such behavior, as well as his rationale for his contempt: "I would rather, God forbid, arrive in eternity with three repented murders on my conscience than as a retired slanderer with this dreadful, incalculable load of crime that had piled up year after year, that may have spread on an almost inconceivable scale, put people into their graves, embittered the most intimate relationships, violated the most innocent sympathizer, defiled the immature, led astray and corrupted both young and old" (p. 291). We know enough to guard against the plague, he says, but we welcome into our homes with open arms the bearers of this far more malignant social infection. In short, the recommendation not to spread tales of faults and weaknesses does not in itself support the criticism that we are being intellectually dishonest or ethically irresponsible. Moreover, this rationale emphasizes Kierkegaard's concern with interpersonal relationships.

Second, love looks for "mitigating explanations" because "every event, every word, every act, in short, everything can be explained in many ways" (WL, p. 291). Here Kierkegaard brings in imagination again, asking us to be creative, ingenious in looking for the good, and generously open to possibility. He suggests that this aspect of his theme has already been broached in part in the deliberations "Love Believes All Things" and "Love Hopes All Things" (p. 294), especially in his challenge that it is not intellectual honesty that causes us to mistrust another, that our "one-sided fear of a certain kind of error" comes from less worthy motives than we might at first think (p. 232). He might also have included the deliberation "Love Builds Up" since all three deliberations have challenged us with the suggestion that love presupposes love in the other, trusts the other, and hopes for the possibility of good for the other. In other words, they have insisted, as this deliberation does, that love does not mistrust others—does not presuppose or expect faults in others. Love insists on persevering in the search for the most lenient explanation, and here again the rationale seems to include the cultivation of relationships and community.

Does the recommendation that we look for mitigating explanations imply that there is no stopping point—no point at which we may legitimately conclude that the search for lenient explanations has become silly? Does the generic mitigating explanation that we are unable to infallibly determine motivation render another's excuse unfalsifiable; does it mean that we can never reach a point at which the search for mitigating explanations is contrived and implausible? Kierkegaard makes two points in this respect. First, he brings in the issue of *justice,* noting that those who are "judges and servants of justice" are called on to discover guilt and crime, that is, to judge and to punish (WL, pp. 292–94). Insofar as that is their station in life, we applaud them when they do a good job. And presumably, if we were "a judge appointed by the state" or a "servant of justice," it would be our responsibility to persevere conscientiously in discovering holes in the mitigating explanations offered for a crime. Kierkegaard assumes, however, that "the rest of us are called to be neither judges nor servants of justice, but on the contrary are called by God to love" (p. 293). Still, he seems to envision the possibility that we may need to step in for the sake of another; he hints at something like this in the passage about the wife who sees her husband being hurt, whereas the husband sees nothing (p. 288).[22]

Second, even when we are not servants of justice, it does seem that there can be a limit to the plausibility of mitigating explanations. That we can and do often reach such a limit is actually indirectly affirmed by Kierkegaard's consequent discussion of "forgiveness," which he puts in a different category from mitigating explanations. If we were never able to judge another, never infer an actual sin, there would never be a reason for forgiveness.

IV. Love's Giving by Forgetting

In one sense, love's not looking for sin, love's being silent about it, or love's finding mitigating explanations for it might all be considered ways of forgiving. They are clearly expressions of a generous and charitable attitude. But Kierkegaard takes the time in this deliberation to introduce and develop the concept of forgiveness as something distinctive: forgiveness is "the most notable way" of hiding sins, and what is distinctive is that forgiveness is a way of *forgetting* the sin.[23] It is important to note, however, that Kierkegaard will put strong qualifications on what forgetting means: it does not mean effacement of the sin.

What does it mean to "forgive" sins?[24] Once again, Kierkegaard takes up the visual metaphor of the seen and the unseen. In forgiving sins, "the one who loves sees the sin he forgives, but he believes that forgiveness takes it away. This cannot be seen, whereas the sin can indeed be seen; on the other hand, if the sin did not exist to be seen, it could not be forgiven either" (WL, p. 295). Thus, the sin is seen, and "forgiveness removes what cannot be denied to be sin" (p. 294). Yet "what is seen is nevertheless not seen"—the one who loves "believes away that which he indeed can see!" (p. 295). What is it to see what is not seen, to see what remains unseen? For Kierkegaard, this paradox is a way to describe forgetting. To forget sin is to remove it, take it away—but not by causing it to cease to exist. He explicitly contrasts what God can do with what we can do: "[F]orgetting, when God does it in relation to sin, is the opposite of creating, since to create is to bring forth from nothing, and to forget is to take back into nothing" (p. 296). We, however, can neither create nor de-create anything. Rather, what we can do is to put it behind our back. Since "it is impossible to see what is behind one's back,"[25] this metaphor is an appropriate one for the forgetting that constitutes forgiveness. In other words, it is not a forgetting that de-creates the sin or takes its being away, as God's forgetting does for us; rather, the figurative way of speaking about how we try not to let the sin come between us, prevent our nearness to the other, is in terms of putting it behind our back: "What is hidden behind my back, that I have seen" but as I turn in love to the other person I cannot see what is behind my back (p. 296). That is, it remains in existence, but it is not in front of us; it is not something we allow to hinder our relationship. The end of forgiveness is reconciliation.

Earlier Kierkegaard told us that we must forget *ourselves,* and he comforted us with the Christian message that if we forget ourselves we will not be forgotten (by God). The purpose of forgetting ourselves is to remember others in their suffering. Here we are being told that we must forget *another person's sin against us,* and here we are brought full circle to the "like for like" involved in forgetting sin—that is, as we forget the sins of others, our sins will be forgotten. Remembering others involves forgetting ourselves, and forgetting ourselves means forgetting the sins of others against us, so remembering others means forgiving others. Moreover, Kierkegaard implies that denying forgiveness is itself a sin when he says that by denying forgiveness we increase sins (WL, p. 296).

Kierkegaard is concerned, too, with the quality of the forgiveness we give. We will see in the deliberation on love's conciliatory spirit more evidence of Kierkegaard's sensitive concern for how we give to others, but even here he tells us that there are ways of forgiving another that are unloving, ways that "increase guilt" or ways in which I try to "make myself important" by forgiving (WL, p. 295). This is a reminder of the first deliberation's emphasis on the hiddenness of love. It is also a reminder of the "as yourself" element of the commandment: if you have ever needed forgiveness you should not wonder whether it can do any good to forgive another (p. 295).[26]

It is clear that we learn how to forgive others in part by considering the kind of forgiveness we seek from others, but we also learn how to forgive by considering the kind of forgiveness we receive from God. This kind of forgiveness is a theme that Kierkegaard very often treated in his religious discourses, but he says explicitly in this deliberation that he is not going to consider forgiveness as we receive it from God: "In Scripture we read, and these are *Love's* own words, that many sins are forgiven one who loved much—because the love in him hides a multitude of sins" (WL, p. 282). But "we shall not discuss that now [because] in this little book we are continually dealing with the works of love; therefore we are considering love in its outward direction." The scriptural passage to which he refers here (the one that supports forgiveness in an inward direction) is one he actually used frequently, both before and after he wrote *Works of Love*: it is the story about the woman of ill repute who interrupts a meal Jesus is having in a Pharisee's house in order to anoint his feet with expensive perfumed ointment (Luke 7:36–50).[27] In a variety of discourses Kierkegaard considers how love hides sin in the context of an individual's relation to God—both the love of the individual for God and God's love (through Christ) for the individual.[28] In Kierkegaard's reading of this story, Jesus makes "the love that was already there" powerful enough to hide her sins—"her many sins were forgiven her, because she loved much."[29] A more recent translation of the scriptural passage reads: "Her sins, her many sins, must have been forgiven her, or she would not have shown such great love," and Kierkegaard addresses this dimension in the discourse "But One Who Is Forgiven Little Loves Little." This is a version of the "like for like": "First you love much, and much is then forgiven you—and see, then love increases even more. This, that you have been forgiven so much, loves forth love once again, and you love much because you were forgiven much! Here love is like faith."[30]

It is interesting that, in one of the early discourses Kierkegaard addresses the question of love's hiding sins precisely in terms of the opposite—the way in which love discovers sin, that is, one's own sin. For example, when people begin truly to love, they discover their previous sinfulness, and because of the love that is in them they are able to hear the comforting message that love covers their sins at the same time as it dis-covers them.[31] The emphasis is on the self's appropriation of the comforting message that because you love much your many sins will be covered and vice versa. But this, Kierkegaard says, is not the kind of forgiveness he wants to discuss in *Works of Love*.

The kind he discusses in *Works of Love* is introduced in another 1843 discourse on hiding sin, which provides a striking contrast by considering the outward or social dimension—the emphasis is on forgiving others. He does this in terms of the story of another sinful woman, the woman taken in adultery by a group of self-righteous scribes and Pharisees and brought before Jesus to test his response (John 8:1–11).[32] We are being shown an example of forgiving another as we would like to be forgiven since in this biblical story Jesus challenges the woman's accusers: "If there is one of you who has not sinned, let him be the first to throw a stone at her." The social import is obvious in Kierkegaard's question: "[W]hen quarreling, malice, anger, litigation, discord, factionalism live in the heart, does one then need to go far to discover the multiplicity of sin."[33] Moreover, in this discourse Kierkegaard suggests that Abraham was covering a multitude of sins when he "pleaded" with God to spare Sodom and Gomorrah: "Love prays for the sins of others."[34]

How is forgiveness supposed to show itself? In this same 1843 discourse, Kierkegaard spends a lot of time discussing the notion of "revenge." He begins with what he calls the pagan belief that 'revenge is sweet' in order to contrast it with the truly loving renunciation of revenge. His examples tells us a great deal about what is at stake for him: "[R]are is the person who forgave in a such a way that the contrite enemy was [seen as] his neighbor," "who loved in such a way that when his enemy prospered" he did not enviously begrudge him his good-fortune, who did not call down God's wrath upon his enemy, because he realized "that no person can quite see through another."[35] Just as an evil eye discovers much that love does not see, so too, love sees much that an evil eye does not see.[36] Thus, in this 1843 discourse, Kierkegaard begins the discussion of forgiveness in an outward direction, which he completes in *Works of Love*'s deliberation on how love hides a multitude of sins.[37]

In the light of Kierkegaard's earlier treatment of neighbor love in terms of blindness and vision, we can say that the metaphor of hiding or covering sin suggests that forgiving is a way of seeing. In his final discourse on love's hiding a multitude of sin (1851), Kierkegaard formulates this as a kind of blindness: love makes one "blind, blind to his neighbor's sins."[38] But given his emphasis in this deliberation on how seeing is a precondition of forgiving, we can say that for Kierkegaard love is a forgiving seeing. That he is not recommending intellectual dishonesty is evident in his early proposal to have God as our model in this loving work. Surely when God forgives, God does not cease to see clearly all there is; God is not deceived when God forgives.[39] The implied inference is that God is not being intellectually dishonest in forgiving sin, so we need not be either. In the end, the only justification Kierkegaard can offer for his recommendation that we hide a multitude of sins is found in the answer to this question: what is the goal of hiding the sins we see? Kierkegaard's defense lies in two of his assumptions: first, the assumption that the ways of hiding sins that he recommends are meant to enhance and facilitate personal relationships with one another and, second, the assumption revealed in the earlier deliberations (2:I–III) that there is a risk of deception in both trust and mistrust and that our unwillingness to believe the best of someone is not necessarily due to pure intellectual honesty after all.

chapter twelve

Love's Faithfulness

"Love Abides" (2:VI)

In the process of introducing the discussion of forgiveness in the preceding chapter, I suggested that this next deliberation, "Love Abides," can also be seen as a study of forgiveness. Through its repeated references to "the moment of forgiveness" and the "transition of forgiveness" (WL, p. 314), its concluding page comes across as the summation of a discussion of forgiveness, but it is forgiveness looked at from a different angle, namely, love's faithful abidingness. Love's fidelity is seen as its continued *openness* to reconciliation with the other.[1]

Kierkegaard introduces this deliberation with an exhilarating affirmation: "Yes, praise God, love abides!" He refers to the abiding love that comforts all those lost and parched in the desert—more literally, those threatened with despondency, listlessness, terror, anxiety, and uncertainty (WL, p. 300–301). It is interesting that such comfort is described in very this-worldly terms: the remembrance that "love abides" allows us to "see the fields and forests become green *again*, see the teeming life in the air and water stirring *again*, hear the singing of the birds begin *again*, *again* and *again* see the busy activity of people in all kinds of work." But this abiding love—this spring in the desert—is God's love, and Kierkegaard acknowledges his obligation to speak in this text of human works of love, so he shifts quite abruptly into the expected discussion of what it means for our love for another person to abide or endure (p. 301).

When he speaks here of abiding in love as "a work of love in faithfulness"

(WL, p. 313) we can complement this discussion with the earlier discussion of the unchangingness and independence of love construed as duty in "You *Shall* Love" (1:II, A).[2] The claim that "love abides" is another version of the requirement that love not vary directly with changes in the one loved: "Such a love stands and does not fall with the contingency of its object . . . it never falls" (p. 39). Moreover, in "Our Duty to Love the People We See" (1:IV) Kierkegaard provides a wonderful description of the faithfulness that is part of loving the person we see, rather than the "imaginary idea of how we think or could wish that this person should be" (p. 164). He refers there to the negative vision in which with one eye we "look at him, testing, searching, criticizing"; this critical "third" takes the distanced stand of an observer, rather than an engaged lover (p. 165). Our loving acceptance of others in their wholeness does not preclude challenging their weaknesses, but it does preclude this kind of 'testing' attitude: "Life certainly has tests enough, and these tests should find the lovers, find friend and friend, united in order to pass the test. But if the test is dragged into the relationship, treachery has been committed" (p. 166). It is precisely "faithlessness" to subject the other to such testing: "Is it loving the person you see if you at every moment look at him, testing, as if it were the first time you saw him?" *Faithlessness* is precisely this way of loving the unseen as opposed to the faithfulness of loving the person one sees (p. 163). Kierkegaard appeals to Peter here, this time not to show the need for love that Jesus had but to illustrate faithfulness—Christ was faithful to the traitor Peter (p. 170).

The theme of love as faithfulness is part of the fabric of *Works of Love*, and we should refer back to these earlier deliberations to fill out the picture of love's abidingness. We should also look ahead to the deliberation on the work of love in recollecting the dead (2:IX), where faithfulness will again become a crucial theme.[3] This sixth deliberation adds two important reminders to those we find elsewhere. First, the phrase "love abides" does not refer to "an inactive characteristic that love has as such" but rather to an "active work" (p. 302). It is not a matter of inertia, keeping on in the absence of an interruption; it is not simple continuance or mere habit. It is a work to "preserve" oneself in love (p. 302). We should consider this to be an explicit reminder of what is implied in all the deliberations thus far—namely, the active striving that is part of all works of love. Second, although one gains by loving abidingly, it is a "work of love in faithfulness" for those whom one loves (p. 313); here, too, we are reminded of what is true of all works of love—that they are *for the other*.

I. The Poet and Love

The claim that love abides is another way of saying that Christian love can only be understood by constant reference to "the eternal," and one strategy Kierkegaard uses to explore this theme is the development of a stark contrast between "poetic" discourse about love and Christian discourse. Kierkegaard refers to the poet's use of language: like Christianity, "poets' tales" praise faithful love, but unlike Christianity, they speak sadly of the misfortune of a love that changes, that ceases, or that can be unilaterally broken (WL, p. 303). Christianity refuses to speak in this way. In the process of considering the limits of poetic discourse about love, Kierkegaard indirectly raises the question of the limits of any discourse about the eternal. Thus, the reference here to the poet gives us an opportunity to consider further Kierkegaard's view of religious language and his differing conceptions of the poetic.

Kierkegaard has numerous references to "the poet" in *Works of Love*, who uses language about love in a way that decisively contrasts with Christian usage, and the discussion of the poet's speech about love in this deliberation relies heavily on references in earlier deliberations (especially 1:I, II). At the outset of the book, Kierkegaard tells us that the poet speaks of a love that wants to be eternal but remains perishable; the sadness in a poet's songs is a function of temporality: "What the poet sings about must have the sadness, which is the riddle of his own life, that it must blossom—and, alas, must perish" (p. 8). Indeed, the poetic understanding of human faithfulness always leaves the poet "disconsolate" (p. 64).

In contrast, Christian love "abides, and for that very reason it *is*" (WL, p. 8).[4] Kierkegaard repeats this peculiar locution: "Something that *is* cannot be sung about—it must be believed and it must be lived."[5] It is worth noting that in the second deliberation (II, A) he contrasts "existence" with "enduring continuance" (p. 31) and speaks condescendingly of what has "only existence" even though it has not (yet) suffered change (p. 34); thus, the claim that Christian love "*is*" aligns it with "enduring continuance" rather than mere existence.[6] Love's abidingness is more than a contingent, unending existence; it is the work characterized by the continuous striving required by the commandment.

Christian love is commanded rather than poetically celebrated. The dimension of eternity is tied to the notion of commandment, and this is lacking both to the love that the poet sings about and to the worldview the poet inhabits. Here the poetic is identified with what is elsewhere considered the aesthetic way of life. The poet is the spokesperson for the love that is not commanded, for "instinctive and inclinational, and spontaneous love"; the poet is the "priest" who celebrates a union of two people with the oath of love (WL, p. 29). But the "poetic misunderstanding" is the failure to recognize that such love is not secured by anything higher than itself—the two people swear their love "*by their love*," instead of swearing to love each other "*by eternity*" (p. 31). The poet is right to believe that anything less than eternal love is not worth talking about, much less singing about, but the poet fails to understand that swearing by eternity, or by duty, is the only way to keep this love from changing, that "*only when it is a duty to love, only then is love eternally secured*" (p. 32). Kierkegaard noted early on that the duty to love "is a change of eternity" (p. 25), a phrase he uses repeatedly. To be seen as a duty is to be seen in the light of eternity, and without the eternal we have either the deadening presence of "habit" (p. 37) or the despairing recognition of perishability (pp. 40—41).[7]

Insofar as he is "true to himself and to his task as a poet," the poet has faith in the "poetic worth of erotic love and friendship, in the poetic view of them" (WL, p. 49); but in that poetic view inclination is idolized and erotic love and friendship "contain no moral task" (pp. 50–51). Thus, "the poet and Christianity are diametrically opposite in their explanations" of love (p. 50). One study of Kierkegaard's account of the poetic divides his authorship into three phases, arguing that he "begins with, then partially but not entirely departs from, and finally returns to a positive concept of the poetic as integrally connected with portrayal and actualization of ethical-religious ideals in human life."[8] *Works of Love* is placed in the middle and predominantly negative group of writings, in which Kierkegaard focuses on the dangers and limitations of the poetic relation to actuality; in fact, it is said to provide "perhaps the most devastating criticism of the poet and the poetic" found in that middle group.[9] Whether or not this evaluation holds true for the whole of *Works of Love*, it is certainly true of this deliberation, for here what the poet teaches about love serves precisely as a negative standard that we should use to determine whether we are speaking about Christian love.[10]

The evaluation of poetic discourse about love in this deliberation, however, needs to be seen against the background of Kierkegaard's earlier suggestion (in 2:I): "All human speech, even the divine speech of Holy Scripture, about the spiritual is essentially metaphorical" (p. 209). This appreciation of the metaphoricity of religious language shows that for Kierkegaard the failure of poetic discourse about love does not lie in its use of metaphors—all religious language is metaphorical.[11] It has been claimed that in rejecting the modern philosophical demand for univocity, in pointing to "the poverty of univocity," Kierkegaard has turned philosophy into poetry.[12] But the sense in which this might be true needs to be carefully assessed in the light of both Kierkegaard's critique of the limits of the aesthetic and his appreciation of the rich multivalence of language. Just as he was not averse to claiming that "God is like a poet,"[13] Kierkegaard would not be averse to affirming the many ways in which our discourse about God and the eternal is poetic (i.e., it cannot be flatfootedly treated as univocal).[14]

This other conception of the poetic is also found in a late journal entry in which Kierkegaard suggests that "the Christian language" is "different from all human language."[15] He acknowledges that "the Christian language uses the same words we men use, and in that respect desires no change. But its use of them is qualitatively different from our use of them; it uses the words inversely, for Christianity makes manifest one sphere more or a higher sphere than the one in which we men naturally live, and in this sphere ordinary language is reflected inversely." He illustrates his thoughts with the words "loss" and "gain," but he could as easily have pointed to the word "love" as an example. It is interesting that Kierkegaard nuances the notion of opposition between Christian and non-Christian uses of language with a musical analogy: "As in music we speak of transposing a part to a key different from that in which it was originally written, so the Christian language is wholly and entirely qualitatively different from our language at every point, even though we use the same words."[16] In other words, the difference between the "celebrated glory of poetry in smiles or in tears" and the "earnestness" of eternity and the commandment (WL, p. 25) is that the latter puts love in an entirely new key. Here the idea of opposition is sustained in the notion of 'inversion,' but it is softened by the new musical analogy. This journal passage thus reveals that the status of religious language is more complex than the simple contrast with the poetic had suggested.

Throughout Kierkegaard's writings we can find a variety of understandings of the poet, including the religious poet, and these are certainly worth exploring for what they might suggest about the way in which Christian love is to be understood. A Nietzschean brand of poetic creation (from nothing) does not exhaust the possibilities for poetically crafting or editing a self or for *letting oneself be* poetically composed.[17] Although this deliberation does not offer much in the way of a positive understanding of the poetic, it is still worth considering the other deliberations in which imagination is seen more positively, for example, 2:I–IV. Kierkegaard's attention to the way in which venturing on possibility is upbuilding is reminiscent of other claims about the religious uses of possibility. Moreover, his attention to the way in which we are to imitate God, who loves the differences and fosters distinctiveness, reflects something of how the aesthetic is preserved and transfigured in the religious, transforming the aesthetic value of imaginative apprehension of concreteness and particularity and sensuality.

Even in an account that contrasts poetic and Christian understandings of love, therefore, we can find an intriguing way in which the aesthetic is preserved in the Christian understanding. In one sense, the imagination performs a similar function in both the aesthetic and the religious—it leads the individual out to possibility and makes him or her a stranger or alien in the world. It does this in opposite ways, however: the aesthetic use of imagination takes one away from actuality, whereas the religious use makes one a stranger or alien within actuality.[18] This latter, "poetic" situation seems to be at the heart of Kierkegaard's various descriptions in *Works of Love* of how the Christian lover faces or provokes opposition from the world.

II. The Threesome and the Unending Dance

Explaining his account of love's faithfulness, Kierkegaard puts forth two rather startling claims. The first is that "when one ceases to be loving, he *has never been loving*" (WL, p. 303). The second, and related, claim is put metaphorically—that, the dance doesn't end just because one of the partners leaves (p. 307). This deliberation is essentially an attempt to make these two claims plausible.

We can all come up with scenarios that are relevant to the question of whether love abides (or should abide), scenarios in which there is a break between two people in a relationship—with an innocent, loving one suffering rejection. Sometimes it is a husband whose wife runs off with another or a friend whose friendship is thrown aside by another, and, of course, we should not forget the one most likely in the front of Kierkegaard's mind—the fiancée who learns that her intended husband has broken the engagement. In all such cases, Kierkegaard argues, "Christian" love will abide.

Underlying all of Kierkegaard's claims about love's abidingness is his deep commitment to the idea that you cannot break with love in a particular case and assume that you can still be loving in other cases. He has already stated this emphatically in the earlier deliberation "Love Hopes All Things" (2:III):

When someone says, "I have given up my love for this person," he thinks that it is this person who loses, this person who was the object of his love. The speaker is of the opinion that he himself retains his love in the same sense as someone who has assisted another person with money and says, "I have stopped giving this assistance to him"—so now the giver keeps the money himself that the other received previously, he who is the loser, since the giver is of course far from losing by this financial shift. (WL, pp. 255–56)

But Kierkegaard insists that "it is not this way with love." One cannot remain loving while excluding anyone. Kierkegaard concludes that "I am not entitled to the adjective 'loving' if I have given up my love 'for this person,' although, alas, I may even imagine that he was the one who lost" (p. 256).

The poet's talk about a break between two people assumes that the one who causes the break is not precluded from being in a loving relation to other people (WL, p. 304). According to Kierkegaard, however, love is a peculiar sort of thing because to refuse to love any person is to withdraw oneself from love as such. He points to the lack of analogy between love and money: "For example, a man may have had money, and when it is gone, when he no longer has money, it still remains just as certain and true that he *has had* money. But when one ceases to be loving, he *has never been loving either*" (p. 303). Kierkegaard is not denying that we can erotically love one person without erotically loving others; he is not denying that we can cease being one person's friend while being someone else's friend. Erotic love and friendship do not abide in the sense he speaks of; they are precisely the changeable. Without a deeper commitment, our romantic infatuations grow dimmer and our friendships can become impatient—which is just how life is. Kierkegaard had already brought to our attention in the second deliberation how "spontaneous love" can lose "its ardor, its joy, its desire, its originality, its freshness," that such love "is dissipated in the lukewarmness and indifference of habit" (p. 36). "Erotic love," he notes, "is temporality's most beautiful but nonetheless most frail invention" (p. 311); obviously, one cannot abide in or be unconditionally faithful in what does not bear duty's stamp of eternity (pp. 312–13). The kind of love that can abide, and that should abide, is the kind of love he has been speaking of earlier—neighbor love, the love that means that I care for the other as an equal before God and will not forfeit my responsibility for him or her. Neighbor love is faithful to the other even when erotic love and friendship (which depend on mutuality) fail (p. 311).

Neighbor love abides; it never wastes away, and if I refuse to love, I am the loser. Kierkegaard's first premise for this conclusion is that all love involves a threesome; even our most intimate relationships are never simply between two, but rather always include a "third"—namely, love (WL, p. 301). This harks back to the notion of "middle term," which we considered in chapter 5. In the case of erotic love and friendship, Kierkegaard noted earlier, preferential love is the third, the middle term (p. 58). When love has the courage to bind itself (p. 38), a husband and wife, or two friends, are related to each other by their loving—that is, each being related to love (p. 304). Love (or God who is Love) is the third.[19]

Here the threesome—you, me, and love—is a way of accounting for the possibility (1) that one can break with another person and yet not break with love and (2) that one can break with another person without automatically preventing the other from holding on to love. It is precisely because our relationships are in fact triadic that rejected love can abide in love. It is because every relationship is in fact a trinity that one cannot break another person's relation to love simply by refusing to love him or her. To abide in love means to refuse to break with love—that is, to refuse to stop loving. Another's rejection of us does not affect our obligation to love that person as an equal before God, which amounts to being responsible for and responsive to such a person in his or her need. Anything else would be breaking the love commandment. Given his affirmation of the love commandment, Kierkegaard has no choice but to describe it in terms of the command to preserve oneself in love—no matter what.

At first glance some of these pages (especially pp. 305–7) in *Works of Love* suggest that Kierkegaard is recommending what we would call a pathological attachment to an other, that he is telling us that the best love is an obsessional, wishful thinking—a failure to face and cope with reality. But he is not talking here about a pathological dependence on the other, about refusing to see that the other no longer loves you. What he said earlier about "habit" shows that he clearly distinguishes "abiding" in love from such habit; duty is understood as an ongoing affirmation of commitment, which fights against habit (pp. 36–37). The recommendation to preserve oneself in love is not an uncritical valorization of inertia or habit. To abide in love is to refuse at every moment to withdraw from love, to refuse to "fall away from love" (p. 305). This need not mean, however, that one cannot withdraw from the other person, that one should never leave another or change a relationship (or break an engagement, for that matter). He is recommending that I continue to love but not that I remain in an abusive relationship, that I pine away forever for an unrequited love, or that I pathetically follow around town the one who rejected me. Neither masochism nor silliness nor stalking is implied in preserving oneself in love. In sum, this discussion needs to be complemented by the consideration in chapter 8 about the limits on self-sacrifice, or it will be entirely misunderstood.

What Kierkegaard seems to be suggesting is something deeper—something we may ourselves have already felt at times, even in our pain and loss—that the one who loves is better off even if he or she gets hurt; to become cynical, angry, hateful, or despairing is the greater loss. The innocent sufferer who holds to love, doesn't give up on love, still trusts in love, and is able to love—he or she has "the better part." We can leave those who mistreat or manipulate or abuse us, without ceasing to see them as children of God: that is, we must refuse to hate the one who tries to harm us because we are commanded not to hate anyone. We can be abandoned by the one we love, while refusing to not love the one who leaves.

What point does Kierkegaard want to make by claiming that a dance cannot be unilaterally ended? He is admittedly fond of dance imagery; he often refers not only to dance as such, but to individual balletic moves.[20] When he asks whether the dance ends because one partner leaves, he answers that in one sense it does (WL, p. 307)—presumably that particular dance ends, at least for the time being.

Yet he insists that the dance is, nevertheless, not ended by the person who leaves. There is a sense in which the one who stays on the floor remains open to the passion of dancing, has not given up on "dance." Love is "the dance" that one still believes in. In this sense, love's abidingness is a reference to the future rather than to the past; it is a kind of expectancy that doesn't close off the further possibility of love (p. 307). Although Kierkegaard does not here refer back to *Fear and Trembling*, there is an echo of Abraham's expectancy—revealed in his ability to take his son Isaac back again with joy, to receive the finite again.[21] Sometimes it is easier to simply give up all expectation and resign oneself in such a way that one would prefer to be left alone after all, perhaps even resenting the return of the other because one is afraid to put oneself at risk again. Although Kierkegaard states that this is not simply a matter of temporal expectancy and that the phrases "love abides" and "immortality" are synonymous (pp. 312, 311), it is nevertheless clear that love abides even in this life by remaining open at all times to reconciliation in neighbor love if the one who rejected us later comes back, wanting reconciliation (e.g., p. 312). The characteristic of love's abidingness is a form of love's hopefulness, and the appropriateness of the ingredient of hope in interpersonal relationships militates against those aspects of the discussion that might otherwise imply a unilateral and disinterested model of neighbor love.[22]

Kierkegaard seems to be fond of using grammatical symbols of interruptions when he describes the works of love. We have already seen his use of the dash as a way of exploring the hiddenness of our loving.[23] Here he uses the metaphor of the "hyphen"—another indeterminate interruption—to suggest the open-endedness, the inability to decide at a given moment whether something is finished or waiting for something else. Although Kierkegaard refers to "the moment of forgiveness" when the faithless one returns, the "transition of forgiveness" already is accomplished by the one who remains loving (WL, p. 314).

III. Not Returning Hatred for Hatred

If we pay close attention to the examples Kierkegaard uses in this deliberation, we can see that his account of what it is to break a relationship is extreme. He describes the situation in which one person breaks the relationship" as "terrible," the person who broke it being filled with "hate, endless, irreconcilable hate" (WL, p. 308). Kierkegaard's description is amazingly detailed and graphic: not only does the one who broke the relationship take care never to see the other person again, but also he hates the one he rejected so much that he "finds it agony to breathe in the same world where the hated one breathes," and "he shudders at the thought that eternity will again hold both of them" (p. 308). In such a case, the person has not simply broken with the other, but with love itself. Whether or not every breakup is that traumatic, Kierkegaard is taking the extreme case to make his point that *even then*, the rejected person's love should abide. Kierkegaard's understanding of the love commandment earlier was that the withdrawal of love should not be met with hatred (p. 34); here it enjoins us not to meet hatred with hatred.

His earlier claim that "love never hates" (WL, p. 34) clearly seems to allow that in some cases what is required by the love commandment is the generalized benevolence that refuses to abandon responsibility for another in need, rather than the attentive caring that is part of love in other kinds of relationships. This deliberation indirectly suggests an important dimension of Kierkegaard's ethic in *Works of Love*—the lack of a single concrete model for what it is to love another. In other words, there seem to be times when Kierkegaard is speaking about a minimal state of love for others, for example, when they hate us or resist or reject our love (as in this deliberation and the upcoming one on reconciliation). This could apply as well to cases in which another is clearly antithetical to our preference and inclination. This understanding of the fulfillment of the love commandment under certain conditions does not, however, mean that such generalized benevolence is the goal in other situations, in which there is friendship or special relations contoured by preference or familial obligations. The faithfulness among friends and lovers that has been put into a different register under the light of the eternal clearly demands more than not hating.

chapter thirteen

Love's Mercifulness

"Mercifulness, a Work of Love Even If It Can
Give Nothing and Is Able to Do Nothing" (2:VII)

At the center of this deliberation is the graphic emblem of 'the heart'—the
"heart that despite poverty and misery still has sympathy for the misery of others" (WL, p. 322). Elements that are important in interpreting its key distinction
between mercy and generosity are found in at least two earlier deliberations,
which it presupposes the reader has understood: first, the deliberation in which
Kierkegaard most explicitly addresses the way in which Christianity is not concerned with "externals" (II, C) and, second, the deliberation on fulfilling the law
through outward action (III, A). Thus, this deliberation provides a striking example of how we should not excise any deliberation from the context in which
Kierkegaard has set it. Moreover, it brings to the fore Kierkegaard's sense of
mercy as taking part in the misery of others—a sympathetic engagement that is
both active and imaginative.

I. Impotent Mercifulness

Adorno, whose criticism of *Works of Love* for its abstraction and inwardness we
met earlier (chapters 4 and 5), found grist for his mill in this deliberation.[1] He
charges that Kierkegaard's ethic implies a dangerous indifference to temporal cir-

cumstances, as shown in his dismissal of the objection that the needy must receive "every possible help" and his assumption that "there is only one danger; the danger that mercifulness is not practiced."[2] Adorno argues that the affirmation of impotent mercifulness reveals the "flippancy of a rigorousness which is ready to leave everything in its status quo."[3] The result of such indifference, according to Adorno, is a "spiteful" and "stubborn maintenance of the 'givenness' of social order [which] is socially conformist and ready to lend its arm to oppression and misanthropy."[4]

Why would a deliberation on mercifulness call up such bitter criticism as Adorno offers? What in the work of loving mercifulness could possibly interfere with the work of helping our neighbor? Why does it seem to some critics to legitimize an indifference to the needs of others? The very title, "Mercifulness, A Work of Love Even If It Can Give Nothing and Is Able to Do Nothing," does, admittedly, give us reason to pause. It seems to divide the inward from the outward in a radical way. Underscoring the value of impotent mercifulness seems to put such a premium on inwardness that it threatens to undermine Kierkegaard's early insistence on the "fruits" of love, love's outwardness. In what follows I will examine (1) Kierkegaard's understanding of mercifulness in relation to the charge that his ethic devalues concrete material needs and interests in favor of either the 'internal' or the 'eternal,'[5] and (2) his understanding of mercifulness as an imaginative taking part in the condition of others, particularly but not exclusively in their suffering.

II. Kierkegaard's Presuppositions

This deliberation is certainly calculated to "awaken" us from our complacent views. It includes some shocking advice : "Be merciful to us more fortunate ones! . . . you have it in your power to alarm the rest of us—so be merciful!" It includes the troubling assessment that "from the point of view of eternity, that someone dies is no misfortune, but that mercifulness is not practiced certainly is." Moreover, it dismisses the "well-intentioned" social conscience, which cries that "the main thing is . . . that need be remedied in every way" (WL, p. 326). And all of this is on a single shocking page! What is the point of such a discussion?

Any assessment of this aspect of Kierkegaard's ethic requires a careful attention to detail. We need to locate the presuppositions that inform his discussion and account for its emphases. The first presupposition is that there is a *distinction between mercy (Barmhjertighed) and financial generosity (Gavmildhed)*. The opening sentence of this deliberation reveals Kierkegaard's irritation with a certain kind of emphasis on generosity, benevolence, or beneficence. He expresses his frustration with temporality's "sensate conception of the size of the gift" (WL, p. 326) and the "large sums that amaze" (p. 319), as well as with the vainglorious and self-congratulatory way in which we pride ourselves on our extravagant generosity in giving financial gifts that far outshine those of others (p. 319). This irritation does not at all question our responsibility "to do good and to share," but it does challenge the particular ways in which we grow up worshiping "money,

money, money!" (p. 319). In short, he begs us to avoid the idolization of money, for "from earliest childhood we are disciplined in the ungodly worship of money" (pp. 320–21), and he urges us to recognize the ways in which we can hide our lack of concern for others behind public displays of financial generosity, displays that are not only gratifying to our egos but also often serve to provide an advantage to ourselves (e.g., a tax advantage). In all of this, Kierkegaard seems to be following in the footsteps of Luther's suggestion in the "Treatise on Good Works" that without faith, generosity is only squandering money.[6]

Kierkegaard's conclusion, "Mercifulness is infinitely unrelated to money" (WL, p. 319), can only be understood in the light of his second presupposition, which is that *if mercifulness is present, generosity will follow*. He says this both explicitly and repeatedly. First, if you know how to instill mercifulness, "then generosity will follow of itself and come by itself accordingly as the individual is capable of it" (p. 315). Once more, he reminds us: "It follows of itself that if the merciful person has something to give he gives it more than willingly" (p. 317). However, "it is not on this that we focus attention, but on this, that one can be merciful without having the least thing to give." Finally, as if anticipating the misunderstandings that would occur, he writes: "It follows naturally of itself that if the merciful person is able to do something, he is only too glad to do it. But that is not what we wanted to focus attention upon, but rather upon this, that one can be merciful without being able to do the least thing" (p. 324). The claim that "mercifulness is infinitely unrelated to money," therefore, does not undermine the expectation that if one has resources one should mercifully be generous.

The third presupposition is that the message is addressed to a *particular audience*—namely, YOU, without the advantages that allow you to be generous. He repeats that "the discourse addresses itself to you, you poor and wretched!" (WL, p. 322); "the discourse addresses itself to you, you wretched ones who are able to do nothing at all" (p. 325). Kierkegaard has deliberately decided "to speak to the poor about practicing mercifulness" rather than "to speak to the rich about practicing generosity" (pp. 321–22). This focus on a particular kind of audience does much, I think, to explain what would otherwise be callous advice. In the next section I will explore why for this audience the reminder of equal obligation to be merciful is *upbuilding* and why the emphasis on the irrelevance of consequences does not serve to promote indifference to the effects of our efforts to help our neighbor.

III. The Rationale: Ought Implies Can; Striving versus Achievement

One can see the point of this deliberation better by looking again at what Kierkegaard accomplished in earlier deliberations. The requirement of indifference to "externals" is actually first introduced in the third part of the deliberation on the love commandment as such (II, C). Those recommendations of blindness to temporal distinctions, as well as statements of the inevitability of temporal distinctions and Christianity's indifference to the "goal of one temporal condition," are the first instances of what fuel the charge that *Works of Love* dictates a conservative preservation of the status quo and callous indifference to unjust social conditions. It is worth recalling this earlier discussion now because I suggest that the way in which the indifference was introduced there can shed light on how this provocative deliberation on mercy can be understood.

In chapter 4, I argued that Kierkegaard's recommendation of indifference to temporal circumstances is part of his strategy for demonstrating the requirement of equality in the obligation to love and follows directly from it, and that it need not, and is not intended to, support an overall attitude of indifference to physical or worldly need. I suggest that the strategy that I highlighted there applies also to this deliberation, and therefore any reading of the deliberation on mercy must be supplemented by the points made in II, C. This is a particularly strong example of the mutual illumination provided by reading deliberations from both series in conjunction with one another.[7]

Insofar as neighbor love is a duty, Kierkegaard must guarantee two things, both of which are made explicit in the second deliberation (II, C) of the first series. First, *ought implies can,* so the duty must *be able to be fulfilled* by all equally. Writing of love of neighbor, he reminds us : "Eternity . . . assumes that every person can do it and therefore only asks if he did it" (WL, p. 79). This same claim is reinforced in this deliberation on impotent mercifulness: the duty cannot be biased in favor of those with financial resources. Kierkegaard's point in II, C (which can be extrapolated to all audiences) was that whatever your temporal circumstances, you are *bound* to fulfill your duty to love the neighbor; it remains your duty in any case. The point that needs to be emphasized for this particular audience (in VII) is that whatever your temporal circumstances, you are *able* to fulfill your duty (and so it remains your duty). He writes in this deliberation: "Oh, be merciful! Do not let the envious pettiness of this earthly existence finally corrupt you so that you could forget that you are able to be merciful" (p. 322). To assume that it is only worthwhile to speak to the rich about mercifulness to the poor means that the poor person "is abandoned by the world's conception of his ability to practice mercifulness and therefore is singled out, given up, as the pitiable object of mercifulness. . . . Merciful God, what mercilessness!" (p. 322)—hence, "Be merciful. This comfort, that you are able to be merciful" (p. 325). His sympathy for "the misery of those who perhaps from childhood or from some time later in life have been so tragically devastated, so badly ravaged, that they are unable to do anything at all, perhaps are even scarcely able to express sympathy in clear words" leads him to ask: "should we now be so merciless as to add this new cruelty to all their misery, to deny them the capacity to be merciful?" (p. 325). These passages clearly suggest that the reminder of equal obligation is used, for this audience, to build up, as a reassurance of equal ability.

The second thing Kierkegaard must guarantee to make sense of a claim that all must and can be merciful is a distinction between *striving* and *achievement*. The consequences of our actions are subject to things outside our control. This is made explicit in II, C: "What a person will or will not achieve is not within his power" (WL, p. 84). In this deliberation he cautions us to "guard ourselves against confusing mercifulness with what is linked to external conditions, that is, what love does not have in its power" (p. 316). The recognition that we cannot always achieve what we set out to does not, however, preclude the responsibility to strive to achieve certain ends.

Kierkegaard's attention to these themes in both deliberations entails an indifference to social (socioeconomic-political) conditions, but only in two very specific senses: (1) indifference about the condition of the one obliged to love and (2) indifference about the condition actually effected by our attempts to fulfill our duty. That is, concerning the determination of one's obligation to be loving, one's physical circumstances can be ignored; moreover, meritorious fulfillment of duty cannot be conditional on one's particular temporal achievements.

There is, undoubtedly, a kind of extreme rhetoric in the following passages: "Be merciful, be merciful toward the rich! Remember what you have in your power, while he has the money! Do not misuse this power; do not be so merciless as to call down heaven's punishment upon his mercilessness. . . . If the rich person is stingy and close-fisted . . . then you be rich in mercifulness! Mercifulness works wonders . . . it makes the stingy gift into a larger sum if the poor person mercifully does not upbraid the rich for it, makes the morose giver less guilty if the poor man mercifully hides it" (WL, pp. 322–23). Likewise, he writes provocatively: "Be merciful to us more fortunate ones! Your care-filled life is like a dangerous protest against the loving Governance; therefore you have it in your power to alarm the rest of us—so be merciful!" (p. 326). He goes on to ask "which is more merciful: powerfully to remedy the needs of others or quietly to suffer and patiently to watch mercifully lest one destroy the joy and happiness of others?" (p. 326). These are, to say the least, unexpected claims in a discourse on love. The only justification is that Kierkegaard, master rhetorician, offers this "in confidence," so to speak, to *this* audience.[8] We need to be reminded that even if we are among the materially disadvantaged, we are able to be a neighbor to others, including those who are socially or materially above us, so far as they need help and so far as we can offer it.[9]

The entire discussion in this deliberation on mercy admittedly puts a premium on the exercise of mercifulness *rather than* generosity, presumably because the distinction between generosity and mercifulness serves to reassure people that all have equal potential to fulfill their duty. It also puts a premium on the exercise of mercifulness *rather than* the alleviation of suffering. But it should be noted that a stark distinction between mercifulness and alleviation of suffering qualifies the relevance of results, given our inability to control all the outcomes of our actions. An emphasis on the alleviation of suffering could be said to have put an undue value on a capacity to provide externals (a capacity not all have to the same degree). In other words, this anticonsequentialist emphasis is in support of the claim that meritorious fulfillment of duty is not conditional on particular temporal circumstances and achievements—fruits of love are equally possible to all.

I argue in chapter 4 that the attempt to deflect concern with temporal conditions (in terms of consequences) because fruits of love may be materially ineffective does not entail acosmic otherworldliness. It need not empty content from the duty to help the neighbor enjoy the fulfillment of the purpose for which each was created and, hence, the duty to help alleviate those conditions that hinder that fulfillment. Here Kierkegaard extends his concern with the disadvantaged to suggest ways of being merciful.

To put the efforts of the poor into perspective, he reminds them that the "well-intentioned" call to remedy temporal need "has a sensate conception of the size of the gift and of the ability to do something to remedy the need" (WL, p. 326). His provocative claim that "from the point of view of eternity, that someone dies is no misfortune, but that mercifulness is not practiced certainly is" must be understood as a response to the cry that "the most important thing is that help be given," where help is understood in terms of "the size of the gift." Given the particular audience he addresses, such reminders encourage each one to see what he or she can do as significant and thus encourage each to do what he or she can. Nothing in this need serve to excuse those with more from doing more. No one can legitimately draw the conclusion from this discussion that one has no duty to help people with fewer resources, which would be committing the fallacy of assuming that because some people (the poor) are told that they ought to love you (the rich), you are excused from the obligation to love them.

In sum, this deliberation does not mitigate the obligation of those with advantages to be loving, nor does it mitigate their responsibility for alleviating the lot of those less fortunate. Its advice is guided by a determination to be even-handed about the ability to perform works of love; this means that it will not focus on externals. One could, of course, argue that Kierkegaard's practical instruction (e.g., the Samaritan) is better than his theorizing or that his theorizing is dangerous precisely because it is able to be misunderstood. In the end, one could still have doubts about whether Kierkegaard makes the right choice when he decides, as the speaker, "to speak to the poor about practicing mercifulness" rather than "to speak to the rich about practicing generosity" (WL, pp. 321–22). But given that choice of audience, the advice is not inappropriate, nor is it able to provide an excuse for the rich not to practice generosity.

IV. The How of Mercifulness

Kierkegaard assumes that the scriptural commendation of the poor widow who gave her few pennies implies that "the greatness of the gift increases in proportion to the greatness of the poverty" (WL, p. 318). He asks us to consider the following question: "Is it mercifulness to give a hundred thousand to the poor?" and he answers: "No." He then asks: "Is it mercifulness to give two pennies to the poor?" Again he answers: "No." Rather than allowing gifts to be measured in absolute amounts, Kierkegaard offers the guideline of proportion; this is a way of showing that the HOW of the giving is decisive. His conclusion is that "mercifulness is *how* it is given" (p. 327), so it may be mercifulness to give the hundred thousand or it may not; it may be mercifulness to give the two pennies or it may not. He is not denying that there may be mercifulness in giving the hundred thousand dollars; mercifulness can and should express itself in generosity to those in need. He is simply trying to point out what we might not find as obvious, which is that one can be merciful even when one gives only two pennies or one or none; it depends on what you have and why you are giving. The mercifulness is not a function of the amount of money given, and the amount of money given can actually distract us from the mercifulness. Kierkegaard once again explicitly appeals to the usefulness of the heuristic device of making something clearer by allowing it to be seen in conditions that are not filled with other distracting elements. If you want to see the circles that a stone produces when it is thrown into the water, you should not throw it into a raging waterfall or a rough sea; you would do better to seek out a quiet pool of water where you can "properly focus your attention upon observing the movements" (p. 328). So, too, with an attempt to focus on the essential character of mercifulness.

This emphasis on the HOW is another way of emphasizing the tension between the seen and the unseen and is relevant to all the deliberations. We find in this deliberation an intriguing reference to the impossibility of portraying a genuine work of love: Kierkegaard writes: "I have often pondered how a painter might portray mercifulness, but I have decided that it cannot be done" (WL, p. 324). I can portray the transfer of a loaf of bread but not the gift of a loaf of bread; or if I can portray the gift of a loaf of bread, I cannot portray that it is the giver's last loaf. It is in this sense that externals are irrelevant. Kierkegaard's remark here on the inwardness of mercy, its invisibility, recalls the judgment by Climacus in the *Postscript* that trying to portray some things is "like wanting to paint Mars in the armor that makes him invisible."[10] Whatever can be portrayed cannot be mercifulness since "mercifulness is *how* it is given."[11]

V. The Practice of Mercy

Early in the deliberation Kierkegaard considers this objection: What good is mercifulness without money? (WL, p. 318) What can it accomplish? We need to ask that, too, because it is important to distinguish between ineffectual, self-indulgent pitying of others and the work of love in actually *"practicing* mercifulness" (p. 322). If mercifulness is a "work," and if it is not the achievement of financial or material assistance to others in their distress, what constitutes its outwardness? We have already noted that striving can be outward even when we cannot guarantee results. But what if we can literally "give nothing" and "do nothing"; what if we cannot even begin to assist someone materially? What then is the work we practice? In the *Concluding Unscientific Postscript*, Climacus anticipates the message of this deliberation when he decisively qualifies his emphasis on the interiority of action: "To have thought something good that one wants to do, is that to have done it? Not at all, but neither is it the external that determines the outcome, because someone who does not possess a penny can be just as compassionate as someone who gives away a kingdom."[12]

What is it to practice mercy? Kierkegaard gives two examples, both variations on the good Samaritan story, which suggest that the outwardness of love is shown in *sympathy*: that is, they illustrate the duty to "keep within your bosom this heart that despite poverty and misery still has sympathy [*Deeltagelse*] for the misery of others" (WL, p. 322). It is interesting that when Kierkegaard speaks of our response to the misery of others here, he uses the word that means to participate, literally *to take part in* (*Deeltagelse*), rather than other common words for sympathy that might have highlighted the notion of feeling with the other. What is it to have such sympathy for others, to take part in, to involve oneself in, their suffering?

Kierkegaard first revises the story of the merciful Samaritan as follows: what if the Samaritan had been walking when he saw the injured man, and so had nothing with him with which to bind up his wounds; what if he had then carried him on his shoulders to the nearest inn and begged the innkeeper to help the injured man but had no money with him to offer the innkeeper for his services? He would still have proved merciful. And what if, because the innkeeper refused to help, he then took the injured man to a further place to rest and tried to staunch his bleeding, but the man died in his arms? He would still have proved merciful, as merciful as the original Samaritan, who was effective in getting help for the wounded man. He would have shown sympathy.

In other words, Kierkegaard is not giving us license to simply feel pity for others, complacent in our conviction that we have nothing to give; the practice of mercifulness is not a simple reflection of how we feel about the other. Rather, he is showing by this example that we are to extend our concern and concretely engage with the other, with the result that we will try to do whatever we can. If Christian love is "sheer action," as he says repeatedly in III, A, then love's expression in merciful sympathy is also action. Such sympathy is not a substitute for action; it is an action that involves us with another person in a unique way. This is shown more clearly in his second variation on the merciful Samaritan. Suppose, he says, that two men were traveling and "both of them were assaulted by robbers and maimed, and no traveler passed by" (WL, p. 324). Mercy can still be shown by one to the other, for suppose that "one of them did nothing but moan, while the other forgot and surmounted his own suffering in order to speak comforting, friendly words, or what involved great pain, dragged himself to some water in order to fetch the other a refreshing drink. Suppose that they were both bereft of speech, but one of them in his silent prayer sighed to God also for the other—was he not then merciful?" Comforting words and silent prayer for another are examples of what we can do even when we can do nothing else and can give nothing else.[13] Mercifulness is not displayed in some interior monologue we have; it is either words spoken to the other or to God about the other.

Kant distinguished between responses to the suffering of others motivated by sympathy and those motivated by respect for the moral law or duty, arguing that only the latter were truly moral.[14] Hume, in contrast, argued that morality is a function of our natural response of benevolent sympathy (corrected by the "general view" taken by the imagination).[15] Kierkegaard, however, seems to go further in the sense of making it a duty to have such sympathy.

VI. Sympathy and Imagination

Since Kierkegaard agrees with Kant that one cannot command an inclination or a feeling, we need to ask what it could mean to have a duty to have sympathy or compassion. It is not a duty to have a particular feeling, but, on the other hand, Kierkegaard does not see a compassionate response as simply a matter of particular actions being performed.[16] In line with the scriptural tendency to transcend any absolute dichotomy between feeling and will, Kierkegaard points to an affective response that demands imaginative activity on our part; as such, it can be subject to a command, at least indirectly. As one modern account of the relation between sympathy and morality puts it: "Sympathy is not a primitive animal feeling but is an exercise of the imagination involving self-consciousness and comparison."[17] Sympathy is necessary to moral response, a "fundamental requirement of morality," precisely because "a certain amount of sympathy is required if anyone is even to *notice* that someone else is *in need* of help."[18] The road to the demand for equal treatment of equal needs cannot even be ventured on unless we have "a being who is able to imagine himself in the place of another so as to realize the other's sufferings as if they were his own," so that "the other man's suffering is not indifferent to him, but exerts a certain pressure for relief comparable with his own natural desire to relieve his own."[19]

Kierkegaard appears to appreciate this imaginative and affective aspect of sympathy; in his journals of 1850, he wrote:

> I have had a deep sympathy for simply and solely being human, especially the suffering, unhappy, handicapped, and the like. I have learned to thank God for this sympathy as a gift of grace. God knows I have become a sacrifice because of this very sympathy, for without it I would never have involved myself so much with the common man and would never have exposed myself to vulgarity, which I did in sympathy for the many, the many who suffer innocently in the vilest manner.—It is still my constant prayer that God will keep me in this sympathy and increase it more and more.[20]

We have a duty not to be so "deadened" by our own suffering that we lose sympathy for the suffering of others (WL, p. 325).

Although the commandment cannot demand a particular feeling of compassion, it can require a disposition to experience compassion, a disposition to engage in the imaginative construal of the other's situation, which motivates us to help the other. This implies an indirect duty to cultivate the conditions that foster a compassionate construal—to develop a repertoire of compassionate interpretations, to "train oneself to feel compassion for people in need, so that this emotional response will occur spontaneously."[21] This construal is neither a simple act by fiat nor a simple feeling; it is informed by an intellectual appreciation, but it remains deeply affective. Although I earlier contrasted Kant's position with Kierkegaard's, there is significant similarity between them in this respect; although Kant rejects sympathy as a motive for moral action, he retains an important role for it in what he calls the "duty of *humanity*."[22] In a section entitled "Sympathetic Feeling Is a Duty in General," Kant maintains that we have an indirect duty to cultivate our natural susceptibility for shared feelings of pleasure or pain at another's condition for the purpose of promoting "active and rational benevolence."[23]

But what does sympathetic engagement consist of? Hobbes had denied its possibility, arguing that we can never transcend self-interest.[24] Others argued in reaction to him that we could go beyond our private interest and extend ourselves in sympathy. Adam Smith's version of sympathy proposed that we imaginatively "place ourselves in [the other's] situation . . . enter, as it were, into his body, and become in some measure the same person with him."[25] He explained that we can form a conception of another's sensations only by the imaginative representation of "what would be our own [sensations], if we were in his case." Bishop Butler suggested that compassion lies in learning to "substitute [others] for ourselves, their interest for our own," to take the "same kind of pleasure in their prosperity, and sorrow in their distress, as we have from reflection upon our own."[26] Hume was critical of the Hobbesean theory of the "selfish origin" of morality, but he was also especially sensitive to the danger that some understandings of sympathetic imagination do not succeed in taking us beyond self-love because they require that we generate an identity between ourselves and another.[27]

Whether we speak of becoming the same person, substituting ourselves for others, or substituting others for ourselves, the danger of assimilation of the other or annihilation of ourselves looms large. The achievement of identity would, however, preclude a genuine relation with another; there would not be two parties to be in relation. Hume was committed to an understanding of sympathy that would allow engagement with another "as different from us"[28] at the same time as it guaranteed sufficient interestedness in the other. Hume conceded that "the sentiments of others can never affect us, but by becoming in some measure, our own," and he allowed that we are able to enter into sentiments "which is no way belong to us, and in which nothing but sympathy is able to interest us."[29] Yet all of this must not issue in an attempted identity with the other that precludes their genuine otherness. What matters is not an identity of interests but an identification with the interests of others, which can be achieved imaginatively.

Hume suggests that we can "take part" with others in their sufferings, that we need to consider others "as they feel themselves,"[30] in contrast to Smith's suggestion that we need to "place ourselves in [the other's] situation." This is an important and plausible distinction between the attempt to feel what another feels and the attempt to feel what I would feel if I were in his or her place. The latter exercise does not sufficiently appreciate others' differences from me—their distinctive likes and dislikes, their sensitivities and idiosyncrasies, and their different beliefs and valuations. If I cannot imagine what it is to have a fear of heights, for example, I do not sufficiently and sympathetically engage with the other if I simply imagine what I would feel in his or her place; in fact, I wouldn't feel frightened in that place. But what is important is what he or she feels in that place. Similarly, if I cannot imagine how others are different from me in the things that cause them suffering, in addition to the way in which we might be the same, then no matter how much I try to imagine how I would feel if I were simply transported into the other's situation, I will not be able either to notice or to attend to the other's distinctive needs. What I need is a way of identifying with another that does not try to achieve an identity with the other (and so either reduce the other to oneself or totally abandon oneself) but succeeds in going beyond the attempt to imagine how I would feel in his or her objective condition.[31]

There may seem to be little in this deliberation with which to develop Kierkegaard's understanding of love's sympathetic imagination, but we have already seen in preceding deliberations a striking appreciation of the role of imagination in several respects: in perceiving the concrete distinctiveness of others, in the imaginative expansiveness that allows us not to need to trim others to our measure, and in the imaginative appropriation of possibility.[32] The references to sympathy in this deliberation recall many of Kierkegaard's other formulations of imaginative engagement, particularly the role of imagination in ethical development.[33] Although he speaks negatively of imagination in *Works of Love,* warning us against trying to refashion people to fit some fantasy notion we have of them, he displays a remarkable sensitivity to the feelings of others, especially to the ways in which they might be humiliated or undermined. Throughout the deliberations on forgiveness and reconciliation he gives us numerous examples to engage our sympathetic imagination, painting pictures that make us more aware of ways in which attempts at forgiveness or reconciliation can hurt others. These suggest that Kierkegaard believes that mercy requires a sensitive awareness of how others might be harmed or helped, and such sensitivity involves an imaginative appropriation.

Although we have focused mostly on sympathy with others in their suffering, sympathy is neutral; it is an imaginative engagement with another in the other's joy or suffering. The latter is, in one sense, of course, the most important. Usually it is not crucial if we fail to rejoice with those who rejoice: when they are rejoicing they, presumably, need no assistance; but if we fail to have compassion for the misery of others, the result is that they will be deprived of necessary help.[34] Still, in line with his equal-minded worry that the poor can be as unloving as the rich, Kierkegaard does not ignore this dimension of sympathetic engagement with others in their good fortune. Indeed, part of the explanation for what would otherwise seem a rather callous bit of advice may well lie in his implicit appeal to the duty to be glad for others in their succees, not to begrudge others their happiness. When Kierkegaard reminds the needy that their "care-filled life" has the power to "alarm" those who are not in need (either by simply raising the unsettling question of God's love for all or by cultivating their guilt), one can imagine a scenario in which the needy are outside looking in at people who are enjoying a banquet. Kierkegaard's advice to the needy here seems to contrast brusquely with his earlier call for sensitivity in feeding the hungry—the reminder that one who feeds the hungry without seeing them as neighbors does not give a "banquet" (WL, p. 82). In this deliberation, he recommends to the needy that love for their neighbors means that they should suffer quietly and patiently lest they "disturb the joy and happiness of others" (p. 326). The apparent harshness of such a recommendation can perhaps only be mitigated if we understood it in the light of Luther's own emphasis on the scriptural recommendation to rejoice with those who rejoice, as well as to mourn with those who mourn (Romans 12:15),[35] and if we see it as located in a context in which this is said to the needy "in confidence," rather than where others can use it as an excuse for their own lack of compassion.

In sum, to those who respond to this deliberation with the criticism that it makes it "seem as if what one does is a matter of indifference," Kierkegaard has already answered: "O, yes, if you are inhuman."[36] This deliberation on practicing mercy needs to be read against the background of earlier deliberations on love's action or outwardness, as well as deliberations that highlight the role of imagination. Otherwise, it will be misunderstood. From the first deliberation's insistence that love must bear fruits, Kierkegaard has insisted on outwardness and action. The necessary relation between inner and outer informs his claim that "when you open the door you shut in order to pray to God and go out the very first person you meet is the neighbor" (WL, p. 51). Kierkegaard mocks all who recognize the neighbor "at a distance" but not up close (p. 79). He condemns the person who is "addicted to promises and good intentions" (p. 94), and he suggests that "the measure of a person's disposition is this: how far he is from what he understands to what he does, how great is the distance between his understanding and his action" (p. 78). Christian love is not any "hidden, private, mysterious feeling"; he insists repeatedly that it is "sheer action" (pp. 98–99). He had already warned us against "seeking alleviation by giving to charity instead of wanting to alleviate poverty" (p. 14) and to "take care lest it become more important to you that you are looked upon as loving them than that you love them" (p. 129). Only when all of that seems quite clear does Kierkegaard begin to speak explicitly and in confidence to those whose actions are limited by their resources, and this is done to encourage and upbuild them.

chapter fourteen

Love's Delight in Reconciliation

"The Victory of the Conciliatory Spirit in Love,
Which Wins the One Overcome" (2:VIII)

Admittedly, the title of this deliberation does not as readily indicate its goal, as do some of the others, but at its heart is a call to reconciliation, the restoration of broken bonds. Such reconciliation, it should scarcely need to be said, is not a renewed relation to God but directly to human persons. Kierkegaard explicitly appeals to the Gospel injunction that points us away from God's altar and back to God's children: "Therefore, if thou art offering thy gift at the altar, and there remember that thy brother has anything against thee, leave thy gift before the altar and go first to be reconciled to thy brother, and then come and offer thy gift" (Matthew 5:23–24). Implicitly, he recalls the message of the Beatitudes: "Blessed are the peacemakers, for they shall be called children of God" (Mark 5:9). What is at stake for Kierkegaard is clarified in the journal comment from the same period, where he insists that "reconciliation itself is the only gift which can be offered upon the altar of God."[1]

Several major moves are accomplished in this short deliberation. Referring most immediately to the two earlier deliberations (2:V, VI) that highlighted forgiveness and faithfulness as openness to reconciliation, it shifts the emphasis here to the practice of reconciliation itself. Kierkegaard veers from forgiveness as such because, he says, the term "forgiveness" actually reminds us of "right and wrong"; so it is preferable to use terms like "reconciliation" and "agreement," words that carry no judicial sting but rather emphasize the meeting of two equal persons (WL, p. 336). If one is reading the deliberations in order, this one seems the capstone of an ethic that shows that Kierkegaard does indeed know something about "sociality."[2] Moreover, the exploration of the "double conflict or double victory" (p. 334) retrieves and transforms the theme of the "double danger" found in the deliberation on love's debt (1:V), this time formulating it in terms of its converse, a double victory, and applying it to the goal of reconciliation. Finally, it tells us about love's "merciful blow" (p. 339)—that is, it tells us that the one who loves doesn't hide the truth from the other person or from oneself; this discussion makes an important contribution to the question raised earlier about what is entailed in the recommendation of love's blindness to weakness, defect, and sin.

We should not expect *Works of Love* to be a 'how to' manual for putting love into practice since Kierkegaard is certainly aware that the awakening potential of a deliberation does not operate directly, by issuing recommendations or imperatives. Still, there is a sense in which these deliberations on forgiveness, faithfulness, and reconciliation do seem to tell us how to respond to wrongdoing, to someone resistant to the good; they tell us about forgiveness and compassionate understanding. Although there are no detailed rules that can be mechanically applied to a given situation, there are important reminders that can serve as general guidelines.

I. The Soft Love of Reconciliation

At the end of "Love Abides" (2:VI), Kierkegaard had noted that forgiveness is "often a difficult collision" but that love, being "softer than the softest," is the medium that prevents a jolting "offense" (WL, p. 314). In the introductory section of this deliberation, in which he undertakes to explain what St. Paul refers to as the struggle "to continue to stand after having overcome everything" (p. 331), Kierkegaard couches the dynamics of interpersonal relationships in the martial idiom of battles and victories, suggesting that love (the softest) transforms a traumatic victory with gentleness. He argues that in spiritual matters, there are two different kinds of battle and two kinds of victory. The first is the battle against evil when another is doing wrong—that is, the struggle in which we must be strong enough to denounce wrongdoing, to expose misdeeds, or to correct another person. The second, more significant, is the "new battle," in which we align ourselves with the other, to win him or her to the good (p. 333). The first victory is termed "overcoming"; the second, "winning."

Although it might seem that, in general, overcoming is equivalent to winning, Kierkegaard is proposing a stipulative definition: overcoming the evil in another is to be followed by winning the other to the good. We may engage in the first struggle for our own glory; it is, after all, gratifying to overcome evil with good. In this second struggle we are asked to take ourselves out of the limelight and direct the other to God and goodness, giving God the credit for winning the battle over evil rather than taking it for ourselves. To be victorious in this second battle specifically means that a person "does not receive the honor of the first victory, because to be victorious means in this context to give God the honor" (WL, p. 333). The battle is no longer the fight against the evil that another does but is the "new battle" (p. 333) to keep oneself from falling "over his own feet" (p. 332)—that is, to keep oneself from gratifying one's natural desire to take the credit for the first victory. The second victory is winning the battle against pride, arrogance, and self-importance (pp. 332–33).

The emphasis on the double victory shows why this entire deliberation is fruitfully read in tandem with the discussion in 1:V; that is, it parallels the treatment of the "double danger," the danger that our gift of love will be met with "ingratitude, opposition, and derision" (WL, p. 194). Kierkegaard is actually criticizing Luther when he laments that "at times we read and hear with sadness Christian addresses that actually leave out the final danger," implying that if you love, all will go well with you in the world (pp. 191–92).[3] The "double danger" is that the sacrifice we suffer in expressing our love for another will be compounded by the sacrifice of not being loved or esteemed for being loving. In parallel fashion, the second victory of which he speaks in this deliberation is a "battle of love" on behalf of the unloving one, which requires that we do not receive "the honor of the first victory." Therefore, it is only in the second struggle that we can discover whether we are really loving the other person (p. 334). For Kierkegaard, loving in order to be loved for loving is comparable to the absurdity of wanting to be praised for being humble, which Climacus alludes to in the *Postscript*: "The same thing happens with faith's crucifixion of the understanding as with many ethical qualifications. A person renounces vanity—but he wishes to be admired because he does it. . . . But it is always dubious to want to have benefit or receive conspicuous benefit from one's religiousness."[4]

The second victory, winning the other to love, entails acting without arrogance or pride and being sensitive to the other's humiliation and difficulties. This "winning" way involves the mercy of being genuinely other-regarding, and Kierkegaard's repeated emphasis on preventing the other's humiliation is striking (WL, pp. 338, 342, 343). He notes the "peculiar difficulty" in relating to the one whom one has corrected or shown to be wrong because "to be one who has been overcome is a humiliating feeling" (p. 338). The loving one must maintain the correction, yet without flaunting or even savoring the victory; Keikegaard adds that "it is indeed simply unloving to want to master another person in this way" (p. 339). The decisive victory is that the one who loves does not relate to the one overcome in terms of victory at all: "[T]he one who loves does not give the impression at all, nor does it occur to him, that it is he who has conquered, he that is the victor—no, it is the good that has conquered" (p. 339). The "winning" way embodies the gentleness of not even referring to forgiveness (p. 343), the gentleness of trying to break the other of the habit of asking for forgiveness (p. 344).

Here we see anther parallel with Kierkegaard's earlier discussion of love as debt—loving without making the other feel indebted or humiliated, making it seem as if it were not a gratuity but given in the knowledge that one owes the other an infinite debt.[5] Kierkegaard's claim here that "the one who loves hides himself" (p. 340) also calls to mind what he has earlier portrayed as the way in which love does not seek its own (2:IV) but loves the other's own. This deliberation elaborates the way in which we are to treat the other with respect, without condescension, esteeming the other's independence and integrity.[6]

The only way for the loving one not to cause or cultivate the humiliation of the other is by not attributing the victory to himself but to the "third" (WL, p. 339). The one overcome does not need to humble himself before the other because both are humbled in the presence of the good (p. 340). "Holy modesty" gives God the credit, assuming that if you think something is a great good, you should thank God for it (p. 341).

It is not clear how much Kierkegaard feels indebted to Luther for his emphasis on giving credit to God rather than allowing it to be given to oneself, but this is clearly a position that Luther holds at least as strongly. Luther's frame of reference is the second commandment, which bids us honor God's name and not take it in vain. Luther equates this with the commandment to "praise God in all his benefits," suggesting that its place in the hierarchy of commandments shows that "after faith we can do no greater work than to praise, preach, sing, and in every way laud and magnify God's glory, honor and name."[7] Luther construes its violation in terms of seeking honor, praise, or approval: "And so the holy name of God, which alone ought to be honored, is taken in vain and dishonored because of our own cursed name, our own self-approval and seeking of our own honor."[8] For Luther, we necessarily dishonor God's name when we seek honor for our own, and he even judges this tendency to take credit and praise to be a more grievous sin than murder and adultery.[9]

Kierkegaard deconstructs the potential power play in forgiving another by reminding us that the one extending forgiveness and the one receiving it are equal before God. One is modest in front of the other when one thinks of "what the presence of the third one makes the other person" (WL, p. 342). That is, the "presence of God makes the two essentially equal"; difference is irrelevant in this respect. For Kierkegaard, the "third" term does not take away from the relationship between the two people; rather it is precisely what makes it clear that both are equally under God, freely created and in need of forgiveness. It is being used to protect the other from the humiliation of having been in the wrong. Moreover, it is used to protect the loving one from the humiliation that could come when it recognized that before God one is always in the wrong (p. 340).[10]

We are asked to see ourselves and others as striving for goodness before God, both needing God's forgiveness. For Kierkegaard, the importance of equality is seen not only in the deliberation on the formal structure of the love commandment (1:II, A–C) but also in the later deliberations that express love in practice. The recognition of equality must inform every act of love, and in this deliberation we see one of the most important ways in which the concern with equality is made concrete. This is in keeping with his later acknowledgment that the theme of equality has been at the center of his life: the "thought of humanity and of human equality" has been "my life, the content of my life, its fullness, it bliss, its peace and satisfaction."[11] He insists that "there is equality, infinite equality, between human beings." Equality is put into practice because Christian forgiveness embodies the desire for reconciliation which is built on the acknowledgment that both are in need and are equal before God.

In effect, Kierkegaard gives us an introductory account of the two battles and two victories so that we can apply the schema to the practice of forgiveness and reconciliation. The goal is reconciliation; we are fighting alongside the other so that he or she will accept forgiveness and allow reconciliation (WL, pp. 335, 336). In this deliberation Kierkegaard's subject is not the person who needs forgiveness but the person who has been offended or treated badly by the other and needs to extend forgiveness. Although he speaks at one point of the one who "does not . . . need forgiveness" (p. 336), this turn of phrase is soon left behind as he goes on to highlight the equality between the two parties. There is no longer anyone who does not need forgiveness because the loving one sees both self and other as equal in the light of the "third" (God, or goodness).

II. Giving Before

When Kierkegaard spoke earlier of love's ability to "hide" sins by forgiveness, he allowed that forgiveness could be done lovingly, that it could occur in such a way that it would not hinder further relationship. Now, however, he seems anxious to contrast this natural understanding with the specifically Christian one, in which one does not wait for the other to admit guilt or seek forgiveness. Christian forgiveness is given *before* the other asks, or even thinks of asking. In other words, in addition to trying to avoid humiliating the other, Kierkegaard suggests another characteristic of love's reconciling spirit—love's willingness to take the initiative. This fits with the assumption Kierkegaard has that love needs to express itself, that it craves expression. We have to be ready to offer reconciliation; it should not have to be wrested from us (WL, p. 336). In fact, we shouldn't actually be waiting; we should be forgiving even before the other requests it (pp. 335, 336). We learn this from the model of God, who—both in the Creation and the Atonement—"loved us first" and did not wait until we requested forgiveness: "It is not human beings who say to God, 'Forgive us.' No, God loved us first" (p. 336). Although the Danish makes clear that forgiving is a kind of giving to another,[12] the English word 'for-giving' makes clear that it is a giving before the other asks.

Our duty is to express forgiveness even in the absence of any sign of repentance or even any request for forgiveness. To make his point, Kierkegaard appeals to the warrant of Christ's sermon on the mount in the Gospel of Matthew. Following the proclamation of the Beatitudes, Christ announces to the crowd that he has come to "fulfill" the law (not destroy it) by elevating its standards. He reminds us of the old law—not to kill, not to commit adultery, and so on—and heightens the requirements: we are not to be angry with another or to lust in our hearts. In the middle of these two reminders, we find the admonition to which Kierkegaard alludes: "Therefore, if thou art offering thy gift at the altar, and there remember that thy brother has anything against thee, leave thy gift before the altar and go first to be reconciled to thy brother, and then come and offer thy gift" (Matthew: 5:23–24). Kierkegaard begins to recite the passage—"if when one goes to the altar to offer one's gift to God, one remembers"—but here he stops with great rhetorical effect. He knows that we often read too fast and see what we expect to see; he alerts us to the fact that what follows in this passage is rather unexpected. It does not read "if you remember that you have something against someone" as we might have expected. It says, rather, "if you remember that someone has something against you." Kierkegaard interprets this passage as emphasizing the radical requirement of taking the initiative in expressing your forgiveness of another's wrong: "[T]he loving one who suffered the wrong needs to forgive or needs agreement, reconciliation" (WL, p. 336). When you remember that another person needs your forgiveness (i.e., needs to be forgiven by you), you are obliged to leave your gift at the altar and seek the other in order to extend that forgiveness.

Kierkegaard's reading of this passage, highlighting the occasion in which you need to forgive another person rather than the situation in which you need to be forgiven, seems to be contoured by another biblical injunction in which what is at stake is clearer: "And when you stand up to pray, forgive whatever you have against anyone, that your Father in heaven may also forgive you your offenses" (Mark 11:25). The one who did the wrong admittedly needs to be forgiven, but here Kierkegaard is emphasizing how the "loving one who suffered the wrong needs to forgive" before she or he can ask God to accept the gift (because that requires God to forgive him or her). In other words, he is suggesting that in the case in which someone has done us a wrong, we are in the debt of love to forgive them; they hold the debt against us. Once again we can see an important connection between this deliberation and the earlier one (1:V) in which Kierkegaard argued that we are in an infinite debt of love to the other—we owe the other forgiveness. In sum, if we remember that someone holds something (a debt) against us, we must first give that person reconciling forgiveness, and only then return to the altar to give our gift to God.

This seems to indicate Kierkegaard's affirmation of the Old Testament message that God prefers mercy over sacrificial offerings.[13] But Kierkegaard departs from at least one Jewish reading of the ethics of forgiveness—namely, that offered by Levinas. In a series of commentaries on the Mishnah, Levinas calls our attention to the way in which the Mishnah distinguishes between forgiveness of sins against God and forgiveness of sins against a human being. He explains that to obtain forgiveness for what I have done to another person, "I must as a precondition appease him"; God cannot forgive the sins I have done to another person until I have expressed my repentance by asking for forgiveness and appeasing him (with restitution if appropriate): '[T]he guilty must recognize his sin . . . no one can forgive, if he has not had forgiveness requested by the offender, if the guilty has not sought to appease the offended."[14] For Kierkegaard, on the contrary, it is clear that fulfilling the law requires us to forgive before the other has asked for it: "[I]t is the conciliatory spirit to need to forgive already when the other person had not had the slightest thought of seeking forgiveness"; indeed, "we are speaking about fighting in love so that the other will accept forgiveness, will allow himself to be reconciled" (WL, p. 336).

There are, of course, dangers in the notion that one should rush to forgive people before they ask for forgiveness or even acknowledge their guilt—dangers of arrogance and conceit. But Kierkegaard, as we have seen, is very aware of the way in which forgiving can be done in an unloving (WL, p. 295) and self-serving way, so he repeatedly emphasizes our obligation to be sensitive to the self-respect of the other person. When he introduces the concept of being "dexterous" with the other, being creative and gentle in the expression of "solicitude" for the person who is in the wrong (p. 340), he is affirming the absolute otherness of the other. The way in which we forgive must put the other's needs first, before our own. He even warns against too much "earnestness"—that is, against creating an uncomfortable 'incident'—and suggests that it is "simply unloving to want to master another person this way" (p. 339). Rather we should do it "as lightly as the truth allows" (p. 340). All of these are intimations of the gracious mercifulness with which a loving one relates to anyone, even to an unloving, recalcitrant person. And Kierkegaard is willing to take the risk of emphasizing this side of forgiveness—our offering forgiveness to another person—because the dangers of conceit and arrogance, once warned against, seem less of a problem than the danger that we will withhold forgiveness from someone.

Our consideration of Kierkegaard's marked sensitivity to the unloving ways in which one can forgive another and to the delicacy with which forgiveness should be exercised cannot end without noting a particularly striking (and perhaps surprising) expression of that sensitivity at the end of the deliberation. Kierkegaard instructs us in the manner of forgiving another as follows: when the other asks us, "Have you forgiven me?" our response should be the question "Do you love me now?" (WL, p. 343). It would not have been surprising if he had urged us to respond with a quick and gracious "Yes, of course," but he doesn't do so. Why is a 'yes' not the most loving response? Something that might account for the peculiarity of Kierkegaard's instruction can be found in the fourth deliberation, in which he notes Christ's question to Peter, "Do you love me?" Kierkegaard suggests that after Christ repeats the question two more times, Peter "does not answer yes anymore" because he realizes that "yes is like an actual answer to an actual question" (p. 156). How can Christ, who knows everything, need to be reassured?[15] Perhaps, then, not saying 'yes' when one is asked to forgive is a way of taking the attention away from the request for forgiveness, preventing it from being an "actual question." Whatever Kierkegaard means by urging us to answer a request for forgiveness with the question "Do you love me?" he is clearly seeing it as a way of being gentle with the other person. Such gentleness is a hallmark of the forgiveness Kierkegaard describes in this deliberation, but gentleness does not stand alone—a rigor must be kept in tension with the compassion of offering forgiveness, and Kierkegaard proceeds to deal with that as well.

III. Hard Love—Love's "Merciful Blow"

For Kierkegaard, offering forgiveness to another is an unconditional obligation; it cannot be conditional on the other's seeking forgiveness or showing repentance. Nevertheless, Kierkegaard insists that the other must be made aware of what he or she has done wrong. Kierkegaard's discussion of how we deal the "merciful blow" of letting the other person see his or her own evil provides additional resources for a response to the criticism that Kierkegaard is advocating moral blindness or intellectual dishonesty.

Kierkegaard insists that it is not love, but indulgence or weakness, that lets the other go on thinking that what he or she has done is good when we think that it is not (WL, p. 338). We need to remember that Kierkegaard has preached long and hard against the idea that we should set ourselves up as judges of other people, and he has indicated the difficulty in determining other people's motivation. Nonetheless, he insists that in our forgiving we cannot hide the truth, which the other person needs to face (WL, p. 340). We must indeed deal that "merciful blow" of helping the truth forward, luring it out of the other, placing it on the other's lips (p. 341). He reminds us that "the one who loves also hides something from the one overcome," but what we are to hide is ourselves, not the truth. Here Kierkegaard reinforces his earlier claim that we actually see the sin we hide and the sin we forgive.[16] We are not urged to be blind to reality or to call good what we see as evil. Kierkegaard thus addresses the question of the relation between moral vision and moral blindness: *"Therefore, the one who loves does not look at the one overcome. This was the first thing;* this was to prevent humiliation. *But in another sense the one who loves does look at him. This is the next thing."* (p. 342). The loving one "does not look" and yet "does look." Love sees, but love abides. Love tells the truth but does so lovingly. Even while one sees the wrong of which one must make the other aware, a "loving look rests so gently" on the other.[17] Once again, gentleness must be held in simultaneous tension with rigor (p. 339). Neither hard love nor soft love can stand alone. Strength is not enough; "the strength must be in weakness" (p. 343).

Kierkegaard thus reinforces the importance of "loving the people we see," as he did in the fourth deliberation of the first series; moral vision is necessary if we are to love people "just as they are." Kierkegaard's account of loving the neighbor does not ask that we abdicate responsibility, which is what it would be to simply fail to distinguish between good and evil. We are responsible for our judgments; love obligates us to work for the other precisely in the consciousness of God's judgment of the difference between good and evil. Moreover, the outwardness of reconciliation entails risk, and here Kierkegaard echoes his earlier appreciation of love's risk in trusting another when he acknowledges that forgiveness is a "venture" (WL, p. 331).

In this particular deliberation (as in 2:V), the accent is on how we should forgive others, not on our own need of forgiveness, although Kierkegaard does not neglect that latter dimension. Indeed, it is implicit in his notion of an infinite debt to the other, as well as in his emphasis on the "like for like" of forgiveness; as the Conclusion will strongly remind us, we will be forgiven only as we forgive. Our need for forgiveness, which looms large in Kierkegaard's Lutheran inheritance, is not an appropriate subject for a deliberation in a book devoted to delineating love in its "outwardness," its other-regardingness, but it is indirectly an important element in the background of this ethic.

Kierkegaard here anticipates the Conclusion in another way as well, when he suggests that our goal is for merciful forgiveness to become "second nature," to be practiced as a work of "art" (WL, p. 340).[18] That is, Kierkegaard does not think that the best way to be merciful is to force oneself to do something, to feel oneself resistant to the commandment. The most mercy comes not from feeling oneself under the heavy hand of a punishing law but from what he later calls in the Conclusion a kind of intimacy with the commandment, so that one has come to love it (pp. 375–76).

The emblem of this deliberation might be said to be the Scriptural account of the gift at the altar. In the year in which he was writing *Works of Love*, Kierkegaard was obviously quite struck by this scriptural story, with its message: "When *in life* you are reconciled with your enemy—then *you* place *on the altar* your gift to God."[19] He notes the ambiguity that "it is presented as if one offered a second gift: first go and become reconciled with your enemy and then come to offer your gift." He takes issue with such a reading, adding in the margin that "where reconciliation takes place, there the altar is, and reconciliation itself is the only gift which can be offered upon the altar of God." In other words, he reads the story as placing a priority on forgiveness of the neighbor, rather than on works of sacrifice directed to God; this shows that in God's own terms the neighbor is not marginalized or devalued or used instrumentally to get to God. But Kierkegaard goes even further. By claiming that reconciliation is the "only gift" that can be offered to God and by locating the altar where the reconciliation takes places, he reveals the centrality of reconciliation to this ethic, its distinctively outward concern with interpersonal relationship and community.

chapter fifteen

Love's Asymmetry

"The Work of Love in Recollecting One Who Is Dead" (2:IX)

The title of this deliberation seems to refer to a classic and unproblematical example of a work of love, in which there are tasks that can be performed to show our love—lovingly cultivating a grave plot, holding memorial services, or more privately cherishing something that was meaningful to the deceased. These tasks require faithfulness and unselfish devotion, and it is difficult to find fault with the recommendation to recollect the dead. Moreover, Kierkegaard makes clear that this deliberation is still focused on love for the living by concluding that if we practice this recollection of the dead we will receive two benefits, that is, "in addition to the blessing that is inseparable from this work of love you will also have the best guidance for rightly understanding life" (WL, p. 358). In other words, the deliberation tells us that there are two dimensions—the value of doing the good deed as such (to honor the dead) and the value of learning from it something about how to love the living.

It is precisely this latter dimension that has caused much consternation. For example, Adorno's 1939 critique of *Works of Love*—calling it an "abstract" and "callous" ethic—focused especially on this deliberation, suggesting that "perhaps one may most accurately summarize Kierkegaard's doctrine of love by saying that he demands that love behave toward all men as if they were dead."[1] For Adorno, this "death-like aspect of Kierkegaard's love," found in perhaps "one of the most important pieces he [Kierkegaard] ever wrote," has a "bad side [which] is obvious": namely, "love of the dead is the one which most rigidly excludes the reciprocity of love."[2] In other words, he charges Kierkegaard with advocating an *asymmetrical* relation in which the response *of* the other is irrelevant; if this were the case, it would mean that our response *to* the other is not a genuine 're'-sponse and there is no genuine relation. Others, too, have singled out this deliberation as a text in which Kierkegaard advocates a total disregard of reciprocity or mutual responsiveness in human relationships.[3]

This deliberation, despite its modest title, thus serves two important functions: first, it highlights the significant dimensions of asymmetry in Kierkegaard's ethic, some of which we have discussed earlier but without noting how they imply asymmetry as such; second, it forces us to look back and reconsider how such asymmetry fits together with Kierkegaard's strident affirmations of equality and the love commandment's "as yourself." The problem of asymmetry versus symmetry in a relationship is not peculiar to Kierkegaard's ethic; it lies at the heart of many prominent modern characterizations of selfhood and the relationship of the self to the other.[4] They disagree about the character of responsiveness and the relevance of mutuality or reciprocity in interpersonal relationships.[5] What is at stake is not only one's response *to* the other but also the response *from* the other, as well as a significant correlation (in kind and degree) between those responses. The issue of asymmetry also arises in discussions of equality and impartiality. It is important, therefore, to reconsider the claims in *Works of Love* that have motivated readers time and again to wonder whether Kierkegaard's ethic implies the ideal of a totally asymmetrical relationship, without mutuality.

In exploring this provocative deliberation, it is important to put it in the context of other parts of *Works of Love* that can illuminate and qualify it. We need to reconsider how Kierkegaard opens himself to this criticism, what pressures him into taking a potentially dangerous position on responsiveness, and whether his discussion of the asymmetrical relationship with the dead implies the annihilation of a responsiveness that we intuitively know is essential to human relationships. I shall argue that although a certain kind of reciprocity is condemned by Kierkegaard, he nevertheless leaves room for and even requires significant dimensions of mutual responsiveness within a relationship because he knows that otherwise responsibility for the other would be emptied of meaning. Moreover, Kierkegaard's deep commitments to both equality and the "as yourself" of the love commandment lead us to expect that he will value a kind of symmetry as essential to a loving relationship. My hope is that by contributing to a clarification of what is at stake for Kierkegaard in regard to symmetry, asymmetry, reciprocity, and mutuality, I will raise the questions that ought to be considered in any account that either endorses or challenges the requirement of symmetry in a relationship.

I. The Asymmetry in Love of the Dead

This deliberation on recollecting[6] those who are dead explores in great detail ways in which love is to be unselfish, free, and faithful. It opens with the suggestion that the relation to one who is dead reveals "a test of what love really is" (WL, p. 346–47). It concludes with this advice: "The work of love in recollecting one who is dead is thus a work of the most unselfish, the freest, the most faithful love. Therefore go out and practice it; recollect the one who is dead and just in this way learn to love the living unselfishly, freely, faithfully. In the relationship to one who is dead, you have the criterion by which you can test yourself" (p. 358). This raises the question of whether or not Kierkegaard's reiterated claim that love of the dead provides a "test" or "criterion" of love amounts to what Adorno charges is the demand that "love behave toward all men as if they were dead," whether or not Kierkegaard is recommending such an asymmetrical relationship as the highest kind of love.

To begin to answer this question, we need to note that in the text we can find two significant qualifications that bear on the answer. The first concerns the object of love, and the second the purpose of a test. These two are in addition to the more fundamental qualification generated by Kierkegaard's crucial distinction between what is required in the realm of "justice" (where reciprocity is an appropriate standard) and what is required in the realm of love as such (WL, p. 265).

A. The Object of Love

Kierkegaard admittedly sets a stark stage for his account of love of the dead. He suggests that "when a person relates himself to one who is dead, there is only one in this relationship, inasmuch as one who is dead is no actuality"; "one who is dead is no actual object," he continues, because one who is dead "has not the slightest influence, neither disturbing nor accommodating, on the one living who relates himself to him" (WL, p. 347). He says repeatedly that the dead one "is no actual object" but is rather "only the occasion that continually discloses what resides in the one living who relates himself to him or that helps to make manifest the nature of the one living who does not relate himself to him" (pp. 347, 355). In other words, in relation to one who is dead, the dead person is only the occasion for a one-sided revelation of the living person. Taken literally as a model of a loving relationship, this deliberation would make normative a radical asymmetry, a total lack of mutuality, which would be troubling; the irrelevance of the response of the other might, in effect, entail an irrelevance of the other.

Kierkegaard, however, does not make the mistake of confusing the dead with the living. In this ninth deliberation, he clearly contrasts cases of loving the dead with those of loving the living; that is, he contrasts cases "when one actual person relates himself to another actual person" with those "when a person relates himself to one who is dead" (WL, p. 347). Thus the claim that the dead one is not an actual being precludes any recommendation that we treat an actual living person in the same way as we treat one who is dead. In fact, Kierkegaard treats as paradigmatic of "relationship" the case of two actual people. He writes explicitly that "when one actual person relates himself to another actual person, the result is two, the relationship is constituted" (p. 347), and more specifically, "when two who are living hold together in love, the one holds on to the other, and the alliance holds on to both of them," whereas "no alliance is possible with one who is dead" (p. 355).[7] In other words, it is precisely because the dead one cannot respond that he or she is excluded from the category of "actual" beings; this means that responsiveness is a necessary characteristic of our relationships with "actual" human beings.

Moreover, the same affirmation of the relevance of an actual other is found in an earlier deliberation in the series, "Love Does Not Seek Its Own" (2:IV). Kierkegaard insists that "without a *you* and an *I*, there is no love" (WL, p. 266). He writes this in the context of ruling out certain kinds of possessiveness: "[T]he more profound the revolution [of love], the more completely the distinction '*mine* and *yours*' disappears," and thus, the following paradoxical picture of relationship results: "Wonderful! There are a *you* and an *I*, and there is no *mine* and *yours*!" But note well the presupposition Kierkegaard puts in place: even though "with *mine* and *yours*, there is no love," still, there must be a 'you' and an 'I' (p. 266). The warning against selfish ways of relating (in which the other is only an 'other I') is reinforced here by the requirement of a genuine 'you.'

By referring to the dead as a test case, Kierkegaard might seem here to reverse the earlier model in which we know that we love the unseen only if we love the seen, but he does so is in the service of emphasizing the living. Kierkegaard puts this work of love into perspective by reminding us that "neither can the duty to those who are dead separate the living from us in such a way that they do not become the objects of our love" (WL, p. 358). He clearly tries to prevent this duty to the dead from becoming either a fetish or obsession, which distracts from our duty to love those we see.

Finally, Kierkegaard reminds us that when there is such a relationship between two actual beings, "observation of the one person is made difficult" because the second person can cover something of the first, and "the second person can have so much influence that the first one appears different from what he is" (WL, p. 347). On the contrary, "when a person relates himself to one who is dead, there is only one in this relationship." The relation to one who is dead is, therefore, one in which it is easier to determine where the initiative comes from and whether it is self-interested or compelled. He illustrates his point with an analogy to dancing: "[I]f you could prevail upon a dancer to dance solo the dance he customarily dances with another, you would be able to observe his motions best, better than . . . if he were dancing with another actual person" (p. 347). That is, love of the dead provides a less complicated situation for consideration, one in which certain dynamics are easier to isolate.[8] Surely we can come to understand a particular movement better by abstracting it from the whole, as we usually do learn steps in dancing in this way, often with the instructor demonstrating it in an exaggerated fashion by himself or herself. But none of this in itself entails that Kierkegaard's ideal is to have the kind of relationship in which "there is only one."

B. Test or Criterion

Once we recognize the heuristic function of a nonactual other in helping us to isolate and focus on certain movements within relationships, it can be plausibly argued that for Kierkegaard the traits of unselfishness, faithfulness, and freedom are natural expectations of our ordinary instances of loving the living and that the point of the deliberation is to highlight their extreme versions for instructional purposes, rather than to present it as a model to be emulated. Thus, Kierkegaard's claim that the work of love in recollecting one who is dead provides a "test" or "criterion" of love does not amount to what Adorno says is the demand that "love behave toward all men as if they were dead."

When one heuristically simplifies the picture of the relation with another, one can see one's own motives more easily. Kierkegaard's appeal to this strategy is shown in his converse example: "[I]f, in conversation with someone, you understand the art of making yourself *no one*, you get to know best what resides in this person" (WL, p. 347). But in the case of a conversation with one living, one cannot truly become "no one," and such an extreme is not the goal. Kierkegaard is right to suggest that one should listen, rather than talk, if one wants to "get to know best what resides" in the other; but this is done precisely to cultivate the relationship and to further the dialogue. This methodological advice, with which we would probably all agree, is, however, distorted unduly if we take it to imply the recommendation that the best conversation for us is the one in which we never speak.

"If, then," Kierkegaard instructs, "you wish to test yourself as to whether you love unselfishly, just pay attention to how you relate yourself to one who is dead" (WL, pp. 350–51); "if you want to test whether you love freely, just watch how over a period of time you relate yourself to one who is dead" (p. 353); "if you want to test whether you love faithfully, just observe how you relate yourself to one who is dead" (p. 355). In other words, we do in fact from this work "learn to love the living" p. (358), but not by learning to love them as if they were dead. What serves the purpose of testing one's love need not be regarded as the model to be uncritically imitated. The situation in which our faithfulness, freedom, or unselfishness can best be isolated and tested because of the radical unresponsiveness of the beloved is not necessarily put forward as the model of relation we should strive to bring about.

II. Justifications for Asymmetry

The value of the totally asymmetrical model of recollecting the dead is that it provides the test question—would you still love even if there were no encouraging or satisfying response to your love, even if the other was unable to reciprocate in some way? This is a test of neighbor love precisely because in many cases the other's need will be so great that he or she cannot reciprocate and in other cases may even misunderstand one's work of love. Kierkegaard deliberately courts the dangers of being misunderstood when he says that the loving work of remembering the dead is one from which we can "learn to love the living" because radical unresponsiveness is simply the best test case. The importance of stressing so vehemently the one-sided initiative in place—the asymmetry—is most clear when we think about the issues of faithfulness, freedom, and debt that he had already spoken of earlier in *Works of Love*. In what follows I want to reconstruct what I take to be two of Kierkegaard's rationales for focusing on asymmetry as a way of illuminating genuine love. I will be arguing that both rationales for asymmetry provide a way to guarantee that the other actual person is responded to most fully.

A. Asymmetry as the Guarantee of Fidelity

The work of recollecting one who is dead is, Kierkegaard says, a work "of the most faithful love" (WL, p. 355). It is plausible to assume that the best "test" for faithfulness would be found in a situation in which is removed any possibility of response from the person to be loved that could help the lover to be faithful. Thus, it is useful to highlight such a situation in teaching us to love the living faithfully. But it is not a model to emulate precisely because in loving the living we are loving one who, in contrast to the dead, *is* an "actual object." How then does the lack of responsiveness in the test case illuminate the way in which we are to love the living?

In his remarks on "change" at the end of this deliberation, we begin to see what is at stake in Kierkegaard's discussion of the asymmetry of one-sided initiative. Here we can see how the heuristic notion of the lack of an actual other, a nonresponsive other, plays its role in an effort to guarantee faithfulness to a living, responsive person. He describes a dialogue in which one person accounts for his own change by blaming the other: "'It was not I who changed; it was he who changed.' Well. What happened then? Did you remain unchanged? 'No, of course it was natural and a necessary consequence that I changed too.'" (WL, p. 355). "At this point we shall not explain how meaningless this presumably necessary consequence is, whereby it necessarily follows that I change *because* another changes." The specific point Kierkegaard makes here is that in the case of a relation to a dead person, one cannot excuse one's lack of faithfulness by blaming the other for changing; the dead cannot change, so one is unable to maintain the illusion that one's change was caused by another. In this way, looking at the relation to the dead is a measuring rod for testing the genuineness of our love. What is at stake in the emphasis on asymmetry in the relation with the dead is the more general message that it is meaningless to speak of love that goes up and down with variations or changes in the other.[9] The lover's faithfulness is not conditional on the love or faithfulness of the one loved in such a way that there is an automatic, corresponding increase or decrease in the faithfulness of the lover.

This understanding of love's faithfulness, its abidingness, is remarkably similar to that found in the early chapter on duty, "You *Shall* Love" (1:II A). Kierkegaard writes at length of the freedom of love in terms of its "blessed independence" (WL, p. 37). He emphasizes how duty can make one free: "Duty, however, makes a person dependent and at the same moment eternally independent" (p. 38); duty "makes love free in blessed independence" because "such a love stands and does not fall with the contingency of its object" (p. 39). This is what recollecting the dead should teach us.

In another dialogue reminiscent of the one in this ninth deliberation, he also insists that "unchangingness is the true independence": "If when another person says, "I cannot love you any longer" one proudly answers, "Then I can also stop loving you."—Is this independence? Alas, it is dependence, because whether he will continue to love or not depends upon whether the other will love. But the person who answers, "In that case I *shall* still continue to love you"—that person's love is made eternally free in blessed independence" (WL, pp. 39–40). Agreeing that "Love is not love which alters when it alteration finds,"[10] Kierkegaard condemns the conditionality of a response to the other that varies directly with variations in the beloved. Duty is what allows independence and guarantees fidelity precisely by *disregarding this kind of response*. He rejects a relationship that involves the dependency of responding in kind and degree to the response of the loved one. We saw a similar message in the deliberation entitled "Love Abides," where the focus was "a work of love in faithfulness" to those whom one loves (p. 313).

The symmetry of a relation in which my love for the other goes up and down in strict correlation with changes in the other leads to the cautious and prudential approach to love condemned in the deliberation "Love Is the Fulfilling of the Law" (III, A). Kierkegaard's claim that the "merely human view of love can never go beyond mutuality [*Gjensidige*]: the lover is the beloved, and the beloved is the lover" (WL, p. 121) might seem to be a denigration of mutuality as such. The specific kind of mutuality he is rejecting is explained, however, a few pages later: "The world is no better than this; the highest that it acknowledges and loves is, at best, to love the good and humanity, yet in such a way that one also looks to one's own earthly advantage and that of a few others" (p.123). To love in such a way that one also looks out for oneself and a few others is to love in a cautious, prudential, and exclusive way. That is, it fails to go beyond the mutuality of preferential relationships. In fact, the way in which this deliberation recapitulates the earlier ones, abbreviating the message that genuine love is faithful, free, and unselfish, provides some evidence for the conclusion that this deliberation serves as a "summary" of the book.[11]

Thus, for Kierkegaard, the rejection of the need of symmetry is a way of guaranteeing the unconditionedness of our response to the neighbor; one underlying explanation of the value of asymmetry in relation lies in its role in preventing our response to the other from going up and down in reaction to variations in the other's response to us. For Kierkegaard, the features of and changes in the other that could condition and cause variation in our response have to be ignored; we have to disregard the symmetry of an exact correspondence between a response by and to the other. Asymmetry ultimately ensures both the unconditionedness of response and the fact that no one is excluded; asymmetry is necessary if we are to love the other equally (i.e., without variation, always) and be sure that we love all others equally.

B. Asymmetry in Terms of Infinite Debt

Another rationale for asymmetry is found in Kierkegaard's characterizations of love in terms of unrepayable debt. As we saw in chapter 8, "Love's Debt," he expresses the relation between love and debt: "[*T*]*his is the distinctive characteristic of love: that the one who loves by giving, infinitely, runs into infinite debt"* (WL, p. 177). He explains: "To give a person one's love is, as has been said, the highest a person can give—and yet by giving it he runs into an infinite debt. . . . It [love] is ashamed to become conscious of its deed as a part-payment on the debt." Seeing the debt as limited means that effectively one gives to another with the unspoken addition "See, now I have paid my debt" (p. 178); the result is that we have then turned the relation into a "bookkeeping arrangement [which] is the greatest abomination to love." It is clear to Kierkegaard that if we claim that we are not always in debt—that is, that our debt to another is not infinite—it implies that there is some way of paying off or at least lessening the debt. The idea of an "infinite debt" to the other thus describes a relationship that is radically asymmetrical.

This asymmetry precludes the kind of reciprocity involved in any repayment. That Kierkegaard has in mind this technical understanding of reciprocity as repayment is made even clearer in this ninth deliberation when he linguistically connects the notion of repayment and repayment love as follows: *"Gjengjeld for Kjerlighed: Gjenkjerlighed"* ["Repayment for love: Repayment (reciprocal) love"].[12] The kind of reciprocity condemned here is the loving back that is intended as repayment. The asymmetry recommended is the sacrifice of a *claim* to reciprocity as repayment.

The Conclusion of *Works of Love* contains an important, though indirect, reference to asymmetry: "In the Christian sense, *you have nothing at all to do with what others do unto you—it does not concern you*; it is a curiosity, an impertinence, a lack of good sense on your part to meddle in things that are absolutely no more your concern than if you were not present. *You have to do only with what you do unto others, or how you take what others do unto you"* (pp. 383–84; emphasis mine). There is a kind of one-sidedness in the relation—I do not have the right to make claims about "what others do unto [me]" or should do unto me. (I shall discuss this passage again when I treat the Conclusion; here the issue is asymmetry; there it will be inwardness and responsibility.)

This kind of asymmetry can be illuminated by reference to Levinas's writings, which—early to late—argue for a similar asymmetry. Levinas writes that one of the "fundamental" themes of *Totality and Infinity* is that "the intersubjective relation is a non-symmetrical relation."[13] He explains: "In this sense, I am responsible for the Other without waiting for reciprocity, were I to die for it. Reciprocity is *his* affair. It is precisely insofar as the relationship between the Other and me is not reciprocal that I am subjection to the Other; and I am 'subject' essentially in this sense. It is I who support all." In response to the question so often asked of his ethic—"But is not the Other also responsible in my regard"[14] (or in the more popular idiom, 'Don't I get to be loved? Isn't the other supposed to love me?')— Levinas's answer is "Perhaps, but that is '*his* affair'." This dismisses our right to *claim reciprocity*.[15] In a sense, it does not even allow the question to be put; there is, in Levinas's eyes, no right to ask whether the other has an infinite obligation to us. There is, moreover, no right to hassle others about their obligations: "To say that the other has to sacrifice himself to the others would be to preach human sacrifice!"[16] Only the other should state his or her obligation to me. All I can do is attend to what I must do, attend to my obligation; I have no right to insist upon or expect anything from you as the condition for my responsibility for you. In sum, "essential asymmetry is the very basis of ethics."[17]

Levinas implies that we could speak about self and others in the same sense (i.e., symmetrically) only if we were capable of "seeing oneself from the outside."[18] He says something similar in an interview entitled "The Paradox of Morality": "[T]he idea that the death of the other is more important than my own is an affirmation that we are not being looked at from outside, but the essential difference between me and the other remains in my look."[19] Levinas also writes that "if I say that 'virtue is its own reward,' I can only say so *for myself*; as soon as I make this a standard for the other I exploit him, for what I am then saying is: be virtuous towards me—work for me, love me, serve me, and so on—but don't expect anything from me in return."[20] I can say to myself (demand of myself) something different from what I can say to (demand of) another person. This is his explanation for the conclusion that "I must always demand more of myself than of the other." Something like this notion may also underlie Kierkegaard's claims about infinite debt. That is, I can only speak from where I stand, from my side. Whatever it looks like from some "outside" perspective, I have only my perspective from the inside; from the inside there is only asymmetry.

Although both Kierkegaard and Levinas affirm this kind of asymmetry, there is a potentially important difference to be noted even at this level. The asymmetry in Kierkegaard's model of the love of the dead highlights the self as the sole center of initiative. It is one-sided in its emphasis on the self as agent; that is, my activity is not conditional on the response of the other. For Levinas, however, the asymmetry seems to go in the opposite direction; it is the other whose presence is the originating source of activity ("It is a matter of an exigency coming from the other").[21] One could argue that the danger of Kierkegaard's view of asymmetry (agent-circumscribed initiative) is that it seems to make the response of the other irrelevant and thus empty of any responsiveness to the other. This is not a problem for an asymmetry like Levinas's, which emphasizes an other-centered initiative, an asymmetry premised on the other's making a demand on me. However, Kierkegaard's emphasis on the way in which our response cannot be conditioned by anything in the other is actually intended to guarantee that there will be a faithful response to the other, no matter what. This kind of asymmetry is intended to make it impossible for us to ignore the other by making it impossible for us to ignore our responsibility for the other.

Both Kierkegaard and Levinas make a deliberate effort to take the attention away from the other in a very specific sense; that is, the infinity of the debt (that the debt can never be repaid or lessened) precludes any claim on our part to reciprocity from the other.[22] The irrelevance of a claim of reciprocity with respect to infinite debt implies, for both Kierkegaard and Levinas, a kind of asymmetry. The resulting asymmetry, precluding our right to demand something from the other or to put the other under obligation to me, is an intriguing way of guaranteeing that responsibility, rather than reciprocity, is the focus of our attention, and this is a way of guaranteeing that the other is responded to most fully.

I have been reconsidering Kierkegaard's affirmations of asymmetry in the light of Levinas's rejection of symmetry and reciprocity in a relationship because it seems to be clearer in Levinas's account that assertions of asymmetry are meant to ensure that the demand on us is more stringent, that is, that the other is responded to most fully. I have tried to show that this allows us to better appreciate how Kierkegaard's assertions of asymmetry are meant to ensure the same thing.

The asymmetry Kierkegaard commends is what is required if we are to love faithfully and freely and if we are to remain in love's infinite debt. It is no more (but no less) than that. We have seen, then, that for Kierkegaard, the issue of reciprocity comes up in two different ways. First, faithfulness excludes ups and downs, which implies the irrelevance of tit-for-tat reciprocity. This kind of asymmetry, however, does not rule out other kinds of responsiveness, and I shall consider them later in this chapter. Second, the infinitude of the demand on us precludes our claim to reciprocity; the response of the other can never be the condition for our assumption of responsibility, the condition for our neighbor love. Nonetheless, love is considered to be a natural response, and it is something, according to Kierkegaard, in which one legitimately takes joy.[23]

It is interesting to note here that both kinds of asymmetry are affirmed by Kierkegaard against the background of a deep commitment to equality; the latter kind of asymmetry in particular, however, raises questions about the relation between equality and asymmetry. In the sense in which one remains in an infinite debt of love to the other, one is not the other's equal. And Kierkegaard acknowledges this when he introduces another kind of asymmetry, this time explicitly tied to the notion of inequality.

C. Asymmetry of a "Heightened Inequality"

In addition to the asymmetrical relationship that is implied in the commandment to be faithful and to remain in an infinite debt, Kierkegaard refers to another source of asymmetry assumed by Christianity: "*Christianity is so rigorous that it even asserts a heightened inequality*" (WL, p. 382, emphasis Kierkegaard's). Alluding to the biblical chastisement "Why do you see the splinter in your brother's eye but do not see the log that is in your own?" Kierkegaard adopts what he calls a "pious" interpretation:

> The log in your own eye is neither more nor less than seeing and condemning the splinter in your brother's eye. But the most rigorous like for like would of course be that seeing the splinter in someone else's eye becomes a splinter in one's own eye. But Christianity is even more rigorous: this splinter, or seeing it judgingly, is a log. . . . You will understand that to see the splinter in your brother's eye in the presence of God (and God is indeed always present) is high treason (pp. 382–83)

The claim that I cannot play judge is a way of saying not only that I am not in a privileged place with respect to the other but also that I am not even the other's equal. Whether or not it is true that only equals can judge each other, Kierkegaard explicitly claims that such inappropriateness of judging reveals a kind of "inequality." Although he does not present this "heightened inequality" through spatial metaphors, it seems to parallel a distinctive formulation of asymmetry (and inequality) presented by Levinas—the asymmetry of "height." It is worth looking at Levinas's account of this dimension of asymmetry in more detail.

In *Totality and Infinity*, Levinas makes the asymmetry between me and the other more specific by appealing to metaphors of "height": he explains that the other "approaches me from a dimension of height and dominates me,"[24] that "the face is not in front of me, but above me."[25] He constantly emphasizes the "moral dissymmetry of the I and the other," which consists in the way "that the Other is placed higher than me."[26] This dimension of "height" is expressed most forcefully in "Transcendence and Height":[27] the other is "lord" over me, commanding me to love (not kill) him or her; in this sense the relationship is not one of equal partners. Levinas later challenges us: "Doesn't the ethical begin when the *I* perceives the *Thou* as higher than itself?"[28] Several things are at stake for Levinas in using this metaphor of height. One is to affirm that my responsibility for the other subordinates me to the other. The demand is not made by an equal; rather than requesting me, the other "commands" me. In other words, it affirms that my responsibility for the other is not the result of my initiative—the other commands me; I do not choose to be commanded. Also at stake is that the notion of "height" precludes any idea of "pity" for the other.[29]

So far we have seen that both Kierkegaard and Levinas affirm structures of asymmetry in relations to ensure that the other is appropriately loved. However, the introduction of this category of "heightened inequality" makes us realize that Kierkegaard's affirmations of asymmetry have their place in an account that is deeply committed to equality. It raises the question of how Kierkegaard's commitment to equality stands in relation to these important forms of asymmetry, one of which is straightforwardly called a kind of inequality. Is equality compatible with asymmetry? Does an emphasis on asymmetry undermine or require qualifications of a commitment to equality?

D. Asymmetry and Equality

Where does Kierkegaard stand on equality? To assess this we need to reconsider deliberations in the first series together with deliberations in the second. In early deliberations, long before notions of reciprocity or symmetry are brought up, Kierkegaard proclaims an unconditional commitment to the equality of all. The affirmation of equality is tied to Kierkegaard's sense of the need for impartiality. Only in love that is "the opposite of preference" (WL, p. 58)—namely, "neighbor love"—can we respond to a genuine other. Love for a genuine other is not based in "passion's preference" but rather in the other's "equality [with you] before God"; "the neighbor is one who is equal" (p. 60). It is important that, for Kierkegaard, this equality is a recognition within love and does not simply concern the separate sphere of justice.[30]

Moreover, although the rejection of reciprocity seems similarly motivated in both Kierkegaard and Levinas by an appreciation of the infinity of love's demand, the infinite responsibility, Kierkegaard, as we saw in chapter 8, adds the interesting twist that the infinity can be seen to come "from both sides." He affirms a kind of reciprocity or symmetry in remaining in love's debt:

> But to be and to remain in an infinite debt is an expression of the infinitude of love; thus by remaining in debt it remains in its element. There is a reciprocal relationship [*Vexel-Forhold*] here, but infinite from both sides. In the one case, it is the beloved, who in every manifestation of the lover's love lovingly apprehends the immeasurability; in the other, it is the lover, who feels the immeasurability because he acknowledges the debt to be infinite. . . . What marvelous like for like in this infinitude! (WL, p. 181)

This "reciprocal relationship [*Vexel-Forhold*] is infinite from both sides." This "like for like," is appreciated, although reciprocity as repayment love (*Gjenkjerlighed*), as an economic tit for tat, is ruled out. It is noteworthy that in the one instance in which we find Kierkegaard's positive evaluation of what is translated in English as reciprocity, he uses a Danish word that is different from the one he uses when he negatively evaluates it. Hence, Kierkegaard has, on the one hand, an affirmation of equality and, on the other hand, a rejection of reciprocity and an affirmation of asymmetry (based on fidelity and infinite debt), coupled with a claim for "heightened inequality."

The issue of symmetry and asymmetry in relationships is the subject of the contemporary 'partiality/impartiality' debate. Acknowledging that many are uncomfortable with the idea of impartiality that seems to follow from the universal or inclusive claim of the love commandment, one contemporary ethicist analyzes the sources of that discomfort and suggests four types of asymmetry.[31] The notion of impartiality or strict symmetry is found troubling for two different types of reasons—those having to do with the other person and those having to do with the self—and each has two expressions. The reasons that have to do with guaranteeing sufficient love of the other person can be expressed in two ways. The first reservation involves the way in which impartiality or strict symmetry fails to do justice to the distinctively Christian notion of cross-bearing or the more general notion of sacrificial love. The second reservation is that such symmetry or impartiality does not effectively take into account our actual preoccupation with our own self; it does not provide an effective counterweight to our de facto bias toward self. That is, for both reasons, if we stay with strict impartiality or symmetry, the other person will not be the recipient of sacrificial love. The second type of discomfort with the idea of impartiality or symmetry is also expressed in two ways. The third reservation about impartiality is that it doesn't do justice to the legitimate value of personal identity and the self's personal projects. The fourth reservation is that impartiality fails to appreciate the importance of the difference between what I can do for myself and what I can do for others. In other words, these two reservations suggest that impartiality does not do justice to the self's needs. All four of these reservations about impartiality suggest that certain kinds of asymmetry might be integral to loving relationships in a theocentric context.[32] Another important kind of reservation about strict impartiality concerns the way in which a close relationship renders the other particularly vulnerable to what I neglect to do.[33] In part this is because I know his or her needs and desires better than do those not in such a close relationship. But it is also true because caretaking conventions are already in place in society, and it if is assumed in a given context that I will help the person related to me, others will then assume that that person is not in need of their help; if I go counter to that general expectation, I deprive my relation of help.

Levinas actually illustrates one kind of commitment to asymmetry that results from dissatisfaction with the notion of equality and impartiality. He would object to impartiality precisely because it would fail to do justice to the de facto bias that we have in our own favor, which therefore would require a counterweight in the form of the "height" or the "command" of the other. He would hold that without that counterweight of asymmetry, the other would never receive sacrificial love. The guarantee that the other person is treated impartially would not be enough to ensure that in the case of conflicting needs, we would sacrifice ourselves for the other. This seems to be the same insight that Kierkegaard expresses in his notion of "heightened inequality."

However, Kierkegaard also adds the critical symmetry of the "as yourself." There is equality even in love. If the "as yourself" is understood to provide an index for the material content of one's love for another person in terms of absolute equality in our day-to-day conduct, it may be difficult to reconcile this claim for equality in a relationship with the claim of an infinite debt or a heightened inequality. But this may not be the way it is supposed to function; Kierkegaard may be indicating a meta-level equality, which he clarifies later: "Christianly, every human being (the single individual), unconditionally every human being, once again, unconditionally every human being, is equally close to God—how close and equally close—is loved by him."[34] This "infinite equality" between human beings is contrasted with the only important difference between people—that some people remember constantly that they are loved by God, and others fail to do so. Levinas's suggestion about the difference in perspectives (inside/outside) is useful here. I can affirm everyone's equality under God at the same time as I affirm my own infinite indebtedness to the other person because the former constitutes a kind of view from outside ourselves, whereas the latter is the view from the concrete place we occupy in relation to an other.

One way to understand Kierkegaard's commitment to the "as yourself" is to compare it with Levinas's refusal to bring it into play. We need to ask what the affirmation of the "as yourself" guarantees for Kierkegaard and what the refusal to affirm it guarantees for Levinas.[35] We have seen that, for Kierkegaard, the emphasis on the "as yourself" reinforces the claim that we are all creatures of God, all equally gifted by God in terms of our being; this entails that differences that obscure that equality have to be ignored (whether they make one want to condescend to the other or to adore the other). It is interesting to note that when Kierkegaard explains that "Christianity presupposes that a person loves himself and then adds to this only the phrase about the neighbor *as yourself*" (WL, p. 18), he is emphasizing "the other as oneself" and not, as Paul Ricoeur would have it, "oneself as another."[36] Kierkegaard's emphasis on equality guarantees that no one is excluded from the scope of those we are unconditionally obliged to love; the guarantee that no one is excluded (i.e., that all are equal) is achieved by guaranteeing that we do not love self *more* than the other. For Levinas, the rejection of claims to equality ensures that we love the other *more* than ourself, but the result is the same: no one will be excluded. Both want to guarantee the ultimate end, that no one is excluded by our selfishness; neither wants the asymmetry that implies the privileged position of the self. But they differ with respect to proximate ends.

It could be argued that they provide a mutual correction of each other: Kierkegaard points out the danger in allowing that one can or should love another more than self, and Levinas points out the danger in emphasizing equality and love of self. For Levinas, the emphasis on dissymmetry may well derive from the fear that an emphasis on equality tends to be exploited by us as license for calculating the other's obligation to us. There is, in the end, something remarkably distinctive about the ways in which Kierkegaard and Levinas proceed to achieve what seems to be a similar goal.

III. The Affirmation of Responsiveness to the Other

Let me now indicate briefly some discussions in *Works of Love* in which the topic of responsiveness is indirectly addressed and affirmed. They help us to appreciate the kind of responsiveness that Kierkegaard allows to stand, even encourages, and they provide indirect textual support for reading the work of love in recollecting the dead as of "criterion" or "test" rather than as of a paradigm to be fostered or uncritically imitated.

A. Recommendations of Responsiveness

First, throughout *Works of Love*, Kierkegaard valorizes responsiveness as constitutive of love. Several instances that we have noted already stand out and can suffice here. One consists in the kind of example he relies on as an illustration of loving the neighbor, for example, the responsiveness of the merciful Samaritan (p. 22). It is clear that the response to the other is both concrete and practical and is directed precisely to the other's material condition. A second example is his recommendation that we pay attention to alleviating the poverty of others for their sake rather than for ours (p. 14). A third is found in his deliberation on "Our Duty to Love the People We See" (IV): included is a lengthy and detailed consideration of the duty to love people precisely "as they are," rather than as we would like them to be. We find, then, throughout *Works of Love* recommendations of compassionate responses to what the neighbor needs and is—not one-sided initiatives that ignore the concrete situation or response of the other. These support the kind of concrete attention to the other's distinctive character and needs that can flesh out the "tender" union of two people, which, Kierkegaard says, constitutes neighbor love (p. 44).

B. The Attack on Self-love's Radical Asymmetry

Second, *Works of Love* as a whole, it could be argued, constitutes a sustained critique of what Kierkegaard terms "self-love, selfishness, self-seeking, or whatever other names the unloving disposition has" (p. 264). The deliberation entitled "You Shall Love *the Neighbor*" (II, B) offers a concentrated version of the attack on "self-love" in its many disguises. The model of nonmutuality, of radical asymmetry, which Adorno attributes to Kierkegaard, would, however, come uncomfortably close to the "self-love" that Kierkegaard repeatedly attacks. That is, one-sided initiatives that ignore the other in his or her concrete actuality constitute a form of pernicious self-love.

C. Mutuality of Claim and Need

Finally, the first deliberation, "Love's Hidden Life and Its Recognizability by Its Fruits," makes a claim that surely bears strongly on any reading of what a loving relationship means for Kierkegaard. As we saw earlier (in chapter 1), Kierkegaard writes, in a passage that deserves close attention, that although words and gestures may deceive, still, to hold back genuine emotion and words "can be the unloving committing of a wrong, just like withholding from someone what you owe him" (WL, p. 12). "Your friend, your beloved, your child, or whoever is an object of your love has a claim upon an expression of it also in words if it actually moves you inwardly. The emotion is not your possession but belongs to the other; the expression is your debt to him, since in the emotion you indeed belong to him."

Similarly, Kierkegaard writes in several contexts about "need" in ways that imply mutuality. As we saw in chapter 2, to our surprise, Kierkegaard insists in the deliberation "*You* Shall Love the Neighbor" (II, C) that "love in a human being is a need, is the expression of riches," and the greater the need, "the greater the riches" (WL, p. 67). When the need is for more than the "one single particular person," "the need is a wealth." In a striking passage, he repeats: "Love is a need, the deepest need, in the person in whom there is love for the neighbor; he does not need people just to have someone to love, but he needs to love people." Moreover, we saw that Kierkegaard's affirmation of the need to love people goes hand in hand with the need to be loved. In the deliberation entitled "You *Shall* Love" (II, A), he condemns the kind of "proud independence that thinks it has no need to feel loved" but rather only "needs other people—not in order to be loved by them but in order to love them, in order to have someone to love" (p. 39). He rails against the way in which the gratification of "proud self-esteem" can try to pass itself off as independence. We can see there that Kierkegaard wants, on the one hand, to appreciate the agent's needs, and he wants, on the other hand, to avoid approving of the kind of need that renders the other instrumental to the agent's satisfaction. In sum, significant textual support leads us to expect that Kierkegaard would not recommend that we treat the living as if they were dead.

IV. Objections Revisited

A. Does Unselfishness Mean Forgoing Mutual Love?

Let us reconsider now how the ninth deliberation looks against this background? What in Kierkegaard's characterizations of the work of love in recollecting one who is dead seems most problematical in terms of what we can learn from it about loving the living?[37] The first—that the expression of love in remembering the dead is "*a work of the* MOST UNSELFISH *love*"—is not itself surprising. Loving the living unselfishly seems an appropriate thing to recommend. Kierkegaard's way of describing such unselfishness, however, may seem extreme: unselfishness lies in the way such recollecting excludes even "the repayment of reciprocal love" (WL, p. 349). A critic could argue that this means that any positive response on the part of the other invalidates our love for him or her; this means that any hope for or expectation of the other's love is considered selfish and hence excluded from love. The work of remembering the dead could appropriately be described as one in which there is no possibility of any response; the dead one, after all, is not an "actual object." In this test situation, love cannot be reciprocated, so we are clearly able to determine what is motivating our work of remembering the dead;—that is, it cannot be the thought of repayment love. But it should be clear by now that what we should learn to avoid in relationships with the living is couched in terms of "repayment," not "response." The idea of "repayment" can characterize a particular kind of attitude to the other—one in which "repayment," even the repayment of 'repayment love,' is seen as the motive for my love, that on which I make my love conditional. But not every response from the other is ruled out as irrelevant because not every response is "repayment" in that technical sense.

Moreover, in "Love Believes All Things—and Yet Is Never Deceived" (2:II), Kierkegaard condemned a view of love that "regards loving as a demand (reciprocal love [*Gjenkjerlighed*] is the demand) and being loved (reciprocal love) as an earthly good, as temporal—and yet, alas, as the highest bliss" (WL, p. 237). It is worth repeating his illustration once more, precisely because it shows so clearly what is at stake for him. He deconstructs the implied analogy between love and the commercial world: "A person pays out money in order to purchase some convenience; he has paid out the money, but he did not get the convenience—well, then he has been duped. He makes a love deal; he barters his love, but he did not receive reciprocal love in exchange—well, then he has been deceived." It is precisely for this reason that Kierkegaard insists that "the one who truly loves regards demanding reciprocal love simply as a defilement, a degradation, and regards loving without the reward of reciprocal love as the highest blessedness."[38] Up to this point in *Works of Love*, the only reciprocity being condemned is that of repayment love [*Gjenkjerlighed*]. In Kierkegaard's mind, his rejection of the "reciprocity" of "repayment love" (or the repayment of reciprocal love) has already been definitively clarified in two preceding deliberations by the time he discusses the asymmetric lack of reciprocity in love of the dead.

Thus, Kierkegaard's comments on the lack of a claim to reciprocity can be dealt with in part by showing that not all response is thereby precluded and by referring to the specific Danish word he uses to condemn that particular kind of response. Although he sees all repayment love as false love, he does not see all loving response as repayment. He alludes to the response of joy in being loved in an 1850 journal comment, drawing an analogy between human love and the divine relation of grace and human "gratitude": "Take the human love-relationship. The lover should not torture himself, wondering whether at every moment he fulfills his beloved's every possible requirement. . . . No, it begins with joy over being loved—and then comes a striving to please."[39] Not all response to love is meant to earn love or to repay love.

B. Does All Influence Constitute Compulsion?

Earlier we saw Kierkegaard's rationale for emphasizing the independence or freedom of love in order to guarantee fidelity. It seems unproblematical to claim as he does that love must be freely given and that "the stronger the compelling, the less free is the love" (WL, p. 351). Kierkegaard's illustrations of such freedom raise questions, however, about whether love of the living is supposed to preclude any influence by the other, any response that could influence us. Probably the harshest claim in this chapter is the one implied in the suggestion that "what can extort from one a work of love can be extremely varied and thus cannot be enumerated. The child cries, the pauper begs, the widow pesters, deference constrains, misery compels, etc. But any love in work that is extorted in this way is not free" (p. 351). A critic could object that Kierkegaard seems to rule out the relevance of anything needed or demanded by the other; this makes it impossible to consider that anything is ever lovingly given to an other, that the other can ever be lovingly responded to. It is easy enough to agree with Kierkegaard that compulsion precludes love since love cannot be extracted against our will. However, it must be admitted that compulsion, for Kierkegaard, is found everywhere along a remarkably broad spectrum of conditions: the vulnerable infant illustrates helplessness "in its most compelling form" (p. 351). Moreover, even "daily sight and habit" are "coercive" and make it difficult to determine whether love is free (p. 354). The question is whether, for Kierkegaard, influence of any kind counts as compulsion, whether anything that could claim our response or call forth a response from us militates against the freedom of our love.[40]

If the extreme scenario of unresponding love for an unresponsive other were the goal toward which we should strive, Kierkegaard's entire ethic of love would be put in jeopardy—as puritan, at best, and hateful, at worst. Extreme nonresponsiveness *of the other to us* would be the most effective way of guaranteeing our nonresponsiveness *to the other* as a concrete being. Such irrelevance of the other evacuates all responsiveness, and hence responsibility, from the agent's side. If nothing about the other were allowed to affect our response to him or her, it would not be genuine response *to* the other. As I have argued, however, the heuristic excessiveness of Kierkegaard's tests, need not be read as if he were proposing that we treat the living as if they were dead.

C. A Charitable Reading

What, then, is Kierkegaard's position? We have seen that in this controversial deliberation Kierkegaard makes a general contrast between love of the dead (who are not "actual" beings) and love of the living (who are "actual" beings). The fact that he makes this contrast shows that the asymmetry concerning the dead need not automatically be a recommendation for our relation with the living. We have also seen him affirm responsiveness within a relation and hint at the "marvelous like for like," infinite from both sides, that enhances a loving relationship. Moreover, we have seen the way in which in other deliberations he uses a narrow technical meaning of reciprocity (as economic exchange or repayment). Thus, one cannot simply say that the relation as such is, for Kierkegaard, either symmetrical or asymmetrical because he affirms a certain kind of asymmetry at the same time as he affirms a certain kind of symmetry (or "like for like," which is "infinite from both sides"). By holding these two in tension, Kierkegaard's account can illuminate the discussion by proposing a number of important distinctions within the category of responsiveness. He distinguishes between two attitudes toward the response to the other: the goal is to love the people we see, just "as they are," yet the other's change cannot carry in its train an automatic change in us. He distinguishes between two attitudes toward a response by the other: the goal is to be independent enough (the relation asymmetrical enough) to preclude love's going up and down with variations in the other, yet dependent enough to admit our need of the other and the claim of the other on us for our expression of love. He distinguishes between two kinds of dependence: he rejects a certain kind of dependence on the other's response, yet allows that we genuinely need the other.

What kind of response from the other can we attach importance to without making our response conditional on the other's response? Let me make three suggestions. The first is that we consider the notion of infinite responsibility to be the hermeneutical principle for interpreting the limits and extent of mutuality. The second is that we look for an idea of mutuality as an ingredient in the claim for equality in a relation. The third is that we read Kierkegaard's extreme sensitivity to what counts as "repayment," as well as his extreme sensitivity to what counts as "compulsion," in the light of the responsiveness that is implied in his affirmation of our need to love and be loved, the claim of the other on us, and our responsibility to take care of others. What we are being urged by Kierkegaard to practice is thus presented indirectly. If every positive response were ruled out as vitiating love, we could not make any sense of his strong affirmation of our need for others, our need to be loved, or the legitimacy of the claim of the other on us. He cannot, therefore, be recommending a relation in which no response of the other can be responded to.

The ninth deliberation shows us only that some forms of mutuality are disguised versions of self-love: (1) fidelity that goes up and down with variations in the beloved and (2) claims to reciprocity. The reminders I have collected together suggest that throughout *Works of Love* Kierkegaard is clarifying a model of a relationship that we should avoid—forms of bartering, tit-for-tat repayment, economic exchange, compelled response, and self-serving response.[41] But warning against making our love conditional on an expected or actual response by the other, against asserting a claim to reciprocity, and against an economic model of reciprocity does not amount to claiming that the response of the other is irrelevant. Significant modes of mutual responsiveness remain in place in Kierkegaard's account of a loving relationship—as we would expect, given his lovely reminder that "what you can have only for yourself alone is never the highest" (p. 27).

chapter sixteen

Love's Transparency

"The Work of Love in Praising Love" (2:X)

Although the title of this deliberation seems to indicate a work parallel to that of memorializing the dead—a work that we can and should perform through a variety of tasks that eulogize love—Kierkegaard immediately sets us straight. We could sing hymns or write discourses that praise love, but the work of love in praising love is not that kind of activity—and a good thing, too, because not all of us can hold a tune or write eloquently. Here Kierkegaard retrieves and recasts several themes from his earlier writings on the ethical: among them, transparency, the universally human, the intensity of passion, and "purity of heart." The burden of this deliberation is to reformulate the dimensions of love's inwardness and outwardness—that is, to suggest that love implies a kind of transparency, that transparency is a kind of self-denial, and that self-denial must show itself outwardly in an unselfishness whose "purpose" is to "reconcile" people in a "community of the highest."

I. Proverb and Practice

The proverb with which Kierkegaard opens the deliberation, "To say it is no art, but to do it is," is put to a use rather different from its usual one. This proverb is usually appropriate when where we want to remind someone that saying some-

thing is not enough; rather, to do it is the important thing. It is, in effect, the reminder that talk is cheap. This is the very same message that we saw earlier in
Kierkegaard's critique of evasive, procrastinating promise making and his insistence that Christianity is "sheer action" (chapter 5). This reminder is not appropriate, however, for the poet because for the poet, who is an artist, "the art actually is 'to say it'" (WL, p. 359). In the activity of praising love, the proverb can
be used in what Kierkegaard calls "a special way"; that is, one could assert: "To
say it is no art, but to do it is," although such a use would be qualified in two
ways. First, we would need to remember that praising love is not an "art" at all
because an art is something conditional on talent and a particular calling, whereas
praising love is something that is possible to every human being, a "universally
human" capability (p. 364). By contrasting a work of love with an art, Kierkegaard again highlights the equality of our createdness. Second, we would need to
remember that in the case of praising love, "'to do it' would mean to say it" (p.
359); in other words, *to love is to praise love.* Just as in an earlier deliberation
Kierkegaard emphasizes how 'what love does, it is,' and 'what love is, it does,'[1]
so, too, he is going to claim here that a work done in love in effect praises love,
that only a work done in love can praise love, and that to praise love we need to
do nothing in addition to the work of loving. Although praising love is not done
by speeches about love, one could speak of a discourse of praising love—our
lives could be a text that praises love.

Here in the final deliberation, Kierkegaard appeals implicitly to the provocative claim with which he ends the first deliberation of *Works of Love:* "Like is
only known by like; only someone who abides in love can know love, and in the
same way his love is to be known" (p. 16). He starts with the premise that only
someone who loves can know love, adds the implied premise that one can only
praise what one knows, and draws the conclusion that only one who loves can
praise love. He then amplifies this reasoning with the rather different conclusion
that all one needs to do to praise love is to love. In other words, the one who is
not loving cannot praise love because she or he does not know love, and the one
who is loving in any work thereby praises love.

Is it plausible to identify praising love with doing something (anything) lovingly? It is if we agree with Kierkegaard's assumption that like is known only by
like, that love is known only by love. In general, I can speak highly of something
I do not myself either do or care about; for example, I can recommend swimming
as a sport that exercises the most muscles with the least amount of stress on the
body, even if I personally detest or am incapable of swimming. Even if I do not
particularly like jazz or abstract art, I can detail some objectively valuable things
about them. But it could be argued that, in one sense, I cannot truly 'praise' them
since I do not truly appreciate them. It is plausible to think that the best praise is
the kind offered by someone who understands and values the object of praise.
Think how differently I would feel about the praise of my cross-court forehand
that is offered by the world's top- ranked tennis player and the praise offered by
someone who never played tennis. Love, Kierkegaard is trying to tell us, cannot
be genuinely praised by an unloving person. An unloving person cannot know
what love is; moreover, our praise of a gift we neglect or refuse to use or enjoy is

empty. I cannot praise love if I am not loving because love is only known by love and only praised by being exercised or actualized.

II. Love's Vision of Love

An interesting aspect of Kierkegaard's claim that only love can know (recognize) love is brought out in a recent article by a French Catholic thinker Jean Luc Marion. Marion claims that "only love can see love" that "only a person who knows from experience what loving means can perceive love."[2] A conclusion similar to Kierkegaard's would follow: if only one who loves can see love, then only one who loves can praise love. Marion argues that if a Christian outlook is to be truly distinctive, it must not only interpret the realities available to everyone but also "reveal" phenomena that might not otherwise be seen (and here he does not mean the "proper domain of revelation," e.g., the Trinity).[3] That is, it must have new phenomena to deal with, or it will be just another interpretation among many. His candidate for a radically new phenomenon is "charity," or agape: "The Christian outlook facilitates the resurgence and appearance in the world of phenomena that have up until then remained invisible, on the basis of which a new interpretation of already visible phenomena becomes thenceforth legitimate. What is this new given and this new interpretation? The answer is charity, which gives itself and only allows itself to be seen by those who love it."[4] Only someone who has undergone a "complete initiation of the soul" can recognize another person "not only as another 'myself,' but rather above all as 'himself,' as one entrusted by God to me." To see the world as "gift" and to see a human being as both "himself" and a "gift" is, Kierkegaard would say, to see rightly.

Marion reinforces this notion of an ethic of vision, echoing words we have already heard from Kierkegaard in the two deliberations on loving the people we see (1:IV) and on love not seeking its own (2:IV): "Man is certainly visible by all men. But the outlooks which see him naturally can also kill him, or more often, render him an object. To see a person as such, with an individuality that is so irreducible that only love can overtake it—this cannot be done by an outlook that is without charity."[5] For Marion, this suggestion of a Christian hermeneutics of love has implications not only for the classic individual instance of the poor man who is begging in the street but also for all who are marginalized by society, including "the sick at the end of their lives or those who are incurable, the physically and mentally handicapped," as well as those exploited by an economy that sees them only as tools.[6] The ethic of vision that Marion is here endorsing recognizes that "certain phenomena in effect disappear either partially or totally from the visibility that the world accords to its privileged ones."[7] For Marion and Kierkegaard, then, it would seem clear that if only love can see love, then only love can praise love.

If only the loving one can praise love, the relevant question is not "What are the special things I should do to praise love?" Although it is a "work" to praise love, rather than an "art" in which the "poet" would have an advantage, it is not the kind of work that requires special forms of expounding love's praises (even if they could be done by anyone who wanted to). Although Kierkegaard describes the work of praising love as a "task," it is done only to contrast it with an art— not to point to special rites, speech acts, behaviors, or even special inner sighs or longings, which are set aside and dedicated to that purpose rather than to another purpose. The question we should ask is, rather, "How should I do what I do so that love is praised, so that love's glory is shown?" Although Kierkegaard's answer in this deliberation may not be what we would expect in relation to the rather upbeat theme of "praise" in the title, his answer is straightforward: do whatever you do "INWARDLY *in self-denial*" and "OUTWARDLY *in self-sacrificing unselfishness*" (WL, p. 360, 365). Love is neither merely inward nor merely outward but exhibits at the same time the two aspects. Here again the theme of the inner/outer, unseen/revealed relation is retrieved for pondering. Whereas it is not yet obvious how "self-denial" is to be understood and how it is distinguished from "self-sacrificing unselfishness," or how to understand what the concepts of inward and outward entail, what is clear is that the work of praising love can be done by anyone who wants to do it because, although only love can praise love, in fact "everyone who wants to have love is given it" (p. 360).

III. Transparency: The Inwardness of Self-denial

When Kierkegaard suggests that the work of love "can be done only . . . *in the love of truth*" (WL, p. 360; emphasis mine), we wonder just how this might apply to all works of love. He has not spoken explicitly about the category of "truth" before, but he focuses on it here and contrasts it to a variety of untruths: "illusion," "little lie," "deception," and "beloved error" (pp. 365, 366, 368, 371). In other words, he is talking about honest appraisal and clear vision. In this way he makes explicit what he had assumed earlier—that loving depends on having a proper understanding of our situation and status as creatures before God. Here Kierkegaard is reconsidering two themes in the ethic proclaimed by Judge William in *Either/Or*. Not only does Judge William hold to an ethic of the universal (universal duty and universal capability), but he also recommends the goal of achieving "transparency," claiming that if we cannot open ourselves we cannot love.[8] In this deliberation, we find that praise of love is a function of the achievement (possible to all) of a kind of transparency, which Kierkegaard identifies with various modes of existential "self-deepening": thinking *one* thought, thinking an *infinite* thought, *essential* thinking, love of *truth*, and *understanding oneself*. As in the earlier deliberation in which he claimed that the inner was the outer and the outer was the inner, insofar as love is what love does, here the transparency is a question of clarity, a transparency in which there is no difference between the inner and the outer:[9] "[T]rue clarity can be only in transparency" (p. 361).

To truly praise love, Kierkegaard begins, "one must persevere for a long time in thinking one thought"; he says unapologetically that "this is the requirement" (WL, p. 360). Love of truth implies seeking truth, and the task is a "strenuous one"—namely, "thinking one thought." If the way to truly praise love is to do a work lovingly, Kierkegaard's account of how to praise love is an account of how to behave lovingly: "[O]ne must persevere for a long time in thinking one thought, persevere in it with the strictest abstemiousness, spiritually understood, in regard to everything heterogeneous, foreign, irrelevant, and intrusive, persevere in it with the most punctilious and obedient renunciation of every other thought." What "one thought" are we supposed to be thinking in this endeavor? Clearly, one that is up to the task of being probed for a lifetime—not a "finite idea," but an "infinite thought" (p. 360).[10] Kierkegaard's contrast does not make it obvious what an "infinite thought" is since it is a contrast between an idea and a thought, as well as a contrast between finite and infinite. We are led, whether by Kierkegaard's design or not, to recall Descartes's treatment of the thought of the "infinite."[11] What is an "infinite thought"? Can we ever have anything more than a finite thought of infinity? Is the alternative infinite thinking? But if infinite thinking means thinking infinitely, clearly we cannot do that. Kierkegaard's notion of an "infinite thought" is of an unending one, and he contrasts that with the thought of something external. To recommend unending thought is to recommend a turn to something that can support unending probing, that is, a turn inward, an attempt at self-understanding. He assumes here the single-mindedness he discussed in "Purity of Heart," the deep and unending probing of the self that calls the self into question by putting the question to the self: is the question (Who am I? What can I do?) real for me and can I answer it? Is such "essential thinking" (p. 361) merely egoistic and self-obsessive navel gazing? Kierkegaard tries to safeguard such thinking from narcissism in two ways. First, it is, to repeat, a "strenuous" task; Kierkegaard points to "the quiet patience, the humble and obedient slowness, the noble renunciation of momentary influence," which are all "necessary to think one thought" (p. 368). Second, it is not meant to affirm and comfort me; it is intended to issue in clarity even if that clarity makes me uncomfortable. Kierkegaard suggests that the outcome is a "humbling" discovery (p. 361).

Kierkegaard describes this thinking as a strenuous alternation, straining and relaxing our spiritual powers; it is a description of passionate intensity, or the passionate maintenance of tension, which calls to mind other places in his writings where Kierkegaard highlights "passion" and paradoxical tension. In particular it calls to mind the paradoxical passion of thought described in *Philosophical Fragments*. There Johannes Climacus construes thought as a passion that, like the passion of love, seeks its own "downfall": "This, then, is the ultimate paradox of thought: to want to discover something that thought itself cannot think."[12] This is a humbling discovery of our limits. In *Philosophical Fragments*, the result of this "ultimate passion of the understanding" is a willed "collision" with the "unknown," to which we give the name "god."[13] Likewise, in *Works of Love*, Kierkegaard is describing a humbling process in which we become transparent to ourselves and we see the truth, which is that of ourselves we are capable of nothing and that God exists. When we single-mindedly probe the only reality that sustains infinite probing, we become aware of our own inability to account for or maintain ourself, and hence, indirectly, we come up against the Ground of our being.[14] Anti-Climacus similarly emphasizes the importance of becoming transparent to our Ground of Being.[15] Kierkegaard has no doubt about it: "When one thinks only one thought, one must in connection with this thinking discover self-denial, and it is self-denial that discovers that God is" (p. 362). That is, if we persist in the self-deepening probing that single-mindedly loves the truth (hence seeks the truth), we MUST experience certain discoveries; we MUST come to a halt, at which we realize that one must lose one's life in order to gain it (p. 362); we MUST discover "self-denial," which discovers God. Kierkegaard uses several phrases interchangeably with the discovery "that God is": what happens when we thus strain our spiritual powers is that we will come to understand ourselves, our "selfishness" will be "broken,"[16] and we will become an "instrument [*Redskab*]" for God.[17]

Transparency, true clarity, and humbling discovery—all of these themes weave themselves in and out of this section on the inwardness of self-denial. This orientation in an inward direction is a relation to self, a coming to a self-understanding; it is deeply inward rather than external and superficial. We see "the truth" clearly, honestly, and without illusion. We probe the "thought," we see "the truth," and the truth is "self-denial." Self-denial is therefore this denial of self as autonomous, as capable—even when, or especially when, things are going our way and we are accomplishing amazing feats. This is the truth, but not the whole truth. Since half-truths are, however, worse than no truths at all, it is crucial to recognize the whole truth about self-denial.

In the first deliberation, Kierkegaard suggests that what appears to be "one thought" may really contain two thoughts. In speaking of the relation between the hiddenness of love and its recognizability in its fruits, he remarks: "The sacred words speak about two thoughts although they hiddenly speak about only one; the statement manifestly contains one thought but also hiddenly contains another" (WL, p. 8). This is a good example of Kierkegaard's Lutheran emphasis on simultaneity—*simul justus et peccator*; *simul* hidden and revealed—and in this deliberation he says that the "one thought" is "self-denial," although in this thought something is experienced that is "a contradiction or is simultaneous" (p. 362). This "one thought" (self-denial) is both "blessedness and terror" because we discover God at the same time as we discover self-denial. The thought that is self-denial is the simultaneous discovery that you are able to do nothing and that you have an omnipotent coworker (p. 362). The simultaneous discovery must be maintained in its simultaneity—that you can do nothing and that God is the one who will help you (p. 365). The statement "manifestly contains one thought but also hiddenly contains another." The terror and blessedness is that you can do nothing (without God) and you can do everything (with God). You cannot separate the two. If you discover the second, you must acknowledge the first; if you acknowledge the first without the second, you will despair (moreover, it will not be the truth). The "one thought" is "self-denial," but it is not appreciated until both aspects of the truth (the thought) are appreciated. By coming to know this dual truth a person will "gain the best powers," but only in self-denial, as "not his own" (p. 362).

How, then, is self-denial related to praising love? First, to praise love is to love the truth, so to praise love is to see oneself truly. Second, the truth has two dimensions—the understanding of self as incapable of anything without God and the understanding of God, as one's coworker, with whom all things are possible. This recognition constitutes self-denial. In self-denial, we hold fast to God. Holding fast to God is knowing Love. One can only praise what one knows or what one is, so the more one knows God, the more one can love and through love praise love. Kierkegaard's claim should now be easier to understand:

> [O]nly in self-denial can one effectually praise love, because God is love, and only in self-denial can one hold fast to God. What a human being knows by himself about love is very superficial; he must come to know the deeper love from God—that is, in self-denial he must become what every human being can become (since self-denial is related to the universally human and thus is distinguished from the particular call and election), an instrument for God. (WL, p. 364).

Seeing ourselves truly is not an ineffective intellectual recognition but a practical transforming of ourselves. Honest vision precludes our remaining the same because we are changed by what we see.[18] This transformation in self-denial, Kierkegaard insists, has to express itself outwardly. Assuming that one has learned the hard lesson of self-denial in relation to God—one has seen one's nothingness before God—there is still the possibility (or even likelihood) that one will desperately cultivate another hope, the hope that at least one is something with respect to, by "comparison" with, others (p. 366). It is here that the "outwardness" of unselfishness comes in, with the purpose of *reconciliation*.

IV. The Outwardness of Self-sacrificing Unselfishness

Kierkegaard does not say that the inward is the recognition that I can do nothing and the outward is the recognition that God helps you; both are part of the inward expression of self-denial. The outward expression of self-denial occurs in the unselfishness that should follow the inward recognition: *in relation to others* I am both able to do nothing and yet able to do everything, with God as my helper. That is, I am nothing, but with God's help I can do everything *for the other*. What I can and should do requires self-sacrificing unselfishness, which is the outward expression of inward self-denial; that is "understood correctly, self-sacrificing unselfishness is one and the same as self-denial" (p.366). Kierkegaard insists that such outward expression is "required" (p. 366); unselfishness in relation to others is not an optional expression of self-denial, contingently related to it, but an essential expression of self-denial. That is, the recognition of this dual truth—that we are both unable to do anything and that God is our coworker—obligates us to help the other (with its attendant self-sacrifice and unselfishness). "Can" implies "ought," in this case. And the ought—the obligation, the duty—is reconciliation: "One who praises love reconciles all . . . in the community of the highest" (p. 365).

Kierkegaard here explicitly distinguishes between the "intrinsic reward" and the "purpose" of praising love (WL, p. 365). In the preceding deliberation, he had concluded that if we practice this recollection of the dead, we will receive two benefits: "[In] addition to the blessing that is inseparable from this work of love you will also have the best guidance for rightly understanding life." In other words, the deliberation tells us that there are two dimensions—the value of doing the good deed as such (to honor the dead) and the value of learning from it something about how to love the living. Here in this deliberation, too, he tells us that there are two benefits: the "intrinsic reward" of praising love and the "purpose," which is, "to win people to it, to make them properly aware of what in a conciliatory spirit is granted to human beings—that is, the highest." To repeat: "[T]he one who praises love reconciles all . . . in the community of the highest." The social implication of such reconciliation has already been made clear by Kierkegaard in the deliberation on love's reconciling spirit (2:VIII), which I discussed in chapter 14. Here Kierkegaard's claim that "true love is self-denial's love" (p. 369) needs to be understood in the context of its "purpose" of winning people to the truth and thus reconciling them with each other.

A. Self-denial and Hatred of the World

Despite the fact that this deliberation combines with others to highlight the various ways in which Kierkegaard understands love in terms of its social expressions, it contains a sentence that has often caused particular consternation: "The world is always offended by the saying that 'love of God is hatred of the world'" (WL, p. 370). Does this mean that, for Kierkegaard, Christianity requires hatred of the world?[19] We are back again with the charge of acosmism or world-denial, which we considered in chapter 5, and that discussion should be kept in mind as we try to put this controversial claim in context.

In this deliberation, Kierkegaard raises the issue of how the loving person is perceived (by those who refuse to be equally loving) in terms of the "loveworthy" person and the "self-lover." His discussion begins with the simple claim that it is not true that the person who praises love "must himself be or come to be loved" (WL, p. 370). This is simply a descriptive generalization about a world that "crucified the one who was Love" and "persecuted and exterminated so many of love's witnesses." There is always the possibility that we, too, will be persecuted or exterminated because what we do in love may threaten others or seem to them as if we hated them or their values.

Kierkegaard then provides a tongue-in-cheek treatment of the so-called "loveworthy" person. The world's conception of the "loveworthy" person is of someone who "is well informed about all the possible excuses and escapes and sagacious rules for higgling and haggling and discounting; and he is loving enough to lend a little of his sagacity to others, by whose help one then advantageously makes one's own life easy and comfortable" (WL, p. 370). He lives this way because he doesn't take to heart God's requirement (eternity's requirement) to love the neighbor as oneself, with its concomitant "strenuous life," and as a result, such a person does not bring us face to face with that requirement either. No, we feel "safe" with him, Kierkegaard says cuttingly, because he helps us forget that God's requirement could have a bearing on what we actually do. We call such a person "loveworthy" because he supports us in our desire to evade the rigor of God's commandments; this kind of loveworthiness is what Kierkegaard calls "treason against the eternal" (WL, p. 370). On the contrary, if someone presses "eternity's requirement . . . home, it looks as if such a person hated everything that most people live for." And our response is to condemn him or her: "How lacking in loveworthiness" (p. 371). It is not comfortable to have in our presence someone "in whose company the excuses and the escapes look less good" (p. 370), even if such a person does not say a word of remonstration. Those who try to dilute the requirement of love of neighbor dub such a person "not loveworthy."

The correlative element in this discussion is the "self-lover." How should we understand Kierkegaard's claim that one should make oneself into a "self-lover," that one should try "to become regarded as the most self-loving of persons" (WL, p. 373)? Does he mean that the goal of our effort should be to be unappreciated and persecuted, as some critics have suggested? Once again it is important to note the difference between a consequence and a goal. Kierkegaard employs two different valuations of the term "self-lover," and even though they coincide in the same person, it is important to distinguish between them. He speaks about the one who is called by others a "self-lover" (meant negatively) because he seems selfishly preoccupied with himself, but this preoccupation amounts to his refusal to be sociable by supportively joining the company of those who want to dilute God's requirement. "Self-lover" thus becomes a pejorative term applied to such a person, the same person who was deemed "not loveworthy." This same so-called "self-lover" is, ironically, a genuine "self-lover" because he is the person who refuses to seek the "approval of the moment" (p. 369) by reducing the Christian requirement; in other words, by remaining true to the rigor of the requirement, he is genuinely doing what is best for himself. This is the sense in which Christ was a paradigmatic "self-lover"—that is, the genuine "self-lover" is the one who lives for God since to love God is to love the self truly. The one whom the world derides as not "loveworthy," as a selfish "self-lover," is in fact the genuine self-lover—the one who loves oneself in the sense appropriate to the "as yourself" of the love commandment. Because such a person refuses to dilute or weaken the love commandment, however, he or she is seen as antisocial, selfishly refusing to be part of the majority opinion that mitigates the commandments. Kierkegaard's critique of Danish Lutheranism takes the form here of his condemnation of the "deception" (pp. 366, 369, 371) that sweetens the Christian message by diluting the requirement of self-denial.

This is not the first time that Kierkegaard has spoken of self-denial. Already in the first series' deliberation on our duty to remain in love's debt (1:V), he was emphasizing self-denial. It is appropriate now to go back and see what kind of background he has laid for this deliberation. He writes: "What Christianity calls self-denial specifically and essentially involves *a double danger*; otherwise the self-denial is not Christian self-denial" (WL, p. 194). Christian self-denial would have no place in either a world that is "essentially good" or in eternity since there is no need in either place for militancy of the sort correlated with self-denial. The or-

dinary idea of self-denial is that you "give up all your self-loving desires, crav-
ings, and plans," and then you are esteemed and honored for your sacrifice. But
Christian self-denial, in contrast, means that you give up all these things in the
service of the good, and then you are probably going to be insulted and ridiculed.
This is the "double danger": that you suffer and then are reviled for your suffering rather than applauded, and so you are twice in danger of losing all. You have
given up the world without getting the world's appreciation and applause. In
other words, you are doubly "abandoned"—you sacrifice and then you are sacrificed. You sacrifice (and so you are abandoned), and you are ridiculed for your
sacrifice; this is the double danger in the "confidential relationship with God"
(p. 195).[20] Genuine self-denial involves this double loss.[21]

B. Self-denial for Its Own Sake?

Løgstrup's critique, which we noted earlier, appeals to the story of the good
Samaritan, cited by Jesus, as an example of a work of love that Kierkegaard's ethic
would preclude because it would not allow us to attend to a person's temporal and
material needs.[22] Given the fact that Kierkegaard, as we have seen, also refers to
the story of the good Samaritan as an example of genuine love for the neighbor, we
need to challenge Løgstrup's refusal to allow that whatever Kierkegaard understands by the self-denial involved in loving another is analogous to the self-denial
entailed by the good Samaritan's responsiveness.[23] We can do this by showing that
Kierkegaard does not regard Christ as a model of self-denial for its own sake.

   Critics fail to take sufficiently into account how Kierkegaard followed in
Luther's footsteps in wanting to learn from the mistakes of the Middle Ages.
Kierkegaard holds that the error of the Middle Ages was its monastic asceticism,
and he explicitly denies that imitation of Christ is meant to promote "ascetic self-
torturing."[24] The goal is not self-torture, not fasting or flagellation; the goal is
not poverty or suffering in themselves.[25] Kierkegaard does often speak of "opposition" and "persecution," but not more than Luther does, and for neither of
them is suffering a goal or end in itself. Luther had made it clear that suffering as
such is not the goal; we are not to artificially seek suffering, although it will in all
likelihood be the result of our imitation of Christ.[26] Kierkegaard agrees that suffering, or collision with the world, will come if we try to follow Jesus' example,
but he reminds us not to seek suffering in itself. In fact, he even recommends that
we use "every permissible means to avoid suffering,"[27] although we must accept
suffering when we cannot avoid it. Self-denial is not what we aim for directly, but
as the compassionate Samaritan who deprived himself to pay for lodging and
medical care for an injured man, we will no doubt find that our love will cause us
hardship and deprivation. Suffering enough will come when we work to console
others in their suffering. When Kierkegaard warns that we shall "die to the
world" or that we must "forsake the world,"[28] he is not recommending self-denial for its own sake; he is simply repeating what he takes to be Luther's message
that when we try to follow Christ's example we will in all likelihood suffer, either
because of the sacrifice we make to help another or because others will probably
be offended by what we do.

It is worth noting here that early in his discussion of the commandment (1:II, C), Kierkegaard argued against what he called a "misunderstanding" of Christianity: "It was thought," he says, that Christianity condemned the bodily aspects of human beings—human drives or the flesh—and posited a "cleft between flesh and spirit" (WL, p. 52). But, he insists, "Christianity is no more scandalized by a drive human beings have indeed not given to themselves than it has wanted to forbid people to eat and drink."[29] Christianity does not want to castrate us, as Nietzsche thought, but rather to guarantee that our drives and preferences will not be the force that dictates our responsibility to others.

V. The Decisive Victory

As in the deliberation on debt (1:V), in which there were "two struggles" (WL, p. 192), and the deliberation on winning the one who is overcome (2:VIII) when two victories were at issue (p. 332), Kierkegaard here points to two levels or degrees of self-denial—the victory of self-denial and the triumph of self-denial (p. 365). This recalls his judgment that self-denial has a "double mark" (p. 204). The initial victory is seeing the double truth of one's nothingness and the concomitant ability to do all with God. The triumph (the decisive victory) of self-denial is finding one's blessedness in that dual truth; this is what it means to deny oneself "decisively" (p. 374). The two levels of victory could also be expressed as (1) knowing the truth and fulfilling the purpose of the work of praising love and (2) avoiding the desire to be praised for doing so. We have already seen several places in which this latter theme is explored, most particularly in 1:V and 2:VIII.

The social implication of self-denial is indirectly brought out by Kierkegaard's standard of "the moment": "True love is self-denial's love. But what is self-denial? It is giving up the moment and the momentary" (WL, p. 369). The momentary means "the approval of the moment" (p. 369).[30] In other words, if we are to express outwardly the dual truth of our nothingness without God and our ability with God to serve others, we will need to forgo the approval of others. The "purpose" of praising love is to win others to "the highest," to "reconcile" all in a "community" of the highest (p. 365); this cannot be achieved if we cling to or seek the approval of the moment, if we have a hankering to win the "approval of people" (p. 367). Love of the truth and of humanity require us to go deeper than the sound bites and photo opportunities that Kierkegaard insightfully anticipates as our modern mode of communication and relation (p.368). What does it mean to win the approval of the majority, of the crowd? Well, one way would be an attempt to be praised for fulfilling the commandment to love our neighbor; another way would be to deny that our responsibility extends beyond those for whom we have preferential love.

In the real world, in "actuality," outward unselfishness in the service of others will cost something. Moreover, Kierkegaard says, even if we wanted to forget the real world and "poetically transfer the whole relation into the realm of the imagination," we would find that "*in the relation between human beings* unselfishness is required for truthfully praising love" (WL, p. 371; emphasis mine). I take the contrast here to be between the nitty-gritty of day-to-day life (with its limited resources) and the abstract conception of the relation between human beings. That is, even if we abstracted human beings from the harsh realities of "the actual world" and placed them in an ideal world, there would still be need for unselfishness in the "thought of praising love" simply because "it is impossible to have any advantage from praising love." The speaker must "make himself into the self-lover," and he must speak about loving the "unlovable object" (pp. 373–74). Here again, Kierkegaard employs the heuristic device of the criterion—the test case, or the uncomplicated scenario in which our motivation is most easily discerned and clarified. The test case is one in which we are not praised for being loving and in which we affirm the need to love the most unlovable object. This is, strictly speaking, a counterfactual part of the thought experiment because, in fact, Kierkegaard repeatedly denies that there can truly be an unlovable person (pp. 157, 159, 172). In the context of the Socratic example he has been elaborating for several pages, the neighbor is the "ugly" one, the nonpreferred; the 'unlovable' one means the one who is not "the choice of passion and inclination."

In other words, the love of neighbor as oneself is praising love, which must be distinguished from preferential love, and the way to ensure that distinction is to emphasize the unlovable object and to work against being esteemed for one's self-denial. This "poetical venture" is "entirely correct" and can shed light on a misunderstanding perpetuated in Christendom: people make both humility and self-denial empty if they refuse to deny themselves "decisively," that is, if they deny themselves in the first degree but cancel that self-denial by either cultivating or allowing themselves to receive the esteem of others for it (WL, p. 374). Kierkegaard is here repeating what he has said often in various ways throughout *Works of Love:* in condemning the desire to "win the approval of the moment," he is condemning the exercise of praising love in order to be praised for being loving.

In sum, Kierkegaard's definition of loving is as follows: "In love of the truth and of humanity to will to make every sacrifice in order to proclaim the truth, and, on the other hand, to will not to sacrifice the least bit of truth" (WL, p. 366). As one of Kierkegaard's critics suggests, this reference to the truth is not by itself a particularly helpful explanation of what we should do.[31] But we do not need to take it by itself; it has been preceded by deliberations that put it in context. In particular, the importance of truth has already been broached in the deliberation on love's reconciling task, which has spoken of our need to deal "mercy's blow" by confronting others when necessary, refusing to call good what is evil, and refusing to go by the majority opinion just because it is the majority one. The apostle, Kierkegaard has told us, wins others for the truth, not for himself, and all for the purpose of reconciliation—that is, for the love of the human community.

chapter seventeen

Love's Repetition

Conclusion

Kierkegaard introduces the Conclusion with an expression of gratitude that he has "succeeded in completing the book" in the way he wished to. The implication is that the full message of *Works of Love* is contained in all the preceding deliberations, and this conclusion will not add anything radically new. We should expect a recapitulation of themes, an evaluation of the project, or a combination of both. In other words, we should expect a kind of repetition. In fact, there has already been much repetition throughout, for if we think about the major themes we have seen—inward/outward, "like for like," love as need—we realize that the whole of *Works of Love* has been like a musical composition that turns over and over on itself. Themes and phrases have been continually recaptured, echoed, and transformed. They have been replayed (repeated), yet they were made new because they were being considered from a new angle in a new place—that is, each time they appeared against a different background of deliberations and in a different proximate surrounding. Another reason for entitling this chapter "Love's Repetition" is that the Conclusion emphasizes the theme of repetition quite explicitly. The aural metaphor of the "echo" is invoked to speak of God's repetition of what we say or do and "eternity's repetition" (WL, p. 384, 385), thus revealing how the category of "like for like" is itself an example of repetition. Before turning to the culmination of earlier themes, however, we ought to note what seems at first glance to be a new theme, although it is not—intimacy with the commandment.

I. Intimacy with the Love Commandment

Kierkegaard begins the Conclusion proper by examining the Apostle John's pregnant exhortation: 'Beloved, let us love one another.' Kierkegaard calls our attention to the fact that the phrasing "let us love" has an "intermediate tone" or "mood." Before elaborating further on how this marks a departure from the strict imperative mood (the "shall"), which governs the commandment as such, he stays for a moment with the dimension of tone and suggests that there is a "sadness" about this exhortation: "It is as if the apostle said, "Dear me, what is all this that would hinder you in loving, what is all this that you can win by self-love! The commandment is that you shall love, but ah, if you will understand yourself and life, then it seems that it should not need to be commanded, because to love people is the only thing worth living for, and without this love you are not really living" (WL, p. 375). By having the Apostle John wondering out loud about what hinders us from loving since, after all, we need to love, Kierkegaard revisits the theme of NEED (the love already in us needs to express itself, and we need companionship—to love and be loved). Here the "apparent contradiction" of commanded love, which he mentioned early in *Works of Love* (p. 24), is attributed to the fact that it is strange (and sad) to think that we need to be commanded to do what we need desperately to do.

The "intermediate" mood or tone of the exhortation "Let us love one another" has neither the "rigorousness of duty" nor the spontaneity of "poet-passion" and "inclination." It must, Kierkegaard strongly insists, be understood in context: "[S]uch words are not the beginning of the discourse about love but are the completion" (WL, p. 376). They are appropriate for the person who "becomes more and more intimate with the commandment, becomes as one with the commandment, which he loves." Such a person needs no harsh reminders about duty; such a person has come to love the commandment to love. The gentleness of this exhortation invites us to a second spontaneity, a spontaneity *after* law; it would not be appropriate at the beginning of *Works of Love* since it could be misunderstood there. Kierkegaard's appreciation of the presupposition of speaking in this way is evident in his advice: "That which is truth on the lips of the veteran and perfected apostle could in the mouth of a beginner very easily be a philandering by which he would leave the school of the commandment much too soon and escape the 'school-yoke'" (p. 376). Kierkegaard includes himself in the category of those who are not perfected in love when he confesses that "we do not dare to speak in this way"; he expresses his closeness to the reader by suggesting that he is not propounding the apostle's words, but rather that they are both "listeners" (p. 376). Once again, his sense of his maieutic service is apparent.

Kierkegaard's reference to perfection in love parallels Luther's assumption in the "Treatise on Good Works" that "if every man had faith we would need no more laws [for] everyone would of himself do good works all the time, as his faith shows him."[1] Elaborating on St. Paul's words that "for the righteous man (that is, the believing man) no law is laid down," Luther divides people into four categories: the first "who need no law . . . do willingly what they know and can, because they alone are distinguished for their firm confidence that God's favor and grace rests upon them in all things"; the other three categories need the disciplining limits and safeguards of laws.

Commentators on Luther's writings have introduced a contrast between "imperative" ethics and "indicative" ethics; they consider the former to be generated by God's law and the latter to be generated by God's grace.[2] Commentators on Kierkegaard often follow suit: imperative ethics is meant to refer to the rigorous demand of the law ("You are required to do this") as opposed to the indicative ethics, which describes our ability—through grace—to fulfill the law ("You are enabled to do this"). Some locate this contrast between Kierkegaard's early writings on ethics and the later *Works of Love*.[3] One could also apply the contrast to *Works of Love* itself by opposing the imperative statement of the commandment to the indicative claims that love does X (builds up, abides, hides sin, etc.). Given Kierkegaard's contrast between the imperative commandment ("Thou shalt") and the "intermediate" mood of the apostolic exhortation ("Let us love one another"), one might also say that the ethic of intimacy with the commandment— the ethic of perfection, where there is no need of harsh reminders of duty—is another way of understanding the term "indicative ethics".[4]

At any rate, Kierkegaard is concerned here to shade the notion of commandment in some way, to suggest that there is a way of conceiving of a commandment other than as an imposed and repressive demand. There is a form of commandment that is not an assertion of duty but rather a sort of exhortation. The idea of intimacy with the commandment means at the very least that it does not feel like duty. Indeed, one could even consider the apostle's exhortation to be a form of invitation—"I invite you to love one another." It contains within it the multivalence of the Danish word *Lov*, which means both law and permission.

An interesting way of elaborating the notion of a commandment that is not simply an imposed and constraining demand is found in the work of both Franz Rosenzweig and Paul Ricoeur. Ricoeur expresses his indebtedness to the Jewish thinker Franz Rosenzweig in describing "a form of commandment that is not yet a law."[5] Ricoeur finds it remarkable that Rosenzweig, in *The Star of Redemption*, does not turn to the usual scriptural places for the formulation of the love commandment (Exodus, Leviticus, and Deuteronomy) but rather turns to the "Song of Songs." Rosenzweig's insight, Ricoeur suggests, is "to show in this way how the commandment to love springs from the bond of love between God and the individual soul. The commandment that precedes every law is the word that the lover addressed to the beloved: Love me!"[6] Rosenzweig's point is that "the arch-commandment was able to command love because it proceeded from the mouth of the lover himself, of him whose love it commanded to requite—because it was a 'love me'."[7] In other words, we can imagine a law ("Thou shalt do X") that can be promulgated by someone other than the one who enables us to fulfill it. However, with God's 'Love me,' we have a case of a distinctive type of command, one that "commands the only kind of love that can be commanded"[8] because it is commanded by the one who loves us first and thus enables us to love.

The "ever-so-subtle distinction" between commandment and law that Rosenzweig proposes "makes sense," to Ricoeur, "only if we admit that the commandment to love is love itself, commending itself, as though the genitive in the 'commandment of love' were subjective and objective at the same time." That is, the commandment *of* love is both the commandment *to love* and the commandment *given by love*. In the plea "Love me!" we find the "conditions for its being obeyed." This is the kind of "commandment, if it can be called such, [which] can be heard in the tone of the *Song of Songs*, in the plea that the lover addressed to the beloved."[9] Ricoeur thus finds in Rosenzweig's distinction between law and commandment a "poetic use of the imperative," which is irreducible to the Kantian moral imperative.[10]

Although Ricoeur and Rosenzweig seem to refer to a commandment that "precedes" or is "not yet" a law, a commandment this side of the law, Kierkegaard's reference to intimacy with the commandment is an understanding of commandment *after* the law has been intimately internalized. For Kierkegaard, the intermediate "tone" of the commandment bespeaks an ethic of perfection, a spontaneity after law, which contrasts with the realm of duty, but from the other side, so to speak, the realm *beyond* duty.

The theological ethic of H. Richard Niebuhr can also illuminate what Kierkegaard calls the "intermediate" tone of the exhortation, the commandment that is not a law. Niebuhr proposes an alternative to the usual dichotomy between teleological (goal-oriented) ethics and deontological (law-oriented) ethics—an ethic of responsibility in which we are seen as responders in a paradigm of conversation.[11] This allows him to make the rather unexpected contrast between an ethic of obedience (law) and an ethic of response or responsibility. Although earlier I considered the notion of responsibility in terms of the commanded dimension of commanded love, as if obedience to command were unproblematically tied to responsibility, it is instructive to note Niebuhr's opposition to a deontological ethic of obedience in favor of an ethic of responsibility. Niebuhr divides the two ethics in terms of their different questions: for an ethic of responsibility the relevant question is 'What is a fitting response to this particular situation in which I find this needy person?' and for an ethic of obedience the relevant question is 'What ought I to do to obey this commandment?' In other words, he suggests that an ethic of obedience responds to the law, whereas an ethic of responsibility responds to the other person. Niebuhr's proposed ethic focuses on three conditions—(1) responsiveness (2) to interpreted actions in relation to us, (3) with accountability[12]; it implies an important difference between loving the neighbor because we are commanded to and loving the neighbor because the neighbor is loved by God, who wants us to love what God loves. The implication is that an ethic of obedience and a divine command ethic occupy a similar place, both to be contrasted with an ethic of responsibility. This is a useful way of highlighting what a simple emphasis on command can obscure, and it supports the claim that Kierkegaard did not hold to a simple divine command ethic. His reference to the merciful Samaritan is a perfect example of the kind of response to another that seems to have been governed by responsibility rather than obedience to law.

Thus, although the perfection of love has the appearance of being a brand new theme, it is an indirect allusion to the theme of need. Moreover, it retrieves and comments further on the authority of the command and the ground of response to the other.

II. The "Christian Like for Like"

A. The New Rule

By way of anticipation, I note in chapter 9 that in the Conclusion Kierkegaard announces that "*the Christian like for like, eternity's like for like*" is "such an important and decisive Christian specification" that he would like to use it to end, "if not every book in which I develop the essentially Christian, then at least one book" (WL, p. 376)—presumably, at least this book. This is one good example of the value of reading the first deliberation and the Conclusion as the frame of the book before going on to the other deliberations; the Conclusion alerts us to the importance of the category of the "like for like."

The Conclusion actually recapitulates most of the permutations of the "like for like" we have already seen.[13] The first appearance of this category was an implicit one—the equality implied in the "as yourself" of the love commandment. The category is introduced explicitly in the deliberation on love's debt (1:V) as the "marvelous like for like" of a "reciprocal relationship, infinite from both sides" (WL, p. 181), and then again explicitly in "Love Builds Up" (2:I), where the "like for like" is said to consist of the tight correlation between the result and what is presupposed: "[T]he more perfect the loving one presupposes the love to be, the more perfect a love he loves forth" (p. 219).[14] This positive, upbuilding "like for like" is inverted in the next two deliberations: an implicit "like for like" is found in 2:II, where Kierkegaard reminds us that "in the very same minute when you judge another person or criticize another person, you judge yourself" (p. 233); in 2:III Kierkegaard proposes "eternity's like for like—to despair over another person is to be in despair oneself" (256).

The Conclusion brings us face to face with the distinctively "Christian like for like" (WL, p. 376). The contrasting object that Kierkegaard terms the "Jewish like for like" is presented in two forms: first, "An eye for an eye and a tooth for a tooth" (p. 376) and, second "As others do unto you, by all means take care that you also do likewise unto them" (p. 383). Kierkegaard is undoubtedly not doing justice to the Jewish interpretation of the love commandment in this rendition of an empirical Golden Rule, of which even Freud would have approved (the mutuality of doing to others what they actually do to you), but he does help locate his alternative by the crude contrast.[15] At the very least, the version he expounds goes further by enjoining us to a more generous Golden Rule: "Do unto others as you would have them do unto you," or "Refrain from doing to others what you would not like them to do to you." In addition, the category of "like for like," which seems at first glance to reinforce that notion of equality in relation to which we have become accustomed by the end of the second deliberation, also extends and deepens this Golden Rule.

B. Leniency and Rigor

The "Christian like for like" is seen as part of the strategy employed by God, the master educator (WL, p. 377). The background is the sorry state of Christendom, of which Kierkegaard will speak with great vehemence at the end of his career. "Christianity," he says somewhat more mildly than usual, "is not infrequently presented in a certain sentimental, almost soft, form of love. It is all love and love; spare yourself and your flesh and blood; have good days or happy days without self-concern, because God is Love and Love" (p. 376). Such a "childish conception" of God's love and such a "sickly-sweet" version of Christ have lost the element of "offense"[16]—"as if Christianity were in its dotage." By contrast, the genuine Christian demand is "simultaneously the greatest comfort and the greatest strenuousness, the greatest leniency and rigorousness" (p. 377).[17]

Both the leniency and the rigor are apparent in the generic structure of the "like for like" found in Kierkegaard's portrayal of Jesus' words to the centurion at Capernaum: "Be it done for you as you have believed" (WL, p. 378). Here, he says, we see both leniency, for "no more joyful tidings can be imagined" (p. 378), and rigorousness, for the phrase "*as* you believe exercises a powerful restraining influence." This "like for like" that Kierkegaard delineates is found first in Augustine's writings.[18] It is found more proximately in Luther's "Treatise on Good Works," where we find Luther's daunting message: "For as faith expects so does it come to pass."[19]

This "like for like" is a version of the earlier formulations—"one who loves receives what he gives" and "I myself receive what I give to another" (WL, pp. 281–82). In the Conclusion these formulations are specified further: "God will do unto you exactly as you do unto others" (p. 383). This is especially true of the claim that you will be forgiven as you forgive others; Christianity's view is that "your forgiveness is your forgiveness; your forgiveness of another is your own forgiveness; the forgiveness you give is the forgiveness you receive" (p. 380). That is, your forgiveness (of others) is your forgiveness (by God), and your forgiveness by God refers both to the forgiveness you have already been given (which enables you to forgive others) and the forgiveness you will be given. This same "like for like" is embodied in the claim that to accuse another is to accuse yourself—that is, as you accuse others, so you will be accused (p. 382). Kierkegaard makes us laugh when he tells the story of the criminal who goes to the police to complain about another criminal's crime against himself, but he pulls us up sharply by reminding us that it is the same with us: "[P]recisely when you come and inform on the other person, God begins to think about how you are involved."

The claim that "God will do unto you exactly as you do unto others" (WL, p. 383) expresses the "echo" and "repetition" involved; in this "like for like" God echoes or repeats exactly what you do to others (384). Underlying this repetition is an explanation that is as heartening as it is terrifying—that "what you do unto people, you do unto God" (p. 384). This is an indirect reference to the scriptural identification of what is done to God and to 'the least of these,' which we have seen Kierkegaard make explicitly before (p. 160). Here Kierkegaard takes up the theme that he has been assuming since he first introduced it in 1:IV—that the only way to know whether we love God is to see how we treat others—and he intensifies it with "what you do unto people, you do unto God."

The "like for like" that Kierkegaard has presented is extremely rigorous, but he points here to a way in which the stakes are even higher: "*Christianity is so rigorous that it even asserts a heightened inequality*" (WL, p. 382).[20] When you see a "splinter" in someone else's eye (i.e., a fault) judging this fault amounts to a "log" (not a splinter) in your own eye. That is, your fault is not a simple equivalent of the fault you find in the neighbor; it is heightened because "God regards it as presumptuous for a human being to pretend purity and to judge the splinter in his brother's eye" (p. 383). In other words, if we remembered that we were presuming to judge another in the presence of the other's Creator (and our own), we would be ashamed to continue, but "God is indeed always present." The "high treason" of presuming to judge others in front of God exposes our assumed self-righteousness, and that constitutes the greater fault. The reminder of the "like for like"—the reminder of the leniency and rigor in both the Gospel and the law—is literally the book's last word of advice to us (p. 386).

C. Alone with God—Inwardness and Externals

With the claim that the Christian "like for like" turns us away from "the external" toward the relationship with God (WL, p. 376), we find the theme of externals considered from a new perspective, with a new approach to "inwardness." In this discussion we come across a standard kind of reference targeted as proof of Kierkegaard's unsocial individualism and religious self-centeredness: "In the Christian sense, a person ultimately and essentially has only God to deal with in everything" (p. 377). In his second contrast to the "Jewish like for like," he says something similar: "In the Christian sense, you have nothing at all to do with what others do unto you—it does not concern you." . . . "The direction is inward; essentially you have to do only with yourself before God" (pp. 383–84). These expressions of "Christian inwardness" admittedly give one reason to pause, but since they are usually taken out of context it is worth stopping for a moment to put them back.

The claim that "essentially you have only to do with yourself before God" must be assessed in the light of its location in *Works of Love*—the *conclusion* of a series of deliberations that remind us of our loving obligation not to judge others, both because we cannot be sure we know what is in their hearts and because, even if we can ever know, we are obligated not to be less forgiving than God. The context is the "like for like" that culminates in the claim that "God will do unto you exactly as you do unto others" (p. 383). Reconsider the earlier passage with a crucial sentence reinserted: "In the Christian sense, you have nothing at all to do with what others do unto you—it does not concern you. . . . *You have to do only with what you do unto others, or how you take what others do unto you.* The direction is inward; essentially you have to do only with yourself before God" (emphasis mine). Thus, seen in context, this claim implies a concern with responsibility, not antisociality: you are responsible for what you are obligated to do; you are not responsible for ensuring that others do what they should. Therefore, the phrase "before God" is more likely to mean "in God's presence"—that is everywhere—rather than what you explicitly direct to God.

What is at stake for Kierkegaard in these claims about inwardness emerges more clearly when we look back at the analysis of a similar-sounding sentiment in Levinas's thought. In chapter 15 I noted that Levinas was often faced with the charge that his ethic of responsibility was too extreme unless it allowed us to remind other people that they were mutually responsible for those who were infinitely responsible for them. When I ask: "Is not the Other also responsible in my regard?"[21] this question (apparently about the other) is actually a concern about myself; that is, is not the other responsible for taking care of me? Levinas's response suggests one way in which to understand Kierkegaard's view: "Perhaps, but that is *his* affair. . . . In this sense I am responsible for the Other without waiting for reciprocity, were I to die for it. Reciprocity is *his* affair." Both Kierkegaard and Levinas agree that there is an important sense in which it can be truly said that you have only to do with what you are supposed to do; the other's responsibility is none of your business. Whether others fulfill or fail to fulfill their responsibility—which you cannot always judge in any case—does nothing to mitigate your own responsibility for them. In both cases, the message seems to be that there is a kind of interest about the other that is not genuine concern but rather a way of trying to abdicate or lessen my responsibility. To suggest that we have "essentially" only to deal with God is a way of deflecting our attention from a concern with the other's responsibility and thus a way of keeping our responsibility for others intact; in neither the work of Levinas nor that of Kierkegaard would it be plausible to read the message as recommending a disregard of the other.

Similarly, the claim that "Christianity turns our attention completely away from the external, turns it inwards, and makes every one of your relationships to other people into a God-relationship" (WL, p. 376) must be taken in the context of the entire book. This is one example of something that can only be understood at the end of the deliberations in which he has reminded us that there can be no certainty based on externals. As if he is aware that despite hundreds of pages of deliberations on works, there is still the possibility of being misunderstood when he speaks of dealing "only with yourself before God," Kierkegaard takes pains to distinguish his appeal to "inwardness" from a self-centered narcissistic concern with God and from selfish preoccupation with one's 'personal' relation to God, one's 'individual' salvation. For example, when he declares that "in everything [the Christian] relates himself to God," he goes on immediately to contrast this with the idea of a "private relation with God," which he emphatically rejects (p. 381). When he claims that we can fulfill our duties to God only if we "remain in the world and in the earthly circumstances assigned to [us]" (p. 377), he is, in the end, appealing to Luther's stress on the demand on us that is announced by our station in life. The option to ignore these qualifications, as commentators often do, amounts to forgetting that such words about dealing "only with yourself before God" come at the end of a lengthy set of deliberations that view Christian love as "sheer action" and recommend "works" based on the model of the Samaritan.[22]

III. Striving and Grace in His Lutheran Heritage

Kierkegaard's descriptions of graceful intimacy with the love commandment and his understanding of the simultaneous leniency and rigor of both Gospel and law put into bold relief the constant reminders of the necessity of striving that have filled the pages of *Works of Love*. That is, since none of us is yet perfected in love, we are reminded indirectly that our effort is necessary. Moreover, his pointing away from "the external" should provoke us into remembering the repeated message that Christianity is, nevertheless, "sheer action" and is expressed in outwardness. Although striving and action are the background, the figure in the Conclusion is the straightforward reminder, retrieving the theme of the Prayer, that none of the works detailed in the preceding deliberations is technically 'meritorious': "Ah, the first thing you learn when you relate yourself to God in everything is that you have no merit whatever" (p. 385).[23] Kierkegaard's steadfast commitment to the Lutheran denial of merit, as well as to the priority of grace, leaves no doubt that his criticism of the Lutheranism of his day did not in fact challenge what is arguably the core of Luther's theology. But his relation to his heritage was complex.[24]

It is noteworthy that in a journal entry from 1847, the year in which *Works of Love* was written, Kierkegaard writes that he has only now begun to "really" read Luther and has discovered that they think alike: "I have never really read anything by Luther. But now I open up his sermons—and right there in the Gospel for the First Sunday in Advent he says 'for you,' on this everything depends."[25] He identifies Luther's use of the 'for you' with his own use of the "category of the 'for you' (subjectivity, inwardness)," which concludes *Either/Or* (that "only the truth which builds up is truth for you"). This affinity is apparently noted with happy amazement, but it should not mislead us about Kierkegaard's familiarity with Luther's teaching. This is, after all, the tradition in which he was painstakingly raised. What he means by not having "really read" Luther may be that he had not yet read his sermons or that he had not technically 'studied' Luther's writings.[26]

Kierkegaard's explicit evaluation of Luther illuminates what is at stake in *Works of Love*. One should take Kierkegaard at his word when he writes in 1850, in "My Position as a Religious Author in 'Christendom' and My Strategy," that he has desperately "wanted to prevent people from taking in vain Luther and the significance of Luther's life."[27] It is not disagreement with Luther that he emphasizes here, but a need to put Luther and the significance of his life in perspective. The attack on Christendom in which Kierkegaard later engages is grounded precisely in this same goal, and his near obsession with the way in which Luther has been taken "in vain" should never be forgotten when we read *Works of Love*. Moreover, Kierkegaard's provocative question: "Is not Protestantism (or the Lutheran principle) really a corrective, and has not a great confusion been brought about by making this normative in Protestantism?" and his claim that "Protestantism [i.e., Luther's protestations] is not qualified to stand alone"[28] are important guides for reading *Works of Love*. One can speculate that although these claims (and most of his other judgments of Luther) were formulated after Kierkegaard finished *Works of Love*, it was precisely the working out of that text that made his relation to Luther clearer to him.

Kierkegaard is actually quite generous in his journal remarks on Luther, more often approving of him than finding fault. Most often a kind of sympathy is apparent: Luther was "exploit[ed]," he was "misused," and he was used for "the opposite" of what he intended.[29] Oh, Luther, poor Luther moans Kierkegaard; sadly, the man was too "innocent," too naïve.[30] This sympathy seems to be in sad anticipation of how his own writing would be misused and exploited. However, Kierkegaard is himself a little naïve about Luther's naïveté. At the very least Luther was well aware of the ways in which he was subject to being misunderstood, and he wrote the "Treatise on Good Works" in response both to a promise he had made to his congregation and to his perceived need to clarify his position for friends and critics alike. Luther's sense of the importance of this treatise is clear in his dedication of the work to John, the brother of Elector Frederick, Luther's sovereign; there he writes that this book needs to be published "perhaps more than any other of my sermons or books" because in it "the greatest question has been raised, the question of good works, where immeasurably more trickery and deception is practiced than anywhere else."[31] Luther laments that "when I exalt faith and reject such works done without faith they accuse me of forbidding good works." But, he retorts, "the fact of the matter is that I want very much to teach the real good works which spring from faith."[32] Luther has much at stake here, and his aim is to be "absolutely clear": works done "apart from faith . . . amount to nothing and are absolutely dead"; all works are included under faith and should "flow from it"; works should not be done for "reward" or to "influence" God or otherwise "lay claim" to something; "faith must cause the works."[33]

In response to those who have defined faith as a state or habit, Luther insists that it is a "work," though of a different sort than traditional works.[34] His point is that faith is an active embrace of grace, involving a continued striving. His repeated tirades against those who make faith a quality or habit is his way of emphasizing that it is not a characteristic or quality of someone but something they do—actively embrace grace and continue to have confidence in God. Kierkegaard, too, will adopt this appreciation of a "work" since he does not limit love's works to the traditional tasks of attending to those in poverty, hunger, or other distress; the examples he gives of love's works include the 'work' of remaining in love's debt to the other; of abiding in love; of forgiving another; of trusting, hoping, and believing. As he says when speaking of love's faithfulness, that love abides "is not an inactive characteristic"; it is a "work" (WL, p. 301). Luther insists that his rejection of works done without faith is meant only to lead people away "from the false, pretentious, pharisaic good works done without faith" on which they try to build their "confidence" in God, and to lead them, instead, "to the right, true, genuine, real works of faith."[35] There is no question that "faith goes out into works and through works comes back to itself, just as the sun goes forth to its setting and comes again at its rising.[36] Works, in this sense, are clearly not able to merit anything, but they are a form of gratitude to God.[37]

Although we have no evidence for claiming that Kierkegaard ever read the "Treatise on Good Works," the instruction found there was also available in Luther's "Short Exposition of the Decalogue, the Creed, and the Lord's Prayer," as well as in "The Freedom of the Christian," and it is unlikely that Kierkegaard was not familiar with them.[38] Moreover, other writings, like the *Lectures on Galatians* (1535), are consistent with an appreciation of the importance of works. Although in these lectures Luther equates the term "works" with 'works-which-merit' and so speaks of "faith without works," he introduces a contrast between "active righteousness" and "passive righteousness" that seems to align the former with what he had earlier called "genuine, real works of faith." The righteousness of faith is "a merely passive righteousness," "which God imputes to us through Christ without works"; this "passive or Christian righteousness . . . says with confidence: 'I do not seek active righteousness'."[39] But concerning this active righteousness it continues immediately: "'*I ought to have and perform it*; but I declare that even if I did have it and perform it, I cannot trust in it or stand up before the judgment of God on the basis of it'."[40] The point is not that active righteousness is unnecessary but rather that one cannot "stand up before the judgment of God on the basis of it." Luther tries to clarify his position:

> This is our theology, by which we teach a precise distinction between these two kinds of righteousness, the active and the passive, so that morality and faith, works and grace, secular society and religion may not be confused. *Both are necessary, but both must be kept within their limits. . . . I am saying this in order that no one may suppose that we reject or prohibit good works*, as the papists falsely accuse us because they understand neither what they themselves are saying nor what we are teaching.[41]

Although Luther provocatively recommends that we live "as though there were no Law whatever" (which amounts to 'ignoring the Law'), he expects that we will continue to finish reading his sentence, which says that "*on the other hand, works and the performance of the Law must be demanded in the world as though there were no promise or grace.*"[42] In other words, Luther admits that it would be undialectical and unjust to recommend either one without the other.

When Kierkegaard suggests that "the place where we really have to begin again is with Luther," it is because "many years earlier Luther quite simply began at the beginning, with works."[43] This assumption that Luther began with actions may well explain what is behind the lengthy journal consideration of works and faith that Kierkegaard, perhaps surprisingly, entitled "That the principle of works is simpler than the principle of faith."[44]

Kierkegaard rightly understood that the question of works is at the heart of the debate about the importance of Christ as an example of a way of life to be followed—a pattern or prototype to be imitated. Or perhaps it should be put conversely, that the relevance of the imitation of Christ as prototype is at the heart of the question of works. Here Kierkegaard reveals his familiarity with Luther's position and his sensitivity to Luther's predicament: "Luther is entirely right . . . about the distinction between Christ as pattern and as gift."[45] "But," he explains, and we should note this huge qualification, "something must be kept in mind in this regard [namely, that] *Luther was confronted by the exaggerated misuse of Christ as pattern; therefore he accentuates the opposite.* But Luther has long since been victorious in Protestantism and Christ has been completely forgotten as the pattern, and the whole thing actually has become pretence in hidden inwardness."[46] This accounts for Kierkegaard's own emphasis on Christ as pattern.

Again, he is not here so much disagreeing with Luther as he is putting Luther's conclusions in perspective; to determine the truth and applicability of Luther's principle, one has to put Luther in his particular historical context. We must remember that "Luther broke out of the monastery."[47] This is Kierkegaard's short way of reminding us that the "pattern" of Christ was exaggerated in the monastic disciplines of poverty, fasting, celibacy, and prayer; we remove the dialectical element from Luther's teaching when we "completely forget that Luther urged faith in contrast to a fantastically exaggerated asceticism," a "mistaken, deluded inflation of asceticism."[48] It is also a reminder that Luther faced a papacy that sold indulgences.[49] Unless we acknowledge and appreciate the falsehood to which Luther was reacting, Lutheranism is entirely senseless.[50]

In Luther's day, according to Kierkegaard, there were "many more who want[ed] to hear the law proclaimed rather than the gospel," and so Luther redressed that one-sidedness with a stark focus on Gospel.[51] Law is left in the background, and with law its implication—works. "In our day," Kierkegaard says with no attempt to disguise his irritation, "it is exactly the opposite. They want to hear nothing at all except gospel, gospel."[52] Example, imitation, striving, works, law: these are all of a piece, and in these days Luther's successor cannot uncritically repeat Luther's message of grace and Gospel.

Kierkegaard consciously distances Lutheranism from Luther, claiming that in nineteenth-century Denmark, Luther's understandably reactionary emphasis on faith has been taken as an excuse not to strive, not to follow Christ as pattern, but to allow ourselves to bask in the light of "hidden inwardness." Our ability to ignore the part of Luther's message about the need for good works is grounded in a self-serving protective mechanism; that is, Kierkegaard suggests that the "real reason we are a little afraid of the principle of works" is that "it will prevent us from unperturbedly imagining all sorts of things about our inwardness while we unperturbedly go on living for secular goals."[53]

Luther's stress on our impotence is the other side of his stress on grace, but he also acknowledged the "requirement to exert myself all the more" just because grace has been given to him; with obvious exasperation Kierkegaard asks: "[T]he genuinely Christian thesis: A man is capable of nothing at all—does not this seem to have become Christendom's password for the discontinuance of all striving?"[54] "Is it Christianity's intention to eliminate striving by means of grace?"

Kierkegaard asks rhetorically. "No, Christianity simply wants to have the law fulfilled, if possible, by means of grace."[55]

If Kierkegaard were merely challenging the one-sided appropriation of Luther by Danish Lutherans, we could assume that Kierkegaard intended to counter Luther's corrective to an exaggerated emphasis on law (which amounted to an exaggerated emphasis on Gospel) with a renewed focus on law and a deemphasis of Gospel. But Kierkegaard believes that he needs to respond not only to Lutheranism but also to Luther himself. Kierkegaard is definitely ambivalent toward Luther. On the one hand, his sense of his own agreement with Luther on important points is obvious. From 1846 on, Kierkegaard writes that Luther said in an "excellent" way what needed to be said on various issues, was "absolutely right," "entirely right," or "absolutely correct."[56] Although Luther is sometimes considered the occasion of great confusion, [57] this is despite his better lights. On the other hand, Kierkegaard accuses him of being confused in his own right.[58] In Kierkegaard's view, Luther's overwhelming and general failing was that "Luther was no dialectician; he always saw only one side of the matter."[59] The criticism that Luther was not "dialectical"—which Kierkegaard repeats almost obsessively[60]—means not only that Luther was naïve about the way in which he could be misunderstood but also that Luther himself misunderstood much. At such times, Kierkegaard charges that Luther failed to recognize how his own proposals about faith were reactions to an exaggeration. This explains those passages in which Luther himself is the target—for example, when Kierkegaard says that Luther had a faulty understanding of the relation between Gospel and law; that he "reduced" Christianity, made it less than sovereign by making "despair" seem like a reasonable justification, or that he interprets Christianity "as if in a certain sense it were the wrath of God."[61] Kierkegaard's criticisms vacillate between the two targets: Luther's naïveté and Luther's genuine confusion.

Kierkegaard's obsessive complaint that Luther is not dialectical must itself be seen in context. True, he charges that Luther is "dialectically confused," and it is on "this point among others that I must concentrate all my strength as I have been doing—the dialectical definition of faith."[62] But Kierkegaard admits that he himself has difficulty in being dialectical enough:

> I must now take care, or rather God will take care of me, so that I do not go astray by all too one-sidedly starting at Christ as the prototype. It is the dialectical element connected with Christ as the gift, as that which is given to us (to call to mind Luther's standard classification). But dialectical as my nature is, in the passion of the dialectical it always seems as if the contrasting thought were not present at all—and so the one side comes first of all and most strongly.[63]

Fully aware of the danger of becoming one-sided—of overemphasizing one thing at the expense of another and of overcompensating in the face of an opponent's exaggerations—Kierkegaard continued to strive to do justice to the relation between Gospel and law, faith and works. As Kierkegaard saw it, Luther exaggerated inwardness in reaction to an exaggerated concern with the merit of outward works,[64] but Luther did not deny the importance of outward imitation and striving as a grateful response. However, Luther's one-sided emphasis on Gospel is a variation on the early theme of the one-sided emphasis on soothing assurances; Luther's vision had been narrowed by the circumstances of his day, which he felt obliged to combat. Whether the fault lay with Luther or with those who had misappropriated him in a self-serving way, Kierkegaard maintains an unflinching commitment to a Luther-inspired principle: "Christianity requires everything, and when you have done this, it requires that you shall understand that you are nevertheless saved simply and solely by grace."[65] This twofold message that effort is required, but is not meritorious, is found in the dialectic of the Conclusion: God is "too sublimely transcendent ever to think that to him a human being's effort should have some meritoriousness. Yet he requires it, and then one thing more, that the human being himself not dare to think that he has some meritoriousness" (WL, p. 379).

IV. Inward/Outward, Unseen/Seen

The claim that the "Christian like for like" "will turn you *away from externality* (but *without taking you out of the world*)" (WL, pp. 383–84; emphasis mine) gives us the opportunity to look back at the development of the relation between inner and outer. The first deliberation has provided an initial statement of incommensurability—inner does not always reveal outer and vice versa. Any word can be unloving; any word can be loving. Any act can be done lovingly or unlovingly. The association between inner and outer is broken in a significant way by the denial that there is a necessary connection of this sort, and this denial continues right up to the end of the book. The last words before the Conclusion begins are the admission that if "someone undertakes to praise love and is asked whether it is actually out of love on his part that he does it, the answer must be: "'No one else can decide this for certain; it is possible that it is vanity, pride—in short, something bad, but it is also possible that it is love'" (p. 374). This reminder that there is something about love that one cannot see goes hand in hand, however, with the equally important claim, running throughout the whole book, that love must express itself outwardly or die. This correlation has also been affirmed in the first deliberation and in numerous deliberations after that. In this way a necessary connection between inner and outer is ultimately affirmed, with the proviso that outer will not always be either externally visible or easily determinable by us.

Thus two concurrent themes inform this book, and they bear to each other the dialectical kind of relation of which Kierkegaard spoke earlier. We can consider them two thoughts in one (WL, p. 8), and we can say that both must be affirmed. Moreover, we can say of these two themes what Kierkegaard said earlier about hope's dimensions of eternity and temporality: "The one expression is no truer than the other; on the contrary, each of the expressions becomes untrue if it is contrasted to the other instead of being united to express the same thing" (WL, p. 249).

In sum, there are several key places in which the relation between inward and outward is made explicit, but even when it is not made explicit it is continually beneath the surface of all the deliberations; the theme of the inner and outer has taken the form not only of the relation between the hidden and the manifest but also the relation between the 'how' and the 'what,' as well as the related theme of ethical blindness and vision. That it would be untrue to speak of one without the other applies not only to inward/outward but also to how and what, to blindness and vision. This is part of Kierkegaard's attempt in *Works of Love* to qualify the extreme emphasis on inwardness or hiddenness that is found in writings preceding it. Given the advantage of hindsight, we are able to consider this work a "bridge," both conceptually and chronologically, between unmitigated condemnations of outwardness (as in the *Concluding Unscientific Postscript*) and strident calls for outwardness (as in *Practice in Christianity* and the later polemical writings).[66]

conclusion

My major goal in the preceding chapters has been a kind of *explication de texte,* a commentary on *Works of Love* that seeks to expose the commitments, rationales, and distinctions at work in the text. Given the purpose of this book and the constraints on length, I have been limited to addressing only briefly and in small part the huge secondary literature on love and ethics. I have used what I found illuminating, and I could not even do justice to all of that. Given that admission, I can only approach this conclusion in fear and trembling because here I want to do something to which I can do even less justice, but which I feel is important to attempt—to try to put *Works of Love* into a broader perspective.

I. A Slightly Bigger Picture

In the last decade discussions about neighbor love or interpersonal ethical relations[1] have tended to assume a classical historical divide between two major opposing positions: these positions represent a contrast between an ethic of self-sacrifice and one of communion, between an ethic that emphasizes impartiality and equality and one that emphasizes mutuality and responsive partiality, or between an ethic that highlights symmetry and one that highlights asymmetry. Although the divide falls roughly between the Protestant and Roman Catholic traditions, it should be noted that Roman Catholic ascetical theology is often grouped with Reformation theology as espousing a self-sacrifice ethic, and both are contrasted with a more mainline Roman Catholic sympathy with an ethic of communion (and mutuality).

The ethic of self-sacrifice and that of mutual communion could also be seen as representing a form of the contrast that C. S. Lewis made between Gift-Love and Need-Love.[2] Gift-Love is associated with the ethic of self-sacrifice because it is best exemplified in a love that is radically unilateral, unmotivated, and unreciprocated. Love as gift is often seen as the natural center of an ethic in which God's love for us is taken to be the norm for love (pure, gratuitous benevolence poured out freely, not in response to any qualities of the receiver), and it is often seen as promoting both a model of disinterested, "pure" love for God and one of self-sacrificial, disinterested love of neighbor.

More recent accounts (often but not always Catholic) of theological ethics have recovered a less unilateral model of God's love for us. Attending carefully to the scriptural sources, both Jewish and Christian, they highlight narratives that reflect a God whose love is responsive to creatures, who rejoices over them and grieves over them, and who desperately seeks reconciliation and communion with them. Such a model of love as the need or desire for communion views sacrifice as part of the cost of restoring a broken bond but not as an end in itself. It appreciates not only God's desire for our fellowship and our desire for fellowship with God but also our needs and the needs of our neighbors. Granting that these descriptions of the two sides are always slanted from the perspective of one particular side, and so may be ungenerous to the other, they do present a picture that can be a useful heuristic device for locating my reading of *Works of Love*.

Moreover, one can consider *Works of Love* in relation to the tradition of 'impartialist' ethics. The long-standing discussion of the merits and limits of impartiality (which I have noted in chapter 15 concerning asymmetry) outlines the reservations about strict impartiality that lead people to find a place for certain kinds of partiality or asymmetry in personal relationships. These reservations about strict impartiality do not concern one side only; the fear is that strict impartiality can deprive the other, as well as the self. On the other hand, even ethicists who are sensitive to the "impracticality" of impartiality have insisted on the dangers of unqualified partiality in a world where wealth and resources are unequally distributed; practices of partiality need to be tempered by impartiality's impulse to redistribute such resources.[3]

Finally, one can try to locate *Works of Love* in relation to the time-honored distinction between 'teleological' and 'deontological' ethics. Although there is something to be gained by initially trying to categorize an ethic in these terms, much of the current literature recognizes the difficulty in making a clear separation between the two categories, as well as the allied difficulty of determining what counts as "disinterestedness" and "interestedness."[4]

The terms of these three frameworks can be helpful in describing what I see as the distinctive contribution of *Works of Love* to this ongoing discussion. Kierkegaard has been assumed to be part of the Reformation tradition of self-sacrificial love, and *Works of Love* has usually been read as an example of an ethic that promotes neighbor love as unilateral, self-denying, impartial, and disinterested. I have been suggesting throughout that *Works of Love* provides resources for an ethic of love of neighbor that does not fall simply on one side or the other of the divide between self-sacrifice or communion, gift or need, asymmetry or symmetry, impartiality or partiality, or deontology or teleology.

Kierkegaard's model of neighbor love includes six crucial elements: proper self-love, the "as yourself," "infinite debt," equality, "like for like," and "heightened inequality." All of these have to be assessed to determine how they mutually qualify and correct and balance one another. The way in which these elements work together is meant, for Kierkegaard, to ensure that the model of God's love for us does not issue in a neighbor love that is indifferent to the concrete distinctiveness of others and their needs, or a neighbor love in which self-denial is seen as a goal in itself. When he asks us: "Have you never thought about God's love?" (WL, p. 65), he is reminding us that we learn from God's love what love is, but the way in which this can be a model for us is complicated. For Kierkegaard, God's love for us is construed as a radical gift, but there are ways in which this is an appropriate model for us and ways in which it is not. God's love as gift means that "God loved us first." But though we are empowered by God's love as gift, we can hardly imitate it in this respect; we cannot ever love God or neighbor "first" because we are always like the child who gives his parent a present purchased with what the parent has already given the child.[5] We can, however, learn from this gift of God that responses of gratitude and hope by the recipient do not invalidate the love of the lover, and we can learn that love is constituted by building up the other. Moreover, we cannot imitate God's model by loving the neighbor "first" because although Kierkegaard claims that our love should not be conditional on anything attractive in the other person and sometimes talks about loving the unlovable person, he nevertheless concedes that no one is actually unlovable (p. 172)[6]; created by God, the other is essentially lovable, and if we do not see that, we do not see the person as he or she is. God's love for us is construed as a radical gift by Kierkegaard precisely so that our love for others will *not* be seen as unmotivated and unresponsive but will be seen as a debt that we owe to them, requiring us to see them just as they are and to respond accordingly. Just as God's love for us is appropriately responded to with gratitude, joy, and hope, love for the neighbor is appropriately responded to with gratitude and joy.

Whereas God's love is radically a gift, it is not only a gift. In keeping with his repeated indications in *Works of Love*, Kierkegaard proposes in a late journal entry that there is a "twofoldness" in Christianity: "God loves—and God wants to be loved. These two in equilibrium make true Christianity."[7] God's love is construed as empowering us with a need to love and a need to be loved by human others, which renders us like God and Christ in terms of need-love; that is, God's love for us confers on us a gift that is a need and a task. Although we cannot imitate God's model of loving first, we can see in it the ideal of our human love as a need-love. Kierkegaard walks the fine line of construing God's love in such a way that it affirms our need-love and of distinguishing this need from what he calls 'seeking our own.' What counts as not seeking our own is presented in a variety of specific illustrations, and they have more to do with not controlling and manipulating others than they do with any self-sacrifice for its own sake. Kierkegaard's understanding of not seeking one's own and of loving what is the other's own distinctiveness provides the counterweight to the bias we have toward self. There are many such counterweights in his ethic, including the notion of infinite debt and heightened inequality.

I have suggested that we look anew at many of the aspects of this ethic that have been criticized and imagine broader possibilities for construing them, possibilities that allow the whole to fit together better than usually thought. I am not arguing that we should not take what Kierkegaard says at face value; I am, however, suggesting that what someone sees at first glance may be what one is conditioned to expect by a history of criticism. I have gleaned from the text what was certainly there but often overlooked because it has been overwhelmed by more dramatic comments or examples. I have gone out of my way to offer a charitable reading of *Works of Love,* not because it is a work by Kierkegaard but because the hermeneutical principle of charity seems to me the most fruitful one to use with any text. If one goes to a text looking for a whipping boy, one will find it, especially if one is determined not to look further, not to look at the whole in context. If one persists in taking the most ungenerous reading possible, especially because it fits in with a position one is against anyway, one is likely to miss possible riches in the text.

If one assumes that the hermeneutic for reading *Works of Love* is a Reformation ethic at its most crude, one is likely to miss the ways in which Kierkegaard challenges both Lutheranism and Luther. In his journals Kierkegaard expresses disagreement with Luther a number of times, but one is particularly telling concerning his model of God's love. Kierkegaard disagrees with Luther's reading of the Gospel parable of the lost sheep.[8] According to him, Luther misreads the parable by imposing on it the view that God does not really love the one saved sheep more than the ninety-nine who obediently remained. Kierkegaard suggests, on the contrary, that the clearest reading of the parable is that God does indeed love the errant but saved sheep more. What is interesting about this interpretive disagreement is that it reveals Kierkegaard's own appreciation of the responsive partiality of God. Here he is in line with those current ethicists who find scriptural resources for rejecting a love that is bound by blind equality. Not a lot can hang on one journal entry, but it seems to reinforce Kierkegaard's openness to an ethic premised on a model of divine love that is both responsive to and loves the differences in the flowers.

The reminders I have collected throughout my study suggest that Kierkegaard retrieves a classical appreciation of proper self-love and the legitimacy of need that allows the love command to be grounded in the ontological relation between persons. At the same time, they suggest a model of neighbor love that is geared to promoting reconciliation between people. Let me summarize the conclusions that follow from these reminders.

Kierkegaard seems to see the model of God's love for us as a radical gift that is the basis for an ethic of absolute indebtedness to the other rather than pure gratuity. This eliminates the unresponsiveness and disinterestedness of pure gratuity. The model of God's love for us promotes an appreciation of our need to love and to be loved. The importance of need highlights the natural foundation of love and is congenial with a view in which grace perfects nature rather than destroys it. Kierkegaard's appreciation of "proper" self-love precludes any need to adopt a model of pure, disinterested love for God or for others. Kierkegaard would most likely see that model as failing to do justice to the roles of both hope and gratitude in our relation to God, and therefore this would not be the model of relation to others. Kierkegaard's ethic is not an ethic of sacrifice for its own sake but of the necessary sacrifice that is asked of us as we seek to promote forgiveness and reconciliation and as we seek to build up love in others. Many of the works of love described in his ethic are attempts to minimize divisiveness and to prevent or restore broken bonds, thus furthering communion. Others are attempts to rebuild broken souls, strengthening them by believing in them, hoping for them, and helping them to be independent. Kierkegaard's understanding of God's love for us and his understanding of what Christ as prototype did do not result in a model of neighbor love that demands self-sacrifice for its own sake. The notion of infinite debt works with the notion of the "as yourself" and proper self-love, so we are motivated to do what we can for others, even when it leads to sacrifice or persecution, but without seeing that as a goal in itself.

In *Works of Love* Kierkegaard is not offering a model of what our love for God should be like; but he is relying on a notion of what God's love for us is like, and that notion includes a sense of God's delight in furthering the distinctiveness of God's creatures. So it is not incompatible with the kind of concrete response to others at the heart of our duty to love the people we see and to love them just as they are. He rejects the equation of impartiality with pure disinterestedness, and he clarifies the kind of interestedness we should express.[9] Moreover, there are good reasons for suggesting that Kierkegaard's ethic appreciates the limits of a divine command ethic and a simple ethic of obedience and is not properly subsumed under either category as such.

Two conclusions seem ironic, given the usual charges of asociality and acosmism. One could argue that Kierkegaard's own emphasis on God as the "middle term" in the triadic relation among me, neighbor, and God presupposes an appreciation of fellowship—the idea that a genuine relation is always a threesome. And, Kierkegaard's emphasis on the impartiality of neighbor love could be construed as a way of doing justice to the limits of partiality in a world where resources are unequally divided.[10]

Finally, let us reconsider the important question of whether disinterested, inclusive love is hopelessly pitted against interested, exclusive love, of whether the commandment's universality allows only a disinterested benevolence toward all persons rather than distinctive, responsive caring.[11] I have been arguing that *Works of Love* rejects this dichotomy, allowing that in different contexts different responses will be appropriate. The neighbor love that is commanded in the case of a spouse or child or friend will in fact be an interested caring, but it will be warm, intimate, or passionate because that is the nature of the relation, not because warmth or intimacy or passion is commanded. The neighbor love that is commanded in the case of the stranger we meet in physical distress will be a benevolence that will address the stranger's distinctive needs rather than some abstract, formulaic attitude; but it need not have the same tenderness that we would show to an intimate relation. We are not commanded to feel the preference we feel in other cases, but we are commanded not to let the lack of preference militate against the other's equality as a child of God. The neighbor love that is commanded for an adversary or an enemy, or one who is resistant to being loved, is probably a more generalized benevolence. Yet even there the context would be decisive; given the model of the good Samaritan it seems that Kierkegaard would allow that if such an enemy were suffering in front of us, we would then be asked for attentive caring. When there is neither passionate love nor friendship, what is commanded is best seen in terms of our responsibility to the other, the infinite debt we owe. The nature of the relationship will shape the response. The commandment cannot command what cannot be commanded; it cannot command the partiality of inclination or preference, but it does not exclude its presence so long as that partiality does not undermine the impartiality that consists in not excluding anyone from our responsibility to build up. Whereas in principle we can exclude no one from the shelter of that responsibility, in practice not everyone will actually come into our empirical moral arena. Seeking the other's own distinctiveness does not amount to the same thing in every case. The answer, then, is that at least a generalized benevolence is required to fulfill our responsibility to the other, and in some cases that benevolence will be enriched by warmth, emotion, and intimacy. Kierkegaard does not render a monolithic judgment about what the relation will look like; he does not homogenize all situations, bringing them down to their lowest common denominator in terms of affection.[12] Nor should one.

It is important to read the whole of *Works of Love* since what Kierkegaard says to us is said in pieces. As any author knows, it cannot all be said at once. In some places the focus is on the need we have for relationship, whereas in others it is on our independence from automatic changes in our response;[13] in some places the focus is on the symmetry, and in others on the asymmetry. In some places the focus is on the way in which differences can be used as excuses for not fulfilling our responsibility, whereas in other places the focus is on the way in which differences and distinctiveness are attended to by love; in some places the focus is on the outwardness of love and vision, whereas in other places it is on the hiddenness of love. In addition to the strong emphasis on the impartiality of neighbor love, there are moving descriptions of love that attest to the legitimacy of a kind of partiality. No single focus can do justice to the characterization of love's works that Kierkegaard offers, and any focus considered in isolation will simply lead to misinterpretation.

II. Neighbor, Nourishment, and Need

Let me now approach the conclusion to this study from another direction, with a brief look at the relation among neighbor, nourishment, and need. In a journal comment in 1849 Kierkegaard remarked somewhat bemusedly: "It is wonderful that in the [Danish] language the word *nourishment* [*Naering*] is related to *near* [*naer*]. To the degree that the need is greater, the nourishment is nearer; the nourishment is in the need, and even if it is not the need, it still is the nearest."[14] He is certainly making a suggestive connection between nourishment and nearness or proximity. Moreover, it is an important point to him since he repeats it in one of his *Christian Discourses*, stating that God would not allow a need unless the nourishment is also available nearby, that part of God's creative mercy is to put near us the nourishment we need:

[T]he need brings its nourishment along with it; what is sought is in the seeking that seeks it; faith is in the concern over not having faith; love is in the self-concern over not loving. The need brings the *nourishment* [*Naering*] along with it—oh, so near [*naer*] (the word indeed says it) it is, so near it is, if only the need is there. The need brings the nourishment along with it, not *by itself,* as if the need produced the nourishment, but by virtue of a divine determination that joins the two, the need and the nourishment.[15]

Whether or not this linguistic connection is borne out in the derivation of the two words, Kierkegaard's point becomes even more intriguing if one recognizes another (much more plausible) connection in many languages, including Danish, between the concepts of neighbor and of near. In Danish, the word for neighbor [*Naeste*] has connotations of nearness insofar as it also means "next," as in the next one, the one next to me, or the one near to me. Kierkegaard explicitly appeals to this derivation in the first deliberation on the commandment as such: "*Who, then, is one's neighbor* [*Naeste*]? The word is obviously derived from 'nearest [*Naermeste*]'; thus the neighbor is the person who is nearer to you than anyone else, yet not in the sense of preferential love" (WL, p. 21). It is impossible not to want to make an association, then, between the neighbor and need and nourishment, so one could say that the neighbor is both our need and our nourishment. This would reinforce Kierkegaard's claim that our deepest need or craving is for companionship, to love and to be loved by another.

One cannot be nourished by what is at a distance; one is nourished only by what is close by (although, of course, not everything close by will nourish). Kierkegaard would be saying—although indirectly—that the demand placed on one by the neighbor comes with its ability to be fulfilled. The need is in one sense continually satisfied, yet in another sense it is never completely satisfied. It is never satisfied in the sense that one can stop seeking or desiring more. The need for love is a never-ending seeking, but one that therein contains its nourishment. The seeking is the finding but not a finding with any closure; rather it is a finding that we desire more. One could say that this theme—that the neighbor is our need and our nourishment—is one of the ways in which these deliberations fulfill their stated goal of turning our "comfortable way of thinking topsy-turvy."

appendix

Table of Contents of Works of Love

notes

1. Dostoyevsky, *The Brothers Karamazov* (1880), Vol. One, Pt. Two, Bk. Five, Sect. 4, "Rebellion," p. 276.

2. Dostoyevsky, *The Idiot* (1868–69), p. 473.

3. Nietzsche, letter to George Brandes, November 20, 1888, *Selected Letters of Friedrich Nietzsche*, p. 327; *Thus Spoke Zarathustra*, Pt. One, Sect. 16.

4. Søltoft argues that EO 2 anticipates WL ("Love and Continuity: The Significance of Intersubjectivity in the Second Part of *Either/Or,*" p. 227). Although it is important to recognize these often overlooked elements, these anticipations are still fragmentary at best and often inconsistent with the main position espoused by Judge William.

5. The most notorious example is MacIntyre's account of Kierkegaard's ethical position, *A Short History of Ethics* (pp. 215–18); the journal literature is full of titles like "Kierkegaard: The Self and Ethical Existence," by George J. Stack, or "Kierkegaard's Ethical Individualism," by Roger S. Gottlieb.

6. For example, Noddings, *Caring: A Feminine Approach to Ethics and Moral Education*, p. 43; Ainley, "The Subject of Ethics: Kierkegaard and Feminist Perspectives on an 'Ethical Self,'" p. 179.

7. Andolsen provides a valuable summary of the ways in which "Feminist ethicists are critical of the emphasis on sacrifice as the quintessence of *agape* and of the denigration of self-love" and propose instead an ethics of mutuality ("Agape in Feminist Ethics," p. 146); Purvis's challenge concerns the area of special relations, and she refers to the deliberation in *Works of Love* about recollecting the dead, proposing to substitute the nursery for "the graveyard as agape's school room" ("Mothers, Neighbors, and Strangers," pp. 21–23). Friedman surveys the partiality/impartiality debate ("The Social Self and Partiality Debates"); note her suggestion that conceptual overlap between feminist and nonfeminist critiques of moral impartialism may mask significantly different concerns (p. 161).

8. See Léon and Walsh, eds., *Feminist Interpretations of Søren Kierkegaard*.

9. See chapter 5 for more on Adorno and Løgstrup; the *Kierkegaard Studies Yearbook 1998* has articles on the Danish, German, and English reception of WL. Barth's criticisms are found in his *Church Dogmatics* IV/2, pp. 747, 782.

10. Løgstrup, "Settling Accounts with Kierkegaard's *Works of Love*," a "Polemical Epilogue" to *The Ethical Demand* (the twelve chapters preceding the epilogue were originally published in English in 1971, but the epilogue is in English for the first time). In the Introduction, Fink and MacIntyre concede that Løgstrup's criticism is "perhaps" more rightly directed against his own contemporaries than against Kierkegaard himself; but because they have appended this explicit critique of Kierkegaard to a work they praise as an insightful contribution to contemporary ethical debate, it is likely to be accepted at face value by those who are not Kierkegaard scholars. Moreover, they note affinities between Løgstrup's thought and that of Emmanuel Levinas; this indirectly supports my conclusion that Løgstrup is actually closer to Kierkegaard than he would ever have wanted to admit.

11. Westphal, *Kierkegaard's Critique of Reason and Society;* Connell and Evans, eds., *Foundations of Kierkegaard's Vision of Community;* Perkins, ed., *International Kierkegaard Commentary 14: Two Ages.* (especially the Introduction).

12. The following were important pioneering efforts: Lindström, "A Contribution to the Interpretation of Kierkegaard's Book, *The Works of Love*"; Müller, *Kierkegard's "Works of Love": Christian Ethics and the Maieutic Ideal;* Walsh, "Forming the Heart: The Role of Love in Kierkegaard's Thought" and "Kierkegaard's Philosophy of Love"; Kirmmse, chapter 19 of *Kierkegaard in Golden Age Denmark* (pp. 306–30); Fendt, *Works of Love?;* Gouwens, Chap. 6 of *Kierkegaard as Religious Thinker* (pp. 186–208).

13. During the period in which I was composing this book I found three examples. The first is a brief study of *Works of Love* that comes at the end of a broader study by Dilman (*Love: Its Forms, Dimensions and Paradoxes,* Chaps. 11 and 12), treating love in the thought of Proust, Freud, D. H. Lawrence, Erich Fromm, and C. S. Lewis. The second is the volume of *Kierkegaard Studies Yearbook 1998,* which has a preponderance of fine essays on *Works of Love.* The third is the excellent *International Kierkegaard Commentary 16: Works of Love,* ed. Perkins, which has just appeared (January 2000).

14. George, "Something Anti-social about *Works of Love*," p. 81.

15. Ibid., pp. 74, 75.

16. Ibid., p. 74.

17. Ibid., p. 78.

18. Ibid., p. 75.

19. See chapter 7, "Love's Vision."

20. JP 5:6111 (1848), p. 436.

21. JP 3:2481 (1849), p. 70

22. Kirmmse notes this in *Kierkegaard in Golden Age Denmark,* p. 311.

23. "My Position as a Religious Author in 'Christendom' and My Strategy" (PV, p. 17).

24. For more detail see chapter 17, section III.

25. The "Paradox of Morality," p. 176 (hereafter "Paradox").

26. I use Levinas because of his interesting commonalities and contrasts with Kierkegaard; I am not at all suggesting that he represents any dominant view in contemporary Jewish ethics about understanding the love commandment. For some indications of the literature in this area, see Radcliffe, "Hanfling on Neighbour Love," p. 499, n. 2; see also Jacobs, "Greater Love Hath No Man—The Jewish Point of View of Self-sacrifice" and "Disinterestedness."

27. Valuable work has already been done by Westphal in exploring the relation between Kierkegaard and Levinas: see "Levinas, Kierkegaard, and the Theological Task";

"The Transparent Shadow: Kierkegaard and Levinas in Dialogue"; "Commanded Love and Divine Transcendence in Levinas and Kierkegaard."

28. For example, Marion's *God Without Being*.

CHAPTER I

1. "I would now like to give a series of twelve lectures on the dialectic of communication. After that, twelve lectures on erotic love, friendship, and love" [JP 5:5996 (1847), p. 374].

2. Further justification for doing this will be apparent in chapter 7, "Love's Vision."

3. WL, Supplement, p. 469. I use this translation—rather than the one in JP 1:641 (1847), p. 263, where *overveielse* is translated as "reflections"—to maintain consistency with the title; Kierkegaard also suggests that its tone should be "impatient" and "high-spirited," involving "irony" and "the comic."

4. WL, p. 265.

5. "The Accounting" and "The Point of View for My Work as an Author" (PV, pp. 29–33).

6. See works by Hartshorne (*Kierkegaard, Godly Deceiver*) and Poole (*Kierkegaard: The Indirect Communication*).

7. PV, Supplement, p. 236.

8. JP 1, "The Dialectic of Ethical and Ethical-Religious Communication," pp. 273–74, 281–82.

9. "A First and Last Explanation" (CUP, pp. 625–30).

10. For example, PF and PC; for further discussion, see the Historical Introductions to PV and BA.

11. JP 1, "The Dialectic of Ethical and Ethical-Religious Communication," pp. 267–80. Müller takes this approach to *Works of Love*, concluding that striving to practice works of love "must necessarily unfold inside the scope of the maieutic, in order to be in harmony with the structure which has already been given in existence" (*Kierkegaard's "Works of Love": Christian Ethics and the Maieutic Ideal*, p. 71; pp. 43–70 present and elaborate four aspects of the maieutic).

12. "Purity of Heart Is to Will One Thing" (A Discourse on the Occasion of a Confession), UDVS, p. 122 (hereafter "Purity").

13. See Chapter 6.

14. "Purity," p. 124.

15. Ibid., p. 125.

16. Ibid., p. 126.

17. JP 3:2423 (1849), p. 44.

18. Andic suggests that the contrast is one between (God's) love and (our) works of love ("Love's Redoubling and the Eternal Like for Like," p. 18, n. 14); elsewhere he suggests that one can read the contrast as one between (our) love (for God) and the works for neighbor which show it ("Is Love of Neighbour the Love of an Individual?" p. 122, n. 6).

19. For a valuable discussion of the Trinitarian and other theological motifs in WL, see Plekon, "Kierkegaard the Theologian: The Roots of His Theology in *Works of Love*."

20. Indeed, God's love provides the model for us (WL, p. 65).

21. John 13:34.

22. Leviticus 19:17–18; Matthew 22:39; Mark 12:31.

23. JP 2:1121 (1847), p. 10.

24. JP 1:993 (1851), p. 434.

25. JP 3:2461 (1846), pp. 63–64.

26. JP 3:2550 (1854), p. 101; JP 3:3617 (1853–54), pp. 669–70.

27. JP 3:2484 (1849), p. 70; that is, it was "in contrast to this adolescent behavior [that] Luther stressed faith"; JP 3:2527 (1850), p. 87.

28. JP 3:2518 (1850), p. 82.

29. See JP 1:709 (1852), p. 332; JP 1:711 (1854), p. 333.

30. JP 3:2481 (1849), p. 70.

31. JP 1:994 (1851), p. 434.

32. "Thou art lightning and love, I found it, a winter and warm" (Hopkins, "The Wreck of the Deutschland," p. 37).

33. JP 3:2551 (1854), p. 101.

34. This phrase is common in the writings of mystics like Meister Eckhart and Marguerite Porete (thirteenth century), as well as Angelus Silesius (seventeenth century).

35. PF, p. 32.

36. Ibid., p. 56.

37. James, "The Will to Believe"; for more on this topic, see chapter 9, "Love's Venture."

38. JP 3:2423 (1849), p. 44.

39. "The Accounting," PV, p. 5.

40. See SV: 9–10, p. 17; he says in the prayer, "There are indeed only some works that human language specifically and narrowly calls works of love [*Kjerligheds-gjerninger*], but in heaven no work can be pleasing unless it is a work of love [*Kjerlighedens Gjerning*]" (SV: 9–10, p. 8).

41. Luther, too, identifies "good works" with "fruits of faith" ("The Judgment of Martin Luther on Monastic Vows," p. 279).

42. CD, p. 244.

43. Levinas contrasts need with desire, which comes from the presence of the other (TI, pp. 62, 103, 114–15, 117, 146, 254, 271).

44. "Trace," p. 351; Levinas writes that "desire for the other . . . proceeds from a being already replenished to overflowing and independent" (p. 350).

45. EI, p. 92.

46. "Trace," p. 350; "Dialogue," FF, p. 24.

CHAPTER 2

1. His appeal to hearing occurs with the 'voice' of conscience (chapter 6) and the "echo" (chapter 15).

2. Kierkegaard's unusual involvement with the typographical layout of his books is documented by Cappelørn and Rohde ("Fra Fractur til Palatino," pp. 76–89).

3. In a passage that was eventually deleted, Kierkegaard wrote: "This discourse no. 2 is omitted from the series and is to be added as an appendix to 'Works of Love'; it is patterned more as a deliberation and also has a definitely didactic element. Therefore, that appendix: that love is a duty, that we shall love" (WL, Supplement, p. 428).

4. JP 3:2403 (1847), p. 38.

5. See chapter 7, section I.

6. This is not to deny that there are interesting ways in which to characterize the deliberations in the second series, ways that do not apply to the first series.

7. He denies that Christianity intends to "teach" us that self-love is "a prescriptive right" (WL, p. 17), yet he allows that we are commanded to love ourselves in the proper way: "The Law is therefore: You shall love yourself in the same way as you love your neighbor when you love him as yourself" (p. 23).

8. Luther, "Lectures on Romans," p. 513.

9. The word "sadly" does not mean that it is unfortunate that we love ourselves but rather that it is unfortunate that our love of self tends to be restrictive and competitive, rather than inclusive.

10. Nygren holds that "Agape recognizes no kind of self-love as legitimate"(*Agape and Eros*, p. 217), and Hallett locates numerous others in that tradition (*Christian Neighbor-Love*). Outka categorizes value judgments about self-love as follows: (1) nefarious; (2) reasonable and prudent—a neutral judgment that covers self-love as an index of what love for another means, as well as the legitimacy of unintended self-fulfillment that follows on loving another; (3) recommendation of deliberate concern for self, which is derived from concern for others (to benefit them or prevent harm to them); (4) obligation to take care of self because of self-respect, self-esteem, and a stand against self-sacrifice (*Agape: An Ethical Analysis*, pp. 55–75). Outka puts Kierkegaard into the category of those for whom self-love is reasonable (because of the 'like for like'; p. 67).

11. "Treatise on Good Works" (hereafter TGW).

12. Ibid., p. 108.

13. "The Law is therefore: You shall love yourself in the same way as you love your neighbor when you love him as yourself" (WL, p. 23). In a 1948 review, David Roberts suggests that "Kierkegaard was exactly a century ahead of [Erich] Fromm in insisting that love for mankind (the neighbor) is conjunctive with self-love, which is the opposite of selfishness" (*"Works of Love:* A Review Article," p. 383).

14. Kant suggests that to "secure one's own happiness is at least indirectly a duty, for discontent with one's condition under pressure from many cares and amid unsatisfied wants could easily become a great temptation to transgress duties" (*Foundations of the Metaphysic of Morals*, p. 15).

15. For example, Aristotle brings out the ambiguity in the phrase "lover of self" and explains the "nature of true self-love"; a good man's being is seen by him to be desirable because it is seen by him to be good; therefore "the good man should be a lover of self" (*The Nichomachean Ethics*, pp. 241, 237). Accounts that emphasize self-respect and self-esteem fall into this category.

16. "Lectures on Galatians," p. 57.

17. "A Short Exposition of the Decalogue, Apostle's Creed, and Lord's Prayer," p. 74.

18. Ibid., p. 75.

19. Ramsey, *Basic Christian Ethics*, p. 100.

20. Whittaker, "'Agape' and Self-Love," pp. 227, 231.

21. Ibid., p. 232.

22. One valuable exception is the discussion by Søltoft in "The Presence of the Absent Neighbor in *Works of Love,"* pp. 117–22. She agrees that this scenario "has the character of a test" and suggests that in this context Kierkegaard's "emphasis is on the concept of the neighbor, not on the neighbor as another concrete human being" (p. 117).

23. *Summa Theologiae* II–II: Q.26.4.

24. For an example of the classical objection to commanded love, see Hanfling, "Loving My Neighbour, Loving Myself."

25. Kierkegaard agrees with Kant that "love as an inclination cannot be commanded" (*Foundations of the Metaphysics of Morals*, p. 16). For further discussion of the contrast and comparison between Kant and Kierkegaard on the love commandment, see Martens, "'You Shall Love': Kant, Kierkegaard, and the Interpretation of Matthew 22:39." For a treatment of their relation more generally, see Green, *Kierkegaard and Kant*.

26. Many read the command in this way (see Pope, "Love in Contemporary Christian Ethics," pp. 13–14).

27. The claim that Christian love is "secured" is not meant as an empirical prediction

(since it is often falsified) but rather as a grammatical rule; that is, Christian love as such is secured, but we can fail to maintain Christian love.

28. Hallett offers the following spectrum of possible positions: Self-denial, Self-forgetfulness, Self-subordination, Other-preference, Parity, and Self-preference (*Christian Neighbor-Love*).

29. This same message is also found in *Either/Or:* "Duty is precisely the divine nourishment love needs, for duty says, 'Fear not; you shall conquer'—says it not just in the future sense, for then it is only a hope, but in the imperative mood, and therein rests a conviction that nothing can shake" (EO 2, p. 146).

30. TGW, p. 60; emphasis mine.

31. Ibid., p. 62.

32. Later on he notes: "If the love in us human beings is not so perfect that this wish is our wish, then the duty will help us to remain in debt" (WL, p. 179); he adds that when Christianity says something is a "duty," it "thereby removes from love everything that is inflamed, everything that is momentary, everything that is giddy" (WL, p. 188).

33. When he later says (II, C) that love "is a need, the deepest need, in the person in whom there is love for the neighbor; he does not need people just to have someone to love, but he needs to love people" (p. 67), this might sound like the arrogance he is denouncing earlier. However, we need to keep this in context, for it has been preceded by the acknowledgment that, he says, was "developed in the preceding discussion"—that the need "to love people" is not the same as the self-referential need "to have someone to love" (p. 39).

34. Christ "humanly felt this need to love and be loved by an individual human being"(WL, p. 155); Levinas affirms that our "desire for another [is] our very sociality" ("Trace," p. 350).

35. Nietzsche, *Human All-Too-Human* I:523, p. 239.

36. Pieper, *Faith, Hope, Love*, pp. 183–84. Pieper suggests that the "general disparagement of wanting to be loved" may be "a typically modern phenomenon, still another form of modern man's claim to equality with God" (p. 184).

37. Outka, *Agape;* "Agapeistic Ethics," p. 481.

38. Quinn, "The Divine Command Ethics in Kierkegaard's *Works of Love*,"pp. 29–44.

39. "A divine command morality holds that the standard of right and wrong is constituted by the commands and prohibitions of God" (Idziak, "Divine Command Ethics," p. 453).

40. Adams, "A Modified Divine Command Theory of Ethical Wrongness" (1973) and "Divine Command Meta-ethics Modified Again" (1979), p. 139; both in *The Virtue of Faith*. Those wanting further discussion of the debate over this ethic should also consult the work of Quinn, "The Recent Revival of Divine Command Ethics," pp. 345–65, and *Divine Commands and Moral Requirements*.

41. I suggest that Quinn's criticism of Kierkegaard for depending on a "perception" that empowers us does not sufficiently acknowledge the importance and role of the gift we are given and the natural embeddedness of the need we thereby have ("Kierkegaard's Christian Ethics," pp. 367–68).

42. "Eternity's *shall* binds and guides this great need so that it does not go astray" (WL, p. 67); "The commandment only forbids loving in a way that is not commanded" (p. 41). The claim that "essentially the commandment is not forbidding but commanding, that you shall love" (p. 41) needs to be read in the light of these other claims.

43. Adams, "Autonomy and Theological Ethics," pp. 126–27.

44. Tillich, *The Protestant Era*, p. 56; cited by Adams, "Autonomy," p. 126.

45. The sketch of such an account is found in MacIntyre's "Which God Ought We to Obey and Why?" pp. 359–71; he concludes that the problem of judging God by some-

thing 'external' to God is precluded if we understand that "natural justice recognized by natural reason is itself divinely uttered and authorized" (p. 370).

46. Charles T. Mathewes reminds me that such a view is still subject to any criticisms that apply to a natural law theory of ethics.

47. See chapter 17, section I, for more on this topic.

48. Kirmmse suggests that the two deliberations (II, A and B) "relate to one another in miniature, in the same way that "Purity of Heart" as a whole relates to *Works of Love* as a whole; or as 'religiousness A' relates to 'religiousness B'; or as philosophical religion relates to revealed religion; or, most significantly, as Law relates to Gospel" (*Kierkegaard in Golden Age Denmark*, p. 310).

CHAPTER 3

1. "The neighbor is one who is equal [*Ligelige*]"; Kierkegaard uses this less common form of the word for (Christian) equality to make a contrast with the more usual *Lighed*, a word that at the time had political or revolutionary overtones.

2. Since, Kierkegaard suggests, loving another as superior to oneself can be a form of self-loving identification and loving another as inferior to oneself can be a self-loving form of condescension (WL, p. 60), the rejection of self-loving partiality can only be achieved through an emphasis on equality.

3. The main contrast is not between *elskov* and *kjerlighed;* this indirectly points to the legitimacy of *elskov.*

4. Quinn suggests that the first claim is plausible enough and not particularly novel, but he rejects the second ("Kierkegaard's Christian Ethics," pp. 358–59); I go on to argue that the second is not particularly novel either; moreover, Kierkegaard distinguishes between proper self-love and selfish self-love (WL, p. 151).

5. Aristotle, *The Nichomachean Ethics*, p. 227.

6. Ibid., p. 200.

7. Ibid., pp. 241, 237.

8. Ibid., p. 228.

9. Ibid., p. 201.

10. Ibid., pp. 228, 238, 241.

11. Aquinas, *Summa Theologiae* I–II, Q.28.1.

12. This is a response to Outka's critique (*Agape*, p. 134) that, for Kierkegaard, preferential and Christian love are antithetical.

13. Green and Ellis argue that neighbor love transforms and fulfills erotic love's desires: "Erotic love for Kierkegaard is less an antitype to Christian love than it is a driving force that leads to it . . . erotic love moves through tumultuous aesthetic expression, through the challenges of married love, until it ultimately finds peace and rest in the religious sphere of existence" ("Erotic Love in the Religious Existence-Sphere," p. 342). Adams argues that there is no dichotomy between self-interested and altruistic, and he rejects the requirement of indifference ("Pure Love," pp. 174–92); he explains that there is eros in agape, and that agape is a combination of eros and benevolence, although benevolence remains *"ethically* the most *important"* and *"essential"* dimension (p. 190). See more on this topic in chapter 15.

14. Hallett (*Christian Neighbor-Love*, p. 2) uses Bultmann's reference to *Works of Love* in *Jesus and the Word* as an example of this Lutheran tradition.

15. Walsh suggests this ("Forming the Heart," p. 176), as does Westphal ("Commanded Love and Transcendence in Levinas and Kierkegaard," p. 15).

16. Kant, *Foundations of the Metaphysic of Morals*, pp. 13–15.

17. "Purity," p. 129.

18. "To love the neighbor" is "to will to exist equally for unconditionally every human being" (WL, pp. 83–84). This is another way of saying that to love "all people" is to will to exist for "unconditionally every" one, which is why renouncing self-love is an indication of love of the neighbor and can occur even if, "so far as thought is concerned" (i.e., in principle), one is alone. Moreover, these chapters do not propose the inflated and impossible demand of substantively expressing love for "all people," which some extreme impartialists advocate but which could rightly be seen as dysfunctional. What is possible and required is that no one be excluded from our loving response because of dissimilarities; whereas for Kierkegaard, this is not humanly possible (without divine grounding), it is possible to human beings (with divine grounding).

19. WA, p. 165.

20. For more on this topic, see chapter 7, "Love's Vision."

21. BPW, pp. 8, 10, 92, 95, 140–43, 167.

22. "Peace and Proximity," BPW, p. 167.

23. "Philosophy, Justice, and Love," EN, p. 103.

24. EI, pp. 95, 96.

25. EI, p. 52; moreover, even that responsibility is spoken of in terms of the negative commandment not to kill.

26. "Philosophy, Justice, and Love," EN, p. 103.

27. OB, pp. 14–15, 18.

28. "God and Philosophy," BPW, p. 140.

29. Ibid., p. 142.

30. "Ethics as First Philosophy," LR, p. 83.

31. See "Transcendence and Height" (BPW, p. 27), where the fear is that the term obscures or obliterates "difference."

32. "Perhaps because of current moral maxims in which the word *neighbor* occurs, we have ceased to be surprised by all that is involved in proximity and approach" (OB, p. 5).

33. "Is Ontology Fundamental," BPW, p. 8; "Peace and Proximity," BPW, p. 167. Levinas does not restrict "face" to the literal body part but equates it with "expression [which] overflows images" (TI, p. 297); for example, "the way in which the other presents himself, exceeding *the idea of the other in me*, we here name face" (p. 50); "the whole body—a hand or a curve of the shoulder—can express as the face" (p. 262); "the face is the other who asks me not to let him die alone, as if to do so were to become an accomplice in his death" (FF, p. 24). He also says that "the idea of the face is the idea of gratuitous love, the commandment of a gratuitous act" ("Paradox," p. 176).

34. "Peace and Proximity," BPW, p. 167; see also "God and Philosophy" on the "face" or "forsakenness" of the neighbor (BPW, p. 141).

35. OB, p. 11; "Peace and Proximity," BPW, p. 167; emphases mine.

36. "Philosophy, Justice, and Love," EN, p. 113.

37. The topic of the individual's responsibility will be addressed again in chapter 6, section II.

38. It may in fact be an objection to Levinas that he does not provide adequate criteria for distinguishing between the generic threat of mortality and other instances of suffering; his view may entail a leveling or raising of all indiscriminately, which is not plausible.

39. "Peace and Proximity," BPW, p. 169.

40. "Paradox," pp. 176, 177, 174.

41. The neighbor is "the persecuted one for whom I am responsible to the point of being a hostage for him" (OB, p. 59), yet "this responsibility against my will . . . is the very fact of finding oneself while losing oneself" (p. 11). This positive notion of hostage is apparent in the claims that "it is through the condition of being hostage that there can be in the world pity, compassion, pardon, and proximity" (p. 117); he notes that "in my essays, the dis-quieting of the Same by the Other is the Desire that shall be a searching, a

questioning, an awaiting: patience and length of time, and the very mode of surplus, of superabundance" ("Questions and Answers," GCM, p. 81).

42. TIME, p. 87.

43. "I was extremely interested in Sartre's phenomenological analysis of the 'other,' though I always regretted that he interpreted it as a threat and a degradation" ("Dialogue," FF, p. 17).

44. "Dialogue" (FF, p. 24); the phrase "the ethics of the welcome" is found in his essay "Dialogue: Self-Consciousness and the Proximity of the Neighbor" (GCM, p. 151). This notion of "welcome" fits with his earliest accounts; for example, in the Preface to *Totality and Infinity*, he writes: "This book will present subjectivity as welcoming the Other, as hospitality" (p. 27). The notion of "greeting" the Other is found in EI, p. 88.

45. Levinas writes that "thus precisely it can welcome that being. The subject is a host" (TI, p. 299).

46. "Hospitality, the one-for-the-other in the ego, delivers it more passively than any passivity from links in a causal chain. Being torn from oneself for another in giving to the other the bread from one's mouth is being able to give up one's soul for another" (OB, p. 79) This refers back to his earlier comment: "To give, to be-for-another, despite oneself, but in interrupting the for-oneself, is to take the bread out of one's own mouth, to nourish the hunger of another with one's own fasting" (OB, p. 56).

47. "The Philosophical Determination of the Idea of Culture," EN, p. 186.

48. "Philosophy, Justice, and Love," EN, p. 108.

49. "Peace and Proximity," BPW, p. 167.

50. "Paradox," pp. 176–77.

51. Chapter 17, section I, addresses the relation between an ethic of responsibility and one of obedience.

52. Nussbaum, *Love's Knowledge*, p. 52.

53. Ibid., p. 188.

54. Ibid., p. 189.

55. Ibid., p. 190.

56. Ibid., p. 189; Nussbaum's final position is more optimistic—see pp. 52–53.

57. As I noted earlier, that Kierkegaard puts both erotic love and friendship in the same category shows that his objections do not concern sexuality but rather selfishness.

58. See Ferreira, "Hume and Imagination: Sympathy and the 'Other'," pp. 39–46.

59. Caring attention to others as genuine others is expressed when one does not simply imagine what one would feel in their place but tries to take account of what *they* feel—in their place (see chapter 13, section V).

60. "Love for the neighbor is love between two beings eternally and independently determined as spirit"; it does not result in a "united self," as do erotic love and friendship (WL, p. 56).

CHAPTER 4

1. Danish *Forskjellighederne* ("dissimilarities").

2. Adorno, "On Kierkegaard's Doctrine of Love," pp. 418–19; for more in response to Adorno's criticisms, see chapters 5, 13, and 15.

3. CUP, vol. 1, p. 249.

4. See chapter 6, section II.

5. Many accounts that stress "the individual," "individuality," or "particularity" fail to make this distinction. Outka cites a variety of accounts of Kierkegaard's stress on individuality that treat it in terms of autonomy and privacy, and he continues the tradition by

focusing on the individual as the "autonomous willing subject" ("Equality and Individuality," pp. 171, 182–87).

6. Outka begins to touch on the issue of concreteness when he considers how Kierkegaard's "dual affirmation inclines him to downplay the religious and ethical importance of meeting given needs" ("Equality and Individuality," p. 193); but since Outka equates "given needs" with "mundane needs for food, drink, shelter, and clothing" and then contrasts the importance of that kind of flourishing with the importance of "individuality," he maintains his rarified notion of individuality and does not really address the question of the relevance of concrete distinctiveness as such.

7. I am not hereby suggesting that any particular difference is in itself alienating or morally relevant; what is at issue is the uses to which the differences are put (to disconnect or to connect).

8. See also his discussion of differences and equality in one of the discourses entitled "Every Good and Perfect Gift Is from Above" (1843), EUD, pp. 142–47.

9. "In the company of rich people, in a setting that in itself makes the advantages of wealth conspicuous, the rich person would perhaps be willing to make every concession to the similarity of human beings—but that, of course, is to remain within the dissimilarity" (WL, p. 77).

10. Eliot deplores the way in which some Christians teach "the love of the *clan*, which is the correlative of antagonism to the rest of mankind"; this limited sense of kinship "gives a charter to hatred" ("Evangelical Teaching: Dr. Cumming," p. 159); Elizabeth McManus has helped me to appreciate Eliot's other-centered ethics.

11. "Purity," p. 124.

12. Robert Gibbs brought this issue about imperatives and indirect communication to my attention, and I agree that it deserves more sustained treatment than I can give it here.

13. Frankfurt suggests the ethical importance of this contrast, arguing that an emphasis on the former can obscure the importance of the doctrine of sufficiency ("Equality as a Moral Ideal," especially pp. 134–35).

14. See Malantschuk's account of Kierkegaard's awareness of the political and social situation in Europe, especially the communistic movements that Kierkegaard feared would exploit the masses by playing on their economic and social needs; Malantschuk concludes that "the whole" of *Works of Love* "is polemically directed against communism" ("Political and Social Aspects of Kierkegaard's Thought," p. 9).

15. Outka's interesting discussion unfortunately focuses on the term "performance" in a way that makes the contrast between effort and achievement more difficult to assess ("Equality and Individuality," pp. 182–83); see his discussion of "natural advantage" (Sect. IV).

16. That Kierkegaard was troubled about such questions is apparent in a journal entry: "Imagine a young man who, for example, is a student; he becomes ill, can accomplish nothing, and is deeply troubled. Now if I were to console him—and how gladly I would do it—I would say: consider that in the eyes of God your life, in spite of everything, is unconditionally just as important and full of meaning as the life of someone who astonishes the world and transforms it with his thinking. Yes, but in order truly to rest in this exaltation, is it not necessary, again, to have a good head, considerable intellectual power? So we are right where we started." Nonetheless, he concludes: "But I cannot escape the thought that every man, unconditionally every man, no matter how simple he is or how suffering, nevertheless can comprehend the highest, specifically, the religious. If this is not so, then Christianity is really nonsense" [JP 1:1017 (1850), p. 446].

17. See chapter 6, section V.

18. WL, Supplement, p. 457.

19. "The person aflame with erotic love, by reason or by virtue of this ardor, can by no means bear redoubling, which here would mean to give up the erotic love if the beloved required it" (WL, p. 21).

CHAPTER 5

1. For example, Mackey's target is CUP ("The Loss of the World in Kierkegaard's Ethics").

2. See my Introduction for examples.

3. Marx, "Introduction to the Critique of Hegel's *Philosophy of Right,* " p. 12.

4. Nietzsche, *Genealogy of Morals: Ecce Homo,* "Why I Am a Destiny," Sect. 8, p. 334.

5. Nietzsche, *The Anti-Christ,* Sect. 43, p. 155; he also insists there that "With the 'Beyond' one *kills life* " (Sect. 58).

6. Levinas, "Trace," p. 355.

7. Bonhoeffer, *Letters and Papers from Prison,* pp. 282, 376.

8. Relevant critiques of Buber can be found in the following articles: Perkins, "The Politics of Existence" and "Buber and Kierkegaard: A Philosophic Encounter," and Rose, "Søren Kierkegaard to Martin Buber—Reply from 'the Single One'."

9. See Kierkegaard's "The Single Individual," in PV, as well as "Purity."

10. Buber, "The Question to the Single One," p. 52.

11. Buber, Afterword to *Between Man and Man,* pp. 211, 213.

12. Adorno, "On Kierkegaard's Doctrine of Love," p. 420; see also chapters 13 and 15.

13. Lalic, *The Works of Love: Selected Poems of Ivan V. Lalic,* p. 53.

14. Webb suggests that Kierkegaard's hyperbolic strategy is "to make love impossible, to make you say no, but to haunt you with the possibility of saying yes" (in "More Than Too Much," p. 56); see also JP 2:1740 (1843), p. 266.

15. Ulrich Lincoln, "Asserung: Studien zum Handlungsbegriff in Søren Kierkegaards *Die Taten der Liebe.* "

16. WL, pp. 57–58, 67, 103, 107, 119, 121, 142, 303, 395, 437–39, 450.

17. Feuerbach, *The Essence of Christianity,* p. 268

18. Note that Aquinas suggests something similar to this "middle term," that "the love of one's friends is not meritorious in God's sight when we love them merely because they are our friends. . . . The love of our friends is meritorious, if we love them for God's sake, and not merely because they are our friends" (*Summa Theologiae* II–II, Q.27.7).

19. "Treatise on Good Works," p. 50; Luther adds that we should offer resistance to evil, regardless of the "distinction" of the persons who commit it, and that the mighty and the rich are unjust; the implication is that we will probably suffer for our obedience to God's command (pp. 50–51).

20. Johannes de Silentio assesses the passage in Luke about "hate" and concludes: "Anyone who in demanding a person's love believes that this love is demonstrated by his becoming indifferent to what he otherwise cherished is not merely an egotist but is also stupid," and obviously this is not "a worthy representation of divinity." "But how to hate?" he goes on to ask: "The absolute duty can lead the knight of faith to do what ethics would forbid, but it can never lead the knight of faith to stop loving" (FT, pp. 72–74).

21. He writes that "it is God who by himself and by means of the middle term 'neighbor' checks on whether the love for wife and friend is conscientious" (WL, p. 142).

22. Løgstrop, "Settling Accounts with Kierkegaard's *Works of Love,* " p. 232 (hereafter SA); his "Opgør med Kierkegaard's *Kaerlighedens Gerninger* " repeats the same charges with more venom.

23. "The essentially Christian is this: truly to love oneself is to love God; truly to love another person is with every sacrifice (also the sacrifice of becoming hated oneself)

to help the other person to love God or in loving God" (WL, p. 114); "to love oneself in the divine sense is to love God, and truly to love another person is to help that person to love God or in loving God" (WL, p. 130).

24. Løgstrup, SA, p. 121.

25. Løgstrup's alternative proposal emphasizes what he calls sovereign life expressions such as trust, fidelity, love, kindheartedness, and so on, and what is crucial is that these are immediate (not mediated by God as the middle term) and given possibilities (rather than existentially created by our decisions); the article by Götke, "Recent Scandinavian Literature on *Works of Love*," is a useful account of how Løgstrup constrained the Danish reception of WL.

26. Løgstrup similarly accuses Kant's ethic of being empty (" Ethics and Ontology," p. 289).

27. Løgstrup, SA, p. 220.

28. Ibid., p. 232.

29. Ibid.

30. Løgstrup asks: "How can it happen that the others' lack of understanding is awarded such a central role that one must ask: but what does self-denial depend on, on the individual's relationship to God or on the others—on their contempt, scorn, and mockery?" (SA, p. 227).

31. "The ingratitude of the world, opposition, and insult are the guarantee that the relationship to God is genuine" (ibid., p. 222).

32. Ibid., p. 227.

33. Kierkegaard is, of course, aware of the ways in which we can fool ourselves into thinking we are "willing" (PC, pp. 252–53).

34. Løgstrup, SA, pp. 226–27.

35. Ibid., p. 221.

36. Ibid., p. 230.

37. JP 3:2407 (1847), p. 39; also WL, pp. 101, 336.

38. JP 2:1121 (1847), p. 10.

39. Kierkegaard writes that "'thanksgiving' is the essentially God-pleasing 'sacrifice'" [JP 3:2497 (1849), p. 74].

40. JP 2:1886 (1850), p. 338; see also JP 2:1892 (1851), p. 340.

41. See chapter 10 for further discussion.

42. Kant, *Critique of Practical Reason*, pp. 28–29, 34–35, 96, 113.

43. Løgstrup demeans it because it seems to place the emphasis on the self again, but this is exactly the point of the shift Christ makes in answering the Pharisee's question: Christ turns the question back on him.

44. JP 3:2434 (1851), p. 47.

45. Again, Kierkegaard is following Luther's lead when in "Treatise on Good Works," Luther points specifically to this verse in Matthew 25 (p. 71).

46. Luther writes: "In this faith all works become equal . . . for the works are acceptable not for their own sake but because of faith, which is always the same and lives and works in each and every work without distinction" (ibid., p. 26).

47. Since there is no question here of the referential opacity of propositional attitudes, we can simply apply the law of transitivity: If X does A and A = B, then X does B.

48. Of course, when the neighbor "stands by himself," he does so as we all do— "through God's help" (WL, p. 278).

49. Løgstrup reads Kierkegaard as putting them in opposition in that "the effort to help the loved one to love God is more important than to fulfill the loved one's most burning wish"; Løgstrup then adds what he thinks is obviously true—that "being helped to love God is not among the loved one's wishes" (SA, p. 223).

50. EO 2, p. 245.

51. Danish *Forbillede* ("prototype"); *Efterfølgelse* ("imitation"). JP 2:1908 (1852), p. 352. "The doctrine of the prototype encompasses everything"—that is, it encompasses both the continual need for striving to imitate along with the impossibility of doing so without grace [JP 2:1857 (1849), p. 322].

52. JP 2:1929 (1854), p. 367.

53. JP 2:1858 (1849), pp. 322–23.

54. JP 1:347 (1849), p. 145.

55. JP 2:1841 (1847), p. 317.

56. JP 2:1902 (1851), p. 347; JP 2:1904 (1851), p. 349.

57. JP 2:1906 (1851), p. 351. "Earnestness lies specifically in the ethical, and if the ethical is taken away and, for example, Christ is made the ideal . . . this is taking him in vain" [JP 2:1853 (1849), p. 320].

58. Løgstrup, SA, p. 225.

59. JP 2:1939 (1854), p. 372.

60. JP 2:1848 (1848), p. 319.

61. JP 2:1884 (1850), p. 337. The *Journals and Papers* contain a complex counterweight to this ability to do what Christ did—namely, a view of Christianity as "superhuman"; a view of imitation as something of which Kierkegaard is "incapable," with the prototype only a source of humiliation; and a view of the ethical as the "extraordinary" [JP 2:1844 (1848), p. 318; JP 2:1899 (1851), p. 344; JP 2:1901 (1851), pp. 345–46].

62. Løgstrup writes that if hate or lack of understanding "fails to arise, what is Christian is missing" (SA, p. 222), but we saw in the earlier section on "hate" that for Kierkegaard opposition is not inevitable, although when it occurs there is an essential connection; perhaps this is why Løgstrup switches from the language of "guarantee" to the periodic admission that love must be willing to be hated (pp. 222, 224). Moreover, Løgstrup does not do justice to the tenth deliberation on which he so heavily relies: he focuses on the thought that one can do nothing, whereas Kierkegaard insists that self-denial brings us to the realization that—at the same time—God is our Omnipotent cohelper.

63. "Dialogue," FF, p. 24; Levinas insists on the "full importance of my fellow human being's need for *food* and *drink*" (Foreword, PN, p. 6). Peperzak notes that "from Levinas's perspective, the satisfaction of human needs is necessarily associated with the fulfillment of our obligations, because I cannot serve the Other concretely without offering the Other a meal, safety, a house, work, education, and sympathy. . . . I cannot be for-the-Other if I do not enjoy the world. But also: the other cannot be served unless I know her needs and at least try to provide food and clothes, etc." (*Beyond: The Philosophy of Emmanuel Levinas*, p. 200).

CHAPTER 6

1. This criticism also derives from Kierkegaard's stress on equality (see chapter 4).

2. FT, p. 39; this marks the incommensurability between the interior and exterior (p. 69).

3. It is generally recognized that the Danish for "conscience" (*Samvittighed*), like the English, implies a co-knowing, a con-science.

4. Kierkegaard writes that "my possible ethical significance is unconditionally linked to the category the *single individual*" (PV, Supplement, "The Single Individual," p. 119, n. 2).

5. Imbrosciano suggests that Kierkegaard's use of the term bears the "Biblically oriented meaning" of *hagios*, the holy, purified "person of outstanding integrity or character, together with a great sense of personal autonomy" ("Kierkegaard's 'Individual'," pp. 444–45).

6. Buber, "The Question to the Single One"; for a sustained and convincing defense of Kierkegaard's position in relation to Buber's critique of this essay, see Perkins, "Buber and Kierkegaard."

7. PV, Supplement, pp. 106–112, n. 1.

8. Westphal, *Kierkegaard's Critique of Reason and Society,* especially pp. 43–44.

9. "Purity."

10. Ibid., p. 129, emphasis mine.

11. Ibid., p. 137.

12. Ibid., pp. 130–31.

13. Ibid., 132.

14. Ibid., p. 139.

15. Ibid., p. 131.

16. Ibid., p. 137.

17. Ibid., p. 134.

18. EI, p. 100; Levinas adds: "Responsibility is what is incumbent on me exclusively, and what *humanly,* I cannot refuse . . . I am I in the sole measure that I am responsible, a non-interchangeable I. I can substitute myself for everyone, but no one can substitute himself for me" (p. 101).

19. Levinas, "Kierkegaard: Existence and Ethics," PN, p. 68; in fact, he attributes this to Kierkegaard.

20. See the fine account of the importance of special relations by Purvis in "Mothers, Neighbors and Strangers"; the model of interested yet unselfish caring she develops is, however, Kierkegaard's own understanding of what the story of the Samaritan recommends.

21. George, "Something Anti-Social about *Works of Love,* "p. 74.

22. Quinn, "Kierkegaard's Christian Ethics," p. 361.

23. Outka, *Agape,* p. 19.

24. Kierkegaard suggests that "such indifference is comparable to someone's going up to another and saying, 'I don't care about you,' to which the other might answer, 'Then why bother to tell me!'" (WL, p. 145).

25. "Purity," p. 129.

26. He says repeatedly that the relationship between husband and wife is the most "intimate," humanly speaking (WL, pp. 151–52).

27. Dilman's valuable two chapters in *Love: Its Forms, Dimensions and Paradoxes* press this question, especially pp. 189–97.

28. "The heart bound infinitely to God has a prior history and therefore understands that erotic love and friendship are only an interlude, a contribution to this, the one and only history of love, the first and last" (WL, pp. 149–50).

29. It is not a "more explicit definition" of pagan love (WL, p. 142).

30. For more detail, see Green and Ellis, "Erotic Love in the Religious Existence-Sphere."

CHAPTER 7

1. In fact, this is precisely the deliberation I would recommend as a starting point for new readers to *Works of Love;* coupling 1:IV and 2:IV ("Love Does Not Seek Its Own") provides an entry into *Works of Love* that will engage the reader enough to want to go back to the beginning, and although these deliberations need to be contextualized by the deliberations on the love commandment as duty, it seems easier to begin there than to begin with the second deliberation, which will also need to be contextualized.

2. Pieper notes that the Russian language "has a word (*lubovatsia*) that seems to mean

approximately 'to love with the eyes': a form of loving that becomes a reality through seeing" (*Faith, Hope, Love,* p. 161).

3. JP 3:2403 (1847), p. 38.

4. JP 1:943 (1847), p. 413.

5. Müller, *Kierkegaard's "Works of Love": Christian Ethics and the Maieutic Ideal,* p. 33.

6. Kirmmse, *Kierkegaard in Golden Age Denmark,* p. 312.

7. Fendt asks: "How does one form a heart? Skip from our present textual locus in Chapter One to Part [Series] Two: believe all things, hope all things, seek not your own . . . every chapter of the first part seeks to drive a reader to embrace the second. Structured like a good Protestant sermon, the first part takes many approaches to the law, a multiplicity of attempts to capture each individual in one way or another. And this capture by the law, however it occurs in an individual case, leads its hearer or reader to realize her utter need for the second part: the good news" (*Works of Love? Reflections on Works of Love,* pp. 45–46). He adds: "The movement of *Works of Love* . . . chas[es] a reader from Law to Gospel" (p. 50); the "logic of the book moves the reader to realize her absolute incapacity, while at the same time the rhetoric fires her desire to have a such a heart as is commanded" (p. 52).

8. Johansen, "The Problem of Knowledge in the Ethics of Kierkegaard's *Works of Love,"* pp. 57–58.

9. Lincoln, "Ausserung: Studien zum Handlungsbegriff in Søren Kierekgaards *Die Taten der Liebe."*

10. JP 5:5996 (1847), p. 374.

11. Levinas usually discusses an aural situation (hearing the command, the call of the other, or being "deaf to the Other"); nevertheless he says that "already *of itself* ethics is an 'optics,'" "ethics is the spiritual optics," and "'vision' here coincides with this work of justice" (TI, pp. 134, 29, 78). He notes, however, that "it is a 'vision' without image, bereft of the synoptic and totalizing objectifying virtues of vision" (p. 23).

12. See also WL, pp. 164, 69, 97.

13. Although it is a case of ethical vision, it is a vision related to the deep embeddedness of our needs rather than some peculiar "perception."

14. EUD, p. 59.

15. EUD, pp. 60–61. He notes that love's blindness is not an imperfection "since only when love had won a place in his soul, only then did he become blind, and then became more and more blind as love became victorious within him" (EUD, p. 59).

16. See my *Transforming Vision.* Judge William also provides an anticipation of the position in *Works of Love* when he challenges the view that love makes one blind, claiming instead that it is "an absolute awakening, an absolute intuiting" (or beholding) (EO 2, p. 42).

17. Kierkegaard speaks often of "illusion" (e.g., WL, pp. 162–63, 171; PV, pp. 41–54).

18. Grøn, "Kærlighedens gerninger og anerkendelsens dialektik," pp. 261–70; see also "The Dialectic of Recognition in *Works of Love,"* pp. 147–57. Grøn also introduces the idea of an ethic of vision in his "Kierkegaards 'zweite' Ethik," pp. 358–68.

19. Grøn, "Dialectic of Recognition," p. 150.

20. See WL, pp. 36, 182–86, 284, 286; see my discussion of "comparison" in chapter 5.

21. See my "Equality, Impartiality, and Moral Blindness in Kierkegaards *Works of Love."*

22. Hucker, "'Who Is My Neighbor?' A Study in the Ethics of Love and Preference," p. 151.

23. Kierkegaard writes that "the neighbor is the person who is nearer to you than anyone else" and that "the Levite and the priest were in a stricter sense the victim's neighbor, but they wished to ignore it" (WL, pp. 21–22).

24. It is worth noting here that Levinas would argue that there is never any one who

is not in need—we are all vulnerable to death, and so always in need of help in preserving ourselves.

25. Derrida, *The Gift of Death*.

26. Levinas criticizes the account in FT ("A Propos of 'Kierkegaard Vivant,'" PN, pp. 76–77).

27. Derrida, *Gift of Death*, pp. 67, 64; it is "a responsibility that doesn't keep account or give an account, neither to man, to humans, to society, to one's fellows, or to one's own. Such a responsibility keeps its secret" (p. 62).

28. Ibid., p. 69.

29. Ibid., p. 70. "There is no language, no reason, no generality or mediation to justify this ultimate responsibility which leads me to absolute sacrifice; absolute sacrifice that is not the sacrifice of irresponsibility on the altar of responsibility, but the sacrifice of the most imperative duty (that which binds me to the other as a singularity in general) in favor of another absolutely imperative duty binding me to every other" (p. 71); "absolute duty towards the unique one means . . . responding where there is no reason to be asked for or to be given" (p. 72).

30. Ibid., p. 68.

31. Ibid., p. 78.

32. See "Love Hides a Multitude of Sins" (WL, 2:V).

33. cummings, *Six Non-Lectures*, p. 11.

34. WL, p. 174; emphasis mine; see also pp. 157–58.

35. See chapter 9.

36. See chapter 14.

37. This is a version of love's faithfulness; see also chapter 15, section II.

38. Buber, Appendix, "Dialogue between Martin Buber and Carl R. Rogers," p. 182.

39. For example, Veatch ("Modern Ethics, Teleology, and Love of Self") and Purvis ("Mothers, Neighbors, and Strangers").

40. This refers back to my earlier discussion of special relations and "one kind of love" (chapter 6) and ahead to the discussion of love's ways of upbuilding (chapter 9).

41. For example, Adorno, George, and Mackey (see bibliography).

42. This has been my own tendency in the past, given my objections to essentialist accounts of human nature (see my "Kierkegaardian Imagination and the Feminine").

43. Adorno, "On Kierkegaard's Doctrine of Love," pp. 418–19; Hucker, "Who Is My Neighbor?" p. 52.

44. Walsh, *Living Poetically*, pp. 251–66. I am trying to develop the sensitive work of Walsh, Andic, and others by showing in detail why the positive assessment of difference we find in *Works of Love* is not an empty assertion.

45. Walsh, "Forming the Heart," p. 241.

46. Andic challenges the opposition between sameness and individualization; he suggests that what is the same, our "humanity" the "image of God," or "conscience," is precisely what individualizes each person because it is a "responsive" "openness" rather than a static image ("Is Love of Neighbour the Love of an Individual?" pp. 116–17).

47. For a discussion of the aural metaphor in other writings, see Viallaneix, "Søren Kierkegaard."

CHAPTER 8

1. Gasché, "Heliocentric Exchange," in Schrift, *The Logic of the Gift*, p. 115.

2. Emerson, "Gifts" (*Essays*, second series, 1844), cited ibid., p. 25.

3. Levinas, "Trace," p. 351.

4. Luther, "Treatise on Good Works," p. 106 (hereafter TGW).

5. Ibid., p. 109; emphasis mine.

6. Luther also sees the debt to love one another as "a debt which is never paid, but rather must continue to be paid forever" ("Lectures on Romans," p. 111).

7. See also WL, p. 134.

8. "Even if it were true, by way of comparison to love more than all other people is—not to love" (WL, p. 184).

9. JP 1:480 (1848), pp. 189–90.

10. It is "impossible to fulfill; such an enormous inflation of love can only lower its value, not get rid of the difficulty" (*Civilization and Its Discontents*, pp. 101–2); Freud's fifth chapter argues that love must be discriminating or it does an injustice to its object, that not all people are worthy of love, and that love must be deserved because it is valuable and imposes sacrifice on me.

11. JP 1:993 (1851), p. 433.

12. "My Position as a Religious Author in 'Christendom' and My Strategy," PV, p. 16.

13. JP 2:1484 (1851), p. 173.

14. See especially chapter 17, section II.

15. JP 2:1884 (1850), p. 337; Kierkegaard's discussion of "Christ the Prototype" in JFY illuminates this theme (Sect. II, especially p. 159).

16. JP 2:1121 (1847), p. 10.

17. JP 2:1475 (1849), pp. 166–67.

18. Ibid.

19. JP 3:2428 (1849), p. 45.

20. PV, p. 49.

21. JP 2:1939 (1854), p. 372; PC develops this theme; see also JP 2:1848 (1848), p. 319.

22. JP 2:1859 (1849), p. 323.

23. It should be clear that we are speaking of the possibility of imitating Christ in his human nature, which Kierkegaard sees, strictly speaking, as the same as ours.

24. Danish *Handling*.

25. Danish *Opgave;* there are repeated references to "task" (WL, pp. 177, 188, 189).

26. JP 1:417 (1835), p. 170.

27. JP 1:993 (1851), p. 433.

28. Kant, *Critique of Practical Reason*, pp. 127–28.

29. JP 2:1489 (1852), pp. 176–77.

30. Ibid. "This does not mean that one is to sneak out of self-denial, no, no. But only that it is not under penalty, which is what makes self-denial so hard and agitates the mind" [JP 2:1490 (1852), p. 177].

31. Levinas, "Kierkegaard: Existence and Ethics," PN, p. 74; also in "Trace," p. 353, and "God and Philosophy," BPW, p. 143.

32. "This passion is abolute in that it takes hold without any a priori," OB, p. 102; see pp. 117, 128.

33. Levinas, OB, p. 113.

34. "Ethics as First Philosophy," LR, p. 84.

35. OB, p. 125. The notion of "gratuity" brings to mind how Kierkegaard, too, speaks of love (WL, p. 242), as a "gift" or "present" (*Forœring*) as contrasted with payment.

36. OB, pp. 125, 124.

37. "God and Philosophy," BPW, pp. 144–45.

38. Ibid., p. 144.

39. EI, p. 105.

40. Ibid.

41. "Questions and Answers," GWM, p. 81; see also his reference to "the simple 'After you, sir'" (OB, p. 117).

42. Kant, *Critique of Practical Reason*, p. 114.

43. For a different perspective on this question, see Marino, "Kierkegaard Contra Freud," pp. 129–44.

44. CUP, especially Pt. Two, Sect. II.

45. Adams, "Kierkegaard's Arguments against Objective Reasoning," pp. 38–39. Even if this were Climacus's understanding of the implications of infinite passion, Adams's objection is off the mark in a way not untypical of analytic philosophers: his reason for doubting "that any human being could have a passion of this sort" is that he doubts "that one could make a sacrifice so great that a greater could not be made, or have a (nonzero) chance of success so small that a smaller could not be had."

46. Ibid., p. 39.

47. PC, p. 67. It may be that the author Climacus did not appreciate the possibility that the author Anti-Climacus did, but it is at any rate an understanding that can be used in Kierkegaard's defense.

48. Ironically, it looks as if this requires them to speak differently about "differences." Levinas warns against reducing the different to the same, whereas Kierkegaard's position includes a reminder to close one's eyes to differences precisely as a way of allowing the other to stand without reduction. In the end, however, Kierkegaard recommends a loving attention to and cultivation of the other's distinctiveness.

49. For example, Kierkegaard's appreciation of "persecuted truth" and the limits of "triumphant truth" is congenial with Levinas's subordination of ontology and system to practice and lived life ("Kierkegaard: Existence and Ethics" and "A Propos of 'Kierkegaard Vivant,'" PN; "Enigma and Phenomena," BPW. Westphal presents a valuable summary of similarities between them in "Levinas, Kierkegaard, and the Theological Task," Sect. I.

50. See "A Propos of 'Kierkegaard Vivant,'" PN, pp. 76–77, for Levinas's critique of the implications of the presentation of the Abraham story in *Fear and Trembling*. See TI, pp. 40, 305, for other evaluations of Kierkegaard by Levinas.

51. See Westphal, "Commanded Love and Divine Transcendence in Levinas and Kierkegaard."

52. On the question of the authority for the demand, the issue between them is more complicated; see Evans, "Authority and Transcendence in *Works of Love.*"

53. See also WL, pp. 58–59.

54. See chapter 5, section III, C.

55. The first question is put to Levinas by Nemo (EI, p. 88).

56. Outka, *Agape*, p. 21.

57. For the sense in which we ought to construe "fulfillment" of the command, see this chapter, section IV.

58. Levinas, "Questions and Answers," GCM, p. 83; "Dialogue," FF, p. 31.

59. TI, p. 247.

60. "Ethics as First Philosophy," LR, p. 85.

61. OB, Chap. IV; also in "Substitution," BPW.

62. Obviously there is a danger of arrogance here, but still there will be times when our best judgment, all things considered, is that X is harmful, and although the judgment is fallible, it would be irresponsible not to follow it.

63. In a draft note that clarifies the text, he writes: "The fact that other men want to exempt you from having duties . . . does not exempt you. It is by no means love to indulge human weakness" [JP 1:944 (1847), p. 414]; he also notes that he is concerned with tracking down illusions (WL, Supplement, p. 440). Of course Kierkegaard reminds us that human judgment must defer to God's judgment about what counts as such a weakness.

64. "Give your gift, keep an eye on it, and even though you yourself are not to blame for it, if you see that the needy one is being led into temptation, then come with the ad-

monition, direct him to God, or preferably abstain entirely from giving to him; in all the prolixity of philanthropy that enables you to rejoice in your wealth, do not forget that it is better and more blessed and infinitely more important to save a soul" ("Every Good and Perfect Gift," EUD, p. 147). Kierkegaard earlier makes the distinction between the intrinsic good of the gift and the way in which it might be used by the recipient—a good gift may be used in a harmful way (p. 39).

65. Indeed, he asks, "How then could your love become the fulfilling of the Law?" if you refrained from loving anyone (WL, p. 129).

66. JP 3:2497 (1849), p. 74.

67. Levinas, TI, p. 89.

68. Ricoeur, *Oneself as Another*, pp. 179, 181, 204; these capacities are "the initiative of acting, choice on the basis of reasons, estimating and evaluating the goals of action."

69. Ibid., p. 168. It is interesting to note that Kierkegaard's version would translate into "loving another as oneself," in contrast to Ricoeur's formulation of "loving oneself as another."

70. Ibid., pp. 189, 138.

71. Levinas, OB, p. 128.

72. "Instead of destroying the *I*, the putting in question binds it to the Other in an incomparable, unique manner" (Levinas, "Kierkegaard: Existence and Ethics," PN, p. 73).

73. "Foreword," PN, pp. 5–6; Levinas adds: "The full importance of my fellow human being's need for *food* and *drink*—all philanthropic mystification aside—bursts forth from the serenity of the categories and commands them."

74. OB, p. 109.

75. Ibid., pp. 108, 115, 117.

76. Levinas, "Kierkegaard: Existence and Ethics," PN, pp. 74, 73; emphasis mine. Indeed, "responsibility confirms the I in its ipseity, in its central place within being, as a supporter of the universe" ("Transcendence and Height," BPW, p. 18).

77. Levinas, OB, p. 127; he even says: "One is for the other what the other is for oneself. . . . The other is known through sympathy, as another (my)self, as the alter ego" (TIME, pp. 82–83).

78. Outka (*Agape*, p. 21) suggests that Kierkegaard considers this rationale only "in part"; I am arguing that it is centrally important for him.

79. I am grateful to Peter Ochs for this suggestion.

80. This is where the issue of resistance to the exploitation of another turns into the issue of restraint or even punishment of another; both restraint and punishment are legitimized.

81. Outka (*Agape*, p. 21) suggests that he "virtually ignores" this dimension.

82. Levinas, "Questions and Answers," GCM, p. 82.

83. OB, p. 128.

CHAPTER 9

1. For further discussion of metaphor and religious language, see chapter 12, section I.

2. See WL, p. 13.

3. See WL, p. 295.

4. Walsh develops this idea in her excellent and detailed essay "Forming the Heart," pp. 234–56.

5. See Chapter 10.

6. Søltoft ("To Let Oneself Be Upbuilt," p. 20) cites this passage from the *Pap.* VIII, 2, p. 296.

7. Pieper, *Faith, Hope, Love*, pp. 171–72.

8. Ibid., p. 174. This is not, of course, to license infantilism but rather, for Kierkegaard, to remind us of what we owe to the other.

9. Ricoeur, *Oneself as Another*, p. 189.

10. Søltoft ("To Let Oneself be Upbuilt," p. 3) argues that the mutually upbuilding relationship is a form of indirect communication without deception, a "*double* dialogical relation"; she suggests that the need that we all have "implicates both the receiver and the communicator."

11. This subject will be considered again in chapter 15.

12. "If a temple is to be erected, *a temple must be destroyed*" (Nietzsche, *On the Genealogy of Morals*, Essay II, Sect. 24).

13. Søltoft ("To Let Oneself be Upbuilt," p. 11.) points to the *Christian Discourses* for Kierkegaard's answer to the question of what is it to let oneself be built up: "The first answer to this is what the upbuilding is at first: it is the *terrifying*" and "the terrifying is that there is sin, and the magnitude of the terror in the inwardness of guilt-consciousness is proportionate to the dimension of the upbuilding" (CD, p. 96).

14. James, "The Will to Believe," pp. 26–27.

15. Nietzsche (*Daybreak*, Bk. V, Sect. 429) writes: "If mankind does not perish of a *passion* it will perish of a *weakness*: which do you prefer?"

16. *Summa Theologiae*, II-II, Q.60.5.4.

17. Aquinas adds: "And though we may judge falsely, our judgment in thinking well of another pertains to our good feeling and not to the evil of the intellect."

18. James ("Will to Believe," p. 17) suggests: "We must know the truth" and "We must avoid error" are "not two ways of stating an identical commandment, they are two separable laws," which dictate two different strategies for believing.

19. Roberts points to this as an example of a grammatical remark, as part of his Wittgensteinian suggestion that "*Works of Love* be read as a grammar book, a collection of rules for the use of the word 'love' in the context of the Christian way of life, and thus of rules governing the Christian concept of love, specifying what does and does not count as Christian love" ("Kierkegaard, Wittgenstein, and a Method of 'Virtue Ethics'," pp. 152, 155).

20. He writes that spiritually only suicide is possible (WL, p. 333).

21. See also CUP, pp. 149, 423–25, 427–29.

22. SUD, p. 167.

23. Meilaender notes the danger of Stoicism more generally in *Works of Love*; see *Friendship: A Study in Theological Ethics*, p. 42.

24. Meilaender (ibid, p. 43) called my attention to this mitigating factor.

25. See chapter 13.

26. See my *Transforming Vision* for a detailed account of these positive appreciations of ethical uses of imagination.

27. Kierkegaard later identified himself publicly with this particular pseudonym, in a newspaper piece entitled "For the new edition of *Practice in Christianity*" (1855): "If it were to come out now, now when both pious consideration for the late bishop has lapsed and I have convinced myself, also by having this book come out the first time, that Christianly the established order is indefensible, it would be altered as follows: it would not be by a pseudonym but by me" (MLW, p. 69).

28. SUD, p. 38.

29. Kant, General Observation," *Religion within the Limits of Reason Alone*, pp. 40–49.

30. SUD, p. 39.

31. The object of belief is "the being of God," but Anti-Climacus explains that "since everything is possible for God, then God is this—that everything is possible. . . . For prayer there must be a God, a self—and possibility—or a self and possibility in a pregnant sense, because the being of God means that everything is possible, or that

everything is possible means the being of God." "Faith is essentially this—to hold fast to possibility" [JP 2:1126 (1848), p. 13].

32. L, p. 262; he notes that "in ordinary speech we often call something hope that is not hope at all but a wish, a longing, a longing expectation now of one thing, now of another" (pp. 250–51).

33. "Hope is not implicit in possibility as a matter of course, because in possibility there can also be fear" (WL, p. 253).

34. Luther put under the rubric of "murder" all the ways in which our hand, heart, and thoughts can kill another ("Sixth Sunday after Trinity," *Sermons of Martin Luther*, pp. 170–71).

35. Although love does not demand "repayment" love, it welcomes and enjoys love that is not given as repayment; our first response is appropriately "joy over being loved" [JP 2:1886 (1850), p. 338].

36. That *Works of Love* presupposes love in us does not contradict the assumption, implied by the term "deliberation," that we do not "know essentially what love is"; the first is an assumption with ontological implications, the second with epistemological implications.

CHAPTER 10

1. "Love is a revolution, the most profound of all, but the most blessed!" (WL, p. 265); note that he fully affirms the ordered world of "justice."

2. See chapters 11 and 13.

3. It just won't be a relationship in which the 'like for like' is a tit for tat (WL, p. 269).

4. He insists that in human relationships a "joy over being loved" should precede any attempt to please the other [JP 2:1886 (1850), p. 338]. Kierkegaard does not say that ingratitude, mockery, and lack of appreciation are proofs or guarantees of self-denial; in 2:IV he merely says that they will never be enough to bring the true lover to capitulate to the need to have a 'mine' in contrast to 'yours.'

5. He writes that "the one who loves, receives what he gives" (WL, p. 281); "I myself receive what I give to another" (p. 282).

6. Kierkegaard repeats this phrase again on p. 362.

7. See chapters 2-7

8. See chapter 5, Section IV, B, 4, and chapter 16, section IV.

9. Luther makes this point repeatedly ("Treatise on Good Works," pp. 24, 33, 40, 45, 85–86, 99, 102); for example, he notes that if parents take care of their children, "they will indeed have their hands full of good works. For what are the hungry, the thirsty, the naked, the sick, the alien if not the souls of your own children?" He goes on to ask: "What use is it if they fast themselves to death, pray, go on pilgrimages, and do all manner of good works?" but fail to take care of the children in their trust (p. 85–86). "If this is what God wants . . . of what use is it then for us to run around performing great works which are not commanded, and to neglect [the works of the commandment]?" (p. 102).

10. JP 2:1251 (1846), pp. 62–63.

11. Matthis ("Kierkegaard and the Problem of the Social Other," pp. 427–31) takes this journal passage to explain the ethical rationale for Kierkegaard's rejection of the social (human) other—that is, only God can relate to us without infringing on our freedom; he argues that although Kierkegaard often inclines toward including the social other, his own position on freedom precludes it.

12. These recall the parallel notions of welcome and hospitality in Levinas's thought; see Dooley, "The Politics of Exodus: Kierkegaard, Derrida, and Levinas, on 'Hospitality'."

13. He repeats that love "gives in precisely such a way that it looks as if the gift were

the recipient's property" (WL, p. 278); both of these formulations are given as explanations of what it means to say "love does not seek its own."

14. We should humble ourselves in giving gifts (WL, pp. 145, 146, 149–50, 157).

15. Note that the little discussion on the top of p. 275 about the man's family thanking his benefactor is mistranslated; it should read as follows: "He and his family and all of them together honor and praise me as his greatest benefactor for having in love made him dependent upon me, or—yes, it is strange, they express their gratitude in an utterly meaningless way, since instead of saying that I have made him dependent [*afhaengig*] on me, they declare that I have helped him to stand by himself " (WL, p. 275; SV 9–10, p. 262).

16. See this chapter, section II.

17. It is interesting to see the same sort of message in Kant (*The Doctrine of Virtue*, Sect. 31, p. 121), who writes about the duty of beneficence: "He must also carefully avoid any appearance of intending to put the other under obligation, for if he showed such an intention (thereby humbling the other in his own eyes) he would not be extending true beneficence. Rather he must make it felt that he is himself obliged by the other's acceptance or honoured by it, hence that the duty is merely something that he owes. But it is still better if he can practice his beneficence in complete secrecy."

18. I am suggesting that Kierkegaard is not himself committed by this phrasing to the idea that what we give is in fact a 'gift'; if it is, it is so only in scare quotes.

19. Kierkegaard hints at this aspect of giving to another without in any way harming the other by reference to the Divine Giver since God prevents the annihilating recognition of our nothingness, which would only harm us (WL, p. 271).

20. God gives the condition (WL, pp. 134, 137).

21. "Christianity equally believes that in the external sense the richest person and the poorest can give equally much, that is, equally little, because riches, of course, are a gift from God" (WL, Supplement, p. 434).

22. Kierkegaard indicates that helping another can be done anonymously without being done lovingly; that is, it can be done with the smile of self-satisfied achievement, which he contrasts with the "fear and trembling" that result from deep "concern" for the other's well-being (WL, p. 277).

23. Luther, "A Short Exposition of the Decalogue, Apostle's Creed, and Lord's Prayer," p. 79; "Treatise on Good Works," p. 109.

24. Kierkegaard is here taking a very Nietzschean approach to the ways in which gifts can be used to manipulate people and put them within our power.

25. When Kierkegaard writes "before God to be oneself," the emphasis is on the "before God" since this is the source and origin of all distinctiveness" (WL, p. 271).

26. See chapter 7, section IV, B.

27. See WL, p. 360.

28. See Schrift, *The Logic of the Gift*; Caputo and Scanlon, *God, the Gift, and Postmodernism*; Hyde. *The Gift*.

29. Although this landscape includes the writings of Bataille and Cixous, I cannot address their contributions here.

30. Levinas also terms it a "movement without return" and a "departure without return" ("Trace," p. 349).

31. TI, p. 75; "God and Philosophy," LR, p. 182. "To recognize the Other is therefore to come to him across a world of possessed things, but at the same time to establish, by gift, community and universality" (TI, p. 76); "if, finally, we recall that this look appeals to my responsibility and consecrates my freedom as responsibility and gift of self" (p. 208). Also see his claim that "suffering signifies in the form of *giving*" (OB, p. 50); also OB, p. 125.

32. "Trace," p. 348.

33. Ibid., pp. 349, 348.

34. Ibid., p. 349.

35. Ibid.

36. Ibid.

37. JP 3:2497 (1849), p. 74; he notes that Christ desired gratitude [JP 2:1518 (1854), p. 190].

38. JP 2:1516 (1851), p. 190.

39. Dooley, "Søren Kierkegaard's Social Philosophy," p. 240 (he is referring to Derrida's *Given Time* and *The Gift of Death*). Dooley also argues elsewhere that "a true understanding of Derrida can be gleaned only by a consideration of the work of that figure in the tradition, whose themes most closely resemble those with which the latter is associated: Søren Kierkegaard" ("Risking Responsibility," p. 140).

40. Derrida, *Given Time: 1. Counterfeit Money*, p. 10; he adds that "if the gift is another name of the impossible, we still think it, we name it, we desire it. We intend it. And this *even if* or *because* or *to the extent that* we never encounter it, we never know it, we never verify it" (p. 29). He says elsewhere that "one might say that a gift that could be recognized as such in the light of day, a gift destined for recognition, would immediately annul itself" (*The Gift of Death*, p. 29).

41. *Given Time*, p. 14.

42. We saw earlier that Levinas, too, fears that we will begin to calculate and focus on what the other gives to (perhaps owes) us in return for some gift we make.

43. Erotic love and friendship are not in this sense a gift; they are rather engagements in which we find ourselves and over which we have less control than we do of a gift. Their very definition seems to include a kind of reciprocity that Kierkegaard does not challenge.

44. JP 2:1121 (1847), p. 10.

CHAPTER II

1. CUP, p. 138; EO 1, p. 3.

2. In the essay entitled "Faith and Knowledge, or the *Reflective Philosophy of Subjectivity* in the complete range of its forms as Kantian, Jacobian, and Fichtean Philosophy," Hegel speaks of the "true identity of the inner and the outer" (p. 58).

3. CUP vol. 1, p. 413; PF, Chaps. 1–2; FT, pp. 68–69.

4. Danish *Fordoblelse*.

5. It is also mentioned in passing in WL, p. 151.

6. For example, "Truth is a redoubling" (CUP, vol. 1, p. 190); for more detail see Andic, "Love's Redoubling and the Eternal Like for Like," and Burgess, "Kierkegaard's Concept of Redoubling and Luther's *Simul Justus*."

7. JP 3:2421 (1849), p. 43.

8. WL, pp. 268, 362

9. This same message is found in *FT* (p. 120): God "sees in secret . . . and counts the tears and forgets nothing."

10. See chapter 9, section III.

11. JP 2:1841 (1847), pp. 316–17.

12. Whittaker, "'Agape' and Self-love," pp. 235–36; the attitude to "craving" in Buddhist ethics may be similar, but obviously differently motivated.

13. This echoes Luther's view of the obligation to the other that comes from acknowledging God's largesse to us ("Treatise on Good Works," pp. 106–9); yet Luther notes that we must not give to scoundrels.

14. Although Kierkegaard here, and in the 1843 and 1851 discourses, takes the actual phrasing of his title from St. Peter's first letter, he follows his goal of elaborating Paul's description of building up since Paul writes that love makes excuses. Luther, too, repeatedly refers to these scriptural recommendations.

15. "Love Will Hide a Multitude of Sins" (hereafter "Love Will Hide"), EUD.

16. "Two Discourses at the Communion on Fridays" (1851), WA.

17. "Love Will Hide," EUD, p. 59.

18. "A Short Exposition of the Decalogue, Apostle's Creed, and Lord's Prayer," pp. 77–79.

19. He points to Christ as "the prototype" (WL, p. 288)—Christ who looked away from the derision and mockery heaped on him, not to spare himself, but so that his glance would not fix his enemies in their hatred, would not make them try to justify themselves by further sinful acts.

20. "Love Will Hide," EUD, p. 63.

21. It is interesting that Kierkegaard uses two examples of children in this discussion—the innocent child in the den of thieves, who will see much but not the sin (WL, pp. 285–86), and the games we play with children in which we pretend not to see what is obviously right in front of our eyes (p. 287).

22. This is similar to Levinas's understanding of justice: justice obtains when there is a third; that is, when I see my neighbor being harmed by a third, I have the right and obligation to prevent that harm if I can. "My 'close relations' or 'my people' are already the others and, for them, I demand justice" (EI, p. 99). "If I am alone with the Other, I owe him everything; but there is someone else . . . thus a necessity to moderate this privilege of the Other; from whence comes justice" (pp. 89–90).

23. In addition to the paradox that Kierkegaard makes explicit concerning what is both seen and not seen, Burgess ("Kierkegaard's Concept of Redoubling," pp. 46–51) examines the tension between the claims that sin is hidden and that it is blotted out (in which case it is not hidden) and suggests that it parallels Luther's uses of the *simul justus et peccator* formulation.

24. Kierkegaard uses two words for forgiviness—*forladelse* and *tilgivelse*—but usually reserves the latter for forgiveness between human beings. This word highlights the way in which forgiving is a kind of giving to another—an actual gift, as opposed to a letting go.

25. At least this is true if we do not take advantage of the artificial assistance of two mirrors.

26. Whittaker, "'Agape' and Self-love," pp. 231–32.

27. Kierkegaard notes that the scriptural citation suggests that a person's love will outweigh or render irrelevant the sins that one has; here the implication is that hiding someone else's sins hides one's own.

28. "Love Will Hide," EUD, pp. 69–78; "The Woman Who Was a Sinner" (1849), in "Three Discourses at the Communion on Fridays; ""The Woman Who Was a Sinner" (1850), in "An Upbuilding Discourse"; "But One Who Is Forgiven Little Loves Little," "Love Will Hide a Multitude of Sins" (written 1849, published 1851), and "Two Discourses at the Communion on Fridays," WA.

29. "Love Will Hide," EUD, p. 77; "Love Will Hide a Multitude of Sins," WA, p. 157.

30. "Two Discourses at the Communion on Fridays" (WA, p. 176).

31. "Love Will Hide," EUD, pp. 72–73.

32. Ibid., pp. 55–68.

33. Ibid., p. 61.

34. Ibid., p. 66.

35. Ibid., p. 58.

36. Ibid., p. 60; one discovers sin when "stinginess lives in the heart, when one gives with one eye and looks with seven to see what one obtains in return" (p. 61).

37. Although most of the communion discourse of 1851 on this theme develops the idea of Christ's love and death as providing the "hiding place" we seek once we recognize our sinfulness, it makes an introductory nod to his treatment in *Works of Love*, emphasizing how by contrast with Christ, the human being derives a "benefit" from forgiving others; that is, "while he lovingly hides a multitude of sins, love in turn does to him what he does to others and covers his sins" (WA, p. 181).

38. "Love Will Hide a Multitude of Sins," WA, p. 181.

39. "Love Will Hide," EUD, p. 66.

CHAPTER 12

1. Chapter 14, "Love's Delight in Reconciliation," addresses in more detail the manner of achieving reconciliation.

2. See chapter 2, section II, B for more detail.

3. See chapter 15, section II, A.

4. "Men den christlige Kjerlighed bliver, og just derfor *er den*" (SV: 9–10, p. 12).

5. González ("Poetics and the 'Being' of Love," p. 133) connects this "emphatical and non-copulative use of the verb 'being' in the third person indicative" with Kierkegaard's discussion of the *Symposium* in *The Concept of Irony*.

6. When Kierkegaard contrasts *Bestaaen* with *Bestandighed,* he aligns the former with what exists, "er til" (SV: 9–10, p. 35).

7. Kierkegaard's claim that despair is to be distinguished from misfortune because despair is a misrelation within the self is in agreement with the picture of despair presented by Anti-Climacus in SUD.

8. Walsh, *Living Poetically*, pp. 15–18.

9. Ibid., p. 179; pp. 167–93 cover this middle period.

10. "Make the test here: forget Christianity for a moment and think of what you ordinarily know as love; call to mind what you read in the poets" (WL, p. 29).

11. Kierkegaard does not distinguish, as Aquinas (*Summa Theologiae* I, Q.13.3, 5, 6) does, between metaphorical and analogical uses of language; for Aquinas, analogy is a literal though not univocal use, whereas metaphor is not literal.

12. Mackey, *Kierkegaard: A Kind of Poet*, p. 269.

13. JP 2:1445 (1854), p. 147.

14. González suggests that "Kierkegaard is inviting us to read, to interpret '*all human speech*' as a poem that breaks against a non-poetic word, a word that is no *longer* poetical" ("Poetics and the 'Being' of Love," p. 132).

15. JP 3:2333 (1854), p. 11.

16. Ibid.

17. I take this to be part of Walsh's point in *Living Poetically*; for another suggestive account of the richness of Kierkegaard's view of the poetic, see González, "Poetics and the 'Being' of Love," pp. 131–41.

18. Walsh, *Living Poetically*, p. 187. She refers to the situation in *Two Ages*, but it holds more generally.

19. This is intriguing given that when Levinas looks at Christianity through Jewish eyes, he sees it as focusing on a twosome, in contrast to the threesome Judaism affirms ("Ideology and Idealism," LR, p. 247).

20. Kierkegaard refers again to dancing in the deliberation on recollecting the dead (2:IX), WL, p. 347. There are references too in PF, pp. 7–8, and FT, p. 41, as well as all the references to the "leap."

21. FT, pp. 35–37.

22. The Christian discourse, "The Expectancy of Faith" (EUD, pp. 7–29), also bears on this deliberation.

23. See chapter 10, section III.

CHAPTER 13

1. Adorno, "On Kierkegaard's Doctrine of Love," pp. 413–29; Adorno also cites the deliberation on recollecting the dead, which I will treat in chapter 15.

2. The reference is to WL, p. 326.

3. Adorno, "On Kierkegaard's Doctrine of Love," p. 422.

4. Ibid., p. 421.

5. Abbreviated versions of this discussion can be found in my "Impotent Mercifulness in *Works of Love*" and in my "Other-worldliness in Kierkegaard's *Works of Love*."

6. Luther, "Treatise on Good Works," p. 109. Kierkegaard's contrast also foreshadows Levinas's suggestion that "*giving* is not the same thing as *giving oneself*" (letter to Buber, March 11, 1963, PN, pp. 37–38).

7. The other obvious one is the conjunction of the fourth deliberation in each series.

8. It is perhaps unexpected to see Kierkegaard drawing attention to the ways in which the disadvantaged could be unloving; however, he clearly feels this is necessary, and he does it in a variety of places in *Works of Love* (see pp. 70, 74, 80, 84, 85).

9. Kierkegaard here anticipates Levinas's (EI, p. 97) insistence that we are responsible whether or not we can do anything for the other.

10. CUP vol. 1, p. 174.

11. The editors of *Works of Love* connect this comment with the journal passage in which Kierkegaard says that neither the eternal nor the temporal can truly be painted or sculpted [JP 1:161 (1847), p. 61].

12. CUP vol. 1, p. 339.

13. Kierkegaard notes earlier that hoping for the other is the best gift when we can do nothing more (WL, p. 258).

14. Kant, *Foundations of the Metaphysics of Morals*, p. 16.

15. Hume, *A Treatise of Human Nature* and *Enquiries Concerning Human Understanding and Concerning the Principles of Morals*.

16. Phillips ("The Christian Concept of Love," p. 321) appeals to Simone Weil's thought on the difficulty of being compassionate: "It is easy enough to give bread to the starving, money to the needy or clothes to the naked. It is not surprising that a person does these things. 'What is surprising,' as Simone Weil says, 'is that he should be capable of doing so with so different a gesture from that with which we buy an object.'"

17. Acton, "The Ethical Importance of Sympathy," p. 66.

18. Ibid., p. 66.

19. Ibid.

20. JP 1:1017 (1850), p. 446; here Kierkegaard uses the Danish word *Sympathie*.

21. Radcliffe, "Compassion and Commanded Love," p. 53.

22. Kant, *The Doctrine of Virtue*, Sect. 34, p. 125.

23. "We have an indirect duty to cultivate the sympathetic natural (aesthetic) feelings in us and to use them as so many means to participating from moral principles and from the feeling appropriate to these principles" (ibid., p. 126).

24. According to Hobbes, the object of every person's voluntary act is "some *Good to himselfe*" (*Leviathan*, Chap. XIV, p. 109). See Veatch ("Modern Ethics, Teleology, and Love of Self") for an interesting discussion of the self-interestedness within altruism.

25. Smith, *The Theory of Moral Sentiments*, Chap. 1, "Of Sympathy," p. 9.

26. Butler "On Compassion," Sermon V, p. 49.

27. I discuss Hume's account at length in "Hume and Imagination: Sympathy and 'the Other.'"

28. Although Hume sounds at first like Butler and Smith, when he suggests that sympathy is "that principle, which takes us so far out of ourselves, as to give us the same pleasure or uneasiness in the characters of others, as if they had a tendency to our own advantage or loss" (*Treatise*, p. 579), he strengthens their view so that it will account for the possibility of loving and esteeming an other person "as different from us" (*Enquiry Concerning Morals*, p. 234).

29. Hume, *Treatise*, p. 589.

30. Ibid., pp. 386, 589.

31. See Cates (*Choosing to Feel*, Pt. III) for an account of compassion that seeks to do justice to all these concerns and is especially useful for the way in which it explores how our desires and beliefs influence what elicits our compassion. Morrison's fascinating and wide-ranging study of empathy, *'I Am You'*, bears on this question.

32. For more on imagination, see Gouwens, *Kierkegaard's Dialectic of the Imagination*.

33. See my *Transforming Vision*.

34. Butler, "On Compassion," Sermon V, pp. 50–53.

35. See Luther's "Lectures on Romans," p. 107.

36. JP 2:1477 (1850), p. 169.

CHAPTER 14

1. JP 2:1208 (1847), p. 46.

2. In January 1847, he writes that despite what people ought to have learned about his "maieutic carefulness," they will "probably bawl out that . . . I know nothing about sociality. The fools! Yet on the other hand I owe it to myself to confess before God that in a certain sense there is some truth in it, only not as people understand it—namely, that continually when I have first presented one aspect clearly and sharply, then the other affirms itself even more strongly. Now I have my theme of the next book. It will be called: Works of Love" (JP 5:5972 (1847), pp. 363–647). For an intriguing way of reading this passage, see Sàez Tajafuerce, "*Works of Love*: Modernity or Antiquity?" pp. 60–71.

3. Writing that "even Luther does not put it together properly" because he undialectically "leaves out the difficulty," Kierkegaard notes that he spoke of this "at the end of part I of *Works of Love*" [JP 3:2502 (1849), p. 75].

4. CUP vol. 1, p. 564.

5. See chapter 8, "Love's Debt."

6. See chapter 10, "Love's Gift."

7. Luther, "Treatise on Good Works," p. 39.

8. Ibid., pp. 42–43.

9. "This sin is more grievous in God's eyes than murder and adultery, but because of its subtlety we do not recognize this wickedness as readily as we do that of murder, for this wickedness is not accomplished in the raw flesh but in the spirit" (Ibid., p. 43).

10. EO 2: Ultimatum.

11. Preface to "Two Discourses at the Communion on Friday," WA, p. 165.

12. *Tilgivelse*.

13. Hosea 6:6.

14. "Toward the Other," NTL, pp. 16–17, 19, 20; I am grateful to Robert Gibbs for his remarks on Levinas's position on forgiveness (Villanova Conference, October 1999).

15. But Kierkegaard acknowledges the paradox: Christ is not truly human if he does not learn something by being reassured (WL, p. 156).

16. See the discussion in chapter 11, section IV.

17. He notes that "it seeks, alluringly and invitingly, to win him!" (WL, p. 342).

18. We see an opening here for a virtue ethics interpretation.

19. JP 2:1207 (1847), p. 46 (the marginal comment is entry 1208).

CHAPTER 15

1. Adorno, "On Kierkegaard's Doctrine of Love," pp. 416, 417, 421.

2. Ibid., pp. 417, 427.

3. Outka (*Agape*, p. 280) notes that this deliberation is a "classic illustration" of Kierkegaard's indifference to response and his tendency to fail to appreciate mutuality in a relation; in an otherwise valuable article, Purvis, ("Mothers, Neighbors, and Strangers," pp. 21, 23) criticizes this deliberation's motif of the graveyard as a school for learning about love.

4. For example, those of Martin Buber, Emmanuel Levinas, and Paul Ricoeur.

5. Although little attention is paid to distinguishing the two terms in such discussions, which is why I will treat them interchangeably, there are some differences.

6. Keeley ("Loving 'No One,' Loving Everyone," pp. 221–25) develops Kierkegaard's distinction between recollecting and remembering.

7. Søltoft ("The Presence of the Absent Neighbor, in *Works of Love*," pp. 122–27) makes a similar point in her insightful discussion of the role of presence and absence in this deliberation.

8. George ("Something Anti-social about *Works of Love*,," p. 80) criticizes this methodological advice, arguing that we cannot understand either dancing or conversation better by such abstraction.

9. See WL, p. 353: "There is so much talk in the world about the necessity for love to be free, that one cannot love as soon as there is the slightest compulsion, that with regard to love there must be no constraint at all. Well, let us see, when it gets down to brass tacks, how it stands with this free love—how the dead are recollected in love, since one who is dead in no way compels anyone."

10. Shakespeare, Sonnet CXVI. For interesting suggestions about Kierkegaard's appropriation of Shakespeare, see Bowen, "Kierkegaard on the Theological Ethics of Love," pp. 30–31.

11. See Keeley "Loving 'No One,'" pp. 219, 224.

12. SV 9–10, p. 331; WL, p. 349.

13. Levinas, EI, p. 98; see also TI, pp. 53, 216, 297, and OB, p. 127.

14. EI, p. 98.

15. It is interesting that at the end of *Otherwise than Being*, Levinas seems to allow that a new kind of reciprocal relation can exist: "[I]t is only thanks to God that, as a subject incomparable with the other, I am approached as an other by the others, that is, 'for myself.' 'Thanks to God' I am another for the others. God is not involved as an alleged interlocutor: the reciprocal relationship binds me to the other man in the trace of transcendence, of illeity" (p. 158).

16. Ibid., p. 126.

17. "Dialogue," FF, p. 31.

18. "What I permit myself to demand of myself is not comparable with what I have the right to demand of the Other. This moral experience, so commonplace, indicates a metaphysical asymmetry: the radical impossibility of seeing oneself from the outside and of speaking in the same sense of oneself and of the others, and consequently the impossibility of totalization" (TI, p. 53). Note that Levinas in other places distinguishes between morality and ethics as follows: "The distinction between the ethical and the moral is very

important here. By morality I mean a series of rules relating to social behavior and civic duty . . . it is ultimately founded on an ethical responsibility towards the other" (Ibid., p. 29).

19. "Paradox," p. 179.

20. "Dialogue," FF, p. 31.

21. OB, p. 125.

22. Levinas, "God and Philosophy," BPW, pp. 144–45.

23. JP 2:1886 (1850), p. 338.

24. TI, p. 214.

25. "Dialogue," FF, p. 24.

26. TI, pp. 279, 291 (where he adds that to see the Other as higher "would be a pure and simple error if the welcome I make him consisted in 'perceiving' a nature").

27. "Transcendence and Height," BPW.

28. "Martin Buber and the Theory of Knowledge," PN, p. 32; one finds the same insistence on dimensions of height in OB, p. 127. See also the interview in which Levinas is asked: "The Other is higher than I am. What do you mean by that?" and responds: "The first word of the face is the 'Thou shalt not kill.' It is an order. There is a commandment in the appearance of the face, as if a master spoke to me. However, at the same time, the face of the Other is destitute; it is the poor for whom I can do all and to whom I owe all. And me, whoever I may be, but as a 'first person,' I am he who finds the resources to respond to the call" (EI, pp. 88–89).

29. "Transcendence and Height," BPW, p. 19.

30. See WL, pp. 265–69.

31. Outka, "Universal Love and Impartiality," pp. 17–72.

32. Such reservations are not limited to the context of theological ethics.

33. See Friedman's "The Practice of Partiality," pp. 822–23, for a discussion of both reasons for vulnerability.

34. Preface, "Two Discourses at the Communion on Fridays," WA, p. 165.

35. I have dealt with this in considering the limits of self-sacrifice in chapter 8, section VIII.

36. Although I cannot do justice to his account here, one could argue that Ricoeur's title—Oneself as Another—betrays the egocentric cast of his model. On the other hand, one could argue that for Ricoeur it is the value we place on another that derivatively gives us value; in that sense it would be a more other-centered ethic than Kierkegaard's.

37. It should be noted that the traits that are said to characterize love (unselfishness, faithfulness, and freedom) are drawn directly from the example of the loving "work of recollecting the dead." The deliberation is describing the loving work of remembering the dead; it is not, as such, a model that could be uncritically imitated in loving the living since the strict parallel for the former would be the loving work of remembering the living.

38. "Just by unconditionally not requiring the slightest reciprocal love, the one who truly loves has taken an unassailable position: he can no more be deceived out of his love than a man can be tricked out of the money he tenders as a gift and gives to someone" (WL, p. 242); there is, of course, the danger of arrogance in this sort of view.

39. JP 2:1886 (1850), p. 338.

40. This recalls his earlier claim that genuine love is not determined by its object, as is the case in erotic love, for the object of genuine love "is without any of the more precise specifications of dissimilarity, which means that this love is recognizable only by love" (WL, p. 66).

41. Adorno ("On Kierkegaard's Doctrine of Love," p. 427) himself recognized that in the very doctrine he so harshly attacked for failing to appreciate reciprocity, a deep ethical insight was present: Kierkegaard describes, he says, "love absolutely void of any

barter, of any 'requital,' and, therefore, the only unmutilated love permitted by our society." Adorno's assessment is particularly interesting in its ambivalence, seeing not only "the worst" but also "the best" of Kierkegaard in his discussion of such love. I have suggested that the best becomes the worst when a test is taken for a condition to be achieved.

CHAPTER 16

1. See chapter 8 (WL, p. 280).
2. Marion, "Christian Philosophy and Charity," p. 471.
3. Ibid., pp. 465–73.
4. Ibid., p. 469.
5. Ibid., p. 471.
6. Ibid., p. 472.
7. Ibid.
8. EO 2, p. 160; the emphasis on transparency (*Gjennemsigtighed*) is also found at pp. 179, 190, 248, 253, 254, 258.
9. This connection between transparency and the identity of inner and outer is brought out by Ake, "'And yet a braver thence doth spring'" p. 102.
10. Not *endelig Forestillung*, but *uendelig Tanke* (WL, p. 360).
11. Descartes, "Third Meditation," pp. 91–108.
12. PF, p. 36; Müller, *Kierkegaard's "Works of Love": Christian Ethics and the Maieutic Ideal*, p. 49, n. 14, makes this connection.
13. PF, p. 39.
14. It has been suggested that Kierkegaard must have in mind the notion of an infinite thinking, a thought whose content rather than whose subject is the infinite; so that when I attempt it, I discover my limits; Ake also considers the notion of the 'self-lover' ("'And yet a braver thence doth spring,'" pp. 98–107).
15. SUD, pp. 14, 82.
16. WL, p. 361; he refers to the selfishness of thinking you are capable (p. 363); this is selfishness because you are not your own, and it is a way of refusing to allow God what is God's.
17. This word, which he uses repeatedly (WL, pp. 362, 363, 364, 365), is literally a tool or appliance, but he gives reason to think of it as a musical instrument: "If you hold only to God, the attack and disparagement and the storm of opposition will help you discover things you otherwise would never discover; they will add new strings to your lyre.—Every man is like an instrument which no doubt can be disturbed and damaged by the world's wretchedness and rudeness—but if you hold to God, it can help you to ever new melody" [JP 4:4596 (1847), p. 374].
18. See my *Tranforming Vision*.
19. It is worth noting that he earlier stipulated that the "world" is equated with "sensuousness" and "selfishness" (WL, p. 52), which means that only that dimension of the world is hated.
20. "The double danger is in encountering opposition precisely where he had expected to find support; thus he has to turn around twice. . . . All self-denial that finds support in the world is not Christian self-denial" (WL, pp. 195–96).
21. Note that deliberations 1:V and 2:X are the two that Løgstrup ("Settling Accounts with Kierkegaard's *Works of Love*") focuses on.
22. Ibid., p. 224.
23. Ibid., p. 200.
24. JP 2:1866 (1850), p. 327; JP 2:1902 (1851), p. 346.
25. JP 2:1904 (1851), p. 348; JP 2:1905 (1851), p. 350. "The mistake of the Middle Ages

was to make asceticism and the like the absolute τεγος. . . . Christ did not teach poverty in and for itself; he taught poverty to enable witnessing to the truth" [JP 2:1893 (1851), p. 341].

26. Luther, "Treatise on Good Works," p. 75.

27. "No human being has the right to think that his sufferings will be atoning or beneficial for others in the sense that he and God alone are aware of it. No, this would make him more than human. No, as a human being he is to let God guide and counsel and even use his reason *and every permissible means to avoid suffering*" [JP 2:1921 (1853), p. 362; emphasis mine]. Kierkegaard notes his agreement with Tauler on imitation: "[R]enunciation of all things is Christian counsel; Christ desires that you do it but does not command it. Nor does he judge every person who does not do it to be no Christian" [JP 2:1844 (1848), p. 318].

28. "Strictly speaking, to be a Christian is: to die (to die to the world)" [JP 2:1899 (1851), p. 344, JP 2:1872 (1850), p. 330].

29. He says earlier that Christianity does not seek to deprive us of the aesthetic (the poetic), just as it does not require of the Christian "that he must not eat ordinary food with others or that he should live apart from other people in the inclosure of separateness"; we cannot, he continues, "live only on the food at the Communion table" (WL, p. 47).

30. Here, too, Kierkegaard retrieves the aesthetic connotations of "the moment" from EO, 2, pp. 179, 201.

31. Løgstrup, "Settling Accounts," p. 230.

CHAPTER 17

1. Luther "Treatise on Good Works," pp. 34–35 (hereafter TGW).

2. Lazareth, "The Christian in Society I," in *Luther's Works*, vol. 44, p. xiii.

3. The editors of *Works of Love* align imperative ethics with the ethics in earlier works (EO 2, "Purity of Heart," and parts of FT) and indicative ethics with the Christian love ethics (WL, p. xii).

4. One might want to qualify the dichotomy between an imperative ethics and an indicative ethics with the introduction of a "subjunctive" ethics, one that in fact relates to the scriptural invitation: "If you love me, keep my commandments" (Brantley Craig reminded me of this formulation).

5. Ricoeur, *Oneself as Another*, p. 351. For Ricoeur this will also turn out to be the difference between an "ethical" sense and a "moral" response.

6. Ricoeur, *Figuring the Sacred*, p. 319.

7. Rosenzweig, *The Star of Redemption*, p. 205. "Love cannot be commanded except by the lover himself" (p. 214); "man loves because God loves and as God loves" (p. 199).

8. Ibid., p. 205.

9. Ricoeur, *Figuring the Sacred*, p. 319. In inverse fashion, he traces the trajectory from invitation or plea to prohibition: 'Thou, love me!' becomes law, and law becomes the prohibition 'Thou shalt not kill' only because "violence taints all the relations of interaction" (*Oneself as Another*, p. 351).

10. Ricoeur, *Figuring the Sacred*, p. 320.

11. Niebuhr, *The Responsible Self*, pp. 47–68.

12. Ibid., pp. 61–65.

13. Andic makes a similar (although not identical) list of implicit and explicit references to the 'like for like,' for the purpose of considering how it is related to the concept of "redoubling" ("Love's Redoubling and the Eternal Like for Like," pp. 14–20).

14. Although it seems not to make his particular point in this passage, he begins: "To him who loves much, much is forgiven."

15. Hall indicates how Christian proposals about agape regularly fail to do justice to Old Testament understandings of agape and the love commandment ("Complicating the Command," pp. 100–5).

16. Timothy Polk, suggesting that "the terminology of offense punctuates *WL*," notes forty-five instances of various forms of the term "offense" (*The Biblical Kierkegaard*, p. 95).

17. One could easily argue that the Jewish law was also an example of both rigor and leniency, because it spelled out both the extent and the limit of legitimate retaliation.

18. For references to the 'like for like' in Augustine's work, see Andic's "Love's Redoubling" p. 11, n.3.

19. TGW, p. 37. Acknowledging with Luther that "the Gospel is not the Law" and that "the Gospel will not save you by rigorousness but by leniency," Kierkegaard gently corrects what he takes to be Luther's one-sided emphasis: "but this leniency will save you, *it will not deceive you; therefore there is rigorousness in it*" (p. 380; emphasis mine).

20. I have discussed this in chapter 15, "Love's Asymmetry."

21. Levinas, EI, p. 98.

22. Like the infamous and oft-cited remark from Kierkegaard's notes on 'the individual' that one should be "careful about becoming involved with 'the others'" (PV, p. 106), such claims seem ripe for criticism, but only if one takes them out of context.

23. For Kierkegaard, the presumption of merit through striving reveals scorn for the Atonement [JP 2: 1469 (1849), p. 163].

24. This topic deserves far more attention than the sketch I provide here.

25. JP 3:2463 (1847), p. 64; this claim is found in the "Ultimatum," the letter from a Jutland pastor that is appended to EO 2.

26. According to the Auction Sales Record of SK's Library, the following works were in Kierkegaard's personal library: Main collection-H: 3–5—Three *Bibel*; 189—*liden Catechismus* (1849) (Kbhv); 225–26—*Tisch-Reden* (Table-Talk), 2 vols. (1745); 283—*Luthers Huuspostil* (in Danish, 1828); 312–16—*Luthers Werke*, 10 vols. Berlin 1840–41; 317–20—*Geist aus Luthers Scriften oder Concordanz* , 4 vols. (1828–31); 634—*Die deutsche Theologie*, mit einer Vorrede (pref) by Martin Luther and Johan Arnd (1839); Appendix 100–4—*Martin Luthers Werke in Auswahl* (selections), 10 vols., Hamburg, 1827–28.

27. PV, p. 17.

28. JP 3:3617 (1853–54), pp. 669, 670. Kierkegaard seems to use the term "Protestantism" and "Lutheranism" interchangeably in these comments, but it is unlikely he would have wanted to lump Lutheranism and Calvinism together.

29. JP 3:2553 (1854), p. 102; JP 2:1877 (1850), p. 334; JP 2:1923 (1853), p. 364.

30. JP 3:2544 (1853–54), p. 96; he also writes: "O, Luther . . . O, you honest man, why did you not suspect how sly we human beings are! Why did you not have eyes in the back of your head so you could have prevented what was going on behind your back!" [JP 2:1904 (1851), p. 349).

31. Luther, TGW, p. 21.

32. Ibid., p. 24.

33. Ibid., pp. 24, 25, 27, 32, 98.

34. Ibid., pp. 25–26.

35. Ibid., p. 29.

36. Ibid., p. 79.

37. In the context of justification and salvation, Luther's concern is to contrast faith with love, but in the different context of the Christian life in society he affirms with Paul and James that faith without love is dead; Gordon Steffey has helped me to appreciate this aspect of Luther's thought, as well as Luther's notion of the "third use of the law."

38. Woolf, the editor of the *Reformation Writings of Martin Luther*, Vol. 1, suggests that "the 'Short Exposition . . . ' gives all the essential, positive instruction of the *Good Works*, and has the advantage that it is even more revealing of Luther's personal religion, and more searching of the reader's conscience" (p. 70). Moreover, "The Freedom of the Christian," also in this volume of *Reformation Writings*, contains a similar message (pp. 371–76).

39. "Lectures on Galatians," p. 4. Luther concedes that although we must continue to distinguish the two kinds of righteousness, the "distinction is easy to speak of," yet "in experience and practice it is the most difficult of all"; "in the hour of death or in other conflicts of conscience these two kinds of righteousness come together more closely than you would wish or ask" (p. 10).

40. Ibid., p. 6; emphasis mine.

41. Ibid., p. 7; emphasis mine. To the question "Then do we do nothing and work nothing in order to obtain this righteousness?" Luther replies: "Nothing at all. For this righteousness means to do nothing, to hear nothing, and to know nothing about the Law or about works but to know and believe only this: that Christ has gone to Father . . . as one who has been made for us wisdom, righteousness, sanctification and redemption from God" (p. 8). This needs to be read, however, in the context of his entire discussion.

42. Ibid., p. 6; emphasis mine.

43. JP 3:2518 (1850), p. 81; JP 3:2543 (1853–54), p. 93.

44. This can be understood in a Pascalian sense, that is, that doing the works might put you in a position and attitude in which you can embrace the gift [JP 3:2543 (1853–54), p. 94].

45. JP 3:2503 (1849), p. 75.

46. JP 3:2503, (1849) p.76; emphasis mine.

47. JP 3:3617 (1853–54), p. 670; Kierkegaard, however, also notes at the same time that breaking out of a monastery does not give one the best "opportunity for seeing with reasonable level-headedness just how much truth lay in the opposite position when it is not overstrained."

48. JP 3:2484 (1849), p. 70; JP 3:2513 (1850), p. 79; for more on this topic, see the discussions of the imitation of Christ (chapter 5, section IV; chapter 8, section V) and of self-denial (chapter 9, section I, E; chapter 16, section IV).

49. "Christianity has never really been more popular than when the Pope stated plainly: If you want to be saved, it will cost 4 marks and 8 shillings and a tip to the priest; if you want to be completely saved, then 5 marks; but that you will be saved is completely guaranteed, and you will get a receipt" [JP 3:2539 (1851), p. 91].

50. "The guilt of the established order is that it has nullified Luther's positive contribution"; it has "taken Luther in vain" [JP 3:2528 (1850), p. 87].

51. JP 3:2527 (1850), p. 87.

52. Ibid.

53. JP 3:2543 (1853–54), p. 95.

54. JP 2:1482 (1851), pp. 170–71.

55. JP 2:1489 (1852), p. 176.

56. P 3:2461 (1846), p. 63; JP 3:2479 (1849), p. 69; JP 1:653 (1847), p. 287; JP 2:1845 (1848), p. 318; JP 3:2476 (1849), p. 68; JP 2:1857 (1849), p. 322.

57. JP 3:2553 (1854), p. 102.

58. P 3:2467 (1848), p. 66; JP 3:2481 (1849), p. 69.

59. JP 3:2541 (1851), p. 92.

60. JP 3:2467 (1848), p. 66; JP 3:2470 (1848), p. 67; JP 3:2474 (1848), p. 68; JP 3:2502 (1849), p. 75; JP 3:2512 (1850), p. 79; JP 3:2521 (1850), p. 83; JP 3:2556 (1855), p. 104.

61. Referring to one of Luther's sermons, Kierkegaard writes that "the way in which

even Luther speaks of the law and gospel is still not the teaching of Christ [because] Luther separates the two: the law and gospel. First the law and then the gospel, which is sheer leniency, etc." [JP 3:2554, (1854), pp. 102–3; JP 3:2551 (1854), p. 102]. Kierkegaard says that Luther interprets it as the wrath of God because he [Luther] believes that "God does not need our love," and God "wants to be loved under the cross and amidst lamentation" [JP 3:2525 (1850), p. 86]. One wonders whether this latter objection is actually in contradiction to Kierkegaard's other objection—that with Luther there is too much emphasis on Gospel.

62. P 3:2467 (1848), p. 66.

63. JP 2:1852 (1849), p. 320.

64. Kierkegaard admitted that "to mention 'works' suggests Catholicism," but "everything that Catholicism has thought up about the meritoriousness of works of course has to be rejected completely" [JP 3:2543 (1853–54), p. 93].

65. JP 2:1480 (1850), pp. 169–70.

66. For example, the position on inwardness in Kierkegaard's writings changes from CUP's true knight of hidden inwardness (p. 508) to the attack on inwardness (PC, pp. 252–53); Stephen Evans uses the terminology of "bridge" (Introduction to Müller, *Kierkegaard's "Works of Love,"* p. viii).

CONCLUSION

1. As examples, I refer the reader to Post, "Communion and True Self-love"; Pope, "Expressive Individualism and True Self-love" and "Love in Contemporary Christian Ethics"; and Hall, "Complicating the Command"; all provide good summaries of the other literature involved in the debate. My unscientific generalization is based on the sort of articles that appear in the *Journal of Religious Ethics* and the proceedings of the Society of Christian Ethics, but current discussions of partiality and impartiality in the literature of moral philosophy seem to cluster in similar ways.

2. Lewis, *The Four Loves*, pp. 1–17.

3. Friedman, "The Practice of Partiality," pp. 828–31.

4. For example, Veatch, "Modern Ethics, Teleology, and Love of Self," especially pp. 54–60, 65–69.

5. JP 2:1121 (1847), p. 10.

6. If you were to see that someone is "no longer worth loving," you would not "really see him (WL, p. 172); indeed, the task is to find the other "lovable," and if we fail we reveal more about ourselves than about the other (pp. 157–59).

7. JP 2:1446 (1854), p. 147.

8. "In God's relationship to the sinner, whom he loves, it is not like this; he does not, after all, love the 99 righteous ones just as much" [JP 3:2473 (1848), p. 67].

9. Although I have suggested that one cannot *uncritically* carry over into WL the position on ethics expressed in CUP, it does seem that the theme of the importance of interestedness and passion to ethics would anticipate and support that in WL.

10. See Friedman, "Practice of Partiality"; she concludes that "by viewing partiality as morally valuable because of what it ultimately contributes to integrity and human fulfillment, and by considering the reality of unequally distributed resources, we are led to a notion that sounds suspiciously like the requirement of moral impartiality" (p. 831).

11. Quinn, "The Divine Command Ethics in Kierkegaard's *Works of Love*," especially pp. 36–37.

12. As I read over my conclusions, I realize that they sound similar to those of Cates (*Choosing to Feel*, pp. 127–207) about Aquinas on certain aspects of special relations and

the scope of the commandment.. The exploration of substantive differences and agreements deserves a closer look.

13. Barrett develops this aspect well in "The Neighbor's Material and Social Well-being in Kierkegaard's *Works of Love*."

14. JP 1:340 (1849), p. 142.

15. CD, pp. 244–45.

bibliography

Acton, H. B. "The Ethical Importance of Sympathy." *Philosophy* 30 (1955): 62–66.

Adams, Robert M. "Autonomy and Theological Ethics." In *The Virtue of Faith and Other Essays in Philosophical Theology*, pp. 123–27. New York: Oxford University Press, 1987.

———. "Divine Command Meta-ethics Modified Again." In *The Virtue of Faith*, pp. 128–43.

———. "Kierkegaard's Arguments against Objective Reasoning." In *The Virtue of Faith*, pp. 25–41.

———. "A Modified Divine Command Theory of Ethical Wrongness." In *The Virtue of Faith*, pp. 97–122.

———. "Pure Love." In *The Virtue of Faith*, pp. 174–92.

Adorno, Theodor W. "On Kierkegaard's Doctrine of Love." *Studies in Philosophy and Social Science* 8 (1939–40): 413–29.

Ainley, Alison. "The Subject of Ethics: Kierkegaard and Feminist Perspectives on an 'Ethical Self.'" *The Oxford Literary Review* 11 (1989): 169–88.

Ake, Stacey Elizabeth. "'And yet a braver thence doth spring': The Heuristic Values of *Works of Love*." In *Kierkegaard Studies 1998*, ed. Niels Jørgen Cappelørn and Hermann Deuser, pp. 93–112. Berlin: de Gruyter, 1998.

Andic, Martin. "Is Love of Neighbour the Love of an Individual?" In *Kierkegaard: The Self in Society*, ed. George Pattison and Steven Shakespeare, pp. 112–24. London: Macmillan, 1998.

———. "Love's Redoubling and the Eternal Like for Like." In *International Kierkegaard Commentary 16*: *Works of Love*, ed. Robert L. Perkins, pp. 9–38. Macon, Ga.: Mercer University Press, 1999.

Andolsen, Barbara Hilkert. "Agape in Feminist Ethics." In *Feminist Theological Ethics: A Reader*, ed. Lois K. Daly, pp. 146–59. Louisville, Ky.: Westminster John Knox Press, 1994.

Aquinas, Thomas. *Summa Theologiae*, trans. Fathers of the English Dominican Province. Benzinger Brothers: 1947; Hypertext Version, New Advent, 1996.

Aristotle. *The Nichomachean Ethics*, trans. Sir David Ross. London: Oxford University Press, 1954.

Barrett, Lee C. "The Neighbor's Material and Social Well-Being in Kierkegaard's *Works of Love*: Does It Matter?" In *International Kierkegaard Commentary 16: Works of Love*, ed. Robert L. Perkins, pp. 137–65. Macon, Ga.: Mercer University Press, 1999.

Barth, Karl. *Church Dogmatics* IV/2, ed. G. W. Bromily and T. F. Torrance. Edinburgh: T. & T. Clark, 1958.

Bonhoeffer, Dietrich. *Letters and Papers from Prison*, ed. Eberhard Bethge. New York: Macmillan, 1971.

Bowen, Gary Starr. "Kierkegaard on the Theological Ethics of Love." *Duke Divinity School Review* 45.1 (1980): 23–32.

Buber, Martin. "Dialogue between Martin Buber and Carl. R. Rogers." In *The Knowledge of Man: A Philosophy of the Interhuman*, ed. Maurice Friedman, pp. 166–84. New York: Harper & Row, [1960] 1965.

———. "The Question to the Single One" and Afterword. In *Between Man and Man*, trans. Ronald Gregor Smith, pp. 40–82. New York: Macmillan, [1936] 1965.

Bultmann, Rudolf. *Jesus and the Word*, trans. Louise Pettibone Smith and Erminie Huntress Lantero. New York: Scribner, 1958.

Burgess, Andrew J. "Kierkegaard's Concept of Redoubling and Luther's *Simul Justus*." In *International Kierkegaard Commentary 16: Works of Love*, ed. Robert L. Perkins, pp. 39–55. Macon, Ga.: Mercer University Press, 1999.

Butler, Joseph. "On Compassion," Sermon V. In *Butler's Fifteen Sermons*, ed. T. A. Roberts. London: SPCK, 1970.

Cappelørn, Niels Jørgen, and Bent Rohde. "Fra Fractur til Palatino: Om udgivelse og tilretteglaeggelse af Søren Kierkegaards Skrifter udgivet af Søren Kierkegaard Forskningscenteret." In *Grafiana 1998: Aarbog for Danmarks Grafiske Museum/Dansk Press Museum*. pp. 76–89. Odense, 1998.

Cappelørn, Niels Jørgen, and Hermann Deuser, eds. *Kierkegaard Studies Yearbook 1998*. Berlin: de Gruyter, 1998.

Caputo, John D., and Michael J. Scanlon, eds. *God, the Gift, and Postmodernism*. Bloomington: Indiana University Press, 1999.

Cates, Diana Fritz. *Choosing to Feel: Virtue, Friendship, and Compassion for Friends*. Notre Dame, Ind.: University of Notre Dame Press, 1997.

Connell, George B., and C. Stephen Evans, eds. *Foundations of Kierkegaard's Vision of Community: Religion, Ethics, and Politics in Kierkegaard*, 2 vols. Atlantic Highlands, N.J.: Humanities Press, 1992.

cummings, e e. *Six Non-Lectures*. New York: Atheneum, 1968.

Derrida, Jacques. *The Gift of Death*, trans. David Wills. Chicago: University of Chicago Press, 1995.

———. *Given Time: 1. Counterfeit Money*, trans. Peggy Kamuf. Chicago: University of Chicago Press, 1992.

Descartes, René. "Third Meditation." In *Discourse on Method and Meditations*, trans. Lawrence J. Lafleur, pp. 91–108. Indianapolis: Bobbs-Merrill, 1960.

Dilman, Ilham. *Love: Its Forms, Dimensions and Paradoxes*. New York: St. Martin's Press, 1998.

Dooley, Mark. "The Politics of Exodus: Derrida, Kierkegaard and Levinas on 'Hospitality.'" In *International Kierkegaard Commentary 16: Works of Love*, ed. Robert L. Perkins, pp. 167–92. Macon, Ga.: Mercer University Press, 1999.

———. "Risking Responsibility: A Politics of the Émigre." In *Kierkegaard: The Self in Society*, ed. George Pattison and Steven Shakespeare, pp. 139–55. London: Macmillan, 1998.

————. "Søren Kierkegaard's Social Philosophy: An Ethics of Responsibility." Ph.D. dissertation, University College, Dublin, 1997.

Dostoyevsky, Fyodor. *The Brothers Karamazov*, trans. David Magarshack. New York: Penguin, 1958.

————. *The Idiot*, trans. Henry Carlisle and Olga Carlisle. New York: Signet Classics, 1969.

Eliot, George. "Evangelical Teaching: Dr. Cumming." In *George Eliot: Selected Writings*, ed. Rosemary Ashton, pp. 138–70. New York: Oxford, [1855] 1992.

Evans, C. Stephen. "Authority and Transcendence in *Works of Love*." In *Kierkegaard Studies 1998*, ed. Niels Jørgen Cappelørn and Hermann Deuser, pp. 23–40. Berlin: de Gruyter, 1998.

Fendt, Gene. *Works of Love? Reflections on* Works of Love. Potomac, Md.: Scripta Humanistica, 1989.

Ferreira, M. Jamie. "Equality, Impartiality, and Moral Blindness in Kierkegaard's *Works of Love*." *Journal of Religious Ethics* 25 (1977): 65–85.

————. "Hume and Imagination: Sympathy and the 'Other.'" *International Philosophical Quarterly* 34.1 (March 1994): 39–57.

————. "Impotent Mercifulness in *Works of Love*." In *Anthropology and Authority in Søren Kierkegaard*, ed. Sven. H. Rossel and Gordon Marino. Amsterdam/Atlanta: Editions Rodopi, 2000.

————. "Kierkegaardian Imagination and the Feminine." *Kierkegaardiana* 16: 79–93.

————. "Moral Blindness and Moral Vision in Kierkegaard's *Works of Love*." *Kierkegaard Revisited: Kierkegaard Studies*, Monograph Series 1, ed. Niels Jørgen Cappelørn and Jon Stewart, pp. 206–22. Berlin: de Gruyter, 1977.

————. "Mutual Responsiveness in Relation: The Challenge of the Ninth Deliberation." In *International Kierkegaard Commentary 16: Works of Love*, ed. Robert L. Perkins, pp. 193–209. Macon, Ga.: Mercer University Press, 1999.

————. "Other-worldliness in Kierkegaard's *Works of Love*." *Philosophical Investigations* 21.1 (1999): 65–79.

————. *Transforming Vision: Imagination and Will in Kierkegaardian Faith*. Oxford: Clarendon Press, 1991.

Feuerbach, Ludwig. *The Essence of Christianity*, trans. George Eliot. Buffalo, N.Y.: Prometheus, 1989.

Frankfurt, Harry G. "Equality as a Moral Ideal." In *The Importance of What We Care About: Philosophical Essays*, pp. 134–58. Cambridge: Cambridge University Press, 1988.

Freud, Sigmund. *Civilization and Its Discontents*, trans. James Strachey. New York: W. W. Norton, 1961.

Friedman, Marilyn. "The Impracticality of Impartiality." *Journal of Philosophy* 86 (1989): 645–56.

————. "The Practice of Partiality." *Ethics* 101 (July 1991): 818–35.

————. "The Social Self and Partiality Debates." In *Feminist Ethics and Politics*, ed. Claudia Card, 161–79. Lawrence: University Press of Kansas, 1999.

George, Peter. "Something Anti-social about *Works of Love*." In *Kierkegaard: The Self in Society*, ed. George Pattison and Steven Shakespeare, pp. 70–81. London: Macmillan, 1998.

González, Darío. "Poetics and the 'Being' of Love." In *Kierkegaard Studies 1998*, ed. Niels Jørgen Cappelørn and Hermann Deuser, pp. 129–46. Berlin: de Gruyter, 1998.

Götke, Povl. "Recent Scandinavian Literature on *Works of Love*." In *Kierkegaard Studies 1998*, ed. Niels Jørgen Cappelørn and Hermann Deuser, pp. 232–44. Berlin: de Gruyter, 1998.

Gottlieb, Roger S. "Kierkegaard's Ethical Individualism." *Monist* 62.3 (July 1979): 351–67.

Gouwens, David J. *Kierkegaard as Religious Thinker.* Cambridge: Cambridge University Press, 1966.

Gouwens, David. "Kierkegaard on the Ethical Imagination." *Journal of Religious Ethics* 10/2 (fall 1982): 204–20.

———. *Kierkegaard's Dialectic of the Imagination.* New York: Peter Lang, 1989.

Green, Ronald. *Kierkegaard and Kant: The Hidden Debt.* Albany: State University of New York Press, 1992.

Green, Ronald M., and Theresa M. Ellis, "Erotic Love in the Religious Existence-Sphere." In *International Kierkegaard Commentary 16: Works of Love,* ed. Robert L. Perkins, pp. 339–67. Macon, Ga.: Mercer University Press, 1999.

Grøn, Arne. "The Dialectic of Recognition in *Works of Love.*" In *Kierkegaard Studies 1998,* ed. Niels Jørgen Cappelørn and Hermann Deuser, pp. 147–57. Berlin: de Gruyter, 1998.

———. "Kærlighedens gerninger og anerkendelsens dialektik." *Dansk Teologisk Tidsskrift* 54.4 (1991): 261–70.

———. "Kierkegaards 'zweite' Ethik." In *Kierkegaard Studies 1998,* ed. Niels Jørgen Cappelørn and Hermann Deuser, pp. 358–68. Berlin: de Gruyter, 1998.

Hall, Amy Laura. "Complicating the Command: *Agape* in Scriptural Context." *Annual of the Society of Christian Ethics* 19 (1999): 97–113.

Hallett, Garth L. *Christian Neighbor-Love: An Assessment of Six Rival Versions.* Washington, D.C.: Georgetown University Press, 1989.

Hanfling, Oswald. "Loving My Neighbour, Loving Myself." *Philosophy* 68 (April 1993): 145–57.

Hannay, Alastair, and Gordon Marino, eds. *The Cambridge Companion to Kierkegaard.* Cambridge: Cambridge University Press, 1998.

Hartshorne, M. Holmes. *Kierkegaard, Godly Deceiver: The Nature and Meaning of His Pseudonymous Writings.* New York: Columbia University Press, 1990.

Hegel, G. W. F. "Faith and Knowledge, Or the *Reflective Philosophy of Subjectivity* in the Complete Range of Its Forms as Kantian, Jacobian, and Fichtean Philosophy." In *Faith and Knowledge,* trans. W. Cerf and H. S. Harris. Albany: State University of New York Press, [1802-3] 1977.

Hobbes, Thomas. *Leviathan.* New York: Dutton, 1950.

Hopkins, Gerard Manley. "The Wreck of the Deutschland." In *A Hopkins Reader,* ed. John Pick, pp. 35–45. Garden City, N.Y.: Image Books, Doubleday, 1966.

Hucker, Bruce M. "'Who Is My Neighbor?' A Study in the Ethics of Love and Preference." Ph.D. dissertation. Princeton Theological Seminary, 1975.

Hume, David. *Enquiries Concerning Human Understanding and Concerning the Principles of Morals,* ed. L. A. Selby-Bigge and P. H. Nidditch. Oxford: Clarendon Press, 1975.

———. *A Treatise of Human Nature,* ed. L. A. Selby-Bigge and P. H. Nidditch. Oxford: Clarendon Press, 1978.

Hyde, Lewis. *The Gift: Imagination and the Erotic Life of Property.* New York: Random House, 1983.

Idziak, Janine. "Divine Command Ethics." In *A Companion to Philosophy of Religion,* ed. Philip L. Quinn and Charles Taliaferro, pp. 453–59. Oxford: Blackwell, 1997.

Imbrosciano, Anthony. "Kierkegaard's 'Individual.'" *International Philosophical Quarterly* 33 (December 1993): 443–48.

Jacobs, Louis. "Disinterestedness." *Judaism* 6 (summer 1957): 202–9.

———. "Greater Love Hath No Man—The Jewish Point of View of Self-Sacrifice." *Judaism* 6 (winter 1957): 41-47.

James, William. "The Will to Believe." In *Essays in Pragmatism,* pp. 88–109. New York: Macmillan, 1948.

Johansen, Kjell Eyvind. "The Problem of Knowledge in the Ethics of Kierkegaard's *Works of Love.*" *Kierkegaardiana* 17 (1994): 52–65.

Jordan, Jeff, and Daniel Howard-Snyder, eds. *Faith, Freedom, and Rationality: Essays on the Philosophy of Religion.* Lanham, Md.: Rowman & Littlefield, 1996.

Kant, Immanuel. *Critique of Practical Reason,* trans. Lewis White Beck. Indianapolis: Bobbs-Merrill, [1788] 1956.

———. *The Doctrine of Virtue,* Part II, *The Metaphysics of Morals,* trans. Mary J. Gregor. Philadelphia: University of Pennsylvania Press, 1964.

———. *Foundations of the Metaphysics of Morals,* trans. Lewis White Beck. Indianapolis: Bobbs-Merrill, [1785] 1959.

———. *Religion within the Limits of Reason Alone,* trans. Theodore M. Greene and Hoyt Hudson. New York: Harper & Row, [1793] 1960.

Keeley, Louise Carroll. "Loving 'No One,' Loving Everyone: The Work of Love in Recollecting One Dead in Kierkegaard's *Works of Love.*" In *International Kierkegaard Commentary 16: Works of Love,* ed. Robert L. Perkins, pp. 211–48. Macon, Ga.: Mercer University Press, 1999.

———. "Subjectivity and World in *Works of Love.*" In *Foundations of Kierkegaard's Vision of Community: Religion, Ethics, and Politics in Kierkegaard,* ed. George B. Connell and C. Stephen Evans, pp. 96–108. Atlantic Highlands, N.J.: Humanities Press, 1992.

Kirmmse, Bruce H. *Kierkegaard in Golden Age Denmark.* Bloomington: Indiana University Press, 1990.

Lalic, Ivan V. *The Works of Love: Selected Poems of Ivan V. Lalic,* trans. Francis R. Jones. London: Anvil Press Poetry, 1981.

Léon, Céline, and Sylvia Walsh. *Feminist Interpretations of Søren Kierkegaard.* University Park, Pa.: Pennsylvania State University Press, 1997.

Levinas, Emmanuel. "A Propos of 'Kierkegaard Vivant.'" In *Proper Names,* trans. Michael B. Smith, pp. 75–79. Stanford: Stanford University Press, [1966] 1996.

———. "Dialogue: Self-Consciousness and the Proximity of the Neighbor." In *Of God Who Comes to Mind,* trans. Bettina Bergo, pp. 137–51. Stanford: Stanford University Press, [1979] 1998.

———. "Dialogue with Martin Buber." In *Proper Names,* trans. Michael B. Smith, pp. 36–39. Stanford: Stanford University Press, [1965] 1996.

———. "Enigma and Phenomenon." In *Basic Philosophical Writings,* ed. Adriaan T. Peperzak, Simon Critchley, and Robert Bernasconi, pp. 61–74. Bloomington: Indiana University Press, [1965] 1996.

———. *Ethics and Infinity,* Conversations with Philippe Nemo, trans. Richard A. Cohen. Pittsburgh: Duquesne University Press, [1982] 1985.

———. "Ethics as First Philosophy." In *The Levinas Reader,* ed. Seán Hand, pp. 75–87. Oxford: Blackwell, [1984] 1989.

———. "God and Philosophy." In *Basic Philosophical Writings,* ed. Adriaan T. Peperzak, Simon Critchley, and Robert Bernasconi, pp. 129–48. Bloomington: Indiana University Press, [1975] 1996.

———. "Is Ontology Fundamental?" In *Basic Philosophical Writings,* ed. Adriaan T. Peperzak, Simon Critchley, and Robert Bernasconi, pp. 1–10. Bloomington: Indiana University Press, [1951] 1996.

———. "Kierkegaard: Existence and Ethics." In *Proper Names,* trans. Michael B. Smith, pp. 66–74. Stanford: Stanford University Press, [1963] 1996.

———. *Otherwise than Being, Or Beyond Essence,* trans. Alphonso Lingis. Pittsburgh: Duquesne University Press, [1974] 1998.

———. "Peace and Proximity." In *Basic Philosophical Writings,* ed. Adriaan T. Peperzak, Simon Critchley, and Robert Bernasconi, pp. 161–70. Bloomington: Indiana University Press, [1984] 1996.

————. "The Philosophical Determination of the Idea of Culture." In *Entre Nous: On Thinking-of-the-Other,* trans. Michael B. Smith and Barbara Harshav, pp. 179–87. New York: Columbia University Press, 1998.

————. "Philosophy, Justice, and Love." In *Entre Nous: On Thinking-of-the-Other,* trans. Michael B. Smith and Barbara Harshav, pp. 103–21. New York: Columbia University Press, [1982] 1998.

————. "Questions and Answers." In *Of God Who Comes to Mind,* trans. Bettina Bergo, pp. 79–99. Stanford: Stanford University Press, [1975] 1998.

————. *Totality and Infinity,* trans. Alphonso Lingis. Pittsburgh: Duquesne University Press, [1961] 1995.

————. "The Trace of the Other," trans. Alphonso Lingis. In *Deconstruction in Context: Philosophy and Literature,* ed. Mark C. Taylor, pp. 345–59. Chicago: University of Chicago Press, [1963] 1986.

————. "Transcendence and Height." In *Basic Philosophical Writings,* ed. Adriaan T. Peperzak, Simon Critchley, and Robert Bernasconi, pp. 11–32. Bloomington: Indiana University Press, [1962] 1996.

Levinas, Emmanuel. With Richard Kearney. "Dialogue with Emmanuel Levinas." In *Face to Face with Levinas,* ed. Richard A. Cohen, pp. 13–34. Albany: State University of New York Press, [1984] 1986.

Levinas, Emmanuel. With Tamra Wright, Peter Hughes, and Alison Ainley. "The Paradox of Morality: An Interview with Emmanuel Levinas." In *The Provocation of Levinas: Rethinking the Other,* ed. Robert Bernasconi and David Wood, pp. 168–80. London: Routledge, [1986] 1998.

Lewis, C. S. *The Four Loves.* San Diego: Harcourt Brace, 1960.

Lincoln, Ulrich. "Äusserung: Studien zum Handlungsbegriff in Søren Kierkegaards *Die Taten der Liebe.*" Ph.D. dissertation, Frankfurt am Main, University of Frankfurt, 1999.

Lindström, Valter. "A Contribution to the Interpretation of Kierkegaard's Book, *The Works of Love,* " *Studia Theologica* 6 (1953): 1–29.

Løgstrup, Knud Ejler. *The Ethical Demand,* ed. Hans Fink and Alasdair MacIntyre. Notre Dame, Ind.: Notre Dame University Press, 1997.

————. "Ethics and Ontology." In *The Ethical Demand,* ed. Hans Fink and Alasdair MacIntyre, pp. 265–93. Notre Dame, Ind.: Notre Dame University Press, 1977.

————. "Settling Accounts with Kierkegaard's *Works of Love,*" a "Polemical Epilogue" to *The Ethical Demand,* ed. Hans Fink and Alasdair MacIntyre, pp. 218-64. Notre Dame, Ind: Notre Dame University Press, 1997. Originally published as "Opgør med Kierkegaard's *Kaerlighedens Gerninger,* " in *Den Etiske Fordring.* Copenhagen: Gyldendal, 1956.

Luther, Martin. "The Judgment of Martin Luther on Monastic Vows." In *Luther's Works,* Vol. 44, "The Christian in Society, I," ed. James Atkinson, pp. 251–400. Philadelphia: Fortress Press, [1521] 1966.

————. "Lectures on Galatians." In *Luther's Works,* Vol. 27, ed. Jaroslav Pelikan. St. Louis: Concordia Publishing House, [1535] 1964.

————. "Lectures on Romans." In *Luther's Works,* Vol. 25, ed. Hilton C. Oswald. St. Louis: Concordia Publishing House, [1515–16] 1972.

————. *Reformation Writings,* ed. Bertram Lee Woolf. New York: Philosophical Library, 1953.

————. *Sermons of Martin Luther: The Church Postils,* Vols. 3–4, trans. John Nicholas Lenker. Grand Rapids, Mich.: Baker Books, 1995.

————. "A Short Exposition of the Decalogue, Apostle's Creed, and Lord's Prayer." In *Reformation Writings of Martin Luther,* Vol. 1, trans. Bertram Lee Woolf, pp. 71–99. New York: Philosophical Library, 1953.

————. "Treatise on Good Works." In *Luther's Works*, Vol. 44, "The Christian in Society, I," ed. James Atkinson, pp. 15–114. Philadelphia: Fortress Press, [1515-16] 1966.

MacIntyre, Alasdair. *A Short History of Ethics*. New York: Macmillan, 1966.

————. "Which God Ought We to Obey and Why?" *Faith and Philosophy* 3.4 (October 1986): 359–71.

Mackey, Louis. *Kierkegaard: A Kind of Poet*. Philadelphia: University of Pennsylvania Press, 1971.

————. "The Loss of the World in Kierkegaard's Ethics." In *Points of View: Readings of Kierkegaard*, pp. 141–59. Tallahassee: Florida State Press, 1986.

Malantschuk, Gregor. "Political and Social Aspects of Kierkegaard's Thought." In *The Controversial Kierkegaard*, trans. Howard V. Hong and Edna H. Hong, pp. 1–17. Waterloo, Ont.: Wilfrid Laurier Press, 1980.

Marino, Gordon. "Kierkegaard Contra Freud: On the Proper Scope of Our Moral Aspirations." *Soundings* 77.1–2 (1994): 129–44.

Marion, Jean Luc. "Christian Philosophy and Charity." *Communio* 19.3 (fall 1992): 465–73.

————. *God Without Being*, trans. Thomas A. Carlson. Chicago: University of Chicago Press, 1991.

Martens, Paul. "'You Shall Love': Kant, Kierkegaard, and the Interpretation of Matthew 22:39." In *International Kierkegaard Commentary 16: Works of Love*, ed. Robert L. Perkins, pp. 57–78. Macon, Ga.: Mercer University Press, 1999.

Marx, Karl. "Introduction to the Critique of Hegel's *Philosophy of Right*." In *The Marx-Engels Reader*, ed. Robert C. Tucker, pp. 11–23. New York: Norton, 1972.

Matthis, Michael J. "Kierkegaard and the Problem of the Social Other." *Philosophy Today* 38 (winter 1994): 419–39.

Matustik, Martin J. "Kierkegaard's Radical Existential Praxis." In *Kierkegaard in Post/Modernity*, ed. Martin J. Matustik and Merold Westphal, pp. 239–64. Bloomington: Indiana University Press, 1995.

Matustik, Martin J., and Merold Westphal, eds. *Kierkegaard in Post/Modernity*. Bloomington: Indiana University Press, 1995.

Meilaender, Gilbert C. *Friendship: A Study in Theological Ethics*. Notre Dame, Ind.: Notre Dame University Press, 1981.

Morrison, Karl F. *'I Am You': The Hermeneutics of Empathy in Western Literature, Theology, and Art*. Princeton: Princeton University Press, 1998.

Müller, Paul. *Kierkegaard's "Works of Love": Christian Ethics and the Maieutic Ideal*, trans. and ed. C. Stephen Evans and Jan Evans. Copenhagen: Reitzel, 1993.

Niebuhr, H. Richard. *The Responsible Self: An Essay in Christian Moral Philosophy*. New York: Harper & Row, 1963.

Nietzsche, Friedrich. *The Anti-Christ*, trans. R. J. Hollingdale. New York: Penguin, 1968.

————. *Daybreak: Thoughts on the Prejudices of Morality*, trans. R. J. Hollingdale. Cambridge: Cambridge University Press, 1982.

————. *On the Genealogy of Morals: Ecce Homo*, trans. Walter Kaufmann. New York: Vintage, 1967.

————. *Human All-Too-Human*, trans. Marion Faber, with Stephen Lehmann. Lincoln: University of Nebraska Press, 1984.

————. *Selected Letters of Friedrich Nietzsche*, ed. and trans. Christopher Middleton. Chicago: University of Chicago Press, 1969.

————. *Thus Spoke Zarathustra: A Book for None and All*, trans. Walter Kaufmann. New York: Penguin, 1966.

Noddings, Nel. *Caring: A Feminine Approach to Ethics and Moral Education*. Berkeley: University of California Press, 1984.

Nussbaum, Martha. *Love's Knowledge*. New York: Oxford University Press, 1990.

Nygren, Anders. *Agape and Eros*, trans. Philip S. Watson. New York: Harper & Row, 1969.

Outka, Gene. *Agape: An Ethical Analysis*. New Haven, Conn.: Yale University Press, 1972.

————. "Agapeistic Ethics." In *A Companion to Philosophy of Religion*, ed. Philip L. Quinn and Charles Taliaferro, pp. 481–88. Oxford: Blackwell, 1997.

————. "Equality and the Fate of Theism in Modern Culture." *Journal of Religion* 67 (1987): 275–88.

————. "Equality and Individuality: Thoughts on Two Themes in Kierkegaard." *Journal of Religious Ethics* 10 (fall 1982): 171–203.

————. "Love." In *Encyclopedia of Ethics*, Vol. 2, ed. Lawrence C. Becker and Charlotte B. Becker, pp. 742–51. New York: Garland Publishing, 1992.

————. "Universal Love and Impartiality." In *The Love Commandments: Essays in Christian Ethics and Moral Philosophy*, ed. Edmund Santurri and William Werpehowski, pp. 1–103. Washington, D.C.: Georgetown University Press, 1992.

Peperzak, Adriaan T. *Beyond: The Philosophy of Emmanuel Levinas*. Evanston, Ill.: Northwestern University Press, 1997.

Perkins, Robert L. "Buber and Kierkegaard: A Philosophic Encounter." In *Martin Buber: A Centenary Volume*, ed. Haim Gordon and Jochanan Bloch, pp. 275–303. New York: KTAV Publishing, 1984.

————. "The Politics of Existence." In *Kierkegaard in Post/Modernity*, ed. Martin J. Matustik and Merold Westphal, pp. 168–81. Bloomington: Indiana University Press, 1995.

Perkins, Robert L., ed. *International Kierkegaard Commentary 14: Two Ages*. Macon, Ga.: Mercer University Press, 1984.

————. *International Kierkegaard Commentary 16: Works of Love*. Macon, Ga.: Mercer University Press, 1999.

Phillips, D. Z. "The Christian Concept of Love." In *Christian Ethics and Contemporary Philosophy*, ed. Ian T. Ramsey, pp. 314–28. New York: Macmillan, 1966.

Pieper, Josef. *Faith, Hope, Love*. San Francisco: Ignatius Press, 1977.

Piety, M. G. "The Place of the World in Kierkegaard's Ethics." In *Kierkegaard: The Self in Society*, ed. George Pattison and Steven Shakespeare, pp. 24–42. London: Macmillan, 1998.

Plekon, Michael. "Kierkegaard the Theologian: The Roots of His Theology in *Works of Love*." In *Foundations of Kierkegaard's Vision of Community: Religion, Ethics, and Politics in Kierkegaard*, ed. George B. Connell and C. Stephen Evans, pp. 2–17. Atlantic Highlands, N.J.: Humanities Press, 1992.

Polk, Timothy. *The Biblical Kierkegaard: Reading by the Rule of Faith*. Macon, Ga.: Mercer University Press, 1997.

Poole, Roger. *Kierkegaard: The Indirect Communication*. Charlottesville, Va.: University of Virginia Press, 1993.

Pope, Stephen J. "Expressive Individualism and True Self-Love: A Thomistic Perspective." *Journal of Religion* 71 (July 1991): 384–99.

————. "Love in Contemporary Christian Ethics." *Journal of Religious Ethics* 23.1 (spring 1995): 1–27.

Post, Stephen G. "Communion and True Self-Love." *Journal of Religious Ethics* 16 (fall 1988): 345–62.

Purvis, Sally B. "Mothers, Neighbors, and Strangers: Another Look at Agape." *Journal of Feminist Studies in Religion* 7 (1991): 19–34.

Pyper, Hugh. "Cities of the Dead: The Relation of Person and Polis in Kierkegaard's *Works of Love*." In *Kierkegaard: The Self in Society*, ed. George Pattison and Steven Shakespeare, pp. 125–38. London: Macmillan, 1998.

Quinn, Philip L. "The Divine Command Ethics in Kierkegaard's *Works of Love*." In *Faith, Freedom, and Rationality: Essays on the Philosophy of Religion*, ed. Jeff Jordan and Daniel Howard-Snyder, pp. 29–44. Lanham, Md.: Rowman & Littlefield, 1996.

———. *Divine Commands and Moral Requirements*. Oxford: Clarendon Press, 1988.

———. "Kierkegaard's Christian Ethics." In *Cambridge Companion to Kierkegaard*, ed. Alastair Hannay and Gordon Marino, pp. 349–75. Cambridge: Cambridge University Press, 1998.

———. "The Recent Revival of Divine Command Ethics." *Philosophy and Phenomenological Research* 50, supplement (1990): 345–65.

Quinn, Philip L., and Charles Taliaferro, eds. *A Companion to Philosophy of Religion*. Oxford: Blackwell, 1997.

Radcliffe, Dana M. "Compassion and Commanded Love." *Faith and Philosophy* 11.1 (January 1994): 50–71.

———. "Hanfling on Neighbour Love." *Philosophy* 69 (1994): 497–502.

Ramsey, Paul. *Basic Christian Ethics*. New York: Scribner, 1950.

Ricoeur, Paul. *Figuring the Sacred: Religion, Narrative, and Imagination*, trans. David Pellauer. Minneapolis: Fortress Press, 1995.

———. *Oneself as Another*, trans. Kathleen Blamey. Chicago: University of Chicago Press, 1992.

Roberts, David E. "*Works of Love*: A Review Article." *Review of Religion* 12 (1948): 382–403.

Roberts, Robert C. "Kierkegaard, Wittgenstein, and a Method of 'Virtue Ethics.'" In *Kierkegaard in Post/Modernity*, ed. Martin Matustik and Merold Westphal, pp. 142–66. Bloomington: Indiana University Press, 1995.

Rodhe, H. P. *Auktions-protocol over SK's Bogsamling*. Copenhagen: Royal Library, 1967.

Rose, Gillian. "Søren Kierkegaard to Martin Buber—Reply from 'the Single One.'" In *Judaism and Modernity: Philosophical Essays*, pp. 155–73. Oxford: Blackwell, 1993.

Rosenzweig, Franz. *The Star of Redemption*, trans. William W. Hallo. Notre Dame, Ind.: Notre Dame University Press, 1970.

Sàez Tajafuerce, Begonya. "*Works of Love*: Modernity or Antiquity?" In *Kierkegaard Studies 1998*, ed. Niels Jørgen Cappelørn and Hermann Deuser, pp. 60–76. Berlin: de Gruyter, 1998.

Santurri, Edmund, and William Werpehowski, eds. *The Love Commandments: Essays in Christian Ethics and Moral Philosophy*. Washington, D.C.: Georgetown University Press, 1992.

Schrift, Alan, ed. *The Logic of the Gift: Toward an Ethic of Generosity*. New York: Routledge, 1997.

Smith, Adam. *The Theory of Moral Sentiments*, ed. D. D. Raphael and A. L. Macfie. Oxford: Clarendon, 1976.

Søltoft, Pia. "To Let Oneself Be Upbuilt." In *Kierkegaard Studies 2000*, ed. Niels Jørgen Cappelørn, pp. 19–39. Berlin: de Gruyter, 2000.

———. "Love and Continuity: The Significance of Intersubjectivity in the Second Part of *Either/Or*." Trans. Marilyn G. Piety. In *Kierkegaard Studies 1997*, ed. Niels Jørgen Cappelørn and Hermann Deuser, pp. 210–27. Berlin: de Gruyter, 1997.

———. "The Presence of the Absent Neighbor in *Works of Love*," trans. Marilyn G. Piety. In *Kierkegaard Studies 1998*, ed. Niels Jørgen Cappelørn, pp. 113–28. Berlin: de Gruyter, 1998.

Stack, George J. "Kierkegaard: The Self and Ethical Existence." *Ethics* 83 (1973): 108–25.

Tillich, Paul. *The Protestant Era*, trans. J. L. Adams. Chicago: University of Chicago Press, 1960.

Veatch, Henry B. "Modern Ethics, Teleology, and Love of Self." *Monist* 75 (January 1992): 52–70.

Viallaneix, Nelly. "Søren Kierkegaard: La Voix et L'Ouïe (A Propos des Quatres Dis-
cours Édifiants de 1843)." *Les Études Philosophiques* (1969): 211–24.

Walsh, Sylvia. *Living Poetically: Kierkegaard's Existential Aesthetics*. University Park,
Pa.: Pennsylvania State University Press, 1994.

Walsh, Sylvia I. "Forming the Heart: The Role of Love in Kierkegaard's Thought." In
The Grammar of the Heart, ed. Richard H. Bell, pp. 234–56. New York: Harper &
Row, 1988.

Walsh Perkins, Sylvia. "Kierkegaard's Philosophy of Love." In *The Nature and Pursuit of
Love*, ed. David Goicoechea, pp. 167–79. New York: Prometheus Books, 1995.

Webb, Stephen. "More than Too Much: Kierkegaard's *Works of Love* Reconsidered." In
Blessed Excess: The Hyperbolic Imagination, pp. 33–58. Albany: State University of
New York Press, 1993.

Westphal, Merold. "Commanded Love and Divine Transcendence in Levinas and Kierkegaard." In *The Face of the Other and the Trace of God: Essays on the Philosophy of Emmanuel Levinas*, ed. Jeff Bloechl. New York: Fordham University Press, 2000.

————. *Kierkegaard's Critique of Reason and Society*. University Park, Pa.: Pennsylvania
State University Press, 1991.

————. "Levinas, Kierkegaard, and the Theological Task." *Modern Theology* 8 (July
1992): 241–61.

————. "The Teleological Suspension of Religiousness B." In *Foundations of Kierke-
gaard's Vision of Community: Religion, Ethics, and Politics in Kierkegaard*, ed. George
B. Connell and C. Stephen Evans, pp. 110–29. Atlantic Highlands, N.J.: Humanities
Press, 1992.

————. "The Transparent Shadow: Kierkegaard and Levinas in Dialogue." In *Kierkegaard in Post/Modernity*, ed. Martin Matustik and Merold Westphal, pp. 265–82.
Bloomington: Indiana University Press, 1995.

Whittaker, John H. "'Agape' and Self-Love." In *The Love Commandments: Essays in Christian Ethics and Moral Philosophy*, ed. Edmund Santurri and William Werpehowski,
pp. 221–39. Washington, D.C.: Georgetown University Press, 1992.

index